About the Author

Richard Tellett is a seasoned finance professional with a diverse background in mathematics, risk analysis, investment management, and accounting. Having developed a strong analytical foundation and a keen interest in quantitative finance during his undergraduate studies at the University of Manchester, where he earned a 2.1 BSc in Mathematics, Richard pursued studies towards the Chartered Financial Analyst (CFA) qualification. This honed his skills in financial analysis, asset valuation, and portfolio management, providing him with a comprehensive understanding of investment principles and strategies.

Richard's professional journey began in investment management, specialising in providing insights and data on global oil movement to institutional investors. Subsequently, he has honed his skills across the insurance sector, private equity investment research, and shipping. He has since founded Nexus Investor, an educational platform with a growing social media presence, where he shares his investment insights and financial expertise. More information can be found at www.nexusinvestor.co.uk.

Outside his professional endeavours, Richard has actively engaged in personal investments, having diversified his investment portfolio across stocks, shares, funds, and property investments, and for nearly a decade, delving into the world of cryptocurrencies and blockchain technologies. With over 15 years of experience through meticulous research and strategic decision-making, he has achieved notable success in generating returns and growing his wealth.

With an active interest in finance, Richard is committed to staying informed about market trends, economic developments, and emerging investment opportunities, continuously seeking to enhance his knowledge and expertise. With his unique blend of academic, professional, and personal insights, Richard brings a wealth of expertise to his writing, offering valuable insights and practical advice to readers navigating the complex world of Bitcoin and Blockchain Technology.

Bitcoin and Blockchain Technology

Shaping the Future of Finance

Richard Tellett

Nexus Investor Editions

Published by Nexus Investor Editions
a trading name of Nexelus Digital Ltd
Registered in England and Wales
Company Number: 16450481
Find more content at:
www.nexusinvestor.co.uk

This book is a work of non-fiction. While every effort has been made to ensure the accuracy of the information, the content is provided for educational and informational purposes only. It does not constitute financial, investment, legal, or other professional advice. Readers should conduct their own research or consult a qualified professional before making financial decisions.

ISBN: 978-1-0682394-0-3
Printed in country of purchase

Disclaimer

The information contained in this book is provided for educational and informational purposes only. It does not constitute financial advice, investment advice, legal advice, or any other professional advice.

While every effort has been made to ensure the accuracy and reliability of the information presented, the author and publisher make no representations or warranties regarding its completeness, accuracy, or suitability for any purpose. The material reflects the author's understanding and views at the time of writing.

Readers should be aware that financial markets, regulatory frameworks, technological developments, and geopolitical conditions are dynamic and subject to rapid change. Consequently, certain information contained within this book may become outdated or superseded after publication.

Readers are strongly encouraged to conduct their own research and seek advice from an appropriately qualified financial professional before making any investment or financial decisions. The author and publisher accept no responsibility or liability for any loss, damage, or other consequences arising directly or indirectly from the use or application of any information contained within this publication. All investments carry inherent risks, including the potential loss of principal. Past performance is not indicative of future results.

The views and opinions expressed are those of the author and do not necessarily reflect the official policies or positions of any other agency, organisation, employer, or company. By reading this book, you acknowledge that you are solely responsible for any investment decisions you choose to make.

Acknowledgements

I would like to thank my family and friends for their constant encouragement and support throughout the writing of this book. Their patience, advice, and belief in this project have been truly invaluable.

I am especially grateful to Jasmin Naim for her editorial guidance and insight, which helped bring this work to a professional standard. Her knowledge, dedication and commitment have been invaluable. Jasmin's thoughtful feedback challenged me to sharpen my ideas and enriched the final result in ways that reflect her experience and expertise.

I would also like to thank the growing community of followers across Nexus Investor's social media platforms. Your engagement, curiosity, and support continue to inspire the content I create and strengthen the mission of making financial education more accessible to all.

"…a swarm of cyber hornets serving the goddess of wisdom, feeding on the fire of truth, exponentially growing ever smarter, faster, and stronger behind a wall of encrypted energy."

— Michael Saylor, Co-Founder of Strategy

Preface

We are on the brink of a technological and financial revolution — one that redefines how we perceive money, value, and trust.

The twenty-first century has seen the world of finance evolve at an unprecedented pace. From the global financial crisis of 2008 to the rise of cryptocurrencies and block-chain technology, we are witnessing a fundamental shift in how economies function, and how individuals interact with money. What was once considered speculative could now be shaping the future of global finance.

This book is not just about Bitcoin or blockchain but about a vision for the future. It is about understanding how these technologies emerged as a response to systemic failures and how they promise to empower individuals and foster a more inclusive, transparent, and efficient financial system.

My aim as author is to demystify the concepts of Bitcoin and blockchain while exploring their transformative poten-tial. I also hope to address the scepticism surrounding these innovations by contextualising their value in the broader arc of economic history.

This is a journey into understanding the technologies themselves and the philosophical and practical challenges they
address. Whether you are a seasoned investor, a curious
sceptic, or someone looking to navigate this rapidly evolving
landscape, this book is for you.

Let us embark on this journey together, exploring the roots
of money, the rise of Bitcoin, and the endless possibilities
of blockchain technology.

Welcome to a new era of finance

Contents

Chapter 1

Introduction

to Bitcoin and Blockchain Technology

"The root problem with conventional currency is all the trust that's required to make it work."

— Satoshi Nakamoto, Bitcoin's anonymous creator, 2009

The winter of 1932 was bitter, but the cold wasn't what people feared most. It was hunger. And silence. The kind that hangs in the air between desperate thoughts and unspeakable choices. In the heart of New York City, a queue stretched along a snow-dusted street, winding past shuttered shop fronts and cracked windows swathed in yellowing newspapers. Men in worn-out coats stared at their boots. Mothers clutched children close, shielding them from a wind that did not care how carefully they had once planned their lives. The soup kitchen's door opened just twice an hour. Some waited all day. Others simply hoped to reach the front before the pot ran dry.

The banks had closed. Lifetime savings vanished overnight. Not stolen with force, but with silence. Numbers erased, promises broken, and trust that would never fully return. A man once proud to be a foreman now bartered his wedding ring for a bag of flour. A retired teacher wept in a queue outside a pawn shop, offering a violin that no one wanted.

Money had stopped working. It no longer moved nor meant what it used to. It couldn't be trusted to hold value, or even to exist the next morning. In that moment, a strange truth emerged, one that had always lingered beneath the surface but now stood exposed: money is belief. A story we all agree to. A system of shared faith. But what happens when belief collapses? Some whispered it was only temporary. Others weren't so sure. Prices soared and fell without warning.

A loaf of bread could cost a few cents on Monday but three times more by Friday. Wages were frozen or gone altogether. And yet, the printing presses on 14th Street in Washington, D.C. rolled on. The real damage wasn't just in lost homes or empty bank accounts. It was in the questions people began to ask.

In the roaring years of the late 1920s, America had seemed unstoppable. Skyscrapers rose like monuments to prosperity. Cars lined the streets, jazz poured from the radios, and stock prices climbed with no ceiling in sight. The future was modern, mechanical, magnificent. Everyone wanted in. Ordinary workers purchased shares on credit, fuelled by easy lending. Headlines promised riches. Confidence was contagious. However, beneath the surface prosperity, strains in the banking system and overextended credit began to stir concerns within the markets. President Hoover, acknowledging the mounting financial tension, moved to reassure the nation.

"The fundamental business of the country… is on a sound and prosperous basis."

— President Herbert Hoover, 25 October 1929

Then, just four days later, on Tuesday 29 October, the New York Stock Exchange imploded, dragging the entire global economy down with it. Black Tuesday wiped out $14 billion in value in a single day. Crowds swarmed Wall Street, racing to discount brokerages and markets to sell their stocks. Prices plummeted throughout the day, eventually leading to a complete stock market crash. Panic choked the air, with people unloading their stock as quickly as they could, even at a loss. In the face of mounting debt and desperate to protect their own assets, banks demanded payment for the loans they had made to individual investors. Those who could not afford to pay found their stocks sold immediately and their life savings wiped out in minutes, yet their debts to the bank remained.

Brokers shouted over one another, while phones rang off the hook and ticker tape rained down in the chaos. Each margin call triggered more selling and fortunes built over decades evaporated in hours, forcing bankers to lock their doors. Police were stationed outside financial buildings to stop investors from throwing themselves out of windows. This wasn't a correction. It was a reckoning.

What we now refer to as the Wall Street Crash wasn't even a single-day collapse. It was a sequence of sharp declines, beginning with Black Thursday (24 October), followed by Black Monday (28 October), and culminating in the devastation of Black Tuesday on 29 October 1929. The Federal Reserve was not even two decades old. It was initially signed into law by President Woodrow Wilson on 23 December 1913 in response to a series of financial panics that had exposed the vulnerabilities of a fragmented and unregulated banking system.

Yet in the three months leading up to the end of November 1929, the stock market lost over half its value, wiping out over $30 billion. By 1933, 9,000 banks had failed in the United States. One in four Americans were unemployed and 9,000,000 savings accounts had been wiped out. The New York Stock Exchange lost around 90% of its value from 1929 to June 1932. The fallout would reverberate around the economy, with GDP in the US dropping by nearly 30% and global GDP dropping by over 15% in just four years. The great depression devastated more than just markets. It devastated lives and shattered trust in money itself.

But that was nearly a century ago, which is plenty of time to learn from this story, right?

A loaf of bread. A bottle of wine. A deposit and a mortgage on a house. A bribe or a bailout. Half of every transaction in human history involves one thing. This thing builds empires and breaks them down. It starts wars and can even send rockets to the moon. You can't eat it. You can't drink it. But you'll give your life chasing it. Some say it's the root of all evil. Others say it's the instrument of all progress. Either way, no one can escape it.

Most people rarely question money. It's simply there, woven into every transaction, every salary, every silent calculation at the till. We earn it. We spend it. We save it. But how many truly understand where it comes from, or what it's built on? From cowrie shells to striking the first coins in ancient Anatolia, and from Rai stones in Yap Island to U.S. dollars, the history of money is very long. We used to trade ivory and obsidian. Then we minted kings' heads into coins. Then we trusted paper and then numbers. So, why does any of this matter?

It matters because money is more than just paper, metal, or numbers on a screen. It is the foundation of our economic freedom and the silent infrastructure underpinning every dream. It also determines the margins we live within. We use it to build families, launch ideas, pay debts, and create safety. Whether we're aware of it or not, money sits at the core of nearly everything we do. It governs what we can give, what we withhold, and what we must protect. Why then does such an integral and useful instrument frequently produce such upheaval?

Trust is the invisible force — a kind of silent agreement — that holds our financial world together. It's there every time we tap a card, sign a loan, or receive a payslip. We trust the numbers on the screen mean something. We trust the value will hold. We trust the institutions behind it all won't falter. But trust, for all its necessity, can be fragile. We place our trust in central banks not to overreach. In governments not to inflate. In commercial banks not to speculate recklessly. In global markets not to freeze credit under pressure. We rely on it, every day, without ever questioning where the limits lie — or what happens when they're breached.

"I don't believe we shall ever have good money again before we take the thing out of the hands of government."

— Friedrich Hayek, author of *The Denationalisation of Money*. From an interview featured in the 1977 documentary, *The Money Masters*.

Throughout history, those limits have been tested. Currencies have collapsed. Savings have vanished. Whole nations have seen their wealth evaporate, not through natural disaster, but often through greed and financial mismanagement. When these events happen, they are often written off as anomalies. External shocks. Rare mishaps. But the truth is, the system itself is not immune. It is, in many ways, designed around risk and control. And the burden of that design rarely falls on those who control it. It falls on the saver watching their nation's currency lose half its value. On the worker locked out of banking. On the retiree whose pension is quietly eroded. In these moments, trust isn't a virtue. It's a risk — one that ordinary people bear while others make the rules.

BITCOIN EMERGES

Bitcoin is a system based on mathematical proofs. A protocol of ones and zeros focused on cryptographic truths. It was a gift to the world whereby trust would no longer be required to facilitate transactions. Traditional banking systems and credit cards were never designed for the internet. They were built around a world of paper, hand-written signatures, and physical presence and not for instant global transactions. Today's digital economy is still running on rails laid decades before the internet even existed.

Outdated. Inefficient. Untrustworthy. Not just because of people's dishonesty, but because these systems were built for a world where trust could be assumed face to face, which is no longer possible online.

> **"I think that the internet is going to be one of the major forces for reducing the role of government. The one thing that's missing, but will soon be developed, is a reliable e-cash — a method whereby on the internet you can transfer funds from A to B, without A knowing B or B knowing A."**
>
> — Milton Friedman, economist, 1999

What the internet did for information, Bitcoin is doing for money and there's nothing that banks or governments can do to stop it. For some, it signals danger. Chaos even. But to others, it represents freedom and opportunity. Either way, just like the first wheels were orchestrated into action in 1885 by Karl Benz, this change is already in motion.

> **"Alistair Darling is preparing to inject billions of pounds into the banking system amid fears that the sector is on the verge of collapse.", "Billions may be needed as lending squeeze tightens", "Britain edges closer to full-blown slump", "Chancellor on brink of second bailout for banks"**
>
> — The front page of UK newspaper, *The Times* on 3 January 2009

It was against this backdrop, not in a conference hall or policy summit, but in a quiet corner of the internet, that something unexpected was emerging. This isn't just a story about technology. It's about the evolution of money and the pursuit of economic freedom. It's a reminder of why any of this still matters. The question is, what other possibilities might lie ahead?

Chapter 2

The Global Financial Crisis

"The truth is no online database will replace your daily newspaper, no CD-ROM can take the place of a competent teacher, and no computer network will change the way government works."

— Clifford Stoll, "The Internet? Bah!", *Newsweek*, 1995

Computer screens flickered in offices across the world, dial-up tones echoed in living rooms, and the promise of the internet was transforming from novelty to necessity. I remember being at school in 1995 and hearing about something called the internet. The world wide web. At the time, I didn't really know what it was. Something you could use to search for information as you would in an encyclopaedia? Back then finding anything out was never easy. You had to rely on what teachers and your family told you was true. But by mid-decade the 1990s were beginning to feel like the start of a new era. A digital age. It wasn't just a new technology; it was spoken about in some quarters as if it were a new frontier. One that promised to change how we lived our everyday lives.

You see, the thing about a transformative technology is that very few people see its true potential until well beyond the point that it is fully established. Scepticism. Resentment. People who stand to lose out financially from an innovation are those who are especially negative about its proposition. It has happened time and time again over history, but this time, the technology was too good to ignore. And importantly, although many people would never have guessed what it would have achieved by 2025, they still saw a way to profit from it.

IN THE WAKE OF THE DOT-COM BOOM

Although the internet is said to have been created in 1983, it wasn't until ten years later that it became widely available to the public. By the late 1990s, mainstream adoption had taken off. Users could now create websites filled with graphics, audio, and hyperlinks for the first time.

New companies were being formed to take advantage of this new technology. The only problem was that many of these start-ups were not yet making any money. Nonetheless, the hype and speculation led to early investment from venture capitalists and institutional investors. As a consequence, many new technology companies launched Initial Public Offerings (IPOs), by offering their shares on a stock exchange for the first time, and their stock prices soared.

Excessive valuations for companies like Amazon, Yahoo, Webvan, eToys, and Pets.com caused their stock prices to skyrocket, despite many lacking a viable way to generate sustainable revenue. The then Federal Reserve Chairman Alan Greenspan in 1996 famously described this period as "irrational exuberance".

When the anticipated profits from these companies failed to materialise, in 2000 the bubble burst. Stock prices fell, wiping out billions in investor wealth. Bankruptcies included Pets.com, Webvan, and Kozmo.com, while tech giants like Yahoo and Amazon saw their valuations collapse.

Despite since becoming a global giant, incredibly Amazon's stock price crashed by about 95%. The dot-com crash was a harsh lesson in the risks of speculative investing. The NASDAQ Composite Index, which is heavily weighted towards tech stocks, had lost nearly 80% of its value from its peak. Investor confidence in equities was shaken, prompting them to move their money elsewhere.

SHIFT TO REAL ESTATE AND CHEAP CREDIT

In the aftermath of the dot-com crash, central banks responded by cutting interest rates to stimulate economic recovery. Interest rates in the U.S. were slashed to historic lows, making borrowing more affordable. This in turn encouraged spending, fuelling economic growth and raising GDP. With stocks considered too risky, investors turned to real estate as a safe investment.

This period of low interest rates, combined with confidence in the housing sector, prompted a rapid rise in house prices. By 2004–05, a housing bubble had started. The greed-driven belief spread that house prices only go up, and financial institutions aggressively expanded mortgage lending. Banks and lenders introduced new mortgages they called "subprime" to provide high-risk loans to borrowers with low credit scores. These borrowers typically had limited income documentation or a history of financial struggles and many of these loans started with low interest rates but increased dramatically after only a few years. Overall, these loans still carried higher interest rates and fees than prime mortgages, making repayments more expensive and potentially putting borrowers under financial strain.

These risky lending practices spread. Subprime mortgages became normal practice as the U.S. government continued to encourage home ownership. Could these people afford to buy these properties? Or was this just a way for the banks and the government to profit as much as possible from this housing boom?

It's honestly hard to comprehend what happened next. Mortgages were issued without requiring a deposit, and some banks even offered 125% mortgages, which meant borrowers received a loan of 25% on top, putting them in negative equity from the start. Banks, convinced that house prices could only rise, saw it as a win-win situation: low interest rates for borrowers and increased profits for lenders. But just think about this for a second. How could this really have been the case? So-called financial innovation also played a significant role in amplifying the crisis. Banks didn't just stop at lending; they securitised these risky mortgages into financial products called Mortgage-Backed Securities (MBS) and Collateralised Debt Obligations (CDOs).

An MBS is a fixed-income financial instrument that bundles home loans together to sell as tradable securities. This means that instead of simply holding onto the mortgages and collecting interest repayments, banks were able to sell these debts to investors, thus freeing up liquidity to issue more mortgages. Liquidity refers to how quickly an asset can be bought or sold without significantly affecting its price. As houses are typically illiquid, MBSs allowed banks quick access to further capital, which intensified the situation even further. Historically, MBSs were offering some of the most attractive risk-adjusted returns compared with high-quality fixed-income investments, such as U.S. Treasury bonds. These securities provided what looked like a profitable way to access capital markets while meeting investor demand for steady cash flows and higher yields.

Compare this to the equity market, where owning a stock makes an investor a partial owner of the company. In the case of a bond, an investor effectively becomes the lender. The investor lends money to a corporation or government for a set period of time in exchange for interest payments and the return of the loan principal at maturity. Generally speaking, U.S. Treasury bonds are regarded as the safest type of bond because they are backed by the full faith and credit of the United States government, which has a proven track record of repaying its debt. However, as investors' appetite for risk increased, they opted to move towards these MBS investments instead.

If this weren't bad enough, CDOs took the concept of mortgage-backed securities even further. These instruments repackaged MBSs into different risk categories that were also sold to investors based on their relative risk appetite. These securities not only included the mortgages from the MBSs but also a diversified pool of other debt assets, such as corporate bonds, car loans, and credit card debt. Assets within CDOs are also divided into tranches, each with varying levels of risk and return, and the income these underlying assets generated, including interest and principal payments, was used to compensate investors. MBSs and CDOs played an important role in the financial crisis because many included both high-quality and subprime assets, making it difficult for investors to assess their risk exposure.

To further aggravate matters, a big flaw in this system was the role of credit rating agencies, which were responsible for assessing the risk of financial products. However, these agencies were incentivised to give favourable ratings to attract business from the very institutions creating these securities. Since the agencies were paid by the issuers of CDOs, there was a clear conflict of interest. As a result, even high-risk CDOs were often classified as low-risk, misleading investors into believing their money was safe.

With banks, hedge funds, pension funds, and insurance companies worldwide buying these products, risk spread across the whole global financial system. Since they carried top-tier credit ratings, many institutions over-leveraged themselves, meaning that they borrowed vast sums of money to invest. With cheap credit available, firms took on massive debt, assuming these securities were a low-risk, high-reward opportunity.

By 2006, market sentiment was still bullish as both institutions and investors could still only see house prices climbing. However, later in the year warning signs began to emerge. Interest rates had started to rise, while the number of unsold houses on the market was also increasing, which was unusual. With interest rates higher, new mortgages were now less affordable for potential buyers. Even worse, current home-owners who had taken variable-rate mortgages were seeing their monthly payments increase significantly. Now, many people couldn't afford to pay their mortgages and demand for properties declined sharply.

THE FINANCIAL CRASH

As mortgage defaults rose, the housing market began to crash. The result was serial defaults to the underlying MBS and CDO securities held by global institutions, triggering a financial domino effect. As more borrowers defaulted, the value of these MBSs and CDOs declined, causing massive losses for the institutions that owned them. The crisis accelerated in 2007 when major financial firms, including Bear Stearns, Lehman Brothers, and Merrill Lynch, began reporting billion-dollar losses. Financial institutions that were over-leveraged found themselves holding worthless assets, contributing to a liquidity crisis that eventually threw the global economy into crisis.

The financial crisis was caused by greed among bankers and financial institutions, made possible by careless or even corrupt regulators and delayed government intervention. This story was famously depicted in Michael Lewis's 2010 book *The Big Short* and the film adaptation of 2015. Christian Bale played Michael Burry, an investor and hedge fund manager who predicted the subprime mortgage crisis and famously shorted the market. Despite initial doubts, Burry's firm, Scion Capital, made profits of hundreds of millions of dollars when the market crashed in 2008.

After collapsing in March 2008 due to its heavy exposure to mortgage-backed securities, Bear Stearns had to be saved by JPMorgan Chase with government support. Similarly, panic spread in the UK when Northern Rock failed in February 2008 due to a severe liquidity crisis. A bank run ensued, with queues of customers desperately rushing to withdraw millions of pounds from their accounts. The crisis underwent a dramatic shift when the British government stepped in and nationalised the bank to prevent more mayhem.

The tipping point occurred in September 2008, when Lehman Brothers, one of the largest investment banks in the United States, declared bankruptcy. This sent shockwaves through the global financial system, provoking panic and a severe credit freeze. Stock prices plummeted, credit markets froze, and businesses and consumers struggled to obtain financing. Governments all over the world rushed to step in, but the damage was already done.

The crisis triggered a deep global recession, freezing economic activity and consumer confidence. At the time, I was made redundant from my job in the City of London, and millions of others were in the same position. Businesses failed, unemployment soared, and families faced growing financial difficulties, all because risk in the system had been overlooked.

HOUSING GLOOM PROMPTED EMERGENCY BAILOUTS

Due to the drop in house prices, many families found themselves with homes worth significantly less than the mortgages they owed. What remained was the heartbreaking prospect of losing their homes. With property values plummeting and widespread repossessions, the housing market struggled with an oversupply of unsold properties. At a friend's birthday party at the time, the main topic of conversation was how many of them were in negative equity and how worried they were about it. I just couldn't believe how wrong this was. But the crisis affected more than just a few countries. Because the institutions and financial system were so interconnected, the impact was felt in every country.

In the chaos, governments and central banks launched dramatic interventions to prevent total economic collapse. This was in sharp contrast to the Great Depression, when authorities allowed banks to fail and markets to unwind brutally on their own.

This time, they provided capital injections and bailouts to banks deemed "too big to fail". For example, in November 2008, the U.S. government bailed out Citigroup, injecting $45 billion amid the banking giant's mounting losses. Also, in October 2008, the UK government rescued Royal Bank of Scotland (RBS) with a £45.5 billion bailout, the largest in British history. Meanwhile, to prevent further instability in the UK banking sector, HBOS was forced to merge with Lloyds TSB in 2009, a deal later supported by another government bailout.

"The Times 03/Jan/2009 Chancellor on brink of second bailout for banks"

This was the message written on the first ever Bitcoin block. It was mined on 3 January 2009, referring to the front-page article written in *The Times* in the UK, regarding the state of the financial industry at the beginning of 2009. This reveals the first clear indication that Bitcoin was created in response to the financial turmoil of the preceding years, but more on this later.

Central banks globally reacted to these bailouts by aggressively slashing interest rates to near zero. To stabilise the system, the U.S. government introduced the Troubled Asset Relief Program (TARP), injecting $700 billion into banks to prevent systemic collapse. Meanwhile, the Federal Reserve and other central banks launched a programme called quantitative easing (QE), a name I am sure you will have heard, as it was all over the news in early 2009.

QE was a crucial component of many of the problems we have faced since the crisis. The idea was first introduced by the Japanese in the late 1990s. Widespread use began in Japan in 2001 in response to prolonged deflation and economic stagnation after its asset bubble burst in the early 1990s. We look at this topic in great detail throughout this book. But in simple terms, it was intended to be a short-term measure only, designed to inject liquidity, or shall we say additional money, into the economy to stabilise the financial system.

When we talk about injecting liquidity, we mean central bank liquidity, which is an important distinction from the market-driven liquidity discussed earlier in this chapter. The difficulty with using QE over extended periods is that it can lead to the devaluation of national currencies, a process commonly known as currency debasement — another fundamental topic covered in this book. And this hasn't only become a major concern in recent years either, but more on this later.

Despite these measures to prevent a complete financial meltdown, the public still felt extremely frustrated. They wondered how these financial institutions managed to get away with what they had done with so few penalties. And why, given their initial role in creating the crisis, were these reckless banks allowed to walk away with taxpayers' money? Like the foreman and the teacher during the great depression in the 1930s, people started to revisit the meaning of money and question just how much influence governments and central banks should have over the monetary system.

REGULATORY REFORMS: WERE THEY ENOUGH?

Governments responded to this backlash with notable legislative changes aimed at preventing another repeat of 2008. The Dodd-Frank Wall Street Reform and Consumer Protection Act aimed to lower systemic risk and boost financial control, by preventing speculative behaviour in the United States. Similarly, European and UK banks were required to maintain strict capital asset ratios, or in other words to balance capital and reserves with total assets. The concept was clear: banks must keep a sufficient buffer to offset any future losses. By maintaining enough in reserve, banks should never need to be bailed out again by the taxpayer.

About 30 million jobs lost worldwide during the crisis. Millions of homes were repossessed globally, with the U.S. alone accounting for 3.8 million of those between 2007 and 2010. $17 trillion decline in U.S. household wealth.

Federal Reserve launched QE under Ben Bernanke during the crisis, later expanded by Janet Yellen and Jerome Powell. 8.8 million jobs lost in the U.S. between 2008 and 2010, peaking at 10% of the workforce.

QE started in 2009 under Mervyn King at the Bank of England, later expanded under Mark Carney and Andrew Bailey.

Estimated cost to UK taxpayers: £150 billion due to QE losses. UK unemployment peaked at 8.4% by 2011 (highest since 1995).

The 2007–09 financial crisis has had long-lasting effects on the world's economy. It demonstrated how unrestricted risk-taking leads to severe weaknesses in centralised financial systems. The crisis made it clear that now certain banks are indeed too large to fail and that governments and central banks will come to the rescue. However, the big question remains: Did the actions and reforms create long-term solutions and financial stability, or long-term consequences that could later prove detrimental? While the collapse was contained, the cost of facilitating this rescue was immense. QE is not free money, but future burden. By absorbing risk and expanding debt, governments may have prevented a complete full-scale deleveraging reset like that of the 1930s, but in doing so, have they merely engineered a delayed deleveraging by shifting private debt to public balance sheets leaving ordinary people to foot the bill?

THE BIRTH OF BITCOIN

Thus far we have laid the groundwork and addressed the possible reasons why decentralised technologies like Bitcoin have emerged. Bitcoin can be seen as a response to the failures of the traditional financial system we have discussed in this chapter. I believe cryptocurrencies were designed as a way to challenge the online payment system, and challenge a financial system plagued by manipulation, bailouts, and currency debasement. But can Bitcoin and blockchain technology be a true revolution? Will they become a true hedge against the very problems that led to the financial crisis? Or will they simply end up being another speculative bubble, destined to collapse like so many have before?

Chapter 3

Decentralisation as a Response

to Financial Crises

Reckless risk-taking. Excessive leverage. And a lack of transparency left ordinary people suffering consequences over which they had no control. Was it fair that hardworking people who acted responsibly had to suffer the consequences of reckless banks, financial institutions and the lack of governmental protection? Should they instead have been given an option to protect their money and take ownership of their own wealth?

Breaking the economy down into its most basic element, a transaction occurs when money or credit is exchanged for goods, services or financial assets, and this process has happened for hundreds of years. Billions of these happen daily, and they make up the entire economy. Every salary. Every purchase. Every investment and every loan. When you take out credit, you borrow money with a promise to pay it back in the future. So, credit increases your ability to spend now but reduces the spending power of your future self. This process leads to short-term booms by boosting demand, but also to debt repayments, which later slows the economy down.

When someone borrows money to spend, that spending becomes someone else's income. As income rises, that person appears more creditworthy, so they can borrow more and spend more — which fuels even more income for others. This self-reinforcing loop drives economic growth and causes short-term booms, but it's built on debt. Over time, the cycle becomes unsustainable when borrowing outpaces the ability to repay and this leads to a short-term bust. People start spending less, which means other people have less income, which makes them less creditworthy. The danger isn't in the borrowing itself, but in how the system from the top down is designed to rely on ever-increasing levels of debt to keep functioning.

These short-term debt cycles: the regular boom and busts that happen every three to eight years, are just smaller movements within a much larger pattern known as long-term debt cycles. There are leveraging phases, which can stimulate growth and expansion and they can last 50 or more years. This longer cycle began after World War II. It was driven by strong productivity growth, and the expansion of credit and global trade, which led to rising living standards.

However, for growth to be sustainable, it must be supported by an increase in productivity. By this we mean the ability to produce more economic output with the same or fewer inputs, so that it can service the debt comfortably. Productivity growth is the real foundation for rising prosperity. However, when debt grows faster than productivity for too long, the imbalance eventually becomes too great, leading to a major deleveraging event, which initiates a long-term bust cycle, where long recessions and major restructuring are required. By 2000, debt had outpaced income and productivity, and I believe this culminated in the 2008 financial crisis.

The issue is that everything in the financial system is leveraged. As we saw in the last chapter, U.S. Treasury bonds are seen to be the safest place in the world to put your money, yet in 2008, the average bond had been leveraged around 30 times. This means that for every $1,000 that you had in the bank, 30 people thought they owned it. For every $1,000 that the central bank had in reserve, 30 people had claim to this money, which is staggering when you think about it.

In the past, when people used gold coins as money, they would store them themselves, perhaps at home or buried in the ground. Then banks came along, offering a seemingly safe place for your gold. The idea was simple; you could deposit your gold coins and withdraw them whenever you needed. But there was a catch. Instead of holding onto the gold for their depositors, banks started lending it out to earn a profit. For instance, in the example above, there might have been 30 people who believed the same gold coin in the bank was theirs. This practice became known as fractional reserve banking, meaning that the bank did not actually hold all of its customers' gold at once. The same principle still applies in modern banking.

To understand how this works, imagine Ted has £1,000 in his bank account. The bank might hold just a fraction of it, say £100, and lends out £900 to Jill. But Ted's account shows £1,000, and Jill's shows £900. Then Jill makes a purchase of a TV for £500, which goes into the retailer's bank account. Of this £500, the bank decides to keep only £50, then lends out £450 to Peter. Then Ted buys a new car on finance, costing £5,000, and this process repeats over and over again. What started with Ted having £1,000 has turned into £7,350. Each time money is spent and re-lent, more digital money appears in the system, which has no reserve backing. This system means that private banks effectively create most of this virtual money in circulation through lending and then earn billions in interest each year in the process.

In the UK and U.S., over 90% of the money supply in circulation is digital and created through debt. None of the money in your bank account really exists and it never did. Money exists as IOUs, with a system built on synthetic claims and unreal reserves.

When you deposit money in a bank, you quite reasonably assume it's sitting safely in your account, ready to be withdrawn at any time. But in reality, banks lend most of it out. If too many people try to withdraw their money at the same time, the bank simply doesn't have enough money available. That's called a bank run, and it's what happened to Northern Rock in 2008.

So, in essence, you don't truly own the money in your bank account. Technically you are a creditor to the bank, much like someone who lends money through a short-term bond, but without earning meaningful interest. Of course, there are government protections in place. For example, in the UK, the Financial Services Compensation Scheme (FSCS) guarantees up to £85,000 per person, per bank, in the event of a failure. But what happens if your balance is higher than this limit?

And more importantly — what happens if the entire financial system reaches a final tipping point and experiences a violent full-scale deleveraging event, where QE and further borrowing simply can't prevent total collapse? As we saw in the Great Depression, systemic re-sets do happen. And in such scenarios, government guarantees may no longer hold true. If all major banks were to collapse, who would actually honour those guarantees? Like the gold coins of the past, the harsh reality is that people today don't truly own anything, regardless of what their bank balance or online statements might suggest.

NEED FOR AN ALTERNATIVE - ENTER BITCOIN

The financial crisis, as well as the devastation which has occurred countless times over the last century, revealed the deep flaws in traditional banking. But what real alternatives existed? Could people have stored their wealth in a way that didn't rely on banks, where access to their own money was never in question? On 31 October 2008, amid the crisis, an unidentified person or group known as Satoshi Nakamoto published the ground-breaking White Paper, *Bitcoin: A Peer-to-Peer Electronic Cash System*. This presented an entirely new concept — a decentralised currency that would allow people to transact directly, without banks or intermediaries.

Bitcoin (BTC) can be described in a variety of ways. Most days I come across new ways to express its meaning and how it works in practice. What is clear is that Bitcoin is an enigmatic concept that is both simple in essence, yet profound in implication. This makes it elusive to capture in just a few lines. Bitcoin is essentially a digital currency that allows peer-to-peer transactions without the need for banks or financial institutions. Instead of a third party processing payments, Bitcoin allows users to send money directly to one another. Securely. Across borders. Without restrictions.

It is basically a layer of technology built on top of the internet, equivalent to email or web apps, but designed for the digital economy. Unlike traditional banking, Bitcoin affords users control over their finances, with the promise that they will "be their own bank". This is especially beneficial in places where traditional banking services are unavailable or unreliable and has become known as banking the unbanked. Bitcoin, like other assets and precious metals, can be used as both a store of value and a medium of exchange.

Even though you may have seen images of Bitcoin or physical coins that bear the Bitcoin logo, including on the cover of this book, I must emphasise that these are just symbolic representations. Bitcoin only exists in the digital space, so you can't hold and see it in the physical world. Similarly, the Bitcoin network and the bitcoins that power it are a digital technology that isn't owned by any company or government. This concept might seem difficult to understand at first, but this will become clearer as we progress through this book. For the time being, the most important takeaway is that Bitcoin is an open-source payment network that anyone with a device and an internet connection can use.

So, what specifically can you do with Bitcoin? First, you can spend it like money, as it is increasingly accepted by businesses that include Starbucks, Virgin Galactic, and at one point, even Tesla for buying cars. Some companies also offer the option to pay salaries in Bitcoin, using platforms like Bitwage, which was anticipated to have paid over $400 million in salaries by the end of 2024. As long as it is accepted, Bitcoin can be used to make everyday purchases, private transactions, or send money to friends or family. It is especially useful for international transfers, as it allows you to send money abroad quickly and cheaply. And this year was the first when donations to runners' charities in the London Marathon could be made in cryptocurrency. Since funds are transferred peer-to-peer, rather than through traditional banking, Bitcoin bypasses large processing fees and the long delays incurred when banks verify transactions through multiple international counterparts. So, for those making frequent transactions across borders, it is especially beneficial.

Even though Bitcoin was initially designed as a peer-to-peer cash system for transactions, it has evolved over time to also serve as a store of value for the future. This approach is similar to traditional hard assets, such as property, which have been used to protect wealth over time. Holding onto traditional currency for too long can lead to a loss of purchasing power due to inflation. A true store of value should maintain or increase its purchasing power over time. One phrase I use many times in this book is that Bitcoin is often referred to as "digital gold". In fact, and as we will explore shortly, its limited supply and unique characteristics make it fundamentally different from any financial system or asset that has previously existed.

Another term that is used frequently in this book is fiat currency. Strangely, most people haven't even heard of it. A fiat currency is any traditional government-issued currency, such as U.S. Dollar (USD), Euro (EUR) and British Pound (GBP) that is controlled by a national central bank. Unlike Bitcoin, fiat currencies have no fixed supply, so central banks can print as much of them as they want, which affects their relative scarcity and purchasing power. This ability to create limitless currency, by using mechanisms such as QE, which we touched upon in the last chapter, explains why large amounts of fiat money continually enters circulation.

CHARACTERISTICS OF BITCOIN

So, now we know that Bitcoin is a decentralised currency, operating independently of banks and governments. How then does it work and what makes Bitcoin unique? Instead of financial institutions controlling and verifying transactions in a bank, Bitcoin relies on a global decentralised network of computers that verify transactions and maintain the protocol.

1. LIMITED SUPPLY

Fixed supply is one of the most distinctive features of Bitcoin. Because it is hardcoded into the software, the maximum supply of bitcoins will never exceed 21 million coins. For this reason, no bank, politician, or developer can ever create any more. Nearly 20 million bitcoins are currently in circulation and this scarcity creates value. It means that Bitcoin is subject to the same laws of supply and demand as any other precious item, including gold, real estate, and rare artwork. And these almost always go up in value over time as demand increases.

When Bitcoin was introduced in 2008, no bitcoins were in circulation. As briefly introduced in the last chapter, Satoshi Nakamoto mined the first block, known as the Genesis Block, on 3 January 2009, creating the first 50 bitcoins. At this stage, it's best just to think of mining as a group of independent participants working together with the goal of upholding and securing the network by confirming transactions. In return, miners are rewarded with newly created bitcoins, which are added to the supply in circulation.

Every new block that has been mined on the Bitcoin network ever since rewards the miner with newly created bitcoins as an incentive to maintain the network. Think of a block on the Bitcoin network like a digital container that holds a list of recent transactions. It's like a digital page in a ledger or spreadsheet that lists Bitcoin transactions, just like the rows that you see on your online bank account. When someone sends Bitcoin, the transaction is grouped with others into a block. Once confirmed, they are permanently added to the blockchain, like a bank statement showing the transactions you made.

In the early days, miners were compensated with 50 bitcoins for each block created. However, Bitcoin's inflation rate was designed so it decreased over time through a process called the halving. Every four years, the amount of newly created Bitcoin gets cut in half. Following the April 2024 halving, the reward was reduced to 3.125 BTC per block. With fewer than 3 million bitcoins left to mine, the final coins are expected to be issued in 2140, at which point the total supply will be in circulation.

2. DIVISIBILITY

Now, let's talk about divisibility, another crucial element of any sound monetary system, and which allows for transactions of any size. It is extremely important that a currency can be broken down into fractional pieces so that it is easy to use. This is the main reason why gold is generally not used to transact any more.

Trying to divide it into tiny values like one penny or one cent wouldn't be feasible.

This is why Bitcoin has a great advantage over precious metals and even fiat currencies, as it can be broken down into 100 million parts. These small fractional units are called Satoshis (sats), obviously named after the currency's famous creator. If someone says they can't afford an entire bitcoin, my response is always the same: you don't have to. This flexibility allows you to purchase or accept any amount, even as small as $1. You can have any fraction of a bitcoin up to eight decimal places. For example, 0.00003545 BTC (3,545 Satoshis) is about £2.50. This key feature makes Bitcoin accessible to anyone, regardless of their financial situation.

3. PORTABILITY

One of Bitcoin's biggest advantages over traditional money is its portability. While physical cash is small and lightweight, large sums become difficult to carry, and by using bank accounts, you must put your trust in a third party. Precious metals like gold are even harder to transport. It wouldn't be possible to carry or transfer heavy metals globally, except by commercial transportation, which is expensive and brings us back to the point regarding counter-party risk from the transporters. In contrast, Bitcoin's portability makes it one of the safest and most flexible forms of money, as it doesn't require you to trust anyone to hold or store it for you. Unlike physical cash or gold, Bitcoin can be stored on a small device, accessed from any location, and transferred worldwide without restrictions.

4. RECOGNISABILITY

One of the traditional qualities of sound money is recognisability — the ability to easily verify that a form of money is genuine and not counterfeit. Think about a gold coin with its distinct shine and weight, or a rare seashell that was once used in ancient trade. A piece of grain. A finely crafted tool used to shape stone or wood.

Finely ground spices from India, or even football stickers traded in the school playground. These items weren't always valued for their stunning appearance or rarity, but because they were hard to fake. They earned trust because they were easily recognisable for what they were.

Bitcoin follows a similar principle, though in digital form. Its recognisability doesn't rely on appearance or touch, but on the cryptographic proof that verifies it. As every transaction is publicly recorded and mathematically verified, anyone securing the network can easily confirm its authenticity. This transparency and cryptographic integrity ensures that every bitcoin circulating on the network is genuine and can't be forged.

5. DURABILITY

Another important aspect of any well-functioning form of money is that it must be durable. Gold and precious metal coins last for centuries, so they possess this quality. However, physical representations of money fade, tear, and deteriorate over time. Although digital cash in a bank account is more durable, you still need to rely on the bank not to fail. Additionally, fiat currencies can be made obsolete.

Remember that many European currencies were converted to euros at the beginning of the century. For some, their savings felt diminished, and they perceived that prices had risen, as businesses often rounded up prices on goods, while savings, wages and pensions were converted more strictly. This led many to feel a loss of purchasing power, making them feel poorer.

Bitcoin is far more durable because it only exists digitally on a global decentralised network. Providing there are computers securing the Bitcoin blockchain, and there are users who want to transact on the network, it cannot be destroyed or made obsolete. Its destiny is not based on government or central bank decisions, but on the entire community who use it. We will look at this in more detail in Chapter 8.

6. FUNGIBILITY

Money should be fungible in design, so that each unit is inter-changeable and always equal to another. Just like one U.S. dollar is equal to another U.S. dollar, one bitcoin is always equal to another bitcoin. This means that Bitcoin can function as a medium of exchange, allowing users to freely trade it without regard for uniqueness or variation.

7. SECURITY

Security is a critical characteristic of Bitcoin and one of its strongest. Unlike traditional banking, Bitcoin eliminates intermediaries and offers users complete control over their funds. There have been instances of fraudulent activity in traditional bank accounts and of banking apps being out of action. Blockchain transactions, however, are cryptographically secure because they rely on mathematical proof. They can't be falsified, altered, or reversed once confirmed. The Bitcoin network runs 24 hours a day, 7 days a week and remains one of the most secure computing networks in the world, with the Bitcoin protocol itself having never been hacked. As we will see later, third-party services have been hacked, which is why self-custody and protection of your private keys are imperative to keeping your digital assets safe.

8. TRANSPARENCY AND IMMUTABILITY

As Bitcoin transactions are public, everyone can view which wallet sent them, when they occurred and which wallet received them. Once transactions are confirmed on the blockchain, they are permanently recorded, making it virtually impossible for anyone to change them. This level of transparency and immutability prevents fraud and is a crucial quality of any sound currency. Compare this with traditional banking, where financial transactions are hidden and can be manipulated.

9. ACCESSIBILITY

One of Bitcoin's most powerful features is its accessibility. Formal identification, proof of address, and minimum balances are not needed. Bitcoin can be accessed by anyone who holds a smartphone and an internet connection. This is especially useful in regions where banking infrastructure is limited or unavailable. It is also useful for someone who is homeless, who is not part of the traditional system, which has become much more common in recent times. Regardless of country, whether living in a city or a remote rural area, and regardless of personal circumstances, no permission is needed. Bitcoin ATMs can facilitate purchase into their mobile wallets with cash, so it redefines who gets to participate in financial markets.

SOME GENERAL NOTES ON STORAGE

So, we now know some of Bitcoin's main characteristics, but not yet how to store it. You can't simply pick it up and put it in your pocket, so how do you keep it safe? Bitcoin can be viewed in your digital wallets, which can be software applications or hardware devices that are designed to store your public and private keys safely. However, these wallets don't actually store your Bitcoin, but rather scan the blockchain using your public key (address) to see how much Bitcoin is associated with it and displays this balance on the wallet interface. These keys grant you access to the Bitcoin, which is recorded on the blockchain. The private key basically grants you ownership of that part of the database. Don't worry too much about that at this stage as we will delve into it in Chapter 9. For now, you just need to know that there are two main types of wallets, hot wallets and cold wallets, and each wallet contains a private key (like a password to access and send Bitcoin) and a public key (to form an address to receive Bitcoin). If you lose your private key, you lose access to your Bitcoin forever, so it is imperative to bear this in mind before using any cryptocurrency network.

THE WHITE PAPER THAT SHOOK THE WORLD

We have now assessed what Bitcoin is and what you can do with it, including its key characteristics. But what exactly did Satoshi Nakamoto's White Paper propose? And what does Bitcoin mining involve?

In general terms, the document explains the idea and technology behind Bitcoin, the first digital currency that didn't need banks or other payment processors to confirm transactions. The paper considers some of the problems that we have already outlined with traditional online monetary systems and the lack of trust in them. By sending money directly, within the boundaries of pre-programmed software, the White Paper explains that cryptocurrency eliminates the chance of human intervention or manipulation.

Instead, it operates using a network of computers, which are called nodes. And these nodes help to keep track of transactions on a public ledger called the blockchain. Transactions on the blockchain essentially move digital money (bitcoins) from one person's wallet to another's.

To understand this better, imagine you have a digital piggy bank (wallet) on your computer or mobile device. Whereas a real-world piggy bank stores cash, this wallet displays your Bitcoin balance and holds the keys that give you access and control over how your Bitcoin is moved or transferred on the blockchain. So, let's say you want to send Bitcoin to your friend, in the way that you would send an email or a WhatsApp message with a photo attached. You open the app, type your message, attach the photo, and make sure that you have their correct email address or phone number. This is broadly similar to sending someone Bitcoin. After opening your wallet app, you enter the amount you wish to send and then enter their correct Bitcoin wallet address. When you click send, your transaction is broadcast to the Bitcoin network. Once confirmed, the Bitcoin is credited to your friend's wallet, just as a picture message would show up in their WhatsApp chat to view.

Focusing on this topic for a second, sending an email is very different to sending cryptocurrency, even though it might seem superficially similar. Even though they are both digital and virtually instantaneous, the underlying mechanics couldn't be more different. An email often passes through multiple servers, routers, and network checkpoints, all dynamically routing the message across the internet, until it reaches its destination. This means it is flexible, forgiving, and can be rerouted around congestion or outages.

Cryptocurrency transactions can't function this way. This is because they must follow a fixed, verifiable path through the blockchain, where every movement of value is cryptographically secured and publicly recorded.

If transactions could bounce between nodes like emails, it would introduce too many vulnerabilities, such as hacking, fraud, and interception. Blockchain's consensus process is slower and more resource-intensive, but that makes it secure. As opposed to email, where the message is duplicated and distributed, a crypto transaction must represent a single, irreversible change to a decentralised ledger.

Overall, the Bitcoin process is efficient, cost effective, cheaper and borderless, often being a much quicker method for international payments, since transactions proceed straight from sender to receiver. When you call your friend on a phone network, as long as you have the correct number, you will reach the intended person. Likewise, a Bitcoin transaction will always reach its intended destination as long as you include the correct wallet address. But it must be correct, as it can't be reversed.

ADDRESSING SOME COMMON QUESTIONS

However, quite possibly, as you have been reading this chapter, some questions may have arisen. Such as, what happens if Bitcoin is lost — wouldn't that mean we'll never reach the full 21 million coins mentioned earlier in 1? What is the effect of fixed supply? Or, as I just explained, what happens if you send BTC to the wrong address? What if a miner steals your digital assets? I also stated that Bitcoin has never been hacked, but perhaps you've heard of hacks in the news that seem to contradict this. So, could Bitcoin actually be lost forever?

1. IS BITCOIN A GIANT DIGITAL SPREADSHEET?

A good way to think about the Bitcoin network is like a giant, digital database that shows every transaction that has ever happened. Each wallet address is one row on this spreadsheet, and next to it is the number of bitcoins that wallet controls. The blockchain itself is like a long-running Excel file with new tab sheets (blocks) added regularly, each recording recent transactions, with the latest one on top. Every time someone sends Bitcoin, it's just a change in numbers between two rows; the sender's row decreases and the receiver's row increases. Nothing physical changes hands. No coins are printed or destroyed. It's simply an update.

2. SO, WHAT HAPPENS WHEN YOU SEND BITCOIN?

When you send Bitcoin, your wallet creates a transaction request and broadcasts it to the Bitcoin network. The nodes running the Bitcoin software check that the correct private key has been used, the transaction follows Bitcoin's rules, and that you have enough Bitcoin available to send. Once these have been verified, mining nodes compile your transaction into a block. Once confirmed, nodes across the network agree on it, and each updates their own copy of the spreadsheet. The balances are updated accordingly, and the block is linked to the one before, forming a permanent chain of records, hence the name blockchain.

That's all Bitcoin really is — a constantly updated ledger that everyone agrees to. And since everyone has their own copy, no one can manipulate it, ensuring that no single entity controls the ledger and that it is transparent and permanent.

3. CAN BITCOIN BE LOST?

Bitcoin isn't like cash or email, which can get lost or delayed in transit. If you send Bitcoin, it simply moves from one row to another. In that sense, Bitcoin can't be lost and nothing disappears. If the address is correct, the transaction is updated on the new row. If the address is invalid, the network usually rejects it, and the Bitcoin stays on your row. If you send it to the wrong valid address, it still gets sent to that row, but only the recipient can choose to return it. Either way, the ledger always records where it is.

4. WHAT IF YOU LOSE YOUR PRIVATE KEY?

It is important to remember that losing your private key doesn't delete your Bitcoin. It doesn't make it disappear — it just makes it inaccessible. You lose the ability to instruct the network to move Bitcoin from your row to another. The amount is still there, visible on the blockchain, but it can't ever be used. If someone with 2 BTC in their wallet loses their private key permanently, they will never be able to move that Bitcoin again. Their line on the spreadsheet will still show 2 BTC and will be visible on blockchain explorers, but they will never be able to use it and that line on the spreadsheet will remain unaltered forever.

5. HOW IS CIRCULATING SUPPLY CALCULATED?

The total amount of Bitcoin on each row of the spreadsheet always equals the total circulating supply. Even if millions of coins are locked in inaccessible rows, they still count. Once all the bitcoins have been mined, the sum across all rows will be fixed at 21 million, and that number will never change.

6. WHAT ABOUT BAD ACTORS?

Miners don't have access to your private key, so they can't move Bitcoin from your row to theirs. They simply confirm transactions and add new spreadsheet tabs (blocks) to the ledger. If a dishonest miner tries to submit a block that manipulates transactions or benefits them, it's rejected by the network. They have effectively updated their spreadsheet differently. However, unless most of the network agrees, their version is ignored. Bitcoin works on majority consensus which means for manipulation to succeed, they would need to convince more than half of the network to follow their version, which is why decentralisation is so crucial to Bitcoin's security.

7. AND WHAT ABOUT HACKING?

The Bitcoin protocol itself has never been hacked. What you may have heard in the media are cases where private keys were stolen. This is often from exchanges or poorly secured wallets. If someone obtains your private key, they can move your Bitcoin to their own address, as in their own row on the spreadsheet. The transaction will still be visible, but the coins will no longer be under your control. That's why protecting your private key is absolutely critical.

We'll look at the mechanics of verification in more detail in Chapter 6, but let's now talk about the mining process. Imagine yourself at a large party, surrounded by people who all want to trade different snacks with one another. Instead of using cash or bank transactions to buy the snacks, everyone keeps a special notebook called the Snack Ledger. When you want to buy or sell snacks, you write down the details of the transaction in your notebook and ask everyone at the party to confirm it is genuine.

To make sure no one cheats and tries to sell the same snack twice, there's a game called Snack Sudoku. Everyone at the party competes to solve complex Sudoku puzzles, and the first person to solve one gets a reward of snacks and a special stamp in their notebook. Then everyone writes down that this transaction is valid in their own notebooks. This way, everyone has a record of the transaction, so it can't be changed or erased as everyone at the party is aware of it. This process is like mining. The Snack Sudoku puzzles are really hard, but they work because they ensure that everyone agrees on which transactions are real and which are fake, as the work has been put in to solve the puzzle, keeping the system fair and secure.

So, in this analogy, the party is the Bitcoin network; the Snack Ledger is the blockchain, and Snack Sudoku is the mining process, using their "proof-of-work" from the sudoku puzzles. The Snack Reward is like the newly minted bitcoins that are given as a reward for working to solve the puzzle. Just like the party, everyone on the Bitcoin network works together to keep track of transactions and make sure the system is reliable.

As highlighted in Satoshi Nakamoto's White Paper, Bitcoin miners must carry out real computational work by using powerful computers to solve complex mathematical puzzles in order to propose the next block. Once a miner solves the cryptographic puzzle, other nodes on the network must then check its validity. If the majority of the network agrees that it follows Bitcoin's rules, the block is confirmed, the miner receives their block reward, and the block is added to the blockchain. This process is known as the Proof-of-Work (PoW) consensus mechanism, and it is this framework that drives Bitcoin's security. Thousands of computers (nodes) across the network, based all around the world, work to uphold the network — this wide distribution is what makes Bitcoin truly decentralised.

PoW is essentially an anti-cheating mechanism, discouraging fraud by making it extremely difficult to alter past transactions. Just as solving a Sudoku puzzle takes effort, mining requires real-world hardware, electricity, and computational power. If someone wanted to rewrite the blockchain, they would not only have to redo all the puzzles but also gain control over the majority of the network, which is thousands of nodes, to even have the ability to get their altered version accepted. Due to the enormous computing power required and the level of coordination that would be needed, such an attack is virtually impossible. This system not only makes Bitcoin secure, decentralised, and tamper-proof, but also guards against the risk of a central authority mismanaging or manipulating the currency.

SATOSHI'S MYSTERY

Up to this point, we have covered the fundamental qualities that make Bitcoin unique. Yet Bitcoin is more than just a theoretical idea. It's something that had to be tested and refined to get to where it is today. Moving from just a concept on an online forum to a functioning currency is where the story becomes even more fascinating. Who created Bitcoin? How did it move from a White Paper to a functioning network? And how did a digital currency with no backing, no central issuer, and no marketing team slowly begin to attract attention? To find out we must step into the earliest days of Bitcoin.

Let's go back to before all the media attention, before institutions embraced Bitcoin, and before anyone could have predicted its impact. Satoshi Nakamoto's brilliance in cryptography and computer science is evident in the intricate design and implementation of Bitcoin. However, unlike many other brilliant innovators, Bitcoin's developer stayed anonymous and never claimed recognition. Nakamoto developed Bitcoin from the beginning to guarantee that it could work independently, even without their oversight. This wasn't just about building a system that could survive, it was about creating one that didn't need a leader at all. Bitcoin's decentralised architecture means that control will always rest with the network itself, not a single individual. We'll explore this more in Chapter 6.

In the early days, Nakamoto actively engaged with cryptographers and developers online, participating in conversations that helped enhance Bitcoin's design and gave the system stability. Among these early contributors was Hal Finney, a well-respected cryptographic activist and developer who immediately saw the potential of Nakamoto's vision. Finney was one of the first to run Bitcoin's software, offering feedback and contributing to its development.

On 12 January 2009, he received the first ever Bitcoin transaction from Nakamoto, demonstrating that Bitcoin's peer-to-peer protocol functioned exactly as intended.

Yet, despite their close collaboration, it is believed Nakamoto never revealed their identity, even to Finney. There were no public appearances, no personal details revealed, only a trail of messages and code. Nakamoto gradually began to withdraw from Bitcoin's development and reduced their online communication. Then, in April 2011, without warning or explanation, they stopped posting on the cryptographic forums and engaging in email correspondence, and their online presence totally disappeared.

Bitcoin was not the only monetary innovation inspired by the frailties in mainstream banking and financial services. In 1998, Bernard von NotHaus created the Liberty Dollar, a private currency backed by precious metals like gold and silver, specifically in response to fiat currency debasement. But in 2007 U.S. federal agents raided his operation, and in 2009 he was arrested and charged with counterfeiting and conspiracy against the U.S. financial system. In 2011 he was convicted, with prosecutors calling his challenge to the government-issued dollar a form of "domestic terrorism". NotHaus was later sentenced to six months of house arrest. Given what had happened to NotHaus and indeed to anyone who challenges the establishment, Nakamoto would have been well aware of the risks of revealing their true identity.

There are many theories and documentaries concerning who Nakamoto might be, why they went away, and why they hid their identity. Over the years speculation has surrounded Finney, Adam Back, Craig Wright, and even three Japanese cryptographers, **Satoshi** Obana, Junko **Naka**jima and Tatsuaki Oka**moto**, which together forms the name of the fabulous creator. Interestingly, all three men were allegedly in the same room with Finney during a cryptography conference prior to Bitcoin's creation. Maybe one day the truth will be revealed, but for now it remains a mystery. Either way, this still adds to the overall intrigue of the story.

Some suggest that Nakamoto just wanted to avoid legal and regulatory scrutiny as Bitcoin was gaining popularity. Others argue that it was purposeful from the start, and they never intended to be a permanent part of Bitcoin's future. I believe it is likely a combination of the two, but one thing is for sure, Bitcoin no longer needs its creator. Nakamoto may have written the software, which is undeniably incredible, but Bitcoin's true power lies in its decentralised nature. And it continues to function and evolve without a central authority, proving that trust in financial systems doesn't require a government, a corporation, or even a visible leader.

BITCOIN PIZZA DAY

In the early days of Bitcoin, one of the most famous moments wasn't a mind-blowing financial deal or the opening of the first Bitcoin exchange, it was a good, old-fashioned pizza trade. On 22 May 2010, a programmer from Florida named Laszlo Hanyecz decided to take a leap into the future by making history with the very first documented real-world transaction using Bitcoin.

At the time, Bitcoin was worth about as much as a soggy copy of *The Times* newspaper. After all, the currency was still in its experimental phase, traded mostly among elite cryptographers on the forums, who saw its potential but had yet to test it in the real world.

Hanyecz, an active participant in Bitcoin's early community, wanted to change that. He posted a wild offer on an online forum, offering to pay 10,000 BTC to anyone brave enough to order and deliver him two large pizzas. It wasn't about convenience as he could easily have ordered them himself and had them delivered in 30 minutes. It was about proving that Bitcoin could function as a real medium of exchange, something people could use to buy goods and services, just like traditional money.

In a twist of fate, a British chap named Jeremy Sturdivant accepted the offer and arranged for the two Domino's pizzas to be delivered to Hanyecz's home, in exchange for the 10,000 BTC. At the time, it must have felt like a steal, considering Bitcoin was about as valuable as a chocolate teapot. But as Bitcoin's value shot up like a rocket in the following years, those 10,000 BTC turned into one of the most expensive meals in history, worth nearly $1 billion today.

Now, 22 May is celebrated each year as "Bitcoin Pizza Day", a tasty reminder of Bitcoin's humble beginnings. It was a moment that proved Bitcoin wasn't just an abstract concept and that it could be used in the real world. Looking back, it shows just how the perception of value can change over time. What was once traded for a couple of pizzas would later be considered a treasure chest of riches. For the Bitcoin community, Bitcoin Pizza Day is more than just a funny anecdote, it's a symbol of just how far the currency has come from its early days as an obscure internet experiment to a recognised financial asset.

BITCOIN'S EARLY PERCEPTIONS

However, we must remember that this recognition took time to materialise. In its first few years, Bitcoin was dismissed by many as a gimmick, a scam or just a temporary curiosity. And its early years did not come without controversy. For many, their first encounter with Bitcoin came not through financial reform or technical innovation — but through headlines linking it to illicit markets and criminal activity.

One of the most infamous examples of this was Silk Road, an online black market, operating on the dark web that allowed users to buy and sell illegal drugs, forged documents, and other prohibited items using Bitcoin. Launched in 2011, Silk Road relied on Bitcoin's pseudonymous nature and borderless transaction model to facilitate anonymous payments. Although all transactions on the Bitcoin blockchain are publicly visible, users could obscure their identities with temporary wallet addresses, making enforcement difficult without further forensic tools.

Critics began to argue that Bitcoin's decentralised structure made it a haven for money laundering, tax evasion, and terrorism financing. This association with crime became one of Bitcoin's most publicised features in its early days, with media narratives portraying it as the currency of hackers, drug dealers, and anarchists.

Alongside its early association with illicit markets, Bitcoin also faced technical and economic growing pains. In the early days, Bitcoin even suffered two outages. An eight-hour downtime occurred in 2010 due to a bug, which created 64 billion Bitcoin in three wallets, an impossibility, as it greatly exceeded the hardcap. Then in 2013, a temporary chain split caused by a software upgrade incompatibility led to a six-hour network disruption, though it was quickly resolved and caused no permanent harm to the network.

Bitcoin's first few years in particular were also extremely volatile, bouncing from fractions of a cent to around $30 in mid-2011 and back to a couple of dollars by the end of the year. In November 2013, it surged past $1,000 for the first time only to crash back below $200 just over a year later.

These wild price swings and criminal associations made it difficult for people to take Bitcoin seriously in its formative years. Beyond the revolutionary technology and the cheerful story of "Bitcoin Pizza Day", lay a more sinister early perception — one that Bitcoin would have to overcome.

Hopefully, you now have a better understanding of what blockchain technology and Bitcoin are, as well as the motivations and challenges it faced during its early development. More importantly, it demonstrates that trust in institutions may previously have been misplaced and that our finances could be returned to our own control. Bitcoin might be more than just another form of digital money. Perhaps it is the answer to financial uncertainty, while also providing extensive opportunities. Could it mark a move towards a financial model that doesn't rely on trust, pushing back against the systems that have controlled economies for centuries?

On that note, we need to go back in time for a better understanding of everything that led to the creation of blockchain technology, to better appreciate its potential as a financial turning point. Looking back at the evolution of money and trade highlights how centralised monetary systems have functioned throughout the ages, and like Bitcoin, what utilities and challenges they have faced along the way. But what lessons can history teach us about financial stability, inflation, and trust? And why have centralised monetary systems consistently faced challenges? The answers lie in their rise and fall throughout history.

Chapter 4

Historic Monetary Standards

Now that we've briefly explored Bitcoin's role in modern finance, let's take a step back, way back, before money as we know it even existed. Before digital ledgers and bank accounts, before anyone could ever have dreamt of tapping a card to buy a coffee. How did people trade? And what systems did they rely on to exchange value?

For thousands of years, human societies have found ways to cooperate, barter, and create systems to measure value. If you think today's financial system is complex, imagine a time when people didn't even have a currency to argue about. Instead of checking exchange rates, they were figuring out how many fish equalled a handful of berries or debating whether it was worth trading a particularly good spear for a warm fur coat. Long before the first coins were minted, before rulers stamped their faces onto bits of metal to signify value, trade was built on trust, necessity, and whatever resources people had at hand.

Money, in its various forms, has always had a big influence on human civilisation. But the way people measure and store value has constantly changed. Could what started as systems of exchange driven by necessity progress into methods that favoured those who could gain the most from them?

As simple exchanges between individuals grew into networks of trade, could the ability to store wealth and enforce rules become just as important as the goods themselves? What can their ways of exchanging value reveal about the systems that followed?

Throughout history, communities have always established their own ways of allocating value to reflect their environment. But how did they organise these systems without coins, without banks, without written agreements? Perhaps some of these systems worked for centuries, while others might have collapsed as quickly as they emerged. But were these shifts always signs of progress, or simply new ways of exercising authority?

Our journey begins before 10000 BCE, prior even to the dominance of agriculture. Human societies relied entirely on the natural world for survival, being predominantly composed of hunter-gatherers. Our early ancestors were on the move, embracing a nomadic or semi-nomadic lifestyle, journeying with the seasons in pursuit of food, water, and shelter. Small societies with 20 to 50 members were common, mostly consisting of extended relatives or close acquaintances. Kings or elites did not rule them, and skill and experience determined leadership, not wealth or prestige.

Large endeavours, such as foraging and hunting huge animals required group teamwork. Hunting, collecting, tool-making, and shelter-building were delegated for daily survival, using stone tools, such as hand axes, knives, and scrapers, and resources were shared. These societies thrived with vibrant and rich cultural traditions. Knowledge was shared through storytelling, songs, and rituals. People crafted amazing cave paintings and carvings, depicting animals, hunts, and other fascinating forms of symbolic art. It reveals a world that goes beyond mere survival, showcasing rich culture and possibly even the beginnings of record-keeping.

For many years these early societies operated without rulers, written laws, or structured economies. They thrived on trust, cooperation, and shared responsibility. There were no central authorities to control wealth or dictate rules, yet they lived in balance with their surroundings. In many ways, this reliance on trust and self-sufficiency mirrors the decentralised ethos of Bitcoin, where systems do not need a central leader, but instead operate under community consensus. In a world now dominated by financial systems, ownership, and competition, it's extraordinary to think that survival once depended on simply working together.

The journey takes an exciting turn around 10000 BCE, when it is believed the hunter-gatherers began to explore the prospect of agriculture, marking the start of the Neolithic Revolution. Small groups who once followed herds and gathered wild plants began planting their own food. At first, it may have been as simple as noticing that seeds left behind near campsites sprouted into edible plants the next season. Over time, this knowledge sparked intentional farming, generating food surpluses and enabling larger populations to thrive.

In contrast to the rapid technological advances we see today, this transition unfolded gradually around the world. Thanks to a more stable food supply, permanent settlements started to flourish. And this laid the groundwork for trade and the eventual development of more organised systems of value. Much of what we know about this period comes from archaeological findings rather than written documents, because writing was not around then. By piecing together what remains, researchers have been able to form a picture of how these early societies lived.

From the earliest known settlements, of Jericho in the West Bank and Göbekli Tepe in modern-day Turkey, we have clear evidence from around 9600 BCE of people living together in early hunter-gather communities that had started to cultivate crops and build structures of spiritual or social significance.

Settlements such as Çatalhöyük in modern-day Turkey show even more advanced early urban living by about 7500 BCE. As one of the best-preserved Neolithic sites, Çatalhöyük features closely packed mud brick buildings with agricultural, herding, and pottery producing activities. Unlike the scattered encampments of their ancestors, these people lived in a structured environment, but this didn't come without problems. Their homes were built so close together that people had to enter through openings in the roofs rather than doors at street level. And although the development of some of these settlements experienced overcrowding and environmental problems, leading to infectious diseases as well as violence, they highlight how societies were evolving. Their progression wasn't just about their ability to grow their own food, but about how they began organising their living spaces, by working together to build long lasting communities.

During the Archaic Period (8000–1000 BCE), comparable developments began in the Americas as the nomadic hunter-gatherer existence gradually shifted to more settled populations. Trade networks grew and populations increased as the indigenous inhabitants of North and South America farmed basic crops, such as maize, beans, and squash. Much like their counterparts across the Atlantic, these societies moved from direct exchange to standardised trade goods, using resources such as shells, salt, and finely crafted tools as early media of exchange. Over time, more structured economies and long-distance trade routes evolved, each uniquely suited to the demands of its specific environment.

Around 7000 BCE, early farmers from the Levant, Mesopotamia, and Central and South Asia began moving to Europe through Anatolia, or what is now the Asian section of Turkey. Agriculture flourished, changing the way people in Europe lived. Trade and social hierarchies were still a long way off, but the shift from a purely subsistence lifestyle to one of stability and surplus was a big turning point. What we know of their lives and the decisions they made gives us insight into the fundamental forces driving human progress, illustrating how these early choices laid the groundwork for the complex economic systems that followed.

As tribes established themselves, food surpluses facilitated early forms of trade. Goods were often shared among hunter-gatherer tribes, but as farming communities gained prominence, the necessity for people and villages to trade with each other increased. In the absence of standardised currencies, systems of bartering sprang up. For example, a farmer with excess grain might swap it for animal skins, or a potter exchange handcrafted bowls for fresh food.

However, this system had its limitations, as a deal could only take place if both parties simultaneously wanted what the other was providing, a difficulty known as the double coincidence of wants. As trade networks grew and products needed to travel longer distances, early societies sought more dependable mechanisms to track transactions. They also needed more standardised methods of exchange, ones that prioritised durability, scarcity, and consistency. It's not a far cry from the way that today's digital currencies have been exploring alternative methods that enforce these sound monetary principles. Bitcoin, for example, doesn't rely on physical form but is still bound by a fixed supply showing scarcity and a system of verification, which mirrors some of the qualities that made early currencies work in the first place. We need to look a bit deeper to understand more about how these ancient methods compare to the ledger style systems we use today, however.

Around 8000–7000 BCE, as agriculture gained in popularity, commercial activities became more complex. Early innovations in record-keeping and trading emerged in and around the Fertile Crescent, including areas of Western Asia, the Balkans, and North Africa. Most prominent among these was Mesopotamia, or present-day Iraq, where clay tokens emerged as the first known system of accounting and trade documentation.

These small, geometrically shaped tokens represented a specific quantity or type of commodity. A cone-shaped token might signify a unit of grain, while a spherical token might represent a sheep. The unique shapes and markings on the tokens helped distinguish between different types of goods and quantities, which is actually very similar to the barcodes we use today. Traders utilised these tokens to track transactions and debts. If someone owed a specific amount of grain, the number of tokens used to represent it constituted a physical record of the debt until it was paid off.

As transactions grew in complexity, merchants and traders began placing the tokens inside hollow clay balls known as bullae, which were then sealed. To serve as an external record, the outside of a bulla was sometimes marked with a summary of its contents. To me, parallels exist between these bullae and the blockchain in this regard at least. For the first time, this technology had enabled secure, long-distance trading by allowing items to be confirmed at the destination without breaking the bullae open. These early systems of inventory management paved the way for more structured economies and the formation of the first civilisations.

Moving forward, in the ancient region of Anatolia, between Europe and Asia, by between 7000 BCE and 5000 BCE people had begun to recognise the importance of various resources, not only for daily survival but also as valuable commodities for trade. Among these were cowrie shells and obsidian. Obsidian, a volcanic glass with razor-sharp edges, was highly prized in Anatolia. This dark, shiny substance was used to make tools and weapons, which were necessary for hunting, survival, and craftsmanship. Its natural scarcity in many areas made it a valuable resource, and it was traded long-distance.

While obsidian was crucial for survival, cowrie shells served an entirely different purpose. These small, intricate shells held intrinsic value as they were lightweight, durable, and aesthetically pleasing. So much so that they became one of the earliest standardised mediums of exchange. Their uniform shape and lightweight nature made them ideal for trade, and they became widely accepted across vast regions. This made them one of the first forms of money, helping early traders transition from simple barter to more structured economic systems. The broad circulation of obsidian and cowrie shells demonstrates evidence of early economic activity that would later be adopted by future great civilisations.

CRADLES OF CIVILISATION

By 3500 BCE a remarkable shift was taking place in various regions of the world. Several human societies were developing from small agricultural villages into large urban centres, giving rise to the first great civilisations. These are often referred to as the Cradles of Civilisation. Despite forming independently, these societies began to dominate trade in their respective regions, spawning the first functioning economies. Mesopotamia led the way, with the Sumerians building some of the world's earliest known cities, including Uruk and Babylon.

However, as trade progressed, it became increasingly difficult to monitor commodities and keep records with clay tokens alone. This led to one of history's most significant breakthroughs: the invention of cuneiform, the world's first fully developed writing system. Instead of carrying physical tokens, now merchants could record transactions on clay tablets, allowing for more advanced tracking of goods and taxes.

Before the emergence of coinage or formal banking systems, writing itself had become an important tool for economic growth. The ability to record debts, taxes, and trade agreements introduced a new level of financial accountability. A stylus was used to inscribe wedge-shaped marks into wet clay tablets, resulting in a durable and permanent economic record. Initially, this script was used for basic lists, which included barley, animals, and textiles. However, by 3200 BCE, it had also been applied to legal contracts, land deals, and advanced taxation.

Concurrently, the Mesopotamians were also constructing ziggurats, the massive, stepped temples that pre-dated the Egyptian pyramids and served as economic and administrative centres. Within these structures, they continued using cuneiform writing to manage trade and taxation, reinforcing the influence of the region's rulers. Much as early societies developed writing systems to formalise transactions and eliminate ambiguity, blockchain technology today provides a decentralised and transparent ledger to ensure financial integrity.

While Mesopotamia flourished, another great civilisation was rising along the Nile River. Ancient Egypt became a highly organised society, renowned for its monumental architecture, including the famous pyramids. The Nile's annual floods ensured a stable food supply, supporting population growth and economic expansion. By 3100 BCE, Egyptians had developed their own hieroglyphic writing system to track agricultural production and taxation. These inscriptions not only facilitated economic management but would also become one of history's most significant artistic and cultural legacies.

Meanwhile, another key civilisation was forming further east. The Indus Valley Civilisation emerged in parts of modern-day Pakistan and northwest India, developing highly advanced urban centres. Cities like Harappa and Mohenjo-Daro featured meticulously planned grid-like street layouts that resembled modern cities like New York. The advanced drainage systems and uniform housing structures reveal impressive attention to detail. Archaeological evidence indicates a highly organised trade system, with standardised weights and seals regulating commerce. The Indus script, developed around 2800 BCE, likely played a crucial role in financial record-keeping. Although it has yet to be deciphered, the evidence of its advanced trading routes and sophistication suggests that it served this purpose. At the time of writing, a prize has been offered to anyone who can successfully interpret the mysterious symbols.

Although other civilisations were emerging around this period, such as those in China and Peru, the most advanced trade networks existed between Mesopotamia, Egypt, and the Indus Valley. They all took advantage of nearby rivers for agriculture and trade, using the fertile ground for growing and exporting crops. Despite their differences, what they had in common was that each had developed their own highly organised economies. The writing and financial innovations they made would set a precedent for all future empires to follow.

These early civilisations demonstrated that as a society grows, so does its need for a structured system of exchange. Without efficient ways to track and record transactions, the development of advanced monetary systems would have been impossible. As trade expanded and bartering became impractical for large-scale economies, economic power increasingly shifted to those who were able to control these systems.

TRANSITION TO METAL-BASED CURRENCIES

Between 600 BCE and 500 BCE, these ancient civilisations transitioned from early forms of commodity-based money, such as cowrie shells and livestock, to metal-based currencies. This was driven by the need for durable, standardised, and widely accepted forms of currency that could accommodate the increasing complexities of trade. Gold, silver, and copper were popular coin materials due to their intrinsic value and scarcity. Unlike prior forms of money, metal coins could be manufactured according to standardised weights and markings, increasing the efficiency of transactions and reducing disputes over value.

Further parallels with the development of cryptocurrency are clearly identifiable. Just as these early societies transitioned to metal currencies for their durability and scarcity, modern digital assets like Bitcoin exhibit these qualities in a decentralised form. Where ancient civilisations sought standardisation through coinage, today's innovations look to cryptographic trust to solve similar challenges. The introduction of coinage marked a turning point in monetary history, imbuing its creators with a more efficient and secure way to store and transfer value. In the same way, digital currencies today offer individuals a new path towards financial sovereignty.

Lydia, which is situated in modern-day Turkey, was one of the first civilisations to use metal currencies. Under King Alyattes (c. 610–560 BCE), the Lydians began minting coins from electrum, a naturally occurring alloy of gold and silver. These standardised coins enabled trade while also serving as emblems of political power, bolstering the ruler's authority and the credibility of the currency. The introduction of metal coinage reduced many of the inefficiencies of barter and soft commodity-based money, setting the groundwork for organised economies based on a more stable and uniform medium of exchange.

Lydia was not the only region experimenting with metal coins. In China, the Guanzhuang mint in Henan Province, which dates back to around 640 BCE, created some of the first regulated metal currencies, including spade coins, which were named for their resemblance to gardening equipment. This transition to metal-based money therefore occurred separately around the Mediterranean and in Asia. The existence of structured mints demonstrates the growing importance of centralised institutions in controlling the production of currency — a clear departure from the parallels with Bitcoin that we have seen so far. This centralisation did, however, improve consistency in trade, which had previously been a challenge.

Even so, the influence of coinage extended far beyond just simplifying transactions. Economically, it promoted the accumulation of wealth and expansion of trade. Culturally, gold and silver coins came to represent wealth and status, cementing social hierarchies. And politically, creating coins bearing state symbols signified rulers' legitimacy, a practice that spread across Greece, Persia, Rome, and China. These coins were also highly portable and durable, making them far easier to store, compared with bulkier barter goods or perishable soft commodities. Gold coins also share many of the characteristics of sound money that we explored with Bitcoin in Chapter 3. For these reasons, they rapidly became the dominant medium of exchange across the ancient world.

After Lydia had introduced coinage, it quickly caught on in neighbouring regions, particularly in Greece, where city-states began minting their own standardised currencies. By 600 BCE, Greek coins were circulating across the Aegean, helping to streamline trade. While largely influenced by the Lydians, the Greeks developed unique monetary systems to suit their own expanding economies and trading networks.

Greek coins were primarily made of silver and valued for their consistent weight, making them a trusted medium of exchange. Two of the most prevalent coins during this period were the drachma and tetradrachm. While the drachma served as a standard unit for daily trade, the tetradrachm, valued at four drachmas, was used for higher value transactions. In some ways, this dynamic isn't so different from digital assets today. Ethereum is often used for everyday transactions and smart contracts, while Bitcoin, with its reputation for stability and scarcity, is preferred for larger transactions or long-term holdings. This reflects how ancient currencies evolved to serve different economic functions by adapting to the needs of the growing economies they supported.

As just mentioned, the consistent weight and value of Ancient Greek coins made transactions smoother and more efficient. This meant merchants no longer had to negotiate inconsistent exchange rates or barter terms, speeding up the expansion of markets and economic growth. A coin's intrinsic metal value played a key role in maintaining trust, something modern currencies no longer deem important. This trust in stable value not only facilitated trade but also encouraged the development of lending and investment, forming the foundations for early banking systems. With tangible backing from these nascent financial institutions, merchants and traders could conduct business with new confidence.

But Greek coinage was not just practical. It also carried cultural and political significance. Coins became a tool for projecting authority, often featuring images of rulers or city-state symbols as a form of propaganda, reinforcing who was in control. By now it was clear that Greek and Lydian money would play an important role in influencing the economic systems of future empires, particularly the Romans, who would build on and enhance these ideas.

THE ROMANS

As the influence of the Roman Republic expanded around 600 BCE, its economic system evolved, drawing inspiration from neighbouring cultures, particularly the Greek colonies in southern Italy (Magna Graecia). Early Roman money, such as aes rude (irregular, unrefined bronze pieces) served as a basic medium of exchange in an economy still reliant on bartering.

By around 400 BCE, Rome had introduced aes signatum (rectangular bronze ingots) and aes grave (round, cast bronze coins), marking an early effort to standardise its currency. However, the most transformative development came in 211 BCE with the introduction of the denarius, which became the most important silver coin in ancient Rome for nearly 500 years. Its uniform weight and purity made it the preferred currency across the Mediterranean, facilitating trade and military expansion. These coins not only adopted the use of political messages from the Greeks, but early Roman coinage often depicted mythological symbols and cultural identity.

As Rome transitioned from Republic to Empire, its monetary system reflected the increasing concentration of power. By 300–100 BCE, Rome's territorial expansion had brought an influx of wealth, particularly gold and silver from conquered lands, allowing the Romans to mint more coins and strengthen the denarius system. A more diverse coinage system evolved, introducing the gold aureus and the bronze sestertius.

With the rise of strong military leaders, Roman coinage became a direct tool for propaganda. Julius Caesar was the first living ruler to feature his own image on coins, breaking from tradition and symbolising the shift towards imperial rule. His assassination in 44 BCE did little to halt this trend and if anything, it reinforced the link between money and power.

When Augustus became Rome's first emperor, he further centralised coin production and used it to cement his authority. Coins now bore inscriptions such as "Son of the Divine", reinforcing his claim to divine status in the eyes of the people and legitimising his rule. From this point forward, Rome's monetary system was no longer just about trade, it was about control.

From firewood and bison to cowrie shells. From obsidian to the gold aureus. Currency has always reflected the meaning of value to the civilisations that use it. What was born of mutual cooperation slowly became a system shaped by influence. In the earliest exchanges, value was conveyed in a conversation. It required silent agreement based on utility, scarcity, and trust. Currency was a language that allowed people to express transactional worth, long before coins or ledgers existed.

These early systems of exchange endured not because they were enforced, but because they worked. They could be carried, divided, and were recognised. They lasted through time and held their worth across distances. People trusted them not because they were told to, but because their value could be seen and shared. Over time, however, that trust started to harden into something else. Into systems that were no longer simply useful but could be controlled. What had once been a tool for cooperation slowly became an instrument of rule. And that shift, from utility to authority cemented a pattern that would dictate economic power for the next 2,000 years.

Chapter 5

The Cycles of Empires

THE ROLE OF MONEY IN SHAPING EMPIRES

Money in its varying forms is the force that has fuelled civilisations and empires through the ages. From the Romans to the fragmented currencies of medieval Europe, monetary systems have been central to the function of exchange and trade. Understanding how these systems operated can offer insights into how new financial technologies, such as Bitcoin and blockchain technology, could support the longevity of modern financial markets.

It's fascinating to observe how humans have continually adapted and evolved throughout the years. The next part of our historical journey explores how empires have built on past civilisations and utilised different forms of currency to expand their influence. The best way to understand any future monetary methods is to look into the past and see what lessons can be learned from these ancient systems. Let's see if this will give us an indication of the true potential of decentralised currencies to create a more stable and inclusive financial future.

Throughout history, empires have not just drawn lines on maps around civilisations; they've also left their mark on trade and monetary exchange. Each empire has introduced clever monetary innovations to help govern their vast territories and manage their ever-expanding populations. By introducing standardised forms of currency, they facilitated smoother trade and greater economic stability, which can only be a positive thing, right?

This enabled those monetary systems to hold consistent value within their borders and therefore, their economic expansion and influence over key trade routes and commodities. Yet, the same economic policies that once strengthened an empire had the potential to create challenges to overcome.

EARLY EMPIRES AND THE STRUGGLE FOR ECONOMIC CONTROL

From Mesopotamia to the Nile, the regions described in the last chapter formed the first known empires and experimented with different economic models, each trying to maintain control over vast territories. The Akkadians (c. 2334–2154 BCE) relied on silver and grain to standardise and facilitate extensive trade networks across Mesopotamia, the Indus Valley, and the Arabian Peninsula. They created one of the first known state-controlled economic bureaucracies to handle taxes and resources. In Egypt (c. 1550–1077 BCE), a barter economy thrived, supported by measured quantities of commodities such as grain and metal, known as debens. Egypt's riches were based on steady agricultural production from the Nile, which ensured economic stability.

Later, the Assyrians (c. 1365–609 BCE) thrived on long-distance trade, and their economy prospered for centuries, from Mesopotamia to Anatolia, using silver as a common unit of exchange across their merchant networks. Each of these systems worked for long periods but eventually ran into problems. The decline of the Akkadian Empire was driven by a combination of overextension, administrative failure, and economic strain.

After being overstretched by military campaigns and struck by climate-induced droughts, inflation eroded their once-thriving economy. Ancient Egypt's reliance on agricultural wealth left it vulnerable to resource mismanagement and foreign invasions. Although the Assyrians were commercially dominant, they disintegrated when conflict disrupted trade lines, cutting off the very system that kept them going. In every case, the same pattern emerged: enhanced monetary and resource control drove expansion, but as economic pressures increased, these empires found themselves unable to handle the weight of their own success. Following their demise, a new force arose in Persia, one that would redefine currency itself.

As empires evolved, so did their currency systems. The Achaemenid Persian Empire (c. 550–330 BCE) introduced one of the first standardised coinage systems, issuing gold darics and silver sigloi to unify trade across territories from the Balkans to the Indus Valley. This early monetary policy stabilised taxation and trade. However, economic triumph came with a cost. Wars with Greece drained resources, while an overreliance on taxation and currency debasement caused inflation and instability. Currency debasement wasn't carried out through multiple rounds of QE, as seen in modern times and discussed in Chapter 2, but rather by physically clipping small parts off the coins or reducing their precious metal content. By the time Alexander the Great conquered Persia in 330 BCE, the empire's coinage had lost most of its original worth, reflecting an economy that had reached its limits. The empire's fall demonstrated that even the most advanced financial systems cannot sustain unrestrained expansion and war.

During the reign of Alexander the Great, the Macedonian Empire (c. 336–323 BCE) expanded from Greece to India, its riches driven by military conquest. Greek coinage spread across newly acquired territories, with silver drachmas and gold staters financing campaigns and broadening the adoption of precious metals as currency. Following Alexander's death in 323 BCE, the once-thriving empire fell into turmoil, breaking into competing kingdoms with no clear succession plan. Without a central authority, regional leaders began minting their own coins, resulting in high inflation and a substantial loss of trust in the currency, a problem that would become all too apparent in the following years. This illustrates that even the most ambitious monetary systems require long-term governance to remain sustainable.

Following the death of Alexander the Great, the Mauryan Empire (c. 321–185 BCE) established one of India's earliest significant centralised economies. Punch-marked silver coins, featuring standardised weights, played a crucial role in enabling the organised trade routes that connected Central Asia with the Middle East. The empire thrived by exporting spices, textiles, and gems, establishing India as a significant power in ancient global trade.

However, prosperity came at a price. Although crucial for supporting the administration, high taxation imposed a burden on local economies. The debasement of silver coins resulted in inflation, undermining public confidence in the monetary system. As provincial leaders queued up to declare their independence, the empire began to fragment. By 185 BCE, the Mauryan Empire had fallen, demonstrating another well-organised economy that suffered inflation and political fragmentation in the face of financial pressures.

So, we can see that monetary policy led to the downfall of some early empires. When currency is managed correctly an empire will prosper and be in a strong position to build a robust economy. Conversely, overstretching oneself, whether we are talking about an empire, or even on a national or personal level, can bring about collapse. When taxation is too high, and currencies are debased, economic output steadily declines. Nonetheless, we can still learn from the way these empires formed such sophisticated trade networks and the different types of coinage they used.

Although these early financial structures supported the empires that created them, none were immune to failure. We must therefore ask, what can truly sustain a whole empire? Does monetary innovation by those in power prevent collapse, or simply delay the inevitable? Back on the shores of the Mediterranean, another empire would attempt to perfect the art of monetary control, and its impact would be felt for centuries. Ultimately, however, would it suffer the same fate?

THE ROMAN EMPIRE AND ITS MONETARY SYSTEM

The Roman Empire, established in 27 BCE, was one of history's most powerful empires, backed by a monetary system that had a long-term impact on international trade. Rome's enormous network of roads, sea routes, and financial systems supported remarkable economic growth, allowing for military expansion and ensuring administrative stability throughout Europe, North Africa, and the Middle East.

As outlined in the previous chapter, when Augustus became Rome's first emperor, he inherited a monetary system that had already experienced major changes. His innovation was to strengthen the bimetallic standard by ensuring a reasonably steady ratio of gold (aureus), silver (denarius), and bronze (sestertius).

This system flourished for many years. Merchants could trade with confidence because Roman money was reliable, and soldiers knew that their wages would hold value. This was essential since an empire as large as Rome relied on financial predictability to properly manage taxation, trade, and the military. At this point, their insights were impeccable and they managed their economy expertly, facilitating the continued dominance of the known world. The reliability of its monetary system enabled seamless trade throughout the empire, from the vibrant markets of Alexandria to the distant coastline of Britannia. It operated in much the same way as today's global reserve currencies, such as the U.S. dollar, promoting economic integration across large regions.

After Tiberius became emperor in 14 CE, Rome continued to thrive. Marketplaces buzzed with life, with merchants haggling over terracotta amphorae of golden olive oil and bolts of deep-purple and crimson-dyed linen. Workers and soldiers put money aside to purchase new togas, wine, and expensive meats. Coins bearing the emperor's image passed confidently from hand to hand, and the standard of living was as good as it ever had been. Artists captured idealised portraits on frescoed walls, and for the next few years, confidence in the Roman economy was as firm as its weathered stone roads.

However, in 33 CE things began to change. It started quietly. A legal technicality. A tightening of credit. But, within months, panic had spread across the entire empire. Defaults rose. Confidence vanished, and the Roman elite scrambled for liquidity, but it was nowhere to be found. In what many historians consider to be the first recorded financial crisis and government bailout; Emperor Tiberius was forced to act. A confluence of the sudden enforcement of Julius Caesar's old law limiting how much cash could be held relative to land investment, as well as rapid loan recalls, and a sharp contraction in the money supply caused Rome's financial system to completely seize up.

Tiberius quickly responded by injecting 100 million sesterces (equivalent to over $1 billion today) into the economy. Interest-free loans, backed not by promises but by land, were distributed by senators over three years — a bold move to restore liquidity and rebuild trust and confidence in the economy. The parallels with modern times are striking. Central bank bailouts. Emergency lending, and a desperate push to keep the system functioning. Even in ancient times, Rome acted swiftly to confront problems which modern economies often fail to anticipate. When trust disappears, and liquidity dries up, even the best-functioning economies can deteriorate.

After this setback, Rome's monetary system fully recovered and provided economic stability for centuries to come, allowing trade to thrive while the empire remained fiscally secure. But eventually it seems no empire, no matter how great, is immune to economic challenges. As Rome expanded, its productivity growth lagged behind and the costs of maintaining its vast empire began to outpace its income. As the army grew larger and administrative expenses increased, the wealth from conquests needed to match these increased costs. It might help to compare it to the expansion of a business, in that a bigger workforce and additional overheads mean that enough income must be generated to cover these costs and sustain the business.

Unfortunately, Rome ran out of ways to bring in enough money to fund its operations. Therefore, the next step was to manipulate the currency, beginning with reducing the silver content of the denarius. Again, the parallels with our monetary system today are clear. Leaders commonly debase their currency to stay in power and maintain control, hoping that growth will start to outpace inflation. And this is exactly what we have been seeing in the modern global economy since 2008. By 300 CE, the denarius, which had been pure silver under Augustus, was debased to less than 5% silver, shattering its purchasing power.

At first, this debasement must have seemed like a good idea, or perhaps just desperate, but it brought an initial economic boost, allowing Rome to mint more coins and meet its immediate financial demands.

However, similar to the debasement of today, the sheer volume of the new coins Rome brought into circulation inevitably prompted rapid inflation. This meant that the denarius had lost most of its purchasing power and trust in the currency dramatically faded. Merchants, no longer confident in Roman money, demanded alternative forms of payment. You see, back then they didn't have other options apart from bartering or requesting payments in goods that they deemed to hold tangible value. Tax revenues became harder to collect in real terms, further crushing the empire's ability to fund its military and infrastructure.

In a final attempt to stabilise the economy and curb inflation, Emperor Diocletian introduced monetary reforms, including a new gold currency, the solidus, and strict price controls. But these measures came all too late. Economic instability. Political fragmentation. And external invasions made recovery impossible. By the time the Western Roman Empire fell in 476 CE, the Byzantine Empire in the east had already established itself, having been founded in 330 CE with its capital in Constantinople. The fragmentation of post-Roman Europe in the west saw trade networks disintegrate, and coinage systems became disparate. This period built the dynamics of medieval trade and currency systems, setting the stage for the rise of modern global powers.

THE BYZANTINE EMPIRE (330–1453 CE): A GOLD STANDARD FOR STABILITY

The continuation of the Eastern Roman Empire preserved much of Rome's economic and financial structure. Like Rome, its robust economy was centred around its gold-based currency. The Byzantine gold solidus, later known as the bezant, maintained a consistent gold content, and served as the empire's primary gold coin for over 700 years. Constantinople's strategic location gave it control over important commercial routes, connecting the Silk Road to Mediterranean markets. The solidus became the primary currency of international trade, with widespread acceptance from Europe to the Middle East. It worked in a similar way to today's reserve currencies, providing merchants and states with a consistent unit of worth for business and taxation.

By 1000 CE, military battles and economic mismanagement had taken their toll on the Byzantine economy. As we see again, a succession of emperors debased the solidus, reducing its gold content in an attempt to cover mounting costs. As trust in the currency was eroded, inflation surged, and Byzantium lost its financial dominance. The sack of Constantinople by the Fourth Crusade in 1204 shook the empire, but by 1453, Constantinople fell to the Ottomans, marking the final collapse of the Byzantine Empire. Despite no longer being at the centre of global trade, Byzantium's influence lived on, and the solidus set the standard for medieval and Renaissance coinage, reinforcing the importance of stable, gold-backed money to the peoples of the time.

ISLAMIC CALIPHATES: A MONETARY SYSTEM BUILT ON GOLD AND SILVER

As Byzantium declined, the Islamic caliphates established a unified monetary system that revolutionised trade and banking. The Umayyad Caliphate (661–750 CE) produced the first distinct Islamic coinage, building a large and interconnected trade network stretching from the Atlantic to Central Asia supported by the gold dinar and silver dirham.

The Abbasid Caliphate (750–1258 CE) strengthened this structure, with Baghdad becoming a key economic point along the Silk Road. Unlike earlier empires, which relied mainly on conquest for economic expansion, the Abbasids invested in trade, infrastructure, and intellectual advancements. Currency stability drove the Abbasid Golden Age, allowing commerce on a scale comparable to Rome at its height. However, internal strife and irregularities in taxes weakened its power. The crusades disrupted trade routes and the Mongol invasions further damaged the economy, causing centralised Islamic control to fall in 1258.

Despite this, the Islamic financial concepts of stable currency, trade facilitation, and banking advances have no doubt paved the way for future economic systems. Even as centralised control faded, successor states including the Mamluks and Ottomans maintained aspects of this monetary system, ensuring its continued role in trade. Bills of exchange and other early banking procedures certainly influenced financial practices in Europe. However, the Mongols would soon impose their own vision of commerce and monetary control. It would be one marked both by innovation and economic challenges.

THE MONGOL EMPIRE: TRADE, MONETARY INNOVATION, AND THE FIRST ATTEMPT AT A GLOBAL CURRENCY

Genghis Khan established the Mongol Empire (1206–1368), and it spanned Eastern Europe to the Sea of Japan. The Mongols encouraged trade and economic integration, presiding over the Pax Mongolica, a period of stability during which merchants and products could freely travel along the Silk Road. To facilitate trade throughout their extensive territory, the Mongols adapted existing financial systems within each region, accepting a combination of regional coinage, silver ingots, and trade credits.

While most parts of the empire continued to rely on traditional metal-based currencies, my main point of focus is the Chinese branch of Mongol rule, namely the Yuan Dynasty (1271–1368), where paper money was formalised and widely used. Though paper money had first emerged during China's Song Dynasty two to three centuries earlier, the Yuan was the first to back it with silver and deploy it as a centralised monetary tool across a vast empire.

The Yuan promoted innovation in trade-weighted currency and standardised silver ingots, aiming to simplify long-distance trade and unify commerce under consistent global currency, centuries ahead of its time. This system certainly showed promise, and is comparable to what underlies global currencies today, however, it was poorly managed. Without the technology to oversee such an advanced system, successive rulers overissued paper currency, with a diminishing amount of silver backing, making it increasingly fiat, leading to extreme inflation and declining confidence. As merchants and foreign traders demanded silver over paper, the economy weakened. The added combination of external factors such as political fragmentation and the way that the Black Death reduced populations and disrupted trade networks, led the Mongol Empire to fall in 1368, ending its short-lived monetary experiment.

This example shows how monetary innovation can falter when its backing with something intrinsic suddenly disappears. It shows a clear comparison to the fiat currencies of today, which were also once backed by precious metals, highlighting the severe potential consequences, when this fiat-style approach has been taken.

THE OTTOMAN EMPIRE: BRIDGING EAST AND WEST

However, the Ottoman Empire would take an entirely different approach, becoming one of history's longest-lasting empires, dominating Southeast Europe, the Middle East, and North Africa from 1299 to 1922. By controlling key trade routes between Europe, Asia and Africa, the Ottomans turned what they called Istanbul into a thriving centre of commerce, facilitating the exchange of gold, silver, silk, and spices.

The empire's monetary system, focused on the silver akçe and later the kuruş, which helped to regulate trade inside its borders. However, its greater significance stemmed from its capacity to control the flow of precious metals, such as gold and silver across continents. As European countries expanded their overseas empires, the Ottomans continued to play an important role in global trade, uniting eastern and western economies by establishing a steady commercial network that fuelled the empire's economy for centuries.

THE BIRTH OF MODERN BANKING: THE MEDICI BANK

While eastern empires dominated overland trade routes and controlled the flow of gold and silver, a quieter financial revolution was unfolding in Europe. Florence was emerging as a new centre of commercial influence, driven not by conquest but by banking innovation. In 1397, Giovanni di Bicci de' Medici founded the Medici Bank, establishing one of the most powerful financial dynasties in European history.

The Medici did not rule an empire in the conventional sense, but their banking operations shaped the continent's economy as effectively as any army could. They introduced double-entry bookkeeping and expanded their network of branches across key European cities, creating one of the earliest models of international finance.

Through instruments like bills of exchange, they enabled merchants and monarchs to transfer large sums across borders without the physical movement of gold or silver, an early precursor to digital value transfer systems. While similar instruments had existed earlier in China and the Islamic world, the Medici's use of bills of exchange appears to have developed independently within the context of European trade and legal systems.

In practice, this worked through trust-based IOUs. For example, a merchant from Bruges might place an order with a Florentine trader for 80 gold florins' worth of fine wool. Instead of sending actual gold, he issued a written promise to pay, known as a bill of exchange. Meanwhile, the Medici might owe a similar amount to a trading partner in Venice for a shipment of glassware and spices. Acting as intermediaries, the Medici facilitated the settlement by transferring the IOU, avoiding the need to physically move gold across Europe. This worked because everyone involved trusted the Medici to honour its value, and that trust itself became the currency. The paper was worth 80 gold florins, not because of the metal behind it, but because everyone believed the Medici would pay.

This system showed that trust could be monetised, eventually overtaking the need to transport the precious metals themselves. It was an early demonstration of how financial confidence, rather than coin content, could underpin entire economies. While kings and emperors had debased their coins and struggled with metal shortages, the Medicis built a paper-based system that proved more stable, more efficient, and more scalable, paving the way for modern banking.

By financing popes, kings, and commercial ventures, the Medici helped lay the foundations for centralised banking and the rise of merchant capitalism. Their system demonstrated how financial control could rival territorial conquest in shaping the modern world. While the Ottomans controlled physical trade routes between Asia and Europe, the Medicis quietly built the financial architecture that would underpin Europe's global economic expansion.

THE SPANISH AND PORTUGUESE EMPIRES

As the Ottoman Empire declined, by the late 15th century Spain and Portugal were emerging as the first truly global empires, fuelled by maritime exploration and a desire to access wealth beyond Europe. The Treaty of Tordesillas in 1494 divided much of the world between these two powers, assigning most of the Americas to Spain and vast territories in Africa, Asia, and Brazil to Portugal. This helps us understand why most of these regions adopted Spanish or Portuguese, and with this global reach they managed to transform international trade by introducing new commodities, markets, and monetary systems.

Between 1500 and 1600, the influx of precious metals initially boosted Spain's economy, but eventually led to severe inflation throughout Europe. Spain's overreliance on colonial income meant that it was unable to create a strong domestic economy, leaving it vulnerable when silver production fell. Portugal, meanwhile, dominated the spice trade and major maritime routes, establishing fortified trading outposts in India, Africa, and the East Indies. Economic mismanagement and extended conflicts began to erode their power, and by the nineteenth century, it too had lost most of its global influence.

Meanwhile, in parts of Europe, merchant banking families like the Medici had already shown how financial networks and trust-based instruments could rival territorial empires in shaping economic influence.

THE DUTCH AND FRENCH EMPIRES: BANKING, TRADE, AND STATE CONTROL

The fall of these empires signalled a change in global dominance from resource-based prosperity to financial and industrial strength. The Dutch Empire (1595–1795) introduced modern financial concepts and banking, establishing the Amsterdam Stock Exchange in 1602 and creating the first multinational corporation, the Dutch East India Company (VOC). The Dutch guilder, stable and widely trusted, became a prominent trade currency across Europe and overseas markets. Unlike Spain and Portugal, which depended on direct colonial extraction, the Dutch focused on financial innovations similar to ours today, like joint-stock companies, bonds, and commercial credit, making them a powerful global economic force.

Alongside this, France was also becoming a dominant European power, fuelled by mercantilist policies based on the idea that wealth came from accumulating precious metals and controlling trade. By storing metals and commodities with strong intrinsic value, France became a much wealthier country.

After Louis XIV became king in 1643, France began to expand its colonial holdings in North America, the Caribbean, India, and Africa. The French livre, and later the franc, became widely utilised in European trade, and France was influential in defining monetary policy in early modern Europe. By the end of Louis' reign in 1715, however, the economy was faltering, and France introduced paper money through John Law's "Mississippi Company" scheme (1716–1720) in response. This would be one of the first complex large-scale experiments with fiat currency.

Meanwhile, the Dutch East India Company continued to rule the seas. Majestic merchant ships bearing the VOC insignia sliced through the vivid turquoise waters between Batavia and Amsterdam, laden with spices, silk, and silver. The Dutch commanded vast trade routes with military precision, believing they had secured global dominance. But beneath the shimmering surface, ripples of disruption were beginning to spread. Competition with the British intensified. Key trade routes intercepted. Dutch ships began to fall. The British began to take control. One by one, their vessels were overtaken, their ports isolated. The VOC, once the most powerful trading company in history, collapsed under mounting debt and British pressure, with its bankruptcy in 1799 marking the end of an era.

By this point, the French fiat experiment had suffered excessive money printing and the speculation that followed, which resulted in a financial crisis. Public trust in French monetary policies was shattered, similar to what many are experiencing today. Financial mismanagement and increasing war debts undermined the French economy, contributing to the French Revolution in 1789 and ultimately reducing its global prominence. By 1815, the monarchy fell, and Napoleon's empire crumbled in the face of financial turmoil.

THE BRITISH EMPIRE AND ITS CURRENCY EVOLUTION

While other European nations saw declines, Britain was expanding. Britain employed some of the techniques used in the Dutch and French economic models but avoided a state-controlled economy with high taxes, creating a more adaptable financial structure. As a result, the country would dominate global trade for decades.

The British Empire (c. 1583 – 20th century) is widely considered the largest and most influential empire in history. Britain's prosperity was built not only on colonial expansion, but also on its ability to construct a financial empire that supported industrial growth and global trade.

Early explorations in the reign of King Henry VII of England in 1497 led to the foundation of many overseas colonies in North America and the Caribbean during the 16th century. The empire continued to grow during the next two centuries, expanding into India, Africa, Australia, and beyond. However, Britain's real strength lay in the combination of territorial conquest as well as financial and trade dominance.

Unlike Spain and Portugal, which extracted wealth from their colonies without reinvesting it effectively, Britain developed a banking system that enabled efficient capital allocation for economic expansion. By using credit markets and financial institutions, it could free up funds to invest in industrial growth and military dominance.

At its peak, the British Empire covered 13 million square miles and governed over 458 million people, which was one-fifth of the then entire world's population. Yet, Britain's true power came from the strength of its financial institutions and the stability of pound sterling currency. Unlike its predecessors' inflationary economies, Britain maintained confidence in its currency through disciplined monetary policy and a gold-backed standard. Sterling was a currency that shaped Britain's economic and imperial influence in remarkable ways. To understand how Britain achieved this, we must first trace its origins.

Pound sterling dates back to Anglo-Saxon England, when King Offa of Mercia introduced the sterling coin in 757 CE. One pound (mass) of silver was divided into 240 silver pennies, forming the £sd system, where one pound (£) equalled 20 shillings (s) and each shilling equalled 12 pence (d). Therefore, £1 equalled 12 x 20 = 240 pennies. The symbols are derived from Latin and come from the Roman coinage names mentioned in Chapter 4. The "£" comes from libra, the Latin word for a unit of weight and currency. The "s" comes from the solidus, a Roman coin, and "d" comes from denarius, originally a silver Roman coin.

Although initially an accounting unit, the exceptional quality and consistency of British silver coins helped establish sterling as a reliable currency, strengthening Britain's reputation as a global trading power.

Even though the £sd system remained the foundation of British currency, coinage evolved over time. King Henry II launched the Tealby penny in 1158, solidifying silver as the main currency. This was overtaken in 1344 by the introduction of the gold noble, reflecting the rising importance of gold in trade, and by 1663, Britain had minted the guinea, a 22-carat gold coin that fluctuated in value, demonstrating gold's growing dominance over silver.

The establishment of the Bank of England in 1694 provided a stable monetary foundation from which to finance wars and encourage industrialisation. It was this ability to control debt and regulate capital flows that distinguished Britain from rival imperial powers, and by the time that Britain's gold valuation had exceeded that of other European countries the result was an outflow of silver for international payments as gold reserves grew domestically. This culminated in 1717, when the guinea's value was officially set at 21 shillings (£1 and 1 shilling), securing the transition to a gold-based economy. By the early nineteenth century, Britain's growing gold reserves led to the formal adoption of the gold standard in 1816, reducing silver to a token currency and paving the way for other countries to follow suit. This cemented the pound's status as the major reserve currency, establishing a reliable worldwide financial system that facilitated international trade and investment.

Britain's worldwide influence peaked in the nineteenth century, when it shaped international business with its gold-backed financial system and control over trade routes. Having transformed itself into a financial empire, the country's global banking network would dominate world trade for over a century. As the Ottoman and Spanish Empires weakened, no longer was wealth tied just to land and commodities, but instead power would increasingly be defined by financial control and global trust in a stable currency. Britain's leadership in the gold standard was significant because it prepared pound sterling to become the main global reserve currency in the nineteenth and early twentieth century.

Despite its dominance, Britain faced rising challenges in the early twentieth century. The First World War put enormous economic pressure on the empire, draining reserves and increasing national debt, setting the stage for long-term economic difficulties. By the time World War II broke out in 1939, Britain was already financially weakened, and the war boosted growth in the United States after the Great Depression by greatly reducing unemployment. When further borrowing was required from the United States, it therefore deepened Britain's reliance on American support.

Following the war, many former colonies achieved independence, further diminishing Britain's global influence while the pound sterling struggled to maintain its status as the global reserve currency. Wartime debts and economic deterioration prolonged British reliance on the United States, reducing Britain to a secondary role in international finance. Repeated devaluations of the pound weakened faith in sterling, highlighting the need for a new global financial system.

U.S. EMPIRE

As British influence declined, the United States emerged as the leading global power, leaning on its industrial strength and military supremacy. The Bretton Woods Agreement of 1944 formalised the shift in global financial dominance, establishing the U.S. dollar as the world's reserve currency, backed by gold. Under this system, other global currencies, including the pound, were pegged to the dollar, and therefore consequently, also pegged to gold, at $35 an ounce. That price had been fixed a decade earlier, after the U.S. government devalued the dollar in 1934. Americans were forced to surrender their gold at $20.67 an ounce, just before the official price was raised to $35 — a move made to address depleting gold reserves compared with the number of issued dollars. This imbalance expanded the monetary base and signalled a shift towards greater U.S. control over global finance — a problem that would quietly resurface decades later.

By the time Bretton Woods was implemented, this framework placed the U.S. at the centre of international trade and finance, effectively ending sterling's dominance. While Britain gradually declined, the U.S. cemented its position in the following decades. However, by the late 1960s, increased government spending, particularly for the Vietnam War and expanding social programmes, put enormous pressure on U.S. gold reserves. Foreign nations, led by France under Charles de Gaulle, grew increasingly anxious about the state of the U.S. economy and its capacity to repay its gold. As a result, they began exchanging their dollar reserves for gold, quickly depleting US gold reserves. This resulted in a catastrophic imbalance, with far more dollars in circulation than gold to back them, putting strain on the entire system — expressing a striking resemblance to the severe problems that the Yuan dynasty began to experience nearly 700 years prior.

Faced with a potential financial crisis, President Richard Nixon abandoned the gold standard in 1971, cutting the dollar's ties to actual assets, and ending the Bretton Woods system. The dollar was now purely a fiat currency, backed only by trust in the U.S. government rather than gold. As the Austrian economist Ludwig von Mises had warned decades earlier:

"The gold standard did not collapse. Governments abolished it in order to pave the way for inflation."

— Ludwig von Mises, *The Theory of Money and Credit* (1912)

I believe the shift to fiat money marked a disastrous twist for global finance. It increased the flexibility of U.S. monetary policy and opened the door to inflation and exchange rate volatility. After 1973, speculative FX (foreign exchange) markets emerged where traders, rather than solely governments and central banks, could influence the exchange rates. This permitted currency manipulation and economic cycles driven by government intervention rather than commodity-based stability.

A fiat currency is named after the Latin word meaning "let it be done", or "it shall be". In this context, "fiat" refers to an order or decree, indicating that the currency has value because the government says so, rather than being backed by a physical commodity like gold or silver. This is significant since a fiat currency has no intrinsic value and relies exclusively on the trust and confidence of the issuing government or central bank.

Over time, many countries abandoned commodity-backed money because it confined the supply of money to the availability of gold or silver. This created considerable leverage in the system. Previously, if there were only one million gold bars, that was it; however, by switching to fiat currency, there could be a trillion gold bars, since more paper gold could be issued and more fiat currency created. Fiat currency gave governments and central banks control over monetary policy, which has become an extremely dangerous thing.

We'll go into greater depth later, but this explains why the financial system has become so contaminated over the last 50 years and the 2008 financial crisis and other significant catastrophes have occurred since 1971. It explains why there is so much leverage and risk within the system, and why debt deficits have built up sharply across the entire global financial system. This event in 1971 was an extremely big deal and perhaps even symbolic that it coincided with the pound sterling moving to a 100 pennies per pound metric system, removing the link between a pound and its original 240 pennies' worth of silver and further dissociating currency from hard-backed precious metals.

Following Nixon's decision in 1973, the fiat petrodollar system was established, tying the U.S. dollar to oil. Secretary of State Henry Kissinger negotiated an agreement with Saudi Arabia, a major participant in the global oil sector, stating that Saudi Arabia would price and sell oil exclusively in U.S. dollars and in exchange, the U.S. would provide military security to the Saudi monarchy. This agreement effectively tied the U.S. dollar to the world's primary energy resource.

PETRODOLLARS AND THE MODERN GLOBAL ECONOMY

The petrodollar system refers to the global practice of exchanging U.S. dollars for oil, instead of any other currency. This means that no matter what country is buying the oil, they must pay the oil-producing country in petrodollars, denominated in U.S. dollars. The petrodollar system originally only applied to Middle Eastern countries and members of the Organization of the Petroleum Exporting Countries (OPEC). However, this has broadened over the years, making U.S. dollars the main source of revenue for these countries. This was a cunning move by the U.S., as it meant that the oil would always back up their governmental trust. By pricing global oil exclusively in U.S. dollars, the petrodollar system created artificial demand for the U.S. dollar, effectively backing it with oil trade and reinforcing its dominance.

The fiat petrodollar introduced a new framework in international finance. It wielded immense power, allowing the United States to finance its deficits through the issuance of its currency, with global demand for dollars driven by the need for oil. Oil-producing countries inevitably end up with large surpluses of U.S. dollars that need to be reinvested in ways that maintain its value and support these nation's economies. This petrodollar recycling can involve channelling these dollars back into their own domestic economies or lending them to other countries. But the real benefit to the U.S. comes when these dollars are invested back into its economy. Countries use their excess U.S. dollars to buy assets and securities like U.S. Treasury Bills, stocks, and real estate, effectively financing U.S. government spending, which helps keep U.S. interest rates low as natural demand for U.S. Treasuries already exists.

This makes the U.S. bond market the cornerstone of the entire global financial system. Foreign governments, central banks, and institutional investors purchase U.S. Treasury bonds not just for returns, but as a signal of confidence in the stability of the dollar and the U.S. economy.

Over the years, however, the U.S. has become increasingly dependent on this demand. If foreign buyers ever begin to hesitate — due to geopolitical shifts, economic pressures, or erosion of trust — the entire system could be destabilised.

Central banks, particularly the Federal Reserve, have stepped in as major buyers when others pull back, but this creates a circular dependency where the system is effectively propped up by its own creator. Confidence — not collateral — is what sustains it. This dynamic strengthens global demand for the U.S. dollar, reinforcing its status as the world's reserve currency.

Since oil transactions generate a continuous flow of dollars worldwide, countries trading in oil need to hold significant dollar reserves, further embedding the U.S. currency at the centre of global finance. High demand for dollars also means that more dollars are held outside the U.S., reducing the amount circulating domestically, which helps control inflation. This in turn creates a stronger dollar as it makes imports cheaper, which keeps inflation lower. All of this gives the U.S. a unique advantage over other nations, which instead must rely on foreign exchange reserves or external borrowing.

Ever since the gold standard was abandoned and the U.S. shifted to a petrodollar system, the government has funded its deficits by issuing debt-backed securities. As a result, the U.S. dollar is often perceived as being "backed by debt", since its global acceptance relies on trust in the U.S. government's ability to repay its obligations.

However, this reliance on petrodollar recycling also creates vulnerabilities. If major oil exporters begin shifting away from the dollar, by pricing oil into other currencies like the Chinese yuan or the euro, demand for U.S. dollars could weaken, challenging its dominant role in global trade. Signs of this shift have already begun, with strained relationships with countries like China and Russia working to conduct energy trade in their own currencies, reducing their dependence on the dollar and forming economic alliances like BRICS (whose founding nations were Brazil, Russia, India, China, and South Africa).

At the same time, beneath the surface of these global trade dynamics, there was growing internal strain within the U.S. and global monetary system. Even after the trillions injected into the system with QE1 between 2008 and 2010 to prevent a full-scale collapse, the private sector has remained hesitant to borrow. Instead of flowing into the real economy, much of that liquidity fuelled asset markets, with banks, financial institutions, and pension funds buying financial assets with this extra liquidity. Meanwhile, most governments have continued to run large deficits — borrowing heavily, with central banks absorbing much of this debt. A subsequent cascade of woes after the 2008 financial crisis means that multiple rounds of QE have been needed, greatly increasing global government debt and central bank balance sheets.

As central banks bought government bonds, their balance sheets ballooned, and this wasn't just accounting; it reflected a major expansion of the monetary base, altering the way that money moved through the system and impacted expectations. The liquidity flowed through commercial banks and ended up on government balance sheets, allowing governments to fund bailouts, stimulus, and basic operations.

Low interest rates made it possible to service this growing debt, but economic growth remained weak. With no room left to reduce interest rates any further, continued rounds of QE were needed every few years. Central banks attempted to balance each round of QE with subsequent periods of Quantitative Tightening (QT), to remove the liquidity from the system. While commendable, these attempts were often short-lived as the economy could not sustain itself without them. It is for these reasons that major liquidity cycles have formed, which now occur every 3–5 years. To compound the wealth inequality narrative, this cheap virtual money has flooded into financial markets, rather than the real economy, because QE primarily benefits financial institutions — causing sharp increases in the price of assets like stocks, property, and eventually cryptocurrencies. Meanwhile, wages stagnated, and productivity remained stubbornly low, leading to worsening wealth inequality; in real terms people had simply become much poorer.

Nonetheless, governments increasingly relied on these rounds of QE, and not for the purpose of stimulating growth, but merely to service existing debt. Debt became so unsustainable that it became normal for deficits in many countries to exceed annual national GDP. Tax revenues remained weak due to low growth and governments couldn't cover spending or reduce debt without relying on new borrowing from further liquidity injections.

This has led global economies to service existing debt and thus require new borrowing, setting off a cycle where short-term financial stability has come at the cost of long-term growth and sustainability. This whole pattern is certainly not one that is showing any signs of turning around. Governments have been returning to the same strategy every few years — injecting liquidity, issuing more debt, and relying on central banks, institutions, the wealthy and pension funds to keep the system afloat. This creation of recurring three-to-five-year liquidity cycles of central bank intervention are not the same as the natural short-term three-to-eight-year boom-and-bust growth cycles, which we discussed at the beginning of Chapter 3. These are purely artificial liquidity-driven cycles because of the timeframes of the debt maturity of the bonds issued by governments, usually two to five years as shorter periods have lower interest rates, and the weak growth fundamentals, mean that productivity is not rising sufficiently to reduce this debt.

Imagine if Derek had £5,000 of credit card debt, and he takes out a 0% balance transfer from another provider, for 36 months. He pays the fee to use this facility and just pays off the minimum payment every month. To ensure the interest rate doesn't go exponentially higher, he must repay the balance at the end of the three-year period. However, when this money becomes due, he can't afford to clear the debt. So, he takes out another balance transfer from another provider, which clears the previous debt, but rolls it over to the new credit card for another two to four years. This is exactly what all major governments have been doing since 2008. The big difference is that the governments have to pay interest on all of this debt, and the debt keeps increasing by the second, as can rather alarmingly be seen on the publicly available U.S. debt clock.

All of these factors combined make the entire financial system extremely fragile. And if, in the case of the U.S., the confidence in the petrodollar system, as well as the bond market were to weaken, it could not only erode the U.S.'s financial dominance but have the potential to drag the entire system down with it. While the U.S. economy remains dominant, its economy is now over $36 trillion in debt, which is increasingly worrying and poses significant systemic risk. Like the concerns raised back in the early 1970s, some are starting to question the long-term reliability of the dollar itself.

GRESHAM'S LAW

So, as we have seen, currency and trade have played a vital role over the centuries in how empires have gained power, and how this power tends to decline over time. In the realms of economics, an important principle which backs up our analysis is Gresham's law. Sir Thomas Gresham, a 16th-century English financier, summarises the complicated dynamics of multiple types of currency inside an economy. Gresham's Law states that "bad money drives out good", providing valuable insight into how an economy perceives its currency. When a less stable, depreciating currency coexists with a more stable, valuable currency, individuals tend to keep the "good" money while spending the "bad".

"Good" money is currency or money that is regarded as valuable, stable, and dependable, such as a commodity or commodity-backed money. In other words, money that takes the form of an actual asset, such as gold or silver, or a currency backed by one of them. This is the type of money that holds its value over time and is chosen for saving or hoarding due to its stability and inflation resistance. Bitcoin and cryptocurrencies, as we will learn in the following chapters, are neither commodity money nor commodity-backed money, but they have perceived value due to their trustless nature and increased adoption. Individuals seeking to hedge against fiat depreciation often view gold and, increasingly, Bitcoin as good money for these reasons.

"Bad" money, on the other hand, is regarded as money with no intrinsic value such as fiat currency, or commodity money made from less valuable materials, such as debased coins, or poorly printed banknotes. It can also even be commodities that are perishable like corn or barley, that will deteriorate in time. Bad money is often prone to devaluation due to inflation or quantitative easing. Gresham's law states that when both are in circulation, bad money drives out the good money, so people hoard the good money for its lasting value and spend the bad money instead.

Our historical journey in this chapter has shone a light on how monetary mismanagement has eroded economic stability and public trust in several major historic empires. As the perception of currency in an economy deteriorates, so does the willingness to hold on to it. This hoarding of good money also often contributes to distrust in the overall financial system.

As we saw in the Roman Empire, as government expenses rose, the Romans began to debase their silver coins by mixing them with less valuable metals. As Roman coins lost so much of their silver content, people began hoarding the older, purer coins while spending the newer, debased ones, which shows an early demonstration of Gresham's Law. This hoarding behaviour reduced trust in the currency overall, contributing to economic instability and a decline in trade, in turn weakening the empire's cohesion and control.

Similarly, in the Byzantine Empire, the debasement of their gold solidus, which had been so strong for 700 years, undermined the stability of their monetary system and traders began turning to alternative currencies. This monetary erosion contributed to the empire's eventual vulnerability to foreign powers and its decline.

Another example of this was in Weimar Republic Germany. After World War I, excessive printing of the German mark to cover war reparations and public spending led to hyperinflation, a topic we will investigate in more detail later. As the mark's value plummeted, people spent it rapidly, fearing it would be worth even less the next day, while they sought good money in the form of foreign currencies or tangible assets like gold. This severe devaluation created economic and social unrest, ultimately setting the stage for political upheaval — and paving the way for the rise of fascism, with Hitler gaining popular support as a supposed solution to the country's financial collapse. This pattern has been repeated in countries such as Zimbabwe and Venezuela, where hyperinflation has similarly driven citizens to rely on foreign currencies or commodities to safeguard their wealth.

After the U.S. and global economies moved from the gold standard onto a fiat-based system, many people have tended to purchase or hold on to other assets. This has vastly devalued fiat currencies since the 1970s. And if we go back to the formation of the Federal Reserve in 1913, the U.S. Dollar has since lost about 97% of its value. During this time, other assets such as gold and property have greatly risen in value, as many people do not want to hold onto a depreciating currency. We saw these previously failed fiat experiments during the Mongol-led Yuan Dynasty in China as well as by the French, both invariably resulting in rapid inflation. Once again, they sought to spend this money as soon as possible while storing their wealth in other assets and currencies that would retain value over time.

Gresham's Law continues to apply in modern economies. The continued injection of trillions by central banks into their economies since 2008 has led to the debasement of various national currencies and a loss of purchasing power. Much of the current system runs on public confidence — in the belief that the currency will hold value, and these debts can be repaid. But, once that confidence falters, the system becomes much more fragile. This dynamic mirrors historical cases where bad currency systems weakened empires, as people today increasingly turn to alternative stores of value to protect their wealth.

This entire behaviour aligns with Gresham's Law: when currency stability is compromised by poor fiscal policies, people naturally seek to preserve their wealth in more stable assets. In empires from Rome to the U.S., debased currency has often marked the beginning of broader systemic decline, as loss of trust in money spreads to institutions and governance, challenging the foundation of economic and political power.

In the digital age, Gresham's Law continues to hold significance, especially in the context of cryptocurrencies. Bitcoin, often referred to as "digital gold", has been the best performing asset over the last 15 years. In fact, it's the best performing asset ever over any similar time-period and is considered by many as good money due to its fixed supply and scarcity. In contrast, fiat currencies are subject to inflationary pressures and so are viewed by many as bad money. This evolution demonstrates that while the forms of money have changed over time, the behavioural patterns supporting Gresham's Law remain timeless.

Gresham's Law serves as a reminder of the complex interplay between different forms of currency in an economy. It highlights the rational behaviour of individuals seeking to protect their wealth and underscores the importance of currency stability and reliability. The choices we make regarding the money we use today will have a profound impact on our financial well-being as we move into the future.

REFLECTING ON THE RISE AND FALL OF EMPIRES

Throughout history, monetary systems have played a defining role in the rise and fall of empires. Yet time and time again, as empires expanded, financial mismanagement and currency debasement signalled their decline. The Roman Empire thrived on a sound currency system, but as territorial ambitions grew, so did financial pressures, with the gradual debasement of the denarius eroding confidence and weakening Rome's economy. Centuries later, Britain followed a similar trajectory, rising to dominance on a solid monetary foundation, only to concede its position as the pound sterling lost global trust.

The shift from gold-backed money to a full-scale fiat currency marked a turning point that exposed the frailties in the financial system that we see today.

This chapter may have taken a lengthy indirect path to uncover these historical economic mistakes, but I believe it is critical to recognise their implications. The fall of previous monetary systems demonstrates a recurring theme: when money loses integrity, economies suffer. Whether through clipping coins, inflating paper currencies, or manipulating interest rates, history has shown that economic power does not last when financial discipline is abandoned. What does this mean for our current fiat economy? And what conclusions can we draw from it?

It is important to remember that we are living in just one moment of time. I have taken you through over 12,000 years over the last two chapters, and history has shown that no empire or monetary system stays in place forever. As with President Hoover's statement back in 1929, collapse often comes when it is least expected. Just because this is all we have known in our lifetimes does not mean it will last indefinitely, just as the people found out who had lived through the heights of past empires.

As we move into the digital era, echoes of these historical cycles are becoming harder to ignore. As central banks continue to print money at unprecedented rates, the same concerns arise as those that plagued past empires. But could an alternative monetary system, free from central control, offer a more resilient future?

Bitcoin, with its fixed supply and decentralised nature, could present a viable alternative, but how can we be sure that it cannot be debased or inflated? How can a system without central oversight truly function on a global scale? If history has shown that every form of money eventually faces challenges, what makes Bitcoin any different?

In the next chapters, we explore these questions by analysing the technical foundations of Bitcoin and blockchain technology to determine whether Bitcoin is truly resistant to manipulation. How does it work? And perhaps most importantly, does it have any value at all?

Chapter 6

Bitcoin's Consensus Mechinism

For centuries, money has been the ultimate puppet master. Kings stamped their faces onto coins. Governments printed bills whenever they pleased. Empires rose and fell on promises backed by nothing but belief. Yet, as we saw in Chapter 5, more control and more power just led to more risk. More recklessness. More pain. Banks constructed elaborate webs of trust, only to break it time and time again. What, then, if trust weren't needed? What if a monetary system did not rely on rulers or middlemen? Imagine a world where we could do without those dubious monetary policies designed solely to serve certain segments of the community.

Bitcoin emerged to challenge all these things, while providing a mathematical means to redefine where we place our trust. To remove manipulation from a system that has been struggling. So, how is this even possible without any oversight? How does Bitcoin guarantee that no one individual can alter its supply? What is the magic technology that allows Bitcoin to function the way it does?

These are the key questions that we address in this chapter. Most people don't understand how Bitcoin works, and that's a major reason it hasn't quite caught on with the average person. There is a big misconception that Bitcoin is risky because of its huge price swings, which make it seem like a scam. Unreliable even. But this is just price action. It has no bearing on the technology underlying the system. If gold or other assets were more volatile then it wouldn't make them bad assets either, what matters is the way people decide to trade them.

As the world slowly shifts away from the inherently broken fiat experiment we've all grown accustomed to, and towards a more robust foundation with digital alternatives, Bitcoin has stepped up to explore this change.

So, what makes Bitcoin so secure? And why do some think it is the most powerful kind of money ever created? On the other hand, even after reading Chapter 3, some will still raise concerns such as, what happens if you send Bitcoin to someone, and it just disappears? Because explanations aside, you can't see it, right? What if it gets lost in the world of the internet, with the ones and zeros never to be seen again? Let's look now at all these questions on the basis of how the technology works.

Bitcoin's security model is rooted in its unique consensus mechanism, which is not unlike how ancient empires relied on tangible methods like coinage to verify and legitimise their currencies. As we know from Chapter 3, consensus is the method used by the network to validate transactions. When we talk about consensus in the context of Bitcoin, it means the way a group collectively agrees on transactions. For example, say that HSBC bank employees all agree that person A has sent £50 to person B, that would be consensus on that transaction. However, unlike physical money, Bitcoin's consensus is totally digital, with no central entity in control.

Whereas past empires wielded weapons and armies to dictate the flow of currency, in the digital world, it is a battle of raw computational power. An electrifying fight of transaction validation upholds the network. It's fascinating how transactions can be verified and recorded in a completely decentralised way, with the aim of making fraud and manipulation a thing of the past. But, what's the secret behind how this system works? How are the incentives to secure the network correctly applied? And why is it that Bitcoin's system ensures reliability and scarcity?

This chapter breaks down the mechanics behind Bitcoin mining and the processes that are used to secure the network. I explore the economic incentives that drive mining competition and its role in Bitcoin's broader monetary system. Understanding this system is crucial, as without it, Bitcoin would be just another digital token, one software upgrade away from failure. With Bitcoin, we can envisage a financial system where the rules are written in mathematics, and not politics.

BITCOIN'S FOUNDING WHITE PAPER

We explored some of Bitcoin's key attributes and use cases in Chapter 3. However, to properly understand how the network operates on a technological level, we must further examine the pivotal 2008 White Paper: *Bitcoin: A Peer-to-Peer Electronic Cash System*. This was not just another research paper. It was a challenge to the entire financial system. A blueprint for a system in which money moves without banks, transactions are finalised without requiring permission, and value is transferred without misplaced trust.

At the heart of this document lies the question: how can we create a financial system that no one can control, yet everyone can verify? The answer lies in Bitcoin's core innovations, which we will now examine, beginning with the White Paper's abstract, the half-page summary that introduced a new kind of money to the world.

Bitcoin: A Peer-to-Peer Electronic Cash System

Satoshi Nakamoto
satoshin@gmx.com
www.bitcoin.org

Abstract. A purely peer-to-peer version of electronic cash would allow online payments to be sent directly from one party to another without going through a financial institution. Digital signatures provide part of the solution, but the main benefits are lost if a trusted third party is still required to prevent double-spending. We propose a solution to the double-spending problem using a peer-to-peer network. The network timestamps transactions by hashing them into an ongoing chain of hash-based proof-of-work, forming a record that cannot be changed without redoing the proof-of-work. The longest chain not only serves as proof of the sequence of events witnessed, but proof that it came from the largest pool of CPU power. As long as a majority of CPU power is controlled by nodes that are not cooperating to attack the network, they'll generate the longest chain and outpace attackers. The network itself requires minimal structure. Messages are broadcast on a best effort basis, and nodes can leave and rejoin the network at will, accepting the longest proof-of-work chain as proof of what happened while they were gone.

1.   Introduction

Commerce on the Internet has come to rely almost exclusively on financial institutions serving as trusted third parties to process electronic payments. While the system works well enough for most transactions, it still suffers from the inherent weaknesses of the trust based model. Completely non-reversible transactions are not really possible, since financial institutions cannot avoid mediating disputes. The cost of mediation increases transaction costs, limiting the minimum practical transaction size and cutting off the possibility for small casual transactions, and there is a broader cost in the loss of ability to make non-reversible payments for non-reversible services. With the possibility of reversal, the need for trust spreads. Merchants must be wary of their customers, hassling them for more information than they would otherwise need. A certain percentage of fraud is accepted as unavoidable. These costs and payment uncertainties can be avoided in person by using physical currency, but no mechanism exists to make payments over a communications channel without a trusted party.

What is needed is an electronic payment system based on cryptographic proof instead of trust, allowing any two willing parties to transact directly with each other without the need for a trusted third party. Transactions that are computationally impractical to reverse would protect sellers from fraud, and routine escrow mechanisms could easily be implemented to protect buyers. In this paper, we propose a solution to the double-spending problem using a peer-to-peer distributed timestamp server to generate computational proof of the chronological order of transactions. The system is secure as long as honest nodes collectively control more CPU power than any cooperating group of attacker nodes.

The abstract for the Bitcoin White Paper is relatively basic. In a few paragraphs, Satoshi Nakamoto describes a financial system that runs without banks, intermediaries, or central control. Fundamentally, it defines Bitcoin as a peer-to-peer digital money that enables transactions over the internet without the need for trust in third parties. Traditional payment systems rely on financial institutions to verify transactions, whereas Bitcoin replaces this trust with mathematical proof. Instead of requiring permission from a central authority, Bitcoin allows direct value transfers between individuals, secured by cryptographic verification. So, how does it do this?

To properly explain these principles, I will go through the Bitcoin White Paper section by section, using examples and analogies along the way to clarify even the most complicated ideas. Doing this will help to demonstrate how Bitcoin works in practice. Some parts may appear difficult at first, but having a general understanding is crucial to appreciating how the protocol works. It is a good idea to read each section of the White Paper at least once, either now, or later as we go through the document, as I will not reproduce every single bit.

PART 1: THE INTRODUCTION

The paper's Introduction addresses the concepts we have previously discussed regarding too much reliance on trusted third parties to process online payments over the internet. It implies that there are weaknesses in the current financial system and a need for a new decentralised payment system that is based on cryptographic proof instead of trust, without requiring a third party to facilitate the transactions.

There is a focus on cryptocurrency transactions having to be immutable and impractical to reverse to protect sellers from fraud, and that escrow mechanisms should protect buyers, to ensure that goods or services are delivered as agreed. The full solution is disclosed as using a peer-to-peer distributed timestamp server to generate computational proof of a chronological order of transactions, which I will come to shortly. The key idea is that the network is secure, provided that the honest nodes have more control than any cooperating group of attacker nodes. As we have previously learnt, Bitcoin nodes are computers that participate in the Bitcoin network, helping to validate transactions and maintain the blockchain's integrity.

The White Paper goes on to consider the problem of transaction costs in the current system rising too high for financial institutions to mediate any disputes, thus limiting the practical size of transactions. There is also no way to reverse transactions on the Bitcoin network, which can be important to protect the sellers of certain non-refundable services. However, as we will see in future chapters, this immutability can also prove problematic if the buyer is defrauded or a transaction is made in error.

So, imagine if you want to buy digital art. Once you pay the artist or dealer and receive the artwork, there should not be a way for you, as the buyer, to claim a refund for this, as you clearly saw what you were purchasing. Or imagine a pay-per-view event, such as a boxing match. On making payment, you get access to the footage and therefore, there wouldn't be any need for it to be reversed.

Finally, picture an online auction where someone places the winning bid on a rare, one-of-a-kind item, such as a signed piece of sports memorabilia, or a luxury watch. The payment is final, and the item gets transferred to the buyer on receipt. The auction house and the seller both require irreversible payment before releasing the asset. Unlike regular card purchases, Bitcoin prevents a buyer from undoing a transaction after receiving an item. In the case of the auction process and transfer of ownership, the service has already been completed, hence an automatic or forced refund makes no sense. This is a completely different category from digital services like pay-per-view, but it demonstrates how beneficial Bitcoin's finality is in high-value, non-reversible transactions.

In traditional payment systems, the cost of mediation raises transaction costs, rendering minor transactions impractical. The prospect of chargebacks and reversals forces retailers to request additional customer information, causing friction and compromising privacy. Moreover, fraud is accepted as an unavoidable cost, adding further inefficiencies and expense. While physical cash overcomes these challenges for in-person payments, until Bitcoin, online transactions lacked a trustworthy alternative. By allowing direct, irreversible payments without intermediaries, Bitcoin eliminates these expenses and uncertainties to provide a digital alternative to cash and traditional e-payment systems.

2. Transactions

We define an electronic coin as a chain of digital signatures. Each owner transfers the coin to the next by digitally signing a hash of the previous transaction and the public key of the next owner and adding these to the end of the coin. A payee can verify the signatures to verify the chain of ownership.

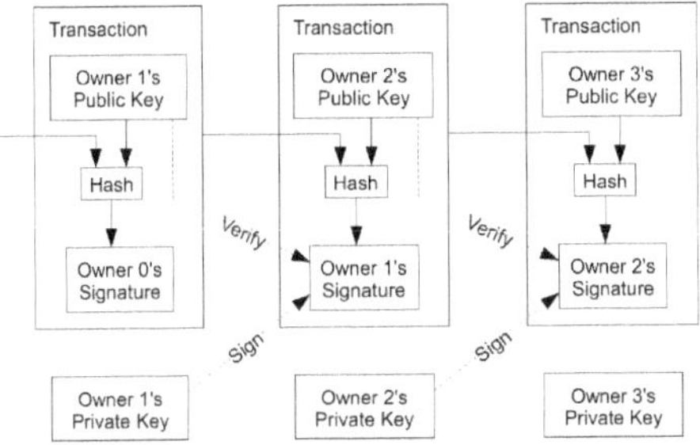

The problem of course is the payee can't verify that one of the owners did not double-spend the coin. A common solution is to introduce a trusted central authority, or mint, that checks every transaction for double spending. After each transaction, the coin must be returned to the mint to issue a new coin, and only coins issued directly from the mint are trusted not to be double-spent. The problem with this solution is that the fate of the entire money system depends on the company running the mint, with every transaction having to go through them, just like a bank.

We need a way for the payee to know that the previous owners did not sign any earlier transactions. For our purposes, the earliest transaction is the one that counts, so we don't care about later attempts to double-spend. The only way to confirm the absence of a transaction is to be aware of all transactions. In the mint based model, the mint was aware of all transactions and decided which arrived first. To accomplish this without a trusted party, transactions must be publicly announced [1], and we need a system for participants to agree on a single history of the order in which they were received. The payee needs proof that at the time of each transaction, the majority of nodes agreed it was the first received.

PART 2: TRANSACTIONS

Before we return to the point regarding cooperating CPU power controlling the majority of the network, first let's look at Part 2 of the White Paper.

The Bitcoin White Paper defines a digital coin as a chain of digital signatures. Each owner transfers their Bitcoin by making a digital signature, authorising the transaction to the next recipient. This ensures that ownership is verifiable and cannot be forged. Everyday digital communication is an effective way to think about this. As previously demonstrated in Chapter 3, when sending an email or WhatsApp message, by simply inputting the recipient's email address or phone number you can ensure that your message is sent to the intended person. This concept is implemented on the Bitcoin network using your Bitcoin address.

PUBLIC AND PRIVATE KEYS

Every Bitcoin user has a private key and a public key, which are cryptographically linked. A user also requires an address to receive Bitcoin. Put simply, this Bitcoin address is created by applying a cryptographic function known as hashing to the public key, along with other data, which makes it shorter and easier to read. This extra step improves security and privacy by guaranteeing that the complete public key is not instantly exposed.

The private key is used to sign transactions and to authorise sending Bitcoin to someone, just as pressing "send" delivers an email. Once a transaction is signed with a private key, the public key is only revealed within the transaction to allow the network to verify its authenticity and ensure it has not been altered. Since transactions are irreversible once confirmed, the integrity of the system relies on the security of these cryptographic signatures and hashing algorithms.

HASHING

A "hash" on the Bitcoin network refers to a special function that is designed to produce a result that is one hundred percent unique. Think of a hash like a digital fingerprint of the data, ensuring authenticity and integrity. These two things are important to understand as they form the basis of the whole system. Let me briefly show you a couple of examples of functions before moving on to hash functions in more detail. For anyone unfamiliar with mathematical functions, a function is like a machine that takes an input, does something to it, and then gives an output. The important thing to know about a function is that it always follows the same set of instructions. No matter how many times you use it, the same input will always give you the same output.

EXAMPLE: A TOASTER AS A FUNCTION

- ⓑ Input: A slice of bread
- ⓑ Function: The toaster heats it up
- ⓑ Output: Toast

If you always put a slice of bread of set properties in for the same amount of time, you will always get the same toast out.

MATHEMATICAL EXAMPLE

A function in maths works the same way. Suppose we have a function that adds 2 to any number:

- ⓑ If we input 3, the function outputs 5
- ⓑ If we input 7, the function outputs 9
- ⓑ The rule of the function is "add 2"

Now, let's go back to Bitcoin's hash function. It does a similar thing as the functions above but there are a few key differences. First, it uses a type of cryptographic hash function called SHA-256 (Secure Hash Algorithm 256-bit). This means whatever the input is, no matter how small or how big the transaction, or how many transactions there are, it always returns a fixed length of 256 ones and zeros. This is because "bit" means binary digit and these are always ones and zeros. A computer reads anything from text to images as a list of binary digits, so everything needs to be presented this way to be understood. If you have transactional data saying Person A sends Person B 0.5 BTC, then when this data is put into the SHA-256 function it always gives you a unique sequence of 256 ones and zeros that represents the parties involved and the amount, among other details that we will come to shortly. While the output may look random, the same input will always produce the same 256-bit hash. Remember that each of these 256-bit sequences of ones and zeros act as a unique digital fingerprint of the original data that was input into the hash function.

All ok so far?

Two important characteristics of these SHA-256 hash functions are that they use complex cryptographic algorithms, and they are one-way functions only. This means that you can't find out what the original data was from a hash.

You wouldn't be able to put the toast back into the toaster and create a slice of bread either. This is an important characteristic to ensure that the original transactional data remains secure, private, and immutable. This is why it is called cryptocurrency; the encryption prevents any possibility of fraud once a transaction has been initiated. Even the smallest change to the input, like altering a single character, produces a completely different hash. This property makes hashes perfect for ensuring a high level of security and preventing tampering in the Bitcoin network.

If you think about the enormous number of possible variations from a random list of 256 ones and zeros, you will appreciate why it would be much easier to win a few lotteries in a row than predicting one of these hash outputs. This leads us onto the next point to consider. The fact that these numbers are so long to represent makes it impractical for humans. Therefore, instead of actually using the 256 binary digits of ones and zeros, these are represented in hexadecimal (hex) format to make it easier for humans to read.

Just remember that the following 16 symbols each represent a unique combination of 4 ones and zeros:

0, 1, 2, 3, 4, 5, 6, 7, 8, 9, A, B, C, D, E, and F.

This is just for human representation; computers use the full 256 binary ones and zeros when processing transactions. For example, 0 in hex = 0000 in binary. 1 in hex = 0001, and A in hex = 1010 in binary. Therefore this 256-bit number of ones and zeros, converts to a 64-character hexadecimal number (256/4 =64). So, from now on, we will use these 64-character hexadecimal numbers to refer to Bitcoin hashes. Let's have a look at an example.

Because SHA-256 always generates a fixed-length output, the size of the input makes no difference; the result will always be a 64-character hexadecimal hash.

For example, if we input the following phrase:

"Bitcoin is decentralised"

We obtain the SHA-256 output hash in hex:

dac998553e9b5bac61b9ed0613f1617c4c28cafc257c766d376 b3d24500bb1cb

Now, if we spell decentralised with a z as in U.S. English, the input becomes:

"Bitcoin is decentralized"

We get the hash:

d320d5b34881f2252e1d0ac87f772373a1299e8c38a0fb743d5 85a3762e1ade2

Even though only one letter changed, we can see that the entire hash is completely different. The outcome is a completely different digital fingerprint. This property is known as the avalanche effect. It ensures that no one can alter a transaction without it easily being detected, so transactions remain tamper-proof and verifiable on the blockchain. Remember as well that by using the U.S. English Hash above (d320….ade2), we can't reverse engineer this to get "Bitcoin is decentralized". This is crucial to Bitcoin to ensure that the output of a hash function cannot be reversed to expose the original transaction details. If attackers were able to reverse-engineer the hash output, they could reveal sensitive transaction data and use it to manipulate the network.

WHY BITCOIN USES DOUBLE HASHING (SHA-256 TWICE)

Ok, now that we understand what hash functions are, it is important to remember that the Bitcoin software always performs the SHA-256 hash function twice on any piece of data, a process known as double hashing. Even though once is already highly secure, applying it twice adds an extra layer of protection against vulnerabilities that could arise from advances in cryptanalysis and computer technology.

TxIDs

Returning to Part 2 of the White Paper, every Bitcoin transaction is processed by taking all of its data and applying the double hash function. This generates a unique transaction ID (TxID) and ensures that all transactions on the blockchain are tamper-proof and immediately recognisable.

Each transaction consists of several essential raw data components, including:

1. The hash of the previous transaction. This links the new transaction to a past one by a particular Bitcoin address (the sender), maintaining an unbroken ledger of Bitcoin ownership.

2. The recipient's Bitcoin Wallet address. This ensures that only the intended recipient can claim the funds by proving ownership.

3. The digital signature. This serves as cryptographic proof that the sender has authorised the transaction.

In addition to these essential components, Bitcoin transactions contain technical information, such as the version number, lock-time, sequence number, and script information, none of which we need to go over here to understand the process. However, what is more important is how the value of the transaction is dealt with. Each transaction follows the UTXO (Unspent Transaction Output) model. This means that the entire amount from the preceding transaction must be spent. At the same time, each transaction remains independent and easier to verify without relying on a central account balance. This parallel validation process makes the network more efficient and scalable.

If the sender does not transfer their entire balance, the remaining amount is returned to them as change output. This works like paying £2.50 for a loaf of bread with a £10 note and receiving £7.50 as change. These are called UTXO and we'll look at them in more detail when we examine Part 3 of the White Paper. Remember that even the slightest change in any of the above input information results in a completely different TxID, and therefore a completely different digital fingerprint of the transactional data, making fraudulent modifications easy to detect.

Now that I have explained how transaction TxIDs are formulated, let me provide an analogy for how the transaction process works and its role in creating a block. Think of a Bitcoin transaction like a person waiting to buy a ticket to enter a busy concert. The transaction pool is like the lobby, where people must wait before being allowed into the concert hall (the blockchain).

1. Before entering the lobby, the person agrees on a fee (i.e. how much they would be willing to pay for the ticket) at the reception desk. This fee is written on a piece of paper and stamped by the receptionist. This stamped paper represents the transaction (Tx) and signifies that the transaction has been verified.

2. The person then waits in the lobby alongside others, each holding their stamped papers, waiting to enter the concert.

3. Miners, like doormen at a concert hall, check the lobby to decide who enters next.

4. They choose transactions based on two key factors:

   a. The transaction fee, recorded in the Tx (i.e. how much people are willing to pay to enter, as written on their stamped piece of paper).

   b. The transaction size, which represents how many people they are bringing in with them (as noted on their stamped paper).

5. Once a miner selects a transaction, they perform the hashing process to create a transaction ID (TxID), and they include it within a block. This is like the doormen collecting the entrance fee, and stamping "paid" onto their piece of paper, and letting the people into the concert.

The transaction is then confirmed, added to the blockchain and it becomes a permanent part of the Bitcoin network.

Now we have an idea of how transactions function in the network, let's look at an example of a Bitcoin transaction and see how the resulting TxID is created after the data has been double hashed. Last year I met Lewis and Abdul while on holiday in Egypt, and explained to them how Bitcoin and cryptocurrency work, so I thought it would be fitting to use them for this example. This simplified example shows Lewis sending Bitcoin to Abdul, highlighting the three key elements needed for the transaction, although I have omitted the additional technical details for simplicity.

Step 1: The hash of the previous transaction (TxID) (Links to the prior transaction when Lewis received the Bitcoin that he now wants to spend. This ensures continuity in the blockchain ledger by referencing this specific unspent output.)

One could look like this:

4a7d1ed414474e4033ac29ccb8653d9b4f2c206a6c6c9d6f5b8
e6c6a7e7a1b1f

Step 2: Abdul's Bitcoin wallet address (This is where Lewis is sending the BTC. It acts as the destination address and is derived from Abdul's public key using hashing and encoding functions.)

One could look like this:

1FfmbHfnpaZjKFvyi1okTjJJusN455paPH

Step 3: Lewis's Digital Signature (Proves Lewis (sender) owns the BTC and authorises the transaction).

One could look like this:

3045022100a6f1b5e3d8f7c6e4b9f1a7d5b3e1a6f4d7c2e1f9b
1a6d4e1c7b3d2f1a5c9e1a5

Again, in practice all nine elements would be included as listed on the previous page, but for this example we will focus on these three for simplicity.

These three elements are then concatenated, which means combined in sequence, to form the full transactional data:

> 4a7d1ed414474e4033ac29ccb8653d9b4f2c206a6c6c9d6f5
> b8e6c6a7e7a1b1f1FfmbHfnpaZjKFvyi1okTjJJusN455paP
> H3045022100a6f1b5e3d8f7c6e4b9f1a7d5b3e1a6f4d7c2e1
> f9b1a6d4e1c7b3d2f1a5c9e1a5

At this stage, the entire transaction data is hashed once using SHA-256. This produces an initial hash:

> 8f604cd9103dd3634ff499a04d6565666c55456fabfb1bcec3b
> 6d1ad734ec914

However, as we know Bitcoin does not stop here. For enhanced security, the result is then hashed a second time with SHA-256:

> 5b80e4bfef4d1de248d41dae90d1a41d6ff0f319ef9f9683a95c
> 01d1be05e129

This is the final transaction ID (TxID).

So far, we have covered Step 1, the hash of the previous TxID and Step 2, the recipient's Bitcoin wallet address. But what about Step 3, Lewis's digital signature? Where does this data come from?

So here is where it starts getting technical. I will not show the exact cryptographic calculation, as it is beyond the scope of this book, but I do try to provide an outline of how it works. The digital signature is a crucial part of the transaction, as it proves the ownership of the Bitcoin being spent and who is authorising the transfer. This digital signature acts like a tamper-proof receipt, ensuring that only Lewis, the rightful owner of the Bitcoin can send it.

Bitcoin secures transactions using the *Elliptic Curve Digital Signature Algorithm (ECDSA)* on a specific curve known as **secp256k1**. This ensures that only the rightful owner of the Bitcoin can authorise a transaction without revealing the private key, while anyone can verify its authenticity.

HOW ELLIPTIC CURVES SECURE TRANSACTIONS

The basis of this cryptographic system is an elliptic curve equation that produces a smooth, elliptic curve:

$$y^2 = x^3 + 7$$

The mathematics behind this curve enable Bitcoin to generate public keys, digital signatures, and verification processes in a way that is practically impossible to reverse-engineer.

UNDERSTANDING DIGITAL SIGNATURES WITH ELLIPTIC CURVES

Going back to our earlier example, when Lewis sends Bitcoin to Abdul, his transaction needs a digital signature to prove ownership. This signature is generated using ECDSA and consists of two essential components:

- Ⓑ The private key, which only Lewis knows and has access to, which is used to sign the transaction.

- Ⓑ The digital signature, represented as a pair of values (r, s), which are mathematically derived from the private key and linked to a unique point on the elliptic curve.

Once Lewis signs the transaction, anyone can verify its authenticity using his public key, without ever needing access to or knowing his private key.

To make things easier to understand, let's extend the analogy. Imagine that Lewis wants to send a sealed envelope containing a contract to Abdul. Not wanting anyone to tamper with it or forge his approval, he does two things. First, he locks the envelope with his private key, which only he knows, to seal it. This is like digitally signing the transaction. Then, he writes a special verification code on the outside, his public key, so that anyone can verify it came from him. When Abdul receives the envelope, he can use Lewis's public key to check that the seal matches. If the seal has been tampered with, or if someone else has tried to forge Lewis's signature, it won't verify correctly.

HOW DOES THE ELLIPTIC CURVE WORK?

An elliptic curve allows mathematical operations where points on the curve are easy to compute in one direction but almost impossible to reverse, a quality that we know is shared by SHA-256. This curve is used to prove that the sender owns the Bitcoin, without revealing their private key.

Here is the process:

1. Generating the Public Key

    - Lewis starts with a large number. This is his random private key.

    - Elliptic curve multiplication is applied via the Bitcoin software using the secp256k1 elliptic curve.

    - This process multiplies the private key by a predefined generator point (G) on the curve, producing a public key, which is a unique point (x, y) on the same elliptic curve, Point A.Creating a Digital Signature

    - When Lewis signs a transaction, the software applies the ECDSA algorithm using his private key.

    - This process generates a unique digital signature (r, s), where r is derived from a point on the elliptic curve, referred to as Point B.

2. Verifying the Signature

    - When Abdul (or any Bitcoin node) receives the transaction, they can use Lewis's public key (Point A) to verify that the signature is valid.

    - The ECDSA verification process checks whether the signature (r, s), corresponds to a valid elliptic curve computation by producing a Point C, which must also lie on the curve. This confirms that the signature was generated by someone who possessed the private key.

⑧ This works because only the private key could have generated this signature, resulting in another valid elliptic curve computation. If someone attempted to forge it without the private key, the resulting point would not satisfy the elliptic curve equation, and the verification would fail.

⑧ Since verification only requires the public key and the digital signature, anyone can confirm that the transaction was signed by the rightful owner, without revealing the private key.

This may seem pretty complicated but just remember that this method is extremely secure. Even if someone knows the public key, they cannot figure out the private key as it is computationally infeasible.

VISUALISING THE ELLIPTIC CURVE

Here is a visual representation of the **secp256k1 elliptic curve** that Bitcoin uses for ECDSA.

Figurwe 6.1: Elliptic Curve

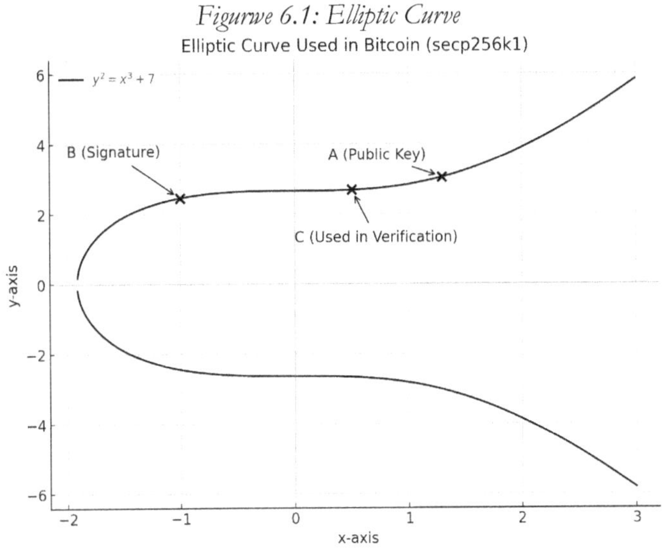

Apologies in advance, because writing what follows almost gave me a headache. To recap, points on the elliptic curve interact in a way that makes encryption secure. Each private key generates a unique public key using elliptic curve multiplication, producing Point A on the curve.

Since elliptic curve multiplication is a one-way function, every public key, and consequently every Bitcoin address (a hashed digital fingerprint version of the public key), is mathematically linked to the original private key. When the Bitcoin software applies the ECDSA algorithm, it uses that private key to generate the digital signature, which consists of values that are derived using elliptic curve mathematics and are linked to a point on the curve, Point B.

For verification, a Bitcoin node uses the sender's public key (Point A) and applies the ECDSA verification formula to compute another point on the curve (Point C). If Point C satisfies the elliptic curve equation and is in fact another point on the elliptic curve, then this could only be the case if the digital signature, used to derive Point B, was also linked to a point on that curve. Hence, this proves that the digital signature (derived using values linked to Point B) could only have been a valid point on the curve if it was derived from the public key, point A.

Therefore, the digital signature must have been obtained through the original elliptic curve multiplication process using the private key. This is the mathematical proof that the node has verified that Point B relates to a correct point on the curve, so it also indirectly confirms that the sender must have used their private key to create the digital signature in the first place, even without actually having access to the private key.

Elliptic curve cryptography is important as it ensures that only the rightful owner of the Bitcoin can spend it. While the underlying mathematics of elliptic curves are complex, the important takeaway is that Bitcoin's digital signatures allow transactions to be verified without revealing private keys, providing both security and decentralisation. This is achieved through the unique properties of the secp256k1 elliptic curve, which ensures that transactions remain tamper-proof, verifiable, and trustless in the cryptographic sense of the word.

These are the properties that make the network so resilient. So, that is the first part of the mining process to verify the transactions. To use Bitcoin in practice you don't need to know the underlying mathematics, as the Bitcoin software takes care of all of this.

Nonetheless, understanding its cryptographic foundation highlights just how secure and technically advanced the Bitcoin network truly is.

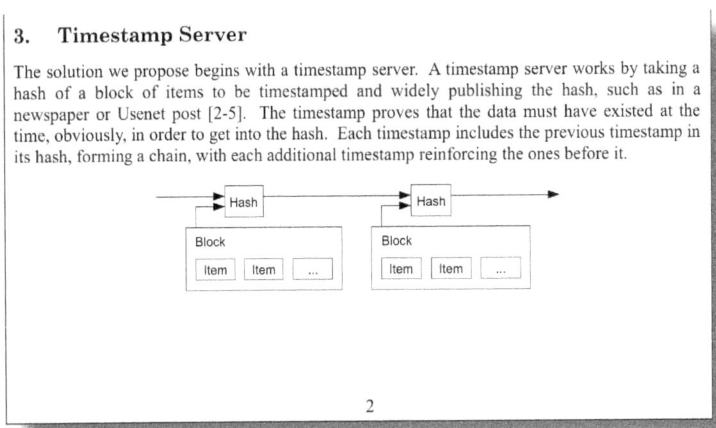

3. Timestamp Server

The solution we propose begins with a timestamp server. A timestamp server works by taking a hash of a block of items to be timestamped and widely publishing the hash, such as in a newspaper or Usenet post [2-5]. The timestamp proves that the data must have existed at the time, obviously, in order to get into the hash. Each timestamp includes the previous timestamp in its hash, forming a chain, with each additional timestamp reinforcing the ones before it.

2

PART 3: THE TIMESTAMP SERVER

Before Bitcoin, digital money systems struggled with double spending, which is the ability to send the same digital currency multiple times. Early attempts like David Chaum's DigiCash and Hal Finney's RPOW tried to solve this but relied on central authorities. Satoshi Nakamoto's breakthrough was to remove trust entirely, replacing it with a decentralised timestamp server that ensures transactions are recorded in an immutable order. So, how does the timestamp server work?

Every Bitcoin transaction must be recorded in a fixed chronological order on the public ledger to prevent double spending. The timestamp server achieves this by:

1. Hashing a block of transactions.

2. Publishing this hash widely, proving the transactions in the block existed at that exact moment.

3. Linking each new block to the previous one, forming a secure, verifiable chain (the blockchain).

Bitcoin does not rely on timestamps alone to prevent double spending. Each transaction references specific unspent outputs (UTXOs), which can only be spent once. Remember the example above of the change you would receive from using a £10 note to buy a loaf of bread?

If two conflicting transactions enter the mempool (transaction pool), nodes will accept the first valid one only and reject the second. When miners select transactions for a block, only the first valid spend is included, while any conflicting transaction is discarded. Consider the situation where two transactions are made in quick succession. Imagine a person (the sender) has 1 BTC and they try to send 0.5 to someone and then 0.8 to someone else. This is clearly not going to be possible as the total exceeds the available balance. Both transactions may enter the mempool, as they are generally verified in isolation. However, miners will need to review the different transactions and select them for their blocks. It is possible for both transactions to be added to competing blocks. However, the only one that would be confirmed would be the one that was part of the winning block. If a miner then tried to add the second one, the software would pick up that the sender's UTXO is less than the amount they are attempting to spend, therefore the second one would be rejected.

Once that block is confirmed, the transactions within it become final, and any attempt to spend the same Bitcoin again is automatically invalidated. The longest valid chain dictates the transaction history, ensuring that no Bitcoin can be spent twice. This system ensures that once a transaction is recorded, it cannot be altered without redoing the work for every subsequent block, making fraud computationally impossible.

PART 4: PROOF-OF-WORK, TIMESTAMPING, AND PREVENTING DOUBLE SPENDING

Bitcoin's security doesn't come from recording timestamps alone, it comes from the way that transactions are validated and secured. This is where Proof-of-Work (PoW) comes in.

4. Proof-of-Work

To implement a distributed timestamp server on a peer-to-peer basis, we will need to use a proof-of-work system similar to Adam Back's Hashcash [6], rather than newspaper or Usenet posts. The proof-of-work involves scanning for a value that when hashed, such as with SHA-256, the hash begins with a number of zero bits. The average work required is exponential in the number of zero bits required and can be verified by executing a single hash.

For our timestamp network, we implement the proof-of-work by incrementing a nonce in the block until a value is found that gives the block's hash the required zero bits. Once the CPU effort has been expended to make it satisfy the proof-of-work, the block cannot be changed without redoing the work. As later blocks are chained after it, the work to change the block would include redoing all the blocks after it.

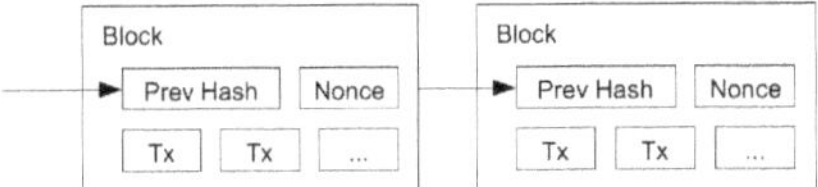

The proof-of-work also solves the problem of determining representation in majority decision making. If the majority were based on one-IP-address-one-vote, it could be subverted by anyone able to allocate many IPs. Proof-of-work is essentially one-CPU-one-vote. The majority decision is represented by the longest chain, which has the greatest proof-of-work effort invested in it. If a majority of CPU power is controlled by honest nodes, the honest chain will grow the fastest and outpace any competing chains. To modify a past block, an attacker would have to redo the proof-of-work of the block and all blocks after it and then catch up with and surpass the work of the honest nodes. We will show later that the probability of a slower attacker catching up diminishes exponentially as subsequent blocks are added.

To compensate for increasing hardware speed and varying interest in running nodes over time, the proof-of-work difficulty is determined by a moving average targeting an average number of blocks per hour. If they're generated too fast, the difficulty increases.

Step-by-Step Process:

1. A transaction is broadcast to the network. For example, when Betty sends 1 BTC to Howard, her transaction is verified (using the elliptic curve ECDSA process explained above) and it enters the mempool.

2. Miners collect transactions from the mempool and package them into a new block. Each miner selects transactions and prepares them for confirmation (based on preset criteria such as transaction fee per byte of data).

3. Miners compete to solve the PoW puzzle. They must find a valid block hash that meets the difficulty target.

4. The winning miner broadcasts the block to the network. Other nodes verify the block and confirm that it follows Bitcoin's rules.

5. The block is added to the blockchain. Once confirmed, all transactions in that block become permanent and irreversible.

So, we have seen how the TxIDs are derived and the general network process, but how are transactions structured into a block?

MERKLE ROOT

A Bitcoin block contains thousands of transactions, but rather than storing them all individually, they are compressed into a single cryptographic summary called the Merkle Root.

Simplified Process:

1. **Transactions (Tx0, Tx1, Tx2, Tx3) are double hashed**, producing TxIDs, as denoted in Figure 6.2 as Hash0, Hash1, Hash2, and Hash3.

2. These TxIDs are then paired together and double hashed.

3. This process keeps reducing the number of TxIDs by half, as remember, any input length always gives a 64-Hexadecimal output.

4. This process continues to boil the data down until a single root hash remains, the Merkle Root, as we can see below in Part 11 of the White Paper.

Figure 6.2: Transactions Hashed in a Merkle Tree

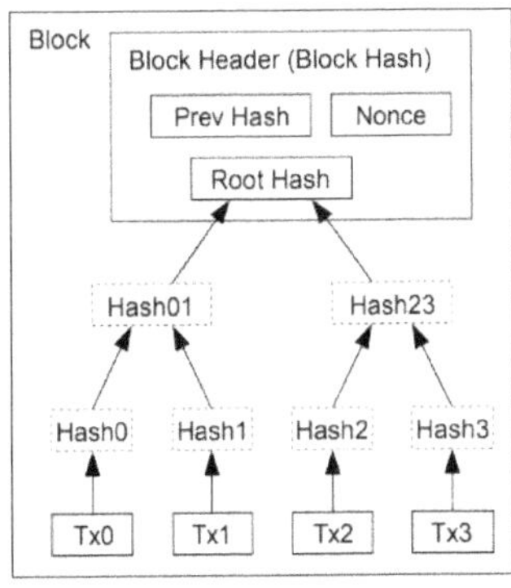

Transactions Hashed in a Merkle Tree

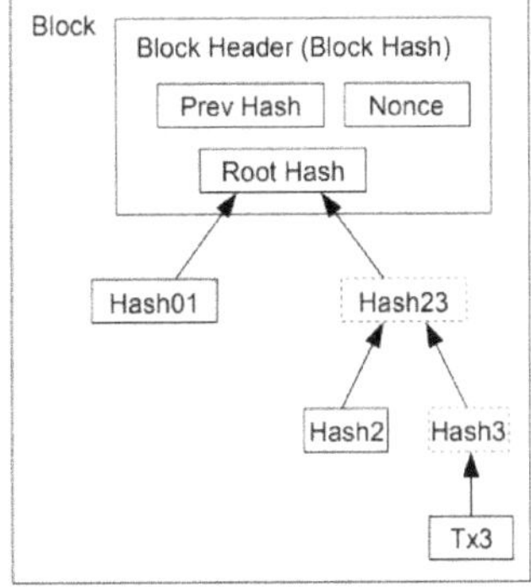

After Pruning Tx0-2 from the Block

The **Merkle Root** is stored in the **block header**, serving as a unique digital fingerprint for all transactions inside that block. Even the smallest change to a transaction would produce a completely different Merkle Root, instantly invalidating the whole block. Once all transactions in a block are processed through the Merkle Tree, the final Merkle Root might look like this:

b3e8b6f4c7c7d5b1e2e1f9b2461a3e8b6f4c7c7d5b6f1a7

The Timestamp server in Part 3 closely relates to Part 4: Proof-of-Work, as before you can create a hash of a block, all of the data in the block needs to be derived, which requires the PoW to be done first.

So, to generate a valid block hash, miners must work with the following elements in the **block header**:

1. **Previous Block Hash**. The digital fingerprint of the previous block and every block before it. This links the new block to the previous one, which is linked in turn to its predecessors, ensuring continuity in the blockchain.

2. **Merkle Root**. A cryptographic summary (hash) of all transactions in the block.

3. **Timestamp**. A record of the exact moment the block was created.

4. **Difficulty Target**. A measure of the current mining difficulty, ensuring blocks are mined at a consistent rate.

There is a final piece of information required to create the block hash:

5. **Nonce**. This is a number that miners must find to generate a valid block hash.

Now, let's turn our attention to Part 4 of the White Paper. This will tell us how the nonce is found and how it ties into Proof-of-Work to secure the blockchain. For a block to be added to the chain, miners must solve a computational puzzle by finding a valid nonce. The nonce is the only unknown variable that must be found to generate a valid block hash. Remember this is the only way for it to obtain a digital fingerprint and to be linked to the chain.

UNDERSTANDING THE NONCE AND PROOF-OF-WORK

As outlined in the White Paper, Bitcoin's PoW system ensures that it requires computational effort to create each new block. This makes it infeasible for attackers to alter past transactions without redoing the PoW for all subsequent blocks. Now that we know how transactions and other data are structured and compiled into a block, the next step is to show how miners use Proof-of-Work.

Their initial goal is to find a valid nonce to solve the cryptographic puzzle and then use it to generate a valid hash for the block.

WHAT IS THE NONCE AND WHY IS IT IMPORTANT?

The nonce (short for "number used once") is a 32-bit variable (ranging from 0 to 4,294,967,295) that miners adjust to find a valid block hash. As stated previously, it is the only part of the block header that changes as miners attempt to solve the PoW puzzle. Bitcoin's PoW system works as follows:

1. Miners take all the known block data (previous block hash, Merkle Root, timestamp, and difficulty target).

2. They combine this data with a nonce and then double hash the entire block header using the SHA-256 function.

3. The goal is to find a hash that meets the difficulty target, meaning it must start with a required number of leading zeros.

THE DIFFICULTY TARGET

The more leading zeros required, the lower the numerical value of the hash, making it exponentially harder to find. But why does a lower target increase the difficulty of finding it?

- Ⓑ Hashes are random, but the network sets a fixed difficulty target (see below for an explanation).

- Ⓑ Bitcoin miners must find a block hash that is lower than the target specified by the network.

- Ⓑ If the target is high, almost any hash will be valid (low difficulty).

- Ⓑ The lower this threshold, the harder it becomes to find a valid hash, as fewer possible solutions will meet the requirement (high difficulty).

- Ⓑ Miners must keep adjusting the nonce and re-hashing the block header millions or billions of times per second to find a valid hash.

Since SHA-256 produces completely random outputs, miners cannot predict or manipulate the result. They must use brute-force, using trial and error with different nonces and then hashing the block header data, over and over until they find one that meets the required difficulty. Bitcoin automatically adjusts its mining difficulty every 2,016 blocks (roughly every two weeks) based on how fast blocks are being found.

- Ⓑ If blocks are being mined too quickly, the network increases the difficulty by requiring more leading zeros.

- Ⓑ If blocks are taking too long, the network reduces difficulty, making mining easier.

- Ⓑ This adjustment ensures that a new block is mined approximately every 10 minutes, regardless of the total computational power in the network.

A straightforward way to understand why more leading zeros make it more difficult is to think of flipping a coin 256 times. Imagine heads means zero and tails means one. If only the first outcome needed to be heads (zero) to satisfy the difficulty target, then on average the hash would be found every couple of tries. If, however, the first five outcomes needed to be heads (five zeros in a row), then finding it would take many more attempts of 256 flips. This is a good way to think about how the difficulty target works.

A valid double hash of the block header could look like this:

SHA-256(SHA-256(Block header data)) → Block Hash:

00000000000000b9f6c9e8a7d3c4e1b24f6c7c7d5b3e1a6f4d7 c2e1f9b1a6d4

If this hash were valid, it would confirm that the number of leading zeros in this example was sufficiently below the difficulty target set by the network.

FINDING THE NONCE

Since the nonce is the only unknown variable, miners must find it through trial and error:

1. A miner usually starts with the statement that nonce = 0 to calculate the block hash.

2. If the resulting hash does not meet the difficulty target, the miner increases the nonce in regular increments (e.g. 1, 2, 3, …), continuously trying to guess the solution.

3. This process is repeated millions or even billions of times per second as miners race to find a valid nonce.

4. Once a miner finds a valid nonce, they broadcast the new block to the network.

5. Other nodes verify that the hash meets the required difficulty level.

6. The first miner to find the correct nonce receives a block reward and transaction fees from all the transactions in the block. We will discuss fees in more detail later in this chapter.

7. The process repeats for the next block, ensuring Bitcoin remains secure, decentralised and resistant to manipulation.

BLOCK VALIDATION AND ADDING THE BLOCK TO THE CHAIN

Now that we understand how miners find a valid nonce, the next step is to examine how the network validates the new block and adds it to the blockchain, building upon Part 5 of the White Paper. Each miner independently selects which transactions to include in their candidate block (new block they are proposing). These transactions come from the mempool, the global waiting area where unconfirmed transactions sit until miners process them.

Miners prioritise transactions based on:

- Ⓑ Transaction fees (higher fees get priority).

- Ⓑ Transaction size (smaller transactions may be included to maximise block space).

- Ⓑ Validity (all transactions must follow Bitcoin's consensus rules).

Because miners choose transactions independently, their proposed blocks will contain different sets of transactions. However, once a miner successfully finds the correct nonce and broadcasts their block to the network, all other miners must:

1. Verify the block to ensure it follows Bitcoin's consensus rules.

2. Accept the block if it is valid.

3. Discard their own versions and begin working on the next block, building on the newly accepted longest chain.

Even though miners may start with different transaction lists, only one block is ultimately accepted per round, ensuring a single, agreed-upon version of history. So, why is proof-of-work (PoW) necessary?

As mentioned in Chapter 3, PoW ensures that miners secure the network and validate transactions by investing real computational work in the form of computer hardware and energy. Due to this great expense, it ensures that it is extremely difficult and costly to manipulate the network, which in turn secures Bitcoin's immutability.

In our previous nonce example above, the valid nonce was 872134. This means the miner's computer had to perform thousands, or sometimes even millions of guesses, double hashing each one, before finding the correct solution.

What is truly extraordinary is that the resulting block hash becomes the digital fingerprint of all the transactions in that block.

This is significant because each block is linked to the previous one, meaning this fingerprint also secures every single transaction that has ever existed on the Bitcoin blockchain. Even back to the first Bitcoin Genesis block that was mined by Satoshi Nakamoto on 3 January 2009.

This is extremely powerful as even the smallest change to any past transaction, even from 15 years ago, would completely change the latest block hash, breaking the chain and exposing tampering. This is what makes Bitcoin's blockchain so secure and immutable.

Let's consider an analogy that further clarifies how the PoW system works. Proof-of-Work can be thought of as a lucky dip lottery where miners continuously pick random numbers, hoping to find the winning one. Each guess is completely random, just like a lottery machine selecting numbers. The first miner to find a valid number, meaning a nonce that meets the difficulty requirement, wins the round and earns the block reward. The more computing power a miner has, the faster they can compute guesses, increasing their chances of solving the puzzle first. Again, this evokes a lottery where having more tickets improves the odds of winning. However, no miner is guaranteed to win every round, and just like a lottery, there is always an element of chance. This system ensures that Bitcoin remains secure and decentralised, as no single entity can manipulate the network without doing the required computational work.

So, we can see that at the heart of Bitcoin's decentralised network lies the Proof-of-Work consensus mechanism, which requires all participants to agree on the validity of transactions. This prevents fraud and ensures that all nodes share the same, consistent version of the blockchain.

To summarise, PoW is the protocol that secures the Bitcoin network, prevents double spending, and guarantees that no single entity can alter transaction history without redoing the required computational work. By requiring miners to expend energy to solve cryptographic puzzles, PoW ensures that consensus is achieved in a trustless and decentralised way.

By this point we have gone through a lot of technical details and calculations. Hopefully, you are forming a clearer understanding of how mining, Proof-of-Work, and block creation function. Let's take a step back and quickly recap on the process described in Part 5 of the White Paper. When a transaction is created, it first enters the mempool, where it is verified, ensuring that it isn't a double-spend and that it has been properly signed using elliptic curve cryptography, before being double-hashed with SHA-256 to generate a unique Transaction ID (TxID). These TxIDs are then grouped into a block, structured into a Merkle Tree where they are paired, concatenated, and double-hashed to form a Merkle Root.

This is best depicted on pages 4 and 5 of the White Paper under Parts 7 and 8, to give the Merkle Root. This is a unique digital fingerprint of all transactions in the block. The block header, which includes the Merkle Root, the previous block's hash (thus linking it to all earlier blocks), a timestamp, the difficulty target, and the nonce, is then double hashed to produce the block's hash. This block hash secures the block and becomes a key piece of information for building the next block in the chain.

5.   Network

The steps to run the network are as follows:

1) New transactions are broadcast to all nodes.
2) Each node collects new transactions into a block.
3) Each node works on finding a difficult proof-of-work for its block.
4) When a node finds a proof-of-work, it broadcasts the block to all nodes.
5) Nodes accept the block only if all transactions in it are valid and not already spent.
6) Nodes express their acceptance of the block by working on creating the next block in the chain, using the hash of the accepted block as the previous hash.

Nodes always consider the longest chain to be the correct one and will keep working on extending it. If two nodes broadcast different versions of the next block simultaneously, some nodes may receive one or the other first. In that case, they work on the first one they received, but save the other branch in case it becomes longer. The tie will be broken when the next proof-of-work is found and one branch becomes longer; the nodes that were working on the other branch will then switch to the longer one.

3

New transaction broadcasts do not necessarily need to reach all nodes. As long as they reach many nodes, they will get into a block before long. Block broadcasts are also tolerant of dropped messages. If a node does not receive a block, it will request it when it receives the next block and realizes it missed one.

PART 5: NETWORK

Part 5 of the White Paper details the process when two miners are working on the same transactions simultaneously. If two blocks are confirmed at the same time, nodes will save both versions and wait for the longest chain to emerge. A useful way to think about resolving conflicts in the Bitcoin network can be done using the analogy of bees and honey. After all, it's feasible for two or more miners to find a block at the same time.

Imagine that Bitcoin nodes are like bees, and two parallel competing blockchain branches are like trees. Usually, the correct tree (longest chain) has honey all over it, while the incorrect one only has a tiny bit. However, if the amount of honey on both trees appears equal, the bees divide themselves between the two trees, just as nodes split between two blockchain versions when a fork occurs.

The competition continues until one tree starts to attract significantly more honey, at which point most of the bees abandon the other tree and flock to the one with the most honey. In the same way, Bitcoin nodes will eventually recognise the chain with the most accumulated Proof-of-Work as the valid one. The longest valid blockchain always wins, and the rejected branch is discarded. This ensures that Bitcoin's consensus remains intact, with all future blocks built on top of the chain that has the most computational work behind it. The chain with the most work behind it always becomes the dominant, correct chain, and all future blocks are built on top of it.

Part 5 also clarifies that Bitcoin's network is designed to be fault-tolerant. Transactions do not need to reach every node immediately. As long as they are received by enough nodes, they will eventually be included in a block. If a node misses a block due to network latency, it simply requests the missing block when it sees the next one and detects a gap, ensuring that it remains in sync. This built-in resilience ensures that Bitcoin remains decentralised, self-correcting, and resistant to network disruptions.

---

6.   Incentive

By convention, the first transaction in a block is a special transaction that starts a new coin owned by the creator of the block. This adds an incentive for nodes to support the network, and provides a way to initially distribute coins into circulation, since there is no central authority to issue them. The steady addition of a constant of amount of new coins is analogous to gold miners expending resources to add gold to circulation. In our case, it is CPU time and electricity that is expended.

The incentive can also be funded with transaction fees. If the output value of a transaction is less than its input value, the difference is a transaction fee that is added to the incentive value of the block containing the transaction. Once a predetermined number of coins have entered circulation, the incentive can transition entirely to transaction fees and be completely inflation free.

The incentive may help encourage nodes to stay honest. If a greedy attacker is able to assemble more CPU power than all the honest nodes, he would have to choose between using it to defraud people by stealing back his payments, or using it to generate new coins. He ought to find it more profitable to play by the rules, such rules that favour him with more new coins than everyone else combined, than to undermine the system and the validity of his own wealth.

PART 6: INCENTIVES

Now that we have explored the full process of how transactions are verified and blocks are created, it is important to ask what incentivises miners to dedicate their computing power and electricity to upholding the network. Mining requires significant investment in hardware and energy, so we must ask why miners continue to participate. Expanding on what we already know, and as we see in Part 6 of the White Paper, the network is designed to reward miners for their efforts, ensuring that Bitcoin remains secure and decentralised.

The first transaction in every new block is called the coinbase transaction, and it generates a block reward for the miner who successfully mines that block. This reward consists of newly minted Bitcoin, which introduces new coins into circulation, whereby the miner receives the amount as if they were being sent Bitcoin by somebody. However, in this case it reduces the number of bitcoins left to mine. This process is analogous to gold mining, where miners expend resources such as labour, machinery, and fuel to extract gold from the ground and add it to the pool of financial assets. In the case of Bitcoin, it is primarily computational power and electricity that are expended to validate transactions and secure the blockchain. This controlled issuance of new Bitcoin follows a fixed schedule that is encoded in the protocol, creating a predictable rate of monetary expansion. Again, the current block reward, as of April 2024, is 3.125 BTC per block, following the most recent halving event. The next is estimated to occur around April 2028, when the reward will fall to 1.5625 BTC.

In addition to the block reward, miners are incentivised by transaction fees. Every Bitcoin transaction commands a fee, which is paid by the sender and collected by the miner who confirms the block of transactions. These fees operate similarly to bank transaction fees but are entirely market-driven. When the Bitcoin network is congested, users often attach higher fees to their trans-actions, as miners tend to prioritise transactions with higher fees. Unlike the fixed block reward, which gradually decreases over time, transaction fees will continue to exist as an economic incentive even after all 21 million bitcoins have been mined.

This gradual phase-out of block rewards means that in the long term, transaction fees will be the primary incentive for miners to secure the network. However, as this transition is expected to take more than a century, Bitcoin is likely to then be a far more mature and stable asset, similar to gold, acting as a digital store of value and transactional currency with lower volatility than it presently experiences. I believe this to be the case because as the value of the asset increases, the more it would cost to substantially move its price. This would give it a stronger reputation, similar to how the gold price has matured over the years. But, for the security of the Bitcoin network to be maintained, there must be enough miners who continue to find it profitable to expend computational work in exchange for the block rewards, and later, just the transaction fees.

7. Reclaiming Disk Space

Once the latest transaction in a coin is buried under enough blocks, the spent transactions before it can be discarded to save disk space. To facilitate this without breaking the block's hash, transactions are hashed in a Merkle Tree [7][2][5], with only the root included in the block's hash. Old blocks can then be compacted by stubbing off branches of the tree. The interior hashes do not need to be stored.

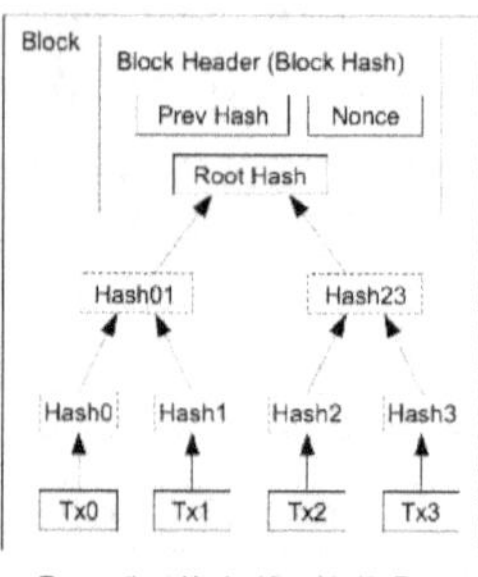

Transactions Hashed in a Merkle Tree

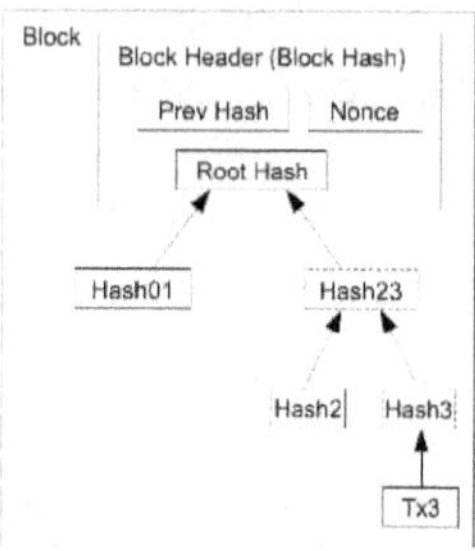

After Pruning Tx0-2 from the Block

A block header with no transactions would be about 80 bytes. If we suppose blocks are generated every 10 minutes, 80 bytes * 6 * 24 * 365 = 4.2MB per year. With computer systems typically selling with 2GB of RAM as of 2008, and Moore's Law predicting current growth of 1.2GB per year, storage should not be a problem even if the block headers must be kept in memory.

4

PART 7: RECLAIMING DISK SPACE

Now that we've covered all the complicated parts, let's finish off the last parts of the White Paper. As Bitcoin continues to grow, so does the amount of data stored in the blockchain.

We know that every full node must maintain a record of all the transactions ever made, which over time results in a significant storage requirement. Therefore, Part 7 of the Bitcoin White Paper addresses this challenge by introducing an optimisation method that allows older transaction data to be discarded in some cases while preserving the integrity of the blockchain.

Once a transaction has been sufficiently confirmed and is buried under multiple new blocks, it becomes practically immutable. At this stage, earlier parts of the blockchain can be pruned, keeping only the critical transaction data that verifies ownership of Bitcoin and prevents double spending. Parts 7 and 8 of the White Paper are closely related, as Bitcoin achieves this through the Merkle Tree structure I mentioned earlier. This enables nodes to discard individual transaction details while retaining the essential Merkle Root in the block header. In this way, even as older transaction data is removed, nodes can still verify the validity of newer transactions by referencing the hashes that remain embedded in the blockchain.

8.   Simplified Payment Verification

It is possible to verify payments without running a full network node. A user only needs to keep a copy of the block headers of the longest proof-of-work chain, which he can get by querying network nodes until he's convinced he has the longest chain, and obtain the Merkle branch linking the transaction to the block it's timestamped in. He can't check the transaction for himself, but by linking it to a place in the chain, he can see that a network node has accepted it, and blocks added after it further confirm the network has accepted it.

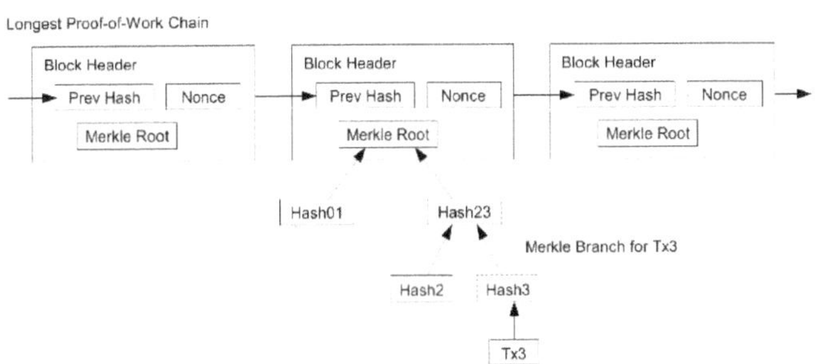

As such, the verification is reliable as long as honest nodes control the network, but is more vulnerable if the network is overpowered by an attacker. While network nodes can verify transactions for themselves, the simplified method can be fooled by an attacker's fabricated transactions for as long as the attacker can continue to overpower the network. One strategy to protect against this would be to accept alerts from network nodes when they detect an invalid block, prompting the user's software to download the full block and alerted transactions to confirm the inconsistency. Businesses that receive frequent payments will probably still want to run their own nodes for more independent security and quicker verification.

PART 8: SIMPLIFIED PAYMENT VERIFICATION (SPV)

This part of the White Paper explains how users can verify transactions without storing the entire blockchain. Instead of downloading and maintaining a full node, SPV nodes rely only on block headers to find the current block's hash. When an SPV node needs to verify a transaction, it requests a Merkle proof from full nodes. This allows the SPV node to confirm that a transaction exists within a specific block without downloading the entire block's transaction history.

Simplified Payment Verification provides a lightweight verification method, making it ideal for mobile wallets and resource-limited devices. However, SPV is less secure than running a full node since it relies on external full nodes to provide transaction proofs. A malicious full node could potentially feed false information to an SPV user, though this risk can be mitigated by querying multiple full nodes for verification.

NODES

Within the Bitcoin network, different nodes play distinct roles in maintaining its crucial decentralisation and security:

- Ⓑ **Full nodes** store the entire blockchain and validate all transactions against Bitcoin's consensus rules, keeping the network trustless, in the cryptocurrency sense of the word.
- Ⓑ **Mining nodes** compete to solve Proof-of-Work puzzles, creating new blocks and securing the blockchain while earning rewards.
- Ⓑ **Archive nodes** maintain a complete historical record of every past block and transaction, serving as long-term storage points for the network.
- Ⓑ **Lightweight nodes** (SPV clients) provide quick transaction verification by relying on Merkle proofs instead of full blockchain storage.

While full nodes are critical for Bitcoin's security and decentralisation, SPV nodes offer a practical solution for users who need to balance efficiency and security. By allowing Bitcoin to be verified without requiring extensive storage capacity, these mechanisms ensure that Bitcoin remains scalable and accessible for everyday use, without compromising its fundamental principles.

Non-mining nodes do not receive direct financial incentives like miners, as they do not compete for block rewards or transaction fees. Instead, their purpose is to independently verify transactions, enforce consensus rules, and enhance network security. Exchanges like Coinbase, payment processors, or Bitcoin wallet providers often run full nodes to verify blockchain data independently without relying on third-party sources.

Even though blockchain.com, for example, now also operates as an exchange, it still functions as a third-party data source from the perspective of other independent entities. Therefore, an exchange operating a full node can verify deposits and withdrawals directly from the Bitcoin network, reducing reliance on external blockchain explorers and preventing inaccurate or fraudulent transactions. This is important when transacting millions of dollars' worth of cryptocurrency daily.

9. Combining and Splitting Value

Although it would be possible to handle coins individually, it would be unwieldy to make a separate transaction for every cent in a transfer. To allow value to be split and combined, transactions contain multiple inputs and outputs. Normally there will be either a single input from a larger previous transaction or multiple inputs combining smaller amounts, and at most two outputs: one for the payment, and one returning the change, if any, back to the sender.

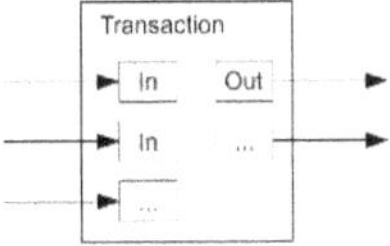

It should be noted that fan-out, where a transaction depends on several transactions, and those transactions depend on many more, is not a problem here. There is never the need to extract a complete standalone copy of a transaction's history.

5

PART 9: COMBINING AND SPLITTING VALUE

Another important difference between Bitcoin and traditional financial systems is the way transactions are viewed. Instead of storing a user's balance as a single number in an account, Bitcoin transactions use a system of inputs and outputs. As introduced earlier, this means that rather than spending a specific bitcoin, a transaction consumes existing unspent transaction outputs (UTXOs) from previous transactions and generates new outputs that become spendable in the future.

Say that a user has three separate UTXOs in their wallet which were received in the following order, worth 0.3 BTC, 0.4 BTC, and 0.5 BTC and they want to send 0.9 BTC. In this case, the transaction will combine the first two UTXOs (0.3 + 0.4 BTC) and a portion of the third UTXO (0.2 BTC from the 0.5 BTC balance) to reach the required amount. The remaining 0.3 BTC from the third UTXO will then be sent back as "change" to the sender's wallet, now becoming the first and only UTXO part of the user's balance (like the £7.50 change from the loaf of bread example earlier).

This system ensures efficient use of resources while allowing transactions to be flexible and scalable. It also means that Bitcoin transactions do not necessarily correspond to a single unit of currency being sent, but rather a collection of smaller pieces that are combined and redistributed. While efficient, the only drawback is that the more inputs and outputs a transaction has, the more bytes it consumes. As fees are based on a fee rate per byte, this causes the transaction fees to rise.

Parts 7, 8, and 9 collectively reinforce Bitcoin's decentralised and scalable design. The use of Merkle Trees helps optimise blockchain storage by allowing older transactions to be pruned while maintaining security. Part 8's Simplified Payment Verification (SPV) enables lightweight wallets to verify transactions without storing the full blockchain. Together, these mechanisms contribute to Bitcoin's efficiency, flexibility, and ability to scale while remaining secure against attacks.

PART 10: PRIVACY AND ANONYMITY IN BITCOIN

As we see in Part 10 of the White Paper, Bitcoin initially aimed to provide a level of anonymity by ensuring that transactions were not directly linked to personal identities. Although Bitcoin transactions are publicly recorded on the blockchain, they only ever reference Bitcoin wallets rather than real names.

10. Privacy

The traditional banking model achieves a level of privacy by limiting access to information to the parties involved and the trusted third party. The necessity to announce all transactions publicly precludes this method, but privacy can still be maintained by breaking the flow of information in another place: by keeping public keys anonymous. The public can see that someone is sending an amount to someone else, but without information linking the transaction to anyone. This is similar to the level of information released by stock exchanges, where the time and size of individual trades, the "tape", is made public, but without telling who the parties were.

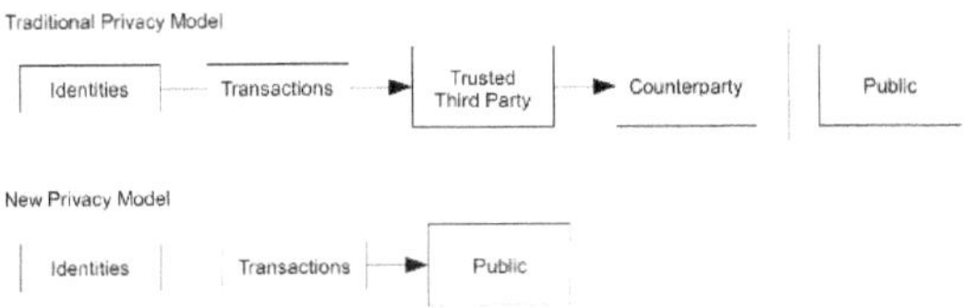

As an additional firewall, a new key pair should be used for each transaction to keep them from being linked to a common owner. Some linking is still unavoidable with multi-input transactions, which necessarily reveal that their inputs were owned by the same owner. The risk is that if the owner of a key is revealed, linking could reveal other transactions that belonged to the same owner.

Despite this, governments and exchanges have reduced Bitcoin's anonymity through Know Your Customer (KYC) and Anti-Money Laundering (AML) regulations, which we return to in Chapter 9. Regulated exchanges require users to verify their identity before buying or withdrawing any digital asset.

Once Bitcoin is withdrawn to an external wallet, authorities can track its movement and link transactions back to individuals if the coins eventually return to a KYC exchange. Although Bitcoin users can generate new addresses for each transaction to enhance their own privacy, certain transaction patterns, such as multi-input transactions, can reveal links between addresses. This means that even though transactions are not tied to real-world identities by default, patterns of usage can sometimes inadvertently expose connections. So, although Bitcoin offers greater privacy than traditional financial systems, it is no longer fully anonymous as Satoshi Nakamoto originally intended, and to combat the cases of fraud or criminal activity, this isn't a bad thing.

11. Calculations

We consider the scenario of an attacker trying to generate an alternate chain faster than the honest chain. Even if this is accomplished, it does not throw the system open to arbitrary changes, such as creating value out of thin air or taking money that never belonged to the attacker. Nodes are not going to accept an invalid transaction as payment, and honest nodes will never accept a block containing them. An attacker can only try to change one of his own transactions to take back money he recently spent.

The race between the honest chain and an attacker chain can be characterized as a Binomial Random Walk. The success event is the honest chain being extended by one block, increasing its lead by +1, and the failure event is the attacker's chain being extended by one block, reducing the gap by -1.

The probability of an attacker catching up from a given deficit is analogous to a Gambler's Ruin problem. Suppose a gambler with unlimited credit starts at a deficit and plays potentially an infinite number of trials to try to reach breakeven. We can calculate the probability he ever reaches breakeven, or that an attacker ever catches up with the honest chain, as follows [8]:

p = probability an honest node finds the next block
q = probability the attacker finds the next block
q_z = probability the attacker will ever catch up from z blocks behind

$$q_z = \begin{cases} 1 & \text{if } p \le q \\ (q/p)^z & \text{if } p > q \end{cases}$$

6

Given our assumption that $p > q$, the probability drops exponentially as the number of blocks the attacker has to catch up with increases. With the odds against him, if he doesn't make a lucky lunge forward early on, his chances become vanishingly small as he falls further behind.

We now consider how long the recipient of a new transaction needs to wait before being sufficiently certain the sender can't change the transaction. We assume the sender is an attacker who wants to make the recipient believe he paid him for a while, then switch it to pay back to himself after some time has passed. The receiver will be alerted when that happens, but the sender hopes it will be too late.

The receiver generates a new key pair and gives the public key to the sender shortly before signing. This prevents the sender from preparing a chain of blocks ahead of time by working on it continuously until he is lucky enough to get far enough ahead, then executing the transaction at that moment. Once the transaction is sent, the dishonest sender starts working in secret on a parallel chain containing an alternate version of his transaction.

The recipient waits until the transaction has been added to a block and z blocks have been linked after it. He doesn't know the exact amount of progress the attacker has made, but assuming the honest blocks took the average expected time per block, the attacker's potential progress will be a Poisson distribution with expected value:

$$\lambda = z \frac{q}{p}$$

To get the probability the attacker could still catch up now, we multiply the Poisson density for each amount of progress he could have made by the probability he could catch up from that point:

$$\sum_{k=0}^{\infty} \frac{\lambda^k e^{-\lambda}}{k!} \cdot \begin{cases} (q/p)^{(z-k)} & \text{if } k \le z \\ 1 & \text{if } k > z \end{cases}$$

Rearranging to avoid summing the infinite tail of the distribution...

$$1 - \sum_{k=0}^{z} \frac{\lambda^k e^{-\lambda}}{k!} \left(1 - (q/p)^{(z-k)}\right)$$

Converting to C code...

```c
#include <math.h>
double AttackerSuccessProbability(double q, int z)
{
    double p = 1.0 - q;
    double lambda = z * (q / p);
    double sum = 1.0;
    int i, k;
    for (k = 0; k <= z; k++)
    {
        double poisson = exp(-lambda);
        for (i = 1; i <= k; i++)
            poisson *= lambda / i;
        sum -= poisson * (1 - pow(q / p, z - k));
    }
    return sum;
}
```

Running some results, we can see the probability drop off exponentially with z.

```
q=0.1
z=0      P=1.0000000
z=1      P=0.2045873
z=2      P=0.0509779
z=3      P=0.0131722
z=4      P=0.0034552
z=5      P=0.0009137
z=6      P=0.0002428
z=7      P=0.0000647
z=8      P=0.0000173
z=9      P=0.0000046
z=10     P=0.0000012

q=0.3
z=0      P=1.0000000
z=5      P=0.1773523
z=10     P=0.0416605
z=15     P=0.0101008
z=20     P=0.0024804
z=25     P=0.0006132
z=30     P=0.0001522
z=35     P=0.0000379
z=40     P=0.0000095
z=45     P=0.0000024
z=50     P=0.0000006
```

Solving for P less than 0.1%...

```
P < 0.001
q=0.10     z=5
q=0.15     z=8
q=0.20     z=11
q=0.25     z=15
q=0.30     z=24
q=0.35     z=41
q=0.40     z=89
q=0.45     z=340
```

12. Conclusion

We have proposed a system for electronic transactions without relying on trust. We started with the usual framework of coins made from digital signatures, which provides strong control of ownership, but is incomplete without a way to prevent double-spending. To solve this, we proposed a peer-to-peer network using proof-of-work to record a public history of transactions that quickly becomes computationally impractical for an attacker to change if honest nodes control a majority of CPU power. The network is robust in its unstructured simplicity. Nodes work all at once with little coordination. They do not need to be identified, since messages are not routed to any particular place and only need to be delivered on a best effort basis. Nodes can leave and rejoin the network at will, accepting the proof-of-work chain as proof of what happened while they were gone. They vote with their CPU power, expressing their acceptance of valid blocks by working on extending them and rejecting invalid blocks by refusing to work on them. Any needed rules and incentives can be enforced with this consensus mechanism.

PART 11: CALCULATIONS

In this section of the paper, Nakamoto provides a statistical explanation of why an attacker attempting to rewrite Bitcoin's transaction history is highly unlikely to succeed. Probability theory is used to demonstrate that the longer a block has been confirmed, the more computationally infeasible it becomes to alter it.

The idea is that if an attack starts behind the honest chain, the attacker must outpace the network's combined mining power to catch up and overtake it. This scenario follows a Binomial Random Walk, a mathematical model in which progress occurs step-by-step, with an expected probability of moving forward or backward. In Bitcoin's case, the honest chain advances steadily since most miners follow the rules, while an attacker has a much lower chance of catching up. Let's look at the other evidence that supports this.

The process aligns with the Poisson distribution, which models rare events over time, suggesting that the likelihood of an attacker successfully surpassing the honest chain decreases exponentially as more blocks are added. Similarly, in the gambler's ruin problem, a player with a smaller bankroll is statistically destined to go bankrupt against a much larger opponent, in the way that a Bitcoin attacker with insufficient hashing power is almost certain to fail in the long run. The probability of an attacker successfully reversing a transaction decreases exponentially with each new block that is added after the target block. In simple terms, the deeper a transaction is embedded in the blockchain, the more difficult it becomes to change.

While a 51% attack, where an entity gains control of more than half of the Bitcoin network's total computing power, is theoretically possible, the cost of acquiring and running the necessary hardware makes it economically impractical. The Bitcoin network consists of thousands of miners spread across the world, all competing to uphold the security of the chain.

Attempting to overpower them would require an enormous investment of energy, with no guarantee of success. Don't worry too much about the mathematics in part 11, as it is there just to prove how statistically difficult it would be to attack the Bitcoin network.

And yes, the mathematics and cryptography underpinning the Bitcoin network may seem daunting. But rather than getting lost in these equations, remember that Bitcoin's security is rooted in its decentralised network and proof-of-work mechanism, and that these features make fraudulent modifications virtually impossible. This contrasts with the many potential vulnerabilities of traditional financial institutions, where internal fraud and human errors can corrupt records.

SOME FINAL THOUGHTS ON PROOF-OF-WORK AND BITCOIN'S SECURITY

I hope all that made sense. There was quite a lot of information to take in, so I would recommend reading it again to let it sink in. We've now explored Bitcoin's full mining process, from transaction validation to block creation, using the Proof-of-Work consensus mechanism. While the technical aspects may seem complicated, the fundamental idea is simple: Bitcoin secures transactions through cryptographic proof and economic incentives, eliminating the need for trust in a central authority. Miners are rewarded for securing the network and every transaction is timestamped before being permanently embedded in the blockchain. This structure makes Bitcoin resistant to fraud and censorship, with its security increasing over time as more blocks are added. And manipulation is near impossible, because any attempt to rewrite history would require redoing all previous work up to the present block, which is a computationally infeasible task.

As we can see, the Bitcoin White Paper is a remarkable document that lays the foundation for a decentralised, trustless financial system. Its creator, or group of creators, demonstrated an extraordinary understanding of cryptography, game theory, and economic incentives. Yet, despite its excellence, Bitcoin remains misunderstood. There are many incumbents that feel threatened because Bitcoin challenges their control over money, as well as the criminal association that Bitcoin is perceived to have. I see many people invest in it purely in the hope of price appreciation, while others dismiss it as a volatile speculative asset, failing to recognise the underlying technological intricacies, or the need for change in our financial system.

Before Bitcoin, numerous attempts at digital currencies failed due to centralisation and security vulnerabilities. Wei Dai's B-money (1998) proposed anonymous transactions but lacked a clear solution to the problem of double-spending. Adam Back's Hashcash (1997) introduced Proof-of-Work but was designed to deter email spam, rather than being a currency. These concepts were important, but it wasn't until Bitcoin in 2008 that Nakamoto managed to bring them all together so perfectly.

Through Bitcoin's Proof-of-Work mechanism, we've seen how a decentralised system can maintain its security, integrity, and scarcity without the need for central oversight. This unique system ensures that every new Bitcoin mined requires computational effort, reinforcing the idea that Bitcoin is a form of "digital gold" which is valuable because of the resources and effort needed to produce it. As Bitcoin continues to expand, its fixed supply and the rules set forth in the White Paper remain foundational, ensuring that it cannot be debased in the way that other currencies have been throughout history. However, Bitcoin is more than just a currency. It is an entirely new way to think about money itself. So, if Bitcoin is a new kind of money, how do we even begin to measure its value?

Chapter 7

What is Bitcoin's Value?

Gold has weight, stocks produce earnings, and traditional currencies are backed by the strength of a government, at least in theory. Bitcoin has none of these. Yet it continues to gain popularity as a store of value, a means of trade, and a system for transferring wealth across borders without middlemen. Instead of simply looking at price charts, to evaluate its worth we need to build on the understanding that we now have of the network itself. In the same way that past civilisations built their economies around trust in tangible goods, Bitcoin is based on trust in decentralisation, security, and in the collective strength of its network.

BITCOIN IS A TECHNOLOGY – WHAT IS ITS VALUE?

As stated at the outset, Bitcoin and blockchain are ultimately technologies built on the internet. Yet unlike commodity money, fiat, or government-backed currency, it is a public ledger, an open financial system where anyone with an internet connection and an understanding of the system can verify transactions. But Bitcoin extends beyond just software, as it is an economic and social system that aims to give people freedom.

We've seen that Bitcoin has created a different monetary system to those depicted in Chapters 4 and 5. It is different to commodity money, such as precious metals or cowrie shells. And it is a different idea to commodity-backed money like U.S. dollars before 1971 or the fiat money of today.

So, how do we value something like Bitcoin in the absence of any physical form or government backing? Is its value simply based on speculation, driven by the hope of getting rich? Or are there deeper economic principles that can truly define its worth?

METCALFE'S LAW: THE NETWORK EFFECT AND BITCOIN'S VALUE

First, Bitcoin has value because thousands of the smartest and most intelligent developers from around the world are collaborating on its open-source technology. They are consistently improving the software and ensuring that Bitcoin can function as efficiently as possible. But that is not all. To grasp the full potential value of Bitcoin, we must also consider Metcalfe's Law, a concept in network theory that states that the value of a network grows exponentially with the number of its users or participants. This law is particularly relevant to Bitcoin, whose value is closely tied to the size and activity of its network.

Think of a mobile phone network and imagine you are the only person with a mobile phone. The value of your mobile phone and the network it is on is virtually nothing, as you would not be able to call anyone. However, if one other person gets a mobile phone, you can now call them and they can call you, making the value of the network increase. As more people join the network, the number of potential phone calls increases exponentially, making the network inherently more valuable with each addition.

Metcalfe's Law was formulated by Robert Metcalfe, the co-inventor of Ethernet, in the early 1980s. The law states that the value of a network is directly proportional to the square of the number of connected users or devices. In other words, as more participants join a network, its value increases exponentially, not linearly. Therefore, in the context of Metcalfe's Law:

If one person has a mobile phone the value of the network is $1^2 = 1$. When a second person gets a mobile phone, the value of the network becomes $2^2 = 4$, and when a third person gets a mobile phone, the total number of connections further increases, and the value becomes proportional to $3^2 = 9$. So, when the number goes from 2 to 3, the value of the network increases from 4 to 9, meaning the network's value more than doubles as it adds just one more user. When it gets to ten people, $10^2 = 100$, or 100 people, $100^2 = 10,000$, the network's value increases exponentially.

Network effects occur when a product or service becomes more valuable as more people use it. The principle is evident in networks that range from social media platforms and telecommunications networks to cryptocurrencies and online marketplaces.

Figure 7.1: Mobile Phone Adoption (users 1990-2025)

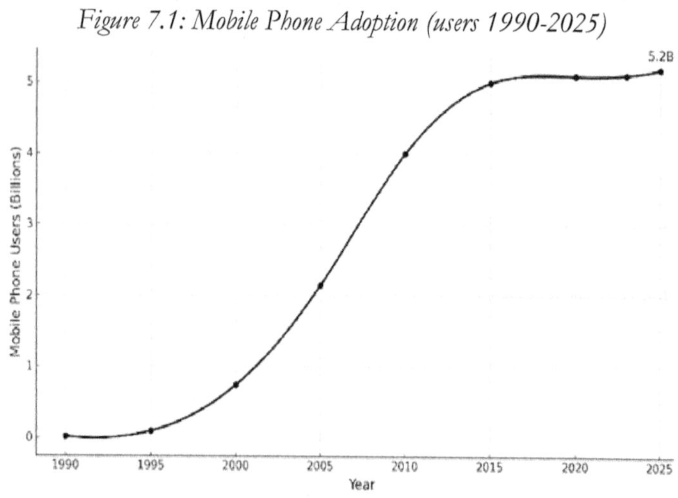

Source: DataReportal.com and prioridata.com

Figure 7.1 depicts this network effect as the mobile phone user base has increased over time. As of 2024, there were over 5 billion unique mobile phone subscribers globally, which accounts for around 70% of the world's population. Figure 7.1 shows the growth with an S-curve pattern, reflecting a gradual rise in the years prior to 2000, and then an emphasis on the period between 2000 and 2010 where the rate of growth accelerated before starting to level off, as seen with many technology adoption trends. The rapid expansion of the user base is consistent with the network effects described by Metcalfe's Law. Other technologies also demonstrate the network effect using Metcalfe's Law:

1. INTERNET

As more users join the internet and as more websites are added to the network, its value increases. With each new user, each website can attract more potential visitors, and each new website adds to the pool of information and services available to them, increasing the utility of the entire web. The growth in the user base is shown in Figure 7.2.

Figure 7.2: Internet Adoption (users 1990-2025)

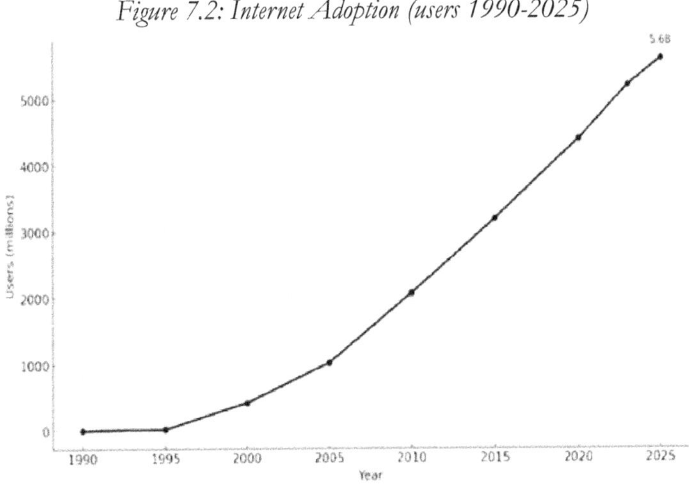

Source: https://www.visualcapitalist.com/visualized-the-growth-of-global-internet-users-1990-2025/

2. EMAIL

The usefulness of email has risen as more people have adopted it. When few people used email, its value was limited. As more individuals, businesses and organisations adopted email for communication, its utility exploded. It could be argued that email use has declined since the boom of WhatsApp and social media. However, it is important to understand the context of these trends. For anything business related or official, email is still the go-to method, effectively diminishing the use of physical letters, as PDF documents can be attached to emails instead. As we'll see later, the blockchain is also finding new solutions for the transmission of official documents. Additionally, in terms of social media for anything entrepreneurial, such as influencers, or aspiring businesses, their primary goal is often to generate email lists, so they can send out promotions to boost sales. An email address is also needed to sign up for virtually every service, whether it be a new cryptocurrency exchange, a gym membership, or even a social media account, so it forms the backbone of everything we do today. In contrast, WhatsApp, has taken over the instant chat space, where it has almost replaced text messages in everyday use. A particularly useful feature of WhatsApp is that you can send documents and pictures, as well as make phone calls, even internationally, where only an internet connection is needed, so it has become a lot more cost effective than it used to be. Therefore, we must always keep in mind that new technological competition is continually arising, posing fresh threats to existing platforms and communication channels.

3. SOCIAL MEDIA

Platforms like Facebook, Instagram, X (Twitter) and LinkedIn thrive on network effects. As more users join, the platforms become more valuable due to the increase in connections, content, and interactions. However, in contrast, platforms like MySpace and Faceparty experienced declines in their user bases, leading to a corresponding decrease in their value. As users left these platforms, the networks became less vibrant and engaging, ultimately diminishing their appeal and relevance.

4. CREDIT CARD NETWORKS

Payment systems like Visa and Mastercard benefit from the network effect because the more merchants that accept the cards, the more valuable it becomes for consumers to hold them. Similarly, the more consumers who have the card, the more merchants are incentivised to accept them. This growth in value also brings about the benefits of scale. As the networks expand, administrative and processing costs can decrease, making the system more efficient, which further increases their dominance. These examples highlight how Metcalfe's Law can apply across various sectors in our everyday life, where the value of a network grows exponentially and is proportional to the square of the number of connected users, enhancing the utility for all users as the network grows.

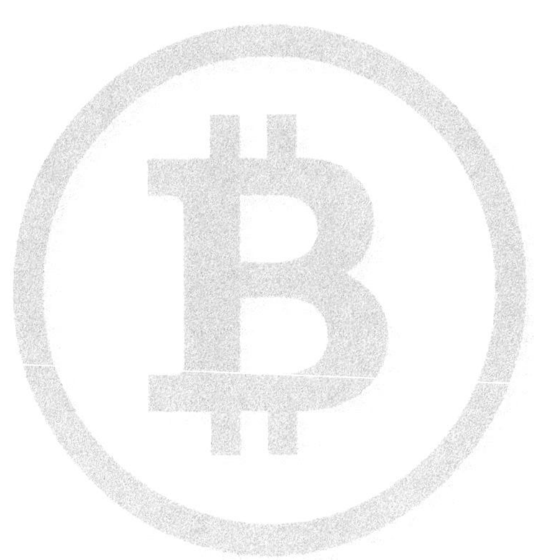

5. Bitcoin

This concept can also be implemented to value the Bitcoin network. When applied to Bitcoin, Metcalfe's Law suggests that wider uptake increases its network value significantly. This is because the utility of Bitcoin grows with the number of users, making it more valuable as a medium of exchange, store of value, and investment. The following graph shows the network effect of the number of Bitcoin users growing over time.

Figure 7.3: Bitcoin Adoption (estimated users (2010-2024)

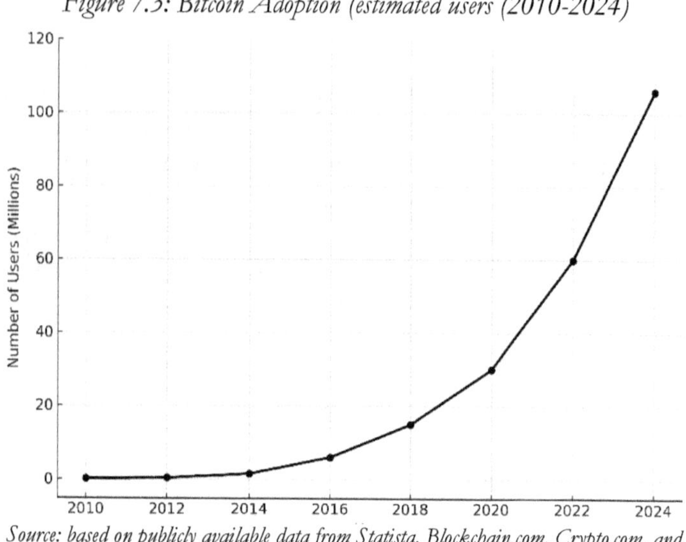

Source: based on publicly available data from Statista, Blockchain.com, Crypto.com, and Keyring Pro.

As of 2024, there were estimated to be around 106 million Bitcoin users globally, representing approximately 1.3% of the world's population, or to put it another way, almost a third of the U.S. population, at around 31.6%. Triple-A estimates the wider crypto market now exceeds 560 million users, showing just how fast digital asset adoption is growing.

Bitcoin's adoption has accelerated, even outpacing the growth rates of other transformative technologies, such as the internet and mobile phones at their same phase of adoption. Compared with mobile phone adoption in 2000, shown in the S-curve above, sources suggest we are currently in the accelerated growth phase for Bitcoin adoption. According to BlackRock-cited data, crypto adoption has grown 43% faster than mobile phones and 20% faster than the internet at comparable stages.

In 2000 there were around 600 million mobile phone users globally. While Bitcoin hasn't yet reached that scale, its adoption rate is growing at a much faster pace. If Bitcoin adoption followed a similar S-curve trajectory to that experienced in the mobile phone industry, then the expected number of Bitcoin users could be over 4 billion globally by 2030. This rapid adoption would be driven by Bitcoin's digital nature, its decentralised infrastructure, and its ability to function as a store of value and medium of exchange. These comparisons highlight that we are still at a very early stage in Bitcoin's adoption cycle and that the value of the network has potential to expand massively in the coming years.

Metcalfe's Law provides a compelling framework for understanding Bitcoin's value and potential. It offers crucial insight into why Bitcoin's value is intrinsically linked to its adoption rate. Like any other network, its value and utility grow with the number of users. And this adoption is driven by the characteristics that we saw in Chapter 3, along with the power of its highly secure consensus mechanism and mining process that we explored in the last chapter. As these qualities continue to boost ownership and participation, Bitcoin's network will likely continue to grow, thereby further increasing its value, driven by the increasing number of participants and the network effects their presence creates.

Additionally, as more nodes join the network and assist with the mining process, the collective tera-hashes per second increase, which combines to improve the security and resilience of the network overall, further expanding user participation on the network.

While Bitcoin's growth over the last few years has been undeniable, there are, however, important caveats that need to be considered when assigning value in this space. First, price doesn't always follow a set pathway as the adoption rate increases. Furthermore, the price doesn't consistently increase as the inflation rate falls after Bitcoins halvings, reducing the amount of newly created bitcoins going into circulation, a factor which we will see in more detail in Chapter 10.

Speculative price swings are often not tied to its scarcity or its genuine network growth. As you can see in Figure 7.4, there were sharp price declines from around $42,000 in January 2021, down to around $28,000 a month later. In November 2021 the price peaked close to $69,000, only to crash to around $15,000 nearly a year later. And this isn't even taking account of the sharp volatility in the early days as discussed in Chapter 3. None of this reflects the adoption rate changing during these periods.

Figure 7.4: Bitcoin Price Volatility (monthly close prices 2020-2025)

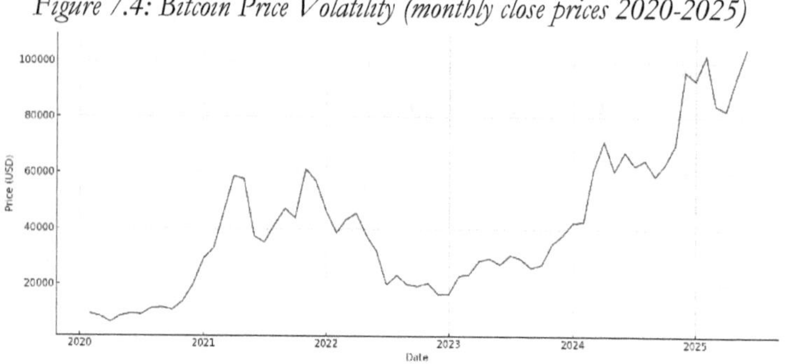

Source: Bitcoin Price History and Historical Data | CoinMarketCap

This is a clear indication that short-term price movements are often influenced by speculation, as well as market cycles, or macroeconomic shocks, which can temporarily inflate or deflate Bitcoin's valuation, regardless of actual adoption. Additionally, network trends don't always guarantee success as we saw with MySpace or Blackberry, as these can be disrupted or overtaken by other technologies. No technology, currency or invention is immune to disruptors coming in and replacing them.

Another important driver is liquidity. As we saw with the multiple rounds of QE and treasury bond issuance in Chapters 2 and 5; liquidity drives asset prices even higher.

Figure 7.5: Liquidity vs Bitcoin

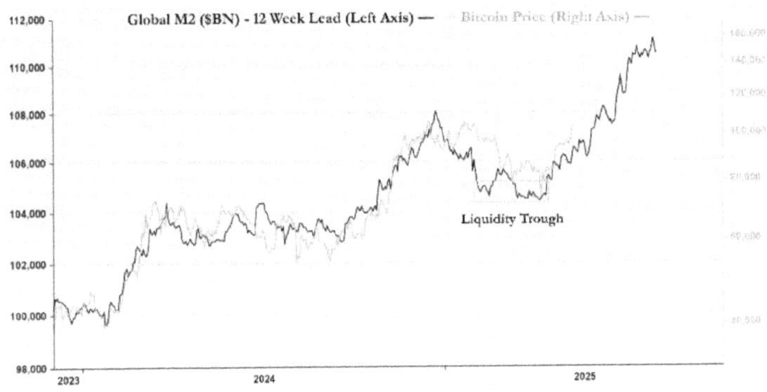

Source: LSEG Datastream – Global Macro Investor

As we can see in Figure 7.5, the Bitcoin price almost perfectly follows the levels of liquidity being pumped into the system. This is a big driver of Bitcoin's price, as well as other hard assets such as gold or property. As more money enters the system, there is more money available to purchase financial assets, and it drives up the price. The data shows a 12-week lead, meaning that the liquidity had entered the system 12 weeks prior to when it appears on the above chart. So, the liquidity trough, followed by a sharp rise in liquidity into the system commenced around August 2024, triggering the crypto prices to skyrocket 3 months later in November 2024, and this looks set to continue in 2025, as more liquidity is needed to contain governmental debt levels, but more on this later.

Additionally, we can see Bitcoin's historic prices in Figure 7.6, where it is undeniable that when looking at the longer-term picture, the technology's adoption and these increasing liquidity cycles are consistently increasing its value over time. Like any monetary system or technology, its strength lies not just in software or statistics, but in the shared belief that it offers something better. And it is this belief that will be tested over time.

Figure 7.6: Bitcoin Price History

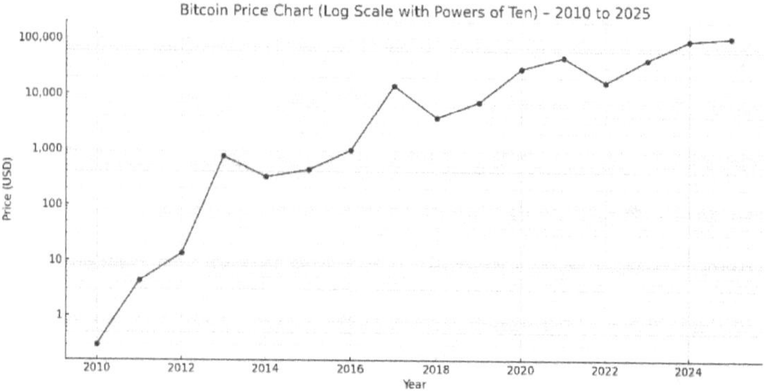

Source: Bitcoin Price History and Historical Data | CoinMarketCap

As more institutions and governments begin moving into the space, the centralisation of holders and power, such as Strategy's increasing ownership could raise questions whether this is good for the network, as we will see in subsequent chapters. Will it centralise control away from the very organic ownership structure that has dominated the space since inception? It also raises questions about whether these network effects are really being driven by long-term conviction or short-term opportunism. Either way, adoption is belief, and as long as this persists, so does the strength of any system. Bitcoin's decentralisation offers a level of resilience, but its value still depends on continued belief in the system.

OWNING A PIECE OF THE INFRASTRUCTURE

While Bitcoin faces the above challenges, including speculative market volatility, as well as regulatory scrutiny, its underlying network effects still suggest that its overall value will continue trending upwards over time as adoption increases. Other transformative technologies have certainly provided vast value to the people that use them. But remember, unlike the Facebooks and Apples of this world, which greatly benefit financially through the use of people's data and sales, Bitcoin's value is solely attributed to the users on the network, and to the holders of Bitcoin. As no central institution benefits financially and only the nodes and miners are rewarded for playing their part, this alleviates the need for profits to go to a large corporation.

In some ways, owning Bitcoin is not too dissimilar to being a shareholder in a company. The value is attributed to the people who own and use the network, and this can be done for less than a dollar, anytime, anywhere in the world. This is what makes the network a highly valuable type of digital property.

This is the first time in history where you can not only own a part of the infrastructure layer, but you can do so at such an early stage. You couldn't own part of the internet. Without being a seed investor, you couldn't have owned part of Apple or Amazon prior to their IPOs, and you would have missed the extraordinary wealth that came from being there right at the beginning. You couldn't own Open AI or any other company initiating the AI language model technology at its inception. This is the first time you can truly front run the governments and institutions and own a part of this infrastructure — before the larger players flood in.

This is not only financially beneficial for those who had belief in the technology early on, and yes, we are still at a really early stage, but it also gives a sense of empowerment.

To own part of the monetary framework is to reclaim control in a system that has long excluded the individual. All of these principles emphasise the importance of network growth in shaping the future of Bitcoin and blockchain technology.

Bitcoin's value is not derived from traditional measures of intrinsic value, such as being backed by physical assets. Instead, its value comes from the network effect, which is generated by its strong characteristics such as security and scarcity, as well as trust in its decentralised infrastructure. Understanding the mechanics of Mining, PoW, and the principles of Metcalfe's Law all help to provide valuable insights into how Bitcoin functions and why it holds value now, and why that value is likely to increase in the future.

However, it is important to appreciate that Bitcoin is just one part of a larger digital financial ecosystem. While its Proof-of-Work system has demonstrated a revolutionary approach to monetary security, the crypto space has evolved rapidly, with alternative cryptocurrencies, or "altcoins", emerging to address Bitcoin's limitations and explore entirely new applications of blockchain technology. In the next chapter we'll examine how these properties compare with other consensus mechanisms and alternative cryptocurrencies and offer a broader perspective on the evolving digital financial space.

Chapter 8

Alternative Cryptocurrencies

The cryptocurrency ecosystem has experienced a compelling transition over the last 15 plus years, as Merkle roots sprawled in countless directions, branching out far more than anyone could ever have imagined. Bitcoin may have set the tone for decentralised currency, but the emergence of alternative cryptocurrencies has introduced a layer of infrastructure that could disrupt even the most established companies and industries worldwide. This has given rise to what is now commonly referred to as Web 3.0 — the next generation of the internet, focused on decentralisation and blockchain technology. Its aim is to give users more control over their data while enabling peer-to-peer interactions and services, without relying on central entities or tech companies.

Unlike today's platforms where central companies store and monetise your data while dictating how you interact, Web 3.0 is being built on decentralised networks that prioritise user ownership, privacy, and individual autonomy. The idea is that you store your personal data on your wallet and it's only in use when connecting to a decentralised website or application. Web 3.0 covers multiple use cases beyond finance, such as decentralised social media or digital identity management, offering a broader vision for how we engage online. Bitcoin laid the foundation, but it is the infrastructure being built around it that is now pushing forward this new decentralised version of the internet. This multitude of use cases, and the undeniable enhancements in efficiency and functionality are nothing short of remarkable. With the very essence of decentralisation and Web 3.0 technology at their heart, altcoins are shattering the confines of the blockchain industry, unleashing waves of ground-breaking innovation that could transform lives across the world, many times over.

So, we've established that Bitcoin has no visible leader and is devoid of any corporate chains, so where did these later altcoins come from? Does anyone claim ownership? And who is left in charge to determine their success? Most importantly, if the new altcoins are alternatives, how do they relate to Bitcoin?

The simple answer is that as the Bitcoin network is fully decentralised without any single owner, altcoins have based their models around this. That said, visible leaders and teams are in charge of their development, although they have tried to copy the core principles of the technology that was explained in the last two chapters. Initially, most tried to rival Bitcoin by making a better version and replacing it as the leading cryptocurrency. But before long, they realised that this wasn't going to work. Bitcoin is unique, which means it has gained a loyal following over the years. Also, its network adoption is hard to ignore. Bitcoin dictates the market, as well as price action and sentiment.

To this day, it is sentiment around Bitcoin that drives the cryptocurrency space, and if its value fluctuates that has a knock-on effect across the whole altcoin market. So, what was needed was to take Bitcoin's technology model and go one step further.

To create something other than just a peer-to-peer medium of exchange or a store of value. Something with totally different benefits and use cases.

In the early days, cryptocurrency exchanges only facilitated the conversion between fiat currency and Bitcoin. But when new altcoins started to emerge, new exchanges then made the conversion between them and Bitcoin possible. In essence, Bitcoin was the gateway. That made owning Bitcoin like holding the key to the rest of the market. Nowadays it is standard practice for cryptocurrency exchanges to enable direct conversion between all altcoins and stable currencies like U.S. Dollars, yet we should still remember that the tradition of Bitcoin being the market leader still holds true.

In this chapter, we'll discover the different categories of altcoins and review their potential for integration into the systems we all use every day. From Layer 1 blockchains to Real World Assets and privacy coins, these innovations are expanding blockchain's capabilities, improving its scalability and real-world utility. We'll see how developers are using the technology to create decentralised applications, unlocking entirely new possibilities. These are not just alternatives to Bitcoin; they represent the potential for an entirely decentralised economy. But with so many projects emerging, each claiming to be unique, how do we determine which ones truly add value and which are based on speculation? Let's now look at a selection of the alternative cryptocurrencies. Some of this may seem hard to understand, but bear with me, because an appreciation of this technology will really help to place Bitcoin in context and see how innovation is taking it forward.

ETHEREUM: THE SECOND-BIGGEST CRYPTOCURRENCY

"Smart contracts have the potential to revolutionize the way we do business by automating processes."

— Vitalik Buterin, Co-Founder of Ethereum

Ethereum, launched in July 2015, has become one of the most popular alternative cryptocurrencies and the second largest by market capitalisation. The Ethereum blockchain, with its native token Ether (ETH), is a decentralised platform that enables developers to build and deploy smart contracts and decentralised applications (dApps). By smart contracts, we mean that developers can create code to automate transactions and agreements. Ethereum's main value proposition is its capacity to serve as a programmable blockchain, unlike Bitcoin, which is primarily a peer-to-peer digital currency. Ethereum had previously used the same PoW consensus mechanism as Bitcoin (see Chapter 6). However, in September 2022, it transitioned to Ethereum 2.0 and adopted the Proof-of-Stake (PoS) consensus mechanism. Let's now look at how that differs from PoW.

PoS is a much simpler concept so there's no need for the same level of detail as with PoW. Instead of relying on miners to solve the complex computational puzzles by finding a nonce and hashing the block to confirm transactions, PoS secures the blockchain on the basis of holding a number of the native tokens. Hence, there is no need for mining hardware, high electricity usage, or to complete hashing puzzles, so it mirrors familiar finance systems, for example in the way that you might put down a security deposit. While Bitcoin uses the SHA-256 hashing algorithm, alternative cryptocurrencies often use different algorithms — but they serve a similar purpose. In PoS, the more you stake as collateral, the more responsibility (and trust) you're given. Then, if you try to cheat the system, you'll lose your deposit. This allows validators to create new blocks and confirm transactions based on the amount of cryptocurrency that they own and are willing to stake.

PROOF-OF-STAKE IN PRACTICE

At this point it's important to clarify that just like Bitcoin's PoW system, Ethereum's PoS mechanism still relies on the same public and private key elliptic curve cryptography to sign transactions and broadcast them to the network. These signed transactions must still be approved by nodes using the elliptic curve cryptography to enter the mempool as valid transactions, where they await inclusion in the next block. What changes in PoS is how those blocks are proposed and how their validation is confirmed. So, let's take a quick look at the steps involved in proof of stake on the Ethereum blockchain:

- Ⓑ Validators: In PoS, miners are replaced by validators, who are selected to propose or vote on any new block consisting of valid transactions in the mempool.

- Ⓑ Staking Ether (ETH): To participate in transaction validation, validators must stake or lock up 32 ETH. (At the time of writing, this is equivalent to just over $59,282, according to cryptoslate.com.) This serves as a form of security, ensuring that validators operate honestly or risk losing their stake.

- Ⓑ Validator selection: The protocol uses a random selection algorithm, with every active validator having an equal chance of being picked. To increase the chances of being selected, a validator can run more than one version of the software, by staking an additional 32 ETH each time. Every 12 seconds, a new slot occurs in which a validator is chosen at random to propose a block. They are the proposer. At the same time, 128 other validators are randomly selected to vote on or attest to that block's validity. These are the attestors.

Ⓑ Confirmation: When roughly two-thirds of the 128 validators agree on a proposed block, it is considered valid and added to the blockchain, much in the way that a jury decides the outcome of a trial. This makes it nearly impossible to change without compromising the majority of the network.

Ⓑ Rewards and Penalties: Validators are rewarded with newly minted ETH and transaction fees for their role in securing the network and validating transactions. Note that proposers are rewarded more generously than the attestors to reflect their greater level of responsibility. However, validators can also be fined through a process known as "slashing" if they deliberately try to compromise the network or fail to execute their duties. This might include actions like proposing contradictory blocks or attempting double-spending. If such behaviour is detected, the Ethereum network can permanently destroy (burn) part or all of the validator's stake, depending on the severity of the offence. In disgrace, that validator will be banned from participating in future validations.

Ⓑ Ethereum's PoS system enhances security by grouping blocks into fixed intervals. These intervals are known as epochs, and each epoch consists of 32 slots, lasting roughly 6.4 minutes. At the end of each epoch, a checkpoint is created, serving as a key reference point. Once a block is finalised, it cannot be altered unless two-thirds of validators agree that it should be, making large-scale attacks extremely difficult.

A good way to think of the PoS process is like buying a raffle ticket, but instead of money, you put down your own cryptocurrency as collateral. The more you stake, the more validators you can run, meaning the more tickets you can hold. This gives you a higher chance of having a winning ticket, allowing you to validate transactions and earn rewards. Any attempt to cheat means forfeiting some or all of your stake. This is the fundamental concept that makes this type of consensus mechanism secure, as it incentivises everyone to participate fairly and so strengthens the network.

THE ETHEREUM BLOCKCHAIN

Now we have an idea of how the proof-of-stake consensus mechanism works, let's look at how transactions are recorded. Like Bitcoin, Ethereum uses a distributed transparent ledger to keep track of transactions. However, Ethereum's ledger is more than just a record of token transfers. Along with transactional data, blocks on the Ethereum network also contain code that relates to smart contracts. Each block contains a header that includes metadata, such as the previous block's hash, a list of transactions, and the state of the Ethereum Virtual Machine (EVM) after executing those transactions.

In case you are wondering what the EVM does, it is the decentralised computational engine that executes smart contracts on the Ethereum network. It's the system that reads and carries out the instructions in smart contracts, which are written in programming languages like Solidity. The EVM is fully capable of running any type of computation, provided it has enough of the resources it requires, including time and memory.

When discussing Ethereum, you might hear reference to the global state. This refers to the status of all the accounts and smart contracts at any given moment. It is the EVM's job to process transactions and update the state accordingly. One important component of the EVM is called Gas, which is a unit of computation. Every operation in a smart contract or transaction consumes gas, so a fee must be paid for this in ETH, and it is these fees that incentivise validators to process and include transactions in blocks.

Hopefully, we have now formed a basic understanding of the EVM and how Ethereum functions, so let me explain smart contracts and their role in creating decentralised applications.

SMART CONTRACTS

Smart contracts are self-executing agreements where the terms and conditions are written directly into the code. These contracts automatically execute and verify actions when predefined conditions are met, eliminating the need for intermediaries like lawyers or banks, unlike traditional payment mechanisms. Once deployed, they are immutable and run exactly as programmed. This ensures that transactions or agreements are transparent and efficient, which means they can be used for a wide variety of purposes.

However, it is worth bearing in mind that these smart contracts only function as well as they have been programmed. Programmers and developers are not infallible, and bugs can lurk within the code. Unlike traditional contracts, which you can read or have reviewed by a legal professional, smart contracts aren't as straightforward. Reliable applications, such as those that are regularly audited are generally safe, and the reputation of such platforms gives the community and users confidence that the contracts are performing as intended. That said, as we'll see in the next two chapters, reliability is not always apparent in digital assets and smart contracts, especially for newer or fraudulent platforms.

Like Bitcoin, the core Ethereum protocol — its consensus mechanism, elliptic curve cryptography, and transaction validation — has never been hacked. However, in 2016, a high-profile hack occurred within a smart contract built on top of Ethereum called DAO, where vulnerabilities caused a large amount of Ether to be stolen. In 2022 a bridge protocol called Ronin was breached due to flaws in the smart contract, so these instances can happen. There have also been cases where malicious actors have written smart contracts designed to take control of users' wallets and drain funds. Therefore, it is important to assess the credibility of any smart contract before interacting with it, if you want to stay safe in the space.

Nonetheless, Ethereum's smart contracts are very powerful because they can interact with other contracts and digital assets and execute tasks without human intervention. For example, in a decentralised finance (DeFi) application, smart contracts can facilitate lending and borrowing without the need for a bank. When specific predefined conditions, such as collateral requirements or interest rate terms are met, the contract executes automatically. So, a smart contract might be written to execute A if it rains four days in a row, but to execute B if it is sunny for five days in a row. Its predetermined conditions therefore function like a programmable agreement to select the appropriate outcome.

Smart contracts were designed to be reusable, meaning the same contract logic can apply to multiple users, as long as the conditions are met. This helps to streamline the contract process and reduce inefficiencies.

Aside from the enhanced efficiency they bring, smart contracts are also more trustworthy. I like to think of it as an automated vending machine for agreements. If you insert the correct input, say, enough collateral for a DeFi loan, or proof of insurance for a claim, the contract delivers the output instantly, with no room for disputes or human interference. It's this level of automation and transparency that makes Ethereum's ecosystem so powerful and one of the most widely used platforms for decentralised applications.

LAYER 1 BLOCKCHAINS

Ethereum is classed as a Layer 1 blockchain because it serves as the base, or foundational layer of a blockchain network. It provides the core infrastructure for the entire ecosystem of dApps and the projects built on top of it. These projects are often referred to as tokens (usually ERC-20 tokens) and they run on top of Ethereum, with their functionalities secured by the underlying blockchain. This is why Layer 1 blockchains are considered self-contained ecosystems, where all core functions, such as consensus mechanisms (like PoW or PoS), network security, and transaction validation, occur directly on the blockchain itself.

Layer 1 blockchains support native tokens (such as BTC or ETH) and often include smart contract functionality, allowing developers to build decentralised applications directly on their networks.

However, an important consideration is that Layer 1 blockchains often face scaling challenges as transaction demand increases. Ethereum can currently handle around 15 Transactions per Second (TPS). However, if congestion is high, users must compete by paying higher gas fees to have their transactions prioritised, which, in turn, effectively slows down the network from a user standpoint. In extreme cases, fees have exceeded the cost of the actual transaction. To remedy this, one option would be to modify the Layer 1 blockchain by using a different consensus mechanism or to increase the block size to give more capacity. Or sharding could be adopted, which divides the network into smaller, more manageable pieces.

However, all of these make significant changes to the underlying infrastructure of how a blockchain operates and could have a negative impact on security or decentralisation. In an effort to solve Ethereum's scalability limitations, Vitalik Buterin has proposed a roadmap to increase the network's capacity to 100,000 TPS by the end of 2025. The goal is to enhance the efficiency of the Layer 2 scaling solutions that Ethereum already uses. So, what exactly are Layer 2 blockchains?

LAYER 2 SCALING SOLUTIONS

Layer 2 solutions are protocols built on top of existing Layer 1 blockchains to increase scalability and lower transaction costs by improving processing capacity. They basically process transactions off the main chain (off-chain), but settle the final result on-chain, while leveraging the security and decentralisation of the Layer 1 blockchain. This helps to reduce congestion, making it faster and cheaper to use while maintaining security.

This can be done using methods such as roll-ups, which process transactions off-chain initially and then submit the result to the Layer 1 blockchain, so it only needs to store the essential data. Think of it like a Merkle root, which represents an entire list of transactions, as we saw in Chapter 6. There are two main types of roll-ups: Optimistic Roll-ups and ZK (Zero-Knowledge) Roll-ups, each taking a different approach to transaction validation.

The Arbitrum and Optimism blockchains both employ optimistic roll-ups, focusing on fraud proofs for validation. Conversely, zkSync and StarkNet conduct validation through zero-knowledge proofs. In case you are wondering, zero-knowledge proofs mean that you can prove something is true without having to reveal any of the specific details relating to it, such as a patient proving they qualify for a clinical trial but without setting out their full medical records.

Another type of Layer 2 scaling solution is the use of a sidechain, a separate blockchain that connects to the main Layer 1 blockchain via a two-way bridge. The bridge is usually built with smart contracts and allows assets to move freely between the two chains. Unlike roll-ups, sidechains generally use their own consensus mechanisms and validators, with the goal of quicker transaction processing and reduced costs. These reduce congestion on the main chain, allowing assets and data to move between the two, keeping the sidechain linked with the main network.

Finally, Celer Network provides an interesting example of a Layer 2 solution that instead, uses a state channel model. Here, transactions occur off-chain and are only recorded on the Layer 1 blockchain when the channel is closed. This considerably reduces congestion and fees, while preserving the underlying security and decentralisation of the main chain. This contrasts with roll-ups, which regularly post batches of transactions to the Layer 1, whereas state channels minimise on-chain interaction until absolutely necessary.

POLYGON

Among Ethereum's most prominent scaling projects, Polygon (formerly Matic Network) began with a widely adopted PoS chain that is fully compatible with Ethereum's EVM and smart contracts. Lower fees. Faster transaction speeds. Processing up to 7,000 TPS — allowing developers to build and deploy dApps within the Ethereum ecosystem. Polygon submits checkpoints back to Ethereum's mainnet, which helps to preserve security and finality while maintaining speed and scalability. This makes it especially popular for use cases like gaming, NFTs, and microtransactions, where low fees and fast confirmations are essential. Over time, Polygon has evolved to support the multiple scaling techniques we discussed above, making it unique in its combined approach. It can also enable secure cross-chain communication between Ethereum and other Layer 2s, helping to create a more cohesive Ethereum ecosystem.

DEFI PLATFORMS

Earlier, we introduced the idea of Decentralised Finance (DeFi) applications, which do away with the need for intermediaries. Many major DeFi platforms built on Ethereum, such as Aave, SushiSwap, and Curve, have integrated Polygon to offer faster and cheaper transactions. Stablecoins like USDT and USDC, which are pegged to a fiat currency, can also operate on Polygon for fast and low-cost transfers. For example, users might turn to Aave to lend or borrow crypto, or use a decentralised exchange (DEX) like Uniswap to swap tokens without using an intermediary. These platforms benefit from combining Ethereum's smart contract capabilities with Polygon's Layer 2 scaling solutions.

Speaking of lending and swapping, how do these digital applications get their liquidity to facilitate these loans or token swaps if there is no central party? These assets must come from somewhere.

This brings us neatly to the topic of liquidity pools. The Ethereum ecosystem contains smart contract-based reserves known as liquidity pools, where holders of certain tokens can deposit them to enable others to trade directly through the pool. For example, if you held ETH and SUI, you could deposit them into a liquidity pool and allow other users to swap between ETH and SUI. Each trade generates transaction fees, which are paid out proportionally to all liquidity providers. As people exchange these tokens back and forth, you earn a share of those fees, which can be a lucrative way to earn yield on your tokens.

That said, liquidity pools involve certain risks, such as impermanent loss, which occurs when the prices of two tokens fluctuate sharply against each other while they are locked up in the pool. This can affect the value of your deposited tokens when you come to withdraw, although the loss may be recovered if the tokens return to their original values. In a similar way, tokens can also be supplied to lending protocols, where users provide liquidity to fund crypto loans. In return, the holder receives yield, which is a bit like earning interest in a bank account.

Polygon is a great example of how providing lower fees and faster transaction times can enhance the Ethereum ecosystem, helping it scale and move closer towards mainstream adoption. Although I must add, that's still a long way off. Either way, there's little point in having smart contracts if there is no way to feed them relevant data to execute correctly. So, we need to look at how this works.

ORACLE NETWORKS: CHAINLINK

This brings us to another important piece of the puzzle — Chainlink (Link). Link is by far the most established decentralised oracle network, which means it ingeniously feeds real-world data into smart contracts in a way that's both secure and resistant to tampering. Several DeFi protocols, including Aave and Uniswap depend on Chainlink to obtain accurate market data and price feeds, which inform key functions such as lending rates, token prices, and automated trading strategies.

Think of this like an excel spreadsheet set up to compute live stock market analysis and financial ratios. This only can work properly when connected to a live data feed. The same way live football betting platforms need constant real-time updates to adjust odds and confirm outcomes. This is what Chainlink does, and in my opinion, is one of the most important cryptocurrencies. Yet, as it isn't as glamorous as a speculative green frog or a flashy new AI gaming token, its true investment potential often gets overlooked. For this space to thrive, it's infrastructure tokens like Chainlink — not hype-driven "shitcoins" with little real-world application — that will do well in the long run.

Chainlink, along with other decentralised oracles like Band or API3, helps bridge the gap between off-chain data sources and on-chain smart contracts. These protocols play an indispensable role in enabling DeFi to function smoothly, especially within Ethereum and its Layer 2 ecosystem. And stepping back to scalability, it's not just Ethereum that uses these solutions to enhance its network. Now that we've seen how this applies across other altcoin ecosystems, let's turn our attention to a scaling solution for Bitcoin.

THE BITCOIN LIGHTNING NETWORK

A well-known initial limitation of Bitcoin was that it could only process about 7 TPS, which is low compared with other payment solutions. Network fees can also spike during periods of high congestion, constricting Bitcoin's ability to function as a medium of exchange. To address this, the Bitcoin Lightning Network was designed to help bring scale and cost-effectiveness to Bitcoin.

The Lightning Network does this by allowing off-chain payment channels to open, facilitating transactions with remarkable speed and minimal fees, all without burdening the Bitcoin blockchain with each and every transaction. Similar in design to the state channels of the Celer Network, only the opening and closing balances of these channels are recorded on-chain. Think of it like a secure network of private tabs between users, capable of theoretically processing millions of transactions per second while the channel remains open. Once the transactions are complete, the final state of the channel is settled back on the Bitcoin blockchain. This significantly reduces the volume of on-chain activity while enhancing both scalability and efficiency. This all makes the Lightning Network primarily suitable for microtransactions and daily purchases, like buying a coffee, rather than being used to store value.

In addition to the Lightning Network, other protocols have been developed to extend Bitcoin's functionality beyond simple transfers. For example, Stacks and RSK (Rootstock) are smart contract platforms built on top of Bitcoin. These networks aim to bring programmability to the Bitcoin ecosystem, enabling features similar to Ethereum, but with Bitcoin as the settlement layer.

Alternatively, Ordinals, another protocol initially developed in 2023 allows individual satoshis to be inscribed with data directly on the blockchain. This makes it possible to create digital collectibles, or Non-Fungible Tokens (NFTs), something which you might have heard of in the news back in 2021, but more on this later. This is notable because Bitcoin is typically considered fungible, meaning each Satoshi is interchangeable with any other. Ordinals challenge that idea by assigning unique identity and meaning to individual units of Bitcoin. While all these protocols are still in their early stages, these innovations reflect the growing effort by the community to expand Bitcoin's utility without altering its core protocol.

OTHER LAYER 1 BLOCKCHAINS

Innovation has not been limited to these scaling solutions and protocols that aim to enhance Bitcoin's and Ethereum's core functionality. Indeed, the Layer 1 blockchain space itself is highly competitive, and several entities are currently trying to displace the others as the go-to infrastructure layer within crypto. Being completely honest, the reason this space is so competitive is because both Bitcoin and Ethereum do contain some fundamental flaws. Some of the following emerging blockchains, in contrast, have been built from the ground up, by taking these scalability issues into account from the start, so they do not require Layer 2 solutions. I will go into more details about these trade-offs in Chapter 10, but for now, it's worth appreciating the strengths of these established protocols while remaining open to the evolution that has followed.

Launched in March 2020 by Solana Labs, Solana has emerged as a formidable, high-performance, multi-purpose Layer 1 blockchain, positioning itself as Ethereum's leading rival. Like Ethereum — and all of the chains that use a form of PoS — energy consumption is minimal compared with PoW networks. Solana was designed to facilitate rapid, scalable, and secure dApps, which it does using a distinctive consensus mechanism known as Proof of History (PoH). PoH uses enhanced elements of PoS to provide a verifiable sequence of events that improves transaction validation speed. I particularly like Solana, as it uses parallel processing to handle multiple transactions simultaneously through a system called Sealevel. This greatly improves on Ethereum's current capacity, with Solana usually averaging 1,000–3,000 TPS, but is capable of processing up to 65,000, making it one of the fastest blockchains in the space, and with its new validator client Firedancer, it has demonstrated the potential to accelerate processing to over 1 million TPS.

Solana's low transaction fees and high speed make it attractive for DeFi applications, NFT projects, and other use cases that demand fast and cost-effective processing, with notable DEXs on the Solana network including Raydium and Jupiter.

Avalanche, created in 2020 by Ava Labs, is another Layer 1 blockchain that emphasises high speed and scalability, making it a powerful platform for DeFi protocols. Avalanche employs a consensus mechanism known as the Avalanche Consensus, which allows the network to achieve fast confirmations. This distinguishes itself from the conventional PoS or PoW systems by employing random sampling and repeated subset sample voting among validators, enabling swift agreements across the network while maintaining a robust security framework.

Avalanche boasts the ability to handle up to 4,500 TPS, showcasing its scalability for various applications, with a focus on gaming. Unlike Solana, Avalanche is notable for its flexible architecture, offering subnets that allow developers to create custom blockchains with specific rules while still benefiting from Avalanche's security and speed. Solana's unique architecture, on the other hand is considerably less flexible, making upgrades or customisation more complex, especially as the ecosystem grows.

We'll see shortly how Avalanche benefits from an interoperability perspective, where developers can use these subnets to launch specialised blockchains while still relying on Avalanche's fast and secure infrastructure for support.

The BNB Chain is a Layer 1 blockchain, originally launched as Binance Smart Chain (BSC) in September 2020 by Binance, one of the world's largest centralised cryptocurrency exchanges. It is designed to provide a high-performance environment for DeFi projects. The BNB Chain operates using a Proof of Staked Authority (PoSA) consensus mechanism, containing aspects of Proof-of-Stake while allowing validators to take turns producing blocks based on their staked BNB, the native token for the Binance smart chain. The BNB chain is capable of processing up to 200 TPS. While this isn't reaching the high numbers of some of the other Layer 1s above, it benefits from compatibility with the EVM for smooth transition from Ethereum-based dApps. Holders also benefit from reduced trading fees on the Binance exchange. PancakeSwap is a prominent DEX on the chain, along with various gaming and lending platforms, embracing its technology as an efficient and cost-effective alternative to Ethereum.

Like Solana, Sui is a multi-purpose, high-performance Layer 1 blockchain that aspires to deliver transactions that are not only fast and scalable, but also remarkably economical, but with less of a focus on DeFi, and with a particular specialisation on dApps, NFTs, and gaming. Developed by Mysten Labs and launched in 2023, Sui employs a rather distinctive consensus mechanism known as Narwhal and Tusk, which separates data availability and consensus processes to achieve high transaction processing speeds. This design enables Sui to process transactions simultaneously in parallel, resulting in explosive speeds compared with traditional blockchain frameworks, with the network potentially capable of reaching up to 300,000 TPS. Sui's architecture showcases scalability and flexibility, with low latency in mind, making it suitable for gaming and other interactive dApps that require swift response times. With its performance focus and developer-friendly tools, Sui is positioning itself as a key platform for the next generation of dApps and Web 3.0.

While Sui has recently focused on gaming and NFTs, its underlying architecture also supports other scalable, high-performance use cases, similar in design ambition to Sei. However, Sei, in comparison, has been much more narrowly focused on DeFi from the outset. Created in 2022 by Sei Labs, the Sei Network has a strong focus on speed, efficiency, and scalability. By leveraging parallel processing and utilising what is known as a Twin-Turbo consensus mechanism to optimise transaction finality and scalability, Sei is capable of processing up to 12,500 TPS. Despite this being lower than Sui or Solana, Sei prioritises fast finality, fairness, and DeFi-specific performance rather than raw TPS. It facilitates high-frequency trading and other complex DeFi use cases, such as a native order matching engine, front-running prevention, and other DeFi-focused capabilities. These features distinguish Sei from other blockchains for enhancing the performance of DEXs. Built using the Cosmos SDK, it also has interoperability benefits that we will come to shortly, giving it a unique advantage as it aims to become the "Layer 1 for DeFi".

Cardano is a Layer 1 blockchain developed in 2017 by Charles Hoskinson, one of the original co-founders of Ethereum. It employs an innovative PoS consensus process known as Ouroboros, which seeks to create a secure and scalable environment for dApps and smart contracts, with seamless interaction between different systems. This blockchain has a multi-layered design, with a settlement layer to process transactions, leaving the computational layer to enable smart contracts and dApps.

Cardano's PoS mechanism allows users to participate in the network by staking ADA, its native token, to validate transactions and produce new blocks. The network can currently handle around 300 TPS, with ongoing efforts to further improve its scalability through initiatives like Hydra, a Layer 2 scaling solution, which aims to increase its capacity up to what would be an impressive 1 million TPS. Although Cardano supports a growing ecosystem of DeFi protocols, in its eight-year history, it has had a reputation in the industry for a lack of developer adoption, and far fewer applications built on its network compared to Ethereum. However, with developer numbers starting to increase and its improved scalability measures, it could yet become a prominent blockchain.

Finally, Litecoin is one of the oldest Layer 1 blockchains, and was developed as a peer-to-peer digital currency that is often regarded as a lighter alternative to Bitcoin. It was created by Charlie Lee, as a hard fork of the Bitcoin network, and launched in October 2011, with the intention of providing faster transactions and lower fees than Bitcoin. Litecoin also uses a PoW consensus mechanism, but it employs a Scrypt hashing algorithm instead of Bitcoin's SHA-256. Litecoin has a block generation time of about 2.5 minutes, four times faster than Bitcoin's 10-minute blocks. This enables quicker confirmations, making it capable of handling approximately 56 TPS, but the speed still falls short of many of the other Layer 1s above. While it does not support smart contracts, Litecoin remains an efficient and low-cost method of transferring value.

CONNECTING LAYER 1 AND LAYER 2 BLOCKCHAINS

So, in terms of interoperability, Layer 0 protocols, are the unsung heroes, working diligently behind the scenes to seamlessly connect Layer 1 blockchains together, and by extension, enable communication between the Layer 2 blockchains built on top. This becomes ever more crucial as the crypto landscape expands, as many new projects are operating on their own networks and need a way to exchange data and interact efficiently. Imagine Layer 0 like the hidden infrastructure of the internet. You don't really see it working, but it's always there, supporting and connecting everything else.

Now, compare this to the current banking system. Banks operate separately, but they're connected by shared payment networks. When you withdraw money from an ATM, make a transfer, or pay with a credit card, these systems work together because they're built on an underlying infrastructure. You don't see the details, but they're essential for making everything run smoothly. In the crypto world, there are two prominent Layer 0 protocols that provide solutions in slightly different ways.

The first of these is Cosmos, which creates what it calls an internet of blockchains, using its Inter-Blockchain Communication (IBC) protocol to allow data and assets to be shared directly, without relying on centralised exchanges. This means that each blockchain built on Cosmos's infrastructure is still an independent chain with its own validators and consensus mechanism, but built within the framework of Cosmos to enable interoperability. Sei, as we mentioned above does this, which gives it an advantage in this respect. Other notable blockchains include Osmosis, which is a DEX, Injective, which provides decentralised derivatives trading, and Akash Network, which focuses on decentralised cloud computing, as well as others that benefit from Cosmos' framework.

Polkadot, on the other hand, uses its relay chain to provide shared security for its parachains, which means developers don't need to build separate security for each new chain. The parachains within Polkadot's framework share Polkadot's validators and have a shared consensus mechanism. Think of this like Apple's App store, where apps are built and created with iphones in mind, using that infrastructure, whereas Cosmos' model could be considered more like Android, with its own individual frameworks. The benefit of Polkadot's model is that it makes it easier for projects to launch, with programmers and developers being confident that the framework they will operate in has been tested and is secure.

As well as the two mentioned above, other new Layer 0 projects are emerging, including LayerZero, Celestia (which helps other blockchains scale more efficiently) and zkLink, among others. It's also worth noting that some Layer 1s, like Avalanche, also offer some Layer 0-like infrastructure within their subnet architecture.

The issue is that many of the Layer 1 blockchains were never built with interoperability in mind. In my opinion, this could be seen as a development flaw. While they do possess many qualities in terms of scalability, speed or decentralisation, their primary focus has been on building their own ecosystems around their chain, rather than considering the seamless integration with other ecosystems from the start. In a similar way that some Layer 1s need enhancements from Layer 2 solutions, options exist for many of the non-native interoperability chains described so far that are designed to combat this problem.

OTHER INTEROPERABILITY OPTIONS

Let's look first at wrapped assets. As Bitcoin is not a yield-producing asset, some holders have sought ways to earn passive income on it. This led to the creation of wrapped versions of Bitcoin such as wBTC (on Ethereum) and sBTC (on Solana), among others. This process involves custodians or bridging protocols holding your BTC in a designated Bitcoin wallet and issuing you with a tokenised version, like wBTC, an ERC-20 token, which can be used within Ethereum's DeFi ecosystem. This allows users to participate in liquidity pools or lending platforms and other dApps to earn yield. The wBTC token is typically backed 1:1 with Bitcoin, meaning that you can redeem it at any time to reclaim your BTC. If you don't return the wBTC, the BTC will stay in the custodian's Bitcoin wallet. However, because there is a custodian or bridging protocol involved, the process is not fully decentralised, and it carries risks relating to trust and potential exploits.

Another interoperability solution is known as a cross-chain bridge, with Wormhole being a prominent example. It facilitates asset transfers and communication between blockchains like Solana, Ethereum, and Avalanche, among others. Other notable cross-chain interoperability protocols include Axelar, LayerZero, and THORChain, which aim to connect various standalone Layer 1s with Layer 0 ecosystems, including Cosmos or Polkadot. However, one of the major risks associated with cross-chain bridges is their vulnerability to security breaches. Wormhole, for instance, suffered a major attack in February 2022, when a vulnerability in its Solana smart contract led to the theft of approximately $325 million in wrapped Ether (wETH). Although the funds were later replenished by Jump Crypto, the breach shows that this method is far from secure.

Modular roll-up infrastructure is also emerging as a key interoperability option. Ethereum aims to become a global settlement layer, supported by roll-ups like zkSync and StarNet, which could eventually connect to other chains. Bitcoin, however, is a lot more difficult to integrate into that type of framework due to its simplicity and lack of smart contract functionality. However, projects like Interlay and tBTC are looking at ways to resolve these issues.

Ultimately, all these solutions aim to solve one of the biggest challenges in blockchain: enabling the secure and seamless movement of value and smart contract functionality across different networks. For cryptocurrencies and web 3.0 technology to move to the next level, cross-chain interoperability is vital, and it is one of the biggest obstacles to progress. Building a decentralised, secure infrastructure that can rival today's interconnected traditional systems will be a key step towards creating a truly open, multi-chain ecosystem.

CROSS-BORDER PAYMENTS

Building on the idea of cross-chain interoperability, blockchain technology is also making significant strides in cross-border payments. As the world becomes more interconnected, demand for faster and more efficient low-cost international payments has never been higher. Moving money across borders can be slow and costly through traditional banking systems, creating a gap that is ripe for improvement. XRP, the native cryptocurrency from Ripple Labs, is designed with this primary goal in mind. Unlike Bitcoin or Ethereum, which have priorities elsewhere, XRP aims to streamline global financial transfers by providing liquidity for cross-border transactions.

XRP transactions are handled through the RippleNet network, which connects banks, payment providers, and digital asset exchanges. One of RippleNet's key advantages is its unique consensus mechanism, which is distinct from both PoW and PoS. Instead of relying on mining or staking, XRP uses the Ripple Protocol Consensus Algorithm (RPCA). In this system, for transactions to succeed, independent validating servers must agree on transaction order and outcomes, with consensus achieved when 80% of validators concur.

Ripple has partnered with over 300 financial institutions globally and is slowly becoming a popular choice as a bridge currency for cross-border payments based on its speed, low gas fees, and energy efficiency. These partnerships have boosted XRP's reputation in the financial sector, with notable institutions using Ripple's technology including:

- Ⓑ Santander
- Ⓑ American Express
- Ⓑ SBI Remi (Japan Remittance)
- Ⓑ PNC Bank

These partnerships demonstrate Ripple's commitment to integrating blockchain technology into traditional finance, offering faster and cheaper alternatives to the current SWIFT system. While international bank transfers can take days to settle, XRP transactions are typically completed in seconds and at a fraction of the cost, making it an attractive option for financial institutions and remittance services. Although XRP is not widely used by major financial institutions for cross-border payments at this stage, many are adopting RippleNet, Ripple's underlying infrastructure to connect and settle transactions more efficiently, even without using XRP.

Nonetheless, Ripple's On-Demand Liquidity (ODL) service uses XRP as a bridge currency, and this is gaining traction among smaller financial institutions and remittance providers. For example, if a company in the U.S. wants to send money to Mexico, ODL can convert U.S. dollars into XRP, send it through Ripple's network, and then change it into Mexican pesos. This process takes mere seconds and removes the need for pre-funded accounts in foreign currencies, cutting costs and saving time for international transfers.

While XRP focuses on large banks and financial institutions, Stellar (XLM) is geared more towards individuals and smaller financial entities, with a consensus mechanism, like XRP's, that allows for fast and low-cost transactions. Created by one of

Ripple's co-founders, Jed McCaleb, Stellar shares many similarities with XRP but places more emphasis on peer-to-peer cross-border transfers and financial inclusion for underserved populations. And it has formed important partnerships, including a notable collaboration with IBM, to enhance cross-border payment solutions.

REAL WORLD ASSETS

Traditional finance's interest in crypto does not stop at cross-border payments. Real World Assets (RWA) are transforming the way traditional finance interacts with blockchain, bringing real-world value to decentralised finance. These projects tokenise physical assets such as real estate, bonds, and commodities, making them more accessible, liquid, and tradable on decentralised networks.

To understand how this works, imagine an expensive artwork being digitised and turned into blockchain tokens, as if shares in a company were being offered. Instead of requiring one person to buy an entire painting, each token represents a fraction of the asset, allowing multiple people to invest in small portions. Ownership history, transactions, and legal documents are permanently recorded on the blockchain, making verification effortless and eliminating the need for intermediaries like banks or brokers.

The same principle applies to real estate. Instead of waiting months to sell a property, tokenised real estate could be traded on decentralised finance marketplaces almost instantly. This not only makes property ownership more liquid, it opens up investment opportunities to smaller investors who lack the capital to buy entire properties outright.

At the forefront of this innovation is Centrifuge (CFG), bringing assets like invoices, real estate, and business loans onto the blockchain. Built on Polkadot, Centrifuge allows these assets to be used as collateral for borrowing, ushering real-world value into decentralised finance markets. Its cross-chain capabilities ensure seamless integration with different blockchain ecosystems, enhancing scalability and security.

SkyDAO, best known for its DAI stablecoin, is also integrating RWAs into decentralised finance by allowing users to mint DAI using tokenised assets as collateral. This bridges traditional finance with blockchain liquidity, offering a stable and decentralised alternative to conventional banking. Pushing this concept even further, Goldfinch (GFI) provides under-collateralised loans to businesses in emerging markets. Unlike conventional decentralised finance lending, which requires crypto collateral, Goldfinch assesses real-world creditworthiness, making capital more accessible to those who need it most. This means that crypto finance could be accessed by holding real-world assets as proof, which means you would be able to benefit and use the assets in the real world to use these DeFi functionalities in the digital space.

These are not the only innovators revolutionising how institutional financial products interact with blockchain. By tokenising bonds and fixed-income assets, Ondo Finance provides liquidity and exposure to traditional markets, while maintaining the benefits of decentralisation. Investors can now diversify portfolios with tokenised bonds and gain access to structured finance in an entirely novel way.

It is of no surprise that institutional interest in RWA tokenisation is growing. Banks and asset managers are exploring tokenised securities and private equity markets, seeing blockchain as a way to modernise outdated financial infrastructure. Putting these assets on the blockchain can not only reduce staffing expenditure, but also function very cheaply, improving their profit margins, so financial institutions clearly see some benefit in incorporating this technology into their operations. However, regulatory frameworks are as-yet undeveloped, and widespread usage of these tokenised financial products will take time to mature.

RWA projects mark one of the most significant shifts in global finance. By transforming once-static assets into dynamic, tradeable digital units, blockchain is not just disrupting finance. It is redefining ownership, liquidity, and making access to wealth more inclusive.

As traditional finance and blockchain continue to merge, the tokenisation of real-world assets could unlock trillions in value, making financial markets more transparent and efficient.

STABLECOINS

Before moving on to other categories of alternative cryptocurrencies, it's important to consider stablecoins, mentioned briefly above, and the role they play in the crypto space. While stablecoins aren't strictly classified as RWAs, they are often included within their related frameworks. This is because they are backed by instruments like U.S. Treasury bills and cash equivalents, tying them closely to RWAs, even if they are primarily a currency.

Stablecoins maintain price stability by being pegged to a reserve asset, often a traditional currency such as the U.S. dollar. Unlike the significant price fluctuations other cryptocurrencies can experience, stablecoins aim to maintain a consistent value.

This makes them ideal for transactions and remittances, as well as being a hedge against market volatility. By bridging traditional finance and digital assets, they offer the stability of fiat with the utility of blockchain technology.

Among the most prominent stablecoins are Tether (USDT), USD Coin (USDC), and DAI. It is important for their integrity that these stablecoins have backing by assets, as other companies could otherwise issue them in unlimited supply. If they went bankrupt without backing, it would have disastrous consequences for the crypto market. The first of these is USDT, issued by Tether Limited, and its value is backed by a mix of cash, short-term deposits, and other assets. It operates on several blockchains, including Ethereum, Tron, and Solana.

Secondly, USD Coin (USDC), issued by regulated financial institutions Circle in collaboration with centralised exchange, Coinbase, is fully backed by cash and short-term government bonds, with regular audits to verify its reserves. It is this that helps to provide transparency and trust to USDC. Finally, DAI is a decentralised stablecoin issued by the MakerDAO protocol, which was renamed Sky in September 2024. It is backed by collateralised assets like Ether (ETH) and maintains its peg using a system of smart contracts and over-collateralisation, rather than relying on traditional custodians. This gives DAI a more decentralised structure than stablecoins like USDT and USDC, which depend on centralised entities to manage reserves.

Overall, stablecoins play a huge role in the cryptocurrency market, providing liquidity and removing volatility from transactions, while utilising the benefits of blockchain technology. We will revisit the regulatory impact of stablecoins in Chapter 13.

MEMECOINS

"Dogecoin was made as a joke to make fun of cryptocurrencies, but fate loves irony. Arguably the most entertaining outcome and the most ironic outcome would be that Dogecoin becomes the currency of Earth in the future."

— Elon Musk, Twitter, April 2021

Having tackled the main altcoin infrastructure, now let's see how some cryptocurrencies have captured the spotlight with a more playful approach. Memecoins have carved out their own quirky niche, proving that internet culture really can drive serious market momentum. What began as a light-hearted joke with Dogecoin back in 2013 has become a full-blown phenomenon, with coins like Shiba Inu (SHIB), PEPE, and Dogwifhat gaining their own devoted fan clubs and cult-like followings. Dogecoin (DOGE), inspired by its loveable Shiba-Inu mascot, became the pioneer of memecoins, and after more than 10 years, remains top dog. Originally created as a parody of Bitcoin, it was never intended to be taken seriously, yet the internet had other ideas. With an ever-growing supply and a high-profile fan in Elon Musk, Dogecoin has become more than a meme. Receiving many favourable words and supportive tweets, this digital currency is primed for tipping and even making payments.

If one dog wasn't enough, SHIB decided in 2023 to up the ante by launching a whole Layer 2 ecosystem known as Shibarium, proving that it's not just riding the meme wave. In contrast to DOGE, SHIB operates on Ethereum as an ERC-20 token, reaping the rewards of the network's scalability enhancements. A generous supply paired with a bargain entry price has lured retail investors on the hunt for the next thrilling price explosion.

Next up is PEPE, drawing inspiration from the iconic Pepe the Frog meme and elevating the viral-hype game to new heights. In 2023 it made quite the entrance, demonstrating that meme-fuelled speculation still packs a punch, as its market cap soared past $7 billion before cooling off. The same year, Dogwifhat (WIF) introduced lightning-speed, low-cost transactions on Solana, demonstrating that even the most fun coins can thrive on a robust blockchain infrastructure. And I haven't even mentioned the wide array of cat-themed projects available. Oh, ok then: Mog. PopCat. And Mew (cat in a dogs world). While memecoins generally lack fundamental use cases, they've become a cultural force in crypto. Their value may be unpredictable, but their popularity reflects a broader confidence in blockchain engagement that can't be ignored.

THE BLOCKCHAIN GAMING ECONOMY

After exploring memecoins, let's shift gears to GameFi, where blockchain and gaming collide. The idea of play-to-earn turned heads in the last cycle, offering players real financial rewards for their in-game efforts, but most of these models have become unsustainable. Axie Infinity kicked things off in 2020 and 2021, allowing players to breed and battle digital pets while earning tokens. But high gas fees on Ethereum led to the development of Ronin, a custom Layer 2 solution that made transactions faster and cheaper, showing that scalability in this sector is essential.

Meanwhile, the metaverse concept took hold with Decentraland and The Sandbox, where virtual real estate became a booming industry. Users could monetise in-game assets, proving that digital property ownership could have real-world value. Gala Games took it a step further, working on its own Layer 1 blockchain, GalaChain, to avoid Ethereum's high fees.

Interestingly, several blockchain games have also crossed over to major gaming platforms like PS5, Xbox, and PC. Games like *Off the Grid*, a cyberpunk battle royale built on Avalanche, have made their way into early access on these platforms, representing a significant milestone for blockchain gaming. While these games are distributed centrally via traditional platforms, the in-game assets and currencies remain decentralised on the blockchain, allowing players to trade and own digital items with real-world value. This hybrid approach merges traditional gaming infrastructure with blockchain technology, giving players true ownership over in-game assets.

More recently, newer projects like SuperVerse, Beam, and Prime are pushing blockchain gaming towards high-quality gameplay rather than just financial incentives, so the quality of the graphics more closely resembles Xbox and PlayStation 5. Prime is targeting AAA-style experiences, leveraging Ethereum's Layer 2 solutions to ensure fast, cheap transactions without compromising quality. Meanwhile, Immutable X is powering a growing number of blockchain games with its gas-free NFT marketplace, making trading seamless.

And then there's GambleFi, a niche but growing sector that applies blockchain to betting and gaming. Platforms like Rollbit offer transparent, provably fair games with instant crypto payouts, attracting users who want to wager without using traditional casinos. With Rollbit even landing a Premier League sponsorship, GambleFi is creeping into the mainstream.

AI COINS

The fusion of artificial intelligence and blockchain is unlocking new possibilities, as AI-driven blockchain projects transform decentralised infrastructure and data processing by combining automation. While still in their infancy, these innovations are already making an impact.

Most AI systems, such as ChatGPT, are controlled by large technology companies. Just as Blockchain projects have unshackled financial markets, they are now working to decentralise AI, shifting power away from centralised control. Instead of a few corporations dictating how AI models function, decentralised AI networks allow contributors to train machine learning models while earning rewards. For example, Bittensor allows users to train AI models collectively, earning its native TAO tokens in return. Similarly, Gensyn is developing AI-powered smart contracts that automate blockchain development, reducing human error and making transactions more secure. This shift distributes AI's power across decentralised networks, making it more transparent, censorship-resistant, and accessible to all.

In gaming, AI is creating smarter, more immersive worlds. Non-playable characters adapt to player behaviour, in-game economies function autonomously, and AI-driven assets evolve over time. NEAR Protocol's high-performance blockchain supports these advances in AI-driven gaming but its broader ambition is to reduce ecosystem fragmentation by offering a unified platform for decentralised applications and users. Meanwhile, Fetch.ai is integrating autonomous AI agents for in-game trading and asset pricing, in what it calls the agentic economy.

AI agents are digital entities capable of acting independently, making decisions, and executing tasks on behalf of users without constant human input. In both gaming and finance, they can manage resources and adapt to dynamic environments. They can even execute buy or sell orders based on real-time data and pre-set strategies and even function as trading bots. These agents can negotiate, optimise outcomes, and interact with digital and real-world systems equally, making them highly versatile tools in decentralised ecosystems.

SingularityNET is pushing the boundaries of AI-as-a-service through a decentralised marketplace, where decentralised AI models can be accessed and integrated across a range of industries, including gaming. These projects are not just enhancing entertainment; they are transforming digital economies into self-sustaining ecosystems.

Aside from gaming, AI is redefining the blockchain infrastructure. AI-driven applications require immense computational power, and decentralised networks are stepping in to meet this demand. Akash Network, which we mentioned earlier, provides access to decentralised cloud computing, allowing AI projects to rent GPU power without relying on centralised providers. Meanwhile, Ocean Protocol solves another problem, by providing access to high-quality data in its marketplace to AI developers seeking to buy and sell datasets without intermediaries. These platforms make AI-driven blockchain applications more efficient, scalable, and secure.

While many of these projects are still at a very early stage, with some viewing them as glorified memecoins, looking ahead, AI and blockchain are natural partners that extend far beyond gaming and finance. We will reignite this discussion later in the book, but for now, it should come as no surprise that AI-driven automation is already being explored in decentralised governance, identity verification, as well as crypto trading.

Blockchain networks are no longer just ledgers; they are becoming intelligent, self-evolving ecosystems where AI and decentralisation merge to redefine digital ownership and automation.

PRIVACY COINS

This chapter would not be complete without examining how privacy-focused cryptocurrencies fit into the broader ecosystem. While transparency is often seen as a strength in finance, privacy coins offer an alternative, one that prioritises confidentiality and financial autonomy, particularly as blockchain analytics tools become more advanced. We've learned that Bitcoin and other public blockchains provide an open, immutable record of transactions, yet this level of visibility is not always ideal. Monero (XMR) and Zcash (ZEC) are at the forefront of this movement. Monero's approach is to ensure complete anonymity by default, concealing transaction details from public view. Zcash, on the other hand, allows users to choose between transparency and privacy through its zk-SNARK (zero-knowledge Succinct Non-interactive Argument of Knowledge) encryption. Both challenge the idea that all blockchain transactions should be traceable, providing individuals with greater control over their financial information.

The question of privacy is more relevant than ever as digital transactions become increasingly scrutinised. Critics argue that privacy coins enable illicit activities, while supporters see them as a necessary safeguard against mass surveillance and financial censorship. The debate will continue as regulatory pressures mount, but their core purpose of ensuring financial privacy remains clear. Whether privacy coins become a niche asset, or a fundamental part of the decentralised economy will depend on how the industry and regulators navigate this evolving landscape. One thing is certain: as digital finance advances, the right to privacy will remain a critical issue. At the same time, ensuring users are protected is just as critical in shaping the future of blockchain technology, in ways we are only just beginning to understand.

As we have explored, alternative cryptocurrencies have expanded far beyond Bitcoin's original purpose. From Ethereum's smart contracts to privacy coins and real-world asset tokenisation, altcoins have pushed the boundaries of blockchain technology, solving challenges that Bitcoin alone cannot address. These innovations are reshaping industries and proving that blockchain's potential extends well beyond its beginnings as a peer-to-peer electronic cash system.

But with this progress comes complexity. While altcoins bring greater efficiency, privacy, and decentralisation, they also introduce new risks, including volatility and security vulnerabilities, as well as regulatory uncertainty. Will these technologies drive the creation of a truly decentralised financial system, or will increasing regulation limit their impact? Can privacy coins survive in a world shifting towards stricter financial oversight? How will real-world asset tokenisation transform global markets, and could it lead to mass blockchain adoption?

Understanding these innovations is only part of the journey. As blockchain-based assets become more prevalent, the question of how to manage and secure them becomes increasingly important. With no central authority to reverse a lost transaction or recover misplaced funds, responsibility falls entirely on the individual. How, then, can users safely navigate this evolving ecosystem? And what tools and strategies will protect digital assets? In the next chapter, we move from blockchain technology to the practical steps of securely managing cryptocurrencies, ensuring that innovation is matched with security and control.

Chapter 9

Crypto Security:

Wallets, Hacks, and How to Stay Safe

- Ⓑ *850,000 Bitcoin was stolen from the Mt. Gox cryptocurrency exchange between 2011 and 2014.*
- Ⓑ *Over $600 million worth of cryptocurrency disappeared from the Ronin Network in 2022.*
- Ⓑ *In a single year, $3.8 billion was stolen through crypto hacks and fraud (Chainalysis, 2022).*

So far this book has only touched upon the underlying security concerns associated with holding and engaging with digital assets. These aren't just isolated events. In the cryptocurrency space, hacks, fraud, and compromised accounts are a real and growing concern. For every story of financial freedom comes with it, a story of in many cases, irreversible loss.

You may recall that Chapter 3 stated that Bitcoin has never been hacked? According to the last chapter, nor has Ethereum. And yet, the facts I have highlighted above seem to contradict this. So how can both be true? Well, both are in fact true and by the end of this chapter hopefully you will see why.

By now you have probably seen one thing very clearly, namely that securing your cryptocurrency assets is not just important, it is essential. Bitcoin, altcoins, and decentralised finance offer unparalleled financial freedom and innovation, but that freedom comes with risks. Unlike traditional banking, where a forgotten password or misplaced card can usually be resolved with a call to customer services, crypto puts you in complete control. That control also means full responsibility, and I can't stress this enough. One of the gravest fears for many people is that a single mistake might result in irreversible loss with no way of recovering their assets. For that reason, this is one of the most important chapters in the book for anyone looking to engage in cryptocurrencies in a practical way. It might not seem the most glamourous of topics but think of it like the crypto road map — vital when navigating the most winding of mountain roads.

This chapter discusses practical security measures and the steps you should take to protect yourself. We'll pose questions like: How do you select the appropriate type of wallet? Is it safe to keep assets on an exchange? How can you defend against hacking and phishing attacks? Every crypto user, whether novice or experienced, must consider these issues carefully throughout their blockchain journey.

The decentralisation that makes cryptocurrency so powerful also means that you, and you alone, are responsible for protecting your assets. That doesn't imply it needs to be difficult or daunting. It implies that with the correct tools and knowledge, securing your investments is simple, and it will give you the confidence to use cryptocurrencies stress-free, without fear or needless deliberation.

At this point it is natural to want to understand the safest way to start to use cryptocurrencies. Together we'll explore the most effective approach to store and manage cryptocurrency assets, including the differences between software and hardware wallets, and how to keep private keys safe. These techniques are more than best practice; they are the very foundation of self-sovereignty in the cryptocurrency arena. By learning them, you will be able to engage with this ecosystem with confidence, no matter what happens in the market. Let's look at the two main ways you can acquire digital assets.

CENTRALISED EXCHANGES

First, consider centralised exchanges (CEXs). These serve as brokers for the purchase, sale, and trading of digital assets and they broadly work like traditional stock exchanges, allowing users to trade cryptocurrencies in a controlled and regulated environment. Established platforms such as Binance, Coinbase, and Kraken provide a user-friendly gateway into crypto, making it easier for investors of all levels to access the market.

One of the main advantages of centralised exchanges is ease of use. These platforms offer high liquidity, enabling rapid conversions between cryptocurrencies and fiat currencies such as USD, EUR, and GBP. Many CEXs also offer advanced trading features, such as margin trading, futures contracts, staking, and lending, making them attractive to investors looking for more complex transactions.

Another benefit lies in the enhanced security features several exchanges have implemented to safeguard users' assets. Coinbase, for example, provides a service called Vault aimed at boosting security for long-term storage of assets. This prevents immediate withdrawals and mandates several authentication steps before any funds can be transferred, including two-factor authentication (2FA) and confirmations from various email addresses.

Moreover, there's a waiting period of 48 hours before withdrawals can be processed. During this time, Coinbase keeps users informed with email updates about the status of their withdrawal, sending them real-time alerts. While not a formal escrow service, this temporary delay acts as a kind of buffer, which is similar in intent to the escrow protection ideas discussed in Chapter 6. This functionality certainly provides reassurance, as users can intervene and cancel any unauthorised transactions as they arise. This additional layer of protection provides real peace of mind against possible hacks or breaches. Note that although these measures enhance security, they cannot replace the complete control of self-custody, where you are the sole guardian of your private keys.

Even with these security features in place, keeping funds on centralised exchanges comes with considerable risks. Storing your assets on a CEX means the platform holds the private keys, effectively transferring direct ownership of your funds to the exchange. In some cases, your displayed balance on a CEX is merely a representation of pooled reserves held in a shared wallet. If that central wallet is hacked or drained, users' individual balances can be impacted even if their own accounts weren't directly compromised.

There is a popular saying in crypto, "not your keys, not your crypto", meaning that if you are not in sole possession of your private keys, you're placing your trust in a third party to manage your assets, similar to using a traditional bank account. Events like the 2014 Mt. Gox collapse, the insolvency of the FTX exchange in 2022, and the Crypto.com security breach in 2022 highlight that even well-established platforms are still vulnerable to hacks and manipulation. In the Crypto.com incident, hackers took advantage of a security flaw to circumvent two-factor authentication, resulting in the theft of over $30 million in Bitcoin and Ethereum combined before the exchange managed to block withdrawals.

These episodes exemplify the dangers of keeping significant sums on a centralised platform, as even reputable exchanges can fall victim to security breaches.

Being subject to regulation is a double-edged sword for centralised exchanges. While it helps to know that these privately-run entities are answerable to regulatory scrutiny, there can also be downsides. Many platforms are required to implement Know Your Customer (KYC) and Anti-Money Laundering (AML) procedures, which require users to verify their identities. This approach has been shown to decrease financial crime, yet it comes at the cost of privacy, a key factor driving some users towards decentralised alternatives in the first place. In some cases, regulatory pressure can place restrictions on exchanges, or force them to suspend operations in specific jurisdictions, as demonstrated by Binance in 2021. Under what some might describe as heavy-handed compliance scrutiny in the UK, many users of Binance were consequently unable to deposit or withdraw GBP through traditional banking methods. Even linking a UK bank account became impossible, and some users had to find workarounds like switching platforms, or using third-party payment services via non-traditional UK high street banks, thus incurring further counterparty risk. It is still possible for existing users in banned countries to use the platform, but the restrictions made it really inconvenient. The frustration of UK users who had traded on the platform was soon felt across several other jurisdictions in the face of compliance concerns in the Netherlands, France, and Cyprus. The U.S. went a step further and convicted the former head of Binance, Changpeng Zhao (CZ) in 2024 for money laundering violations.

Centralised exchanges remain an essential entry point for many users, providing both convenience and liquidity, as well as advanced trading tools. However, in my opinion, they are not the safest place to store large amounts of cryptocurrency, as well as being subject to regulatory scrutiny. Understanding how to use them wisely, such as withdrawing assets to a self-custody wallet when not actively trading, can help balance accessibility with security.

DECENTRALISED EXCHANGES

Another option for trading and exchanging tokens securely is to use decentralised exchanges (DEXs). These platforms offer users far greater freedom and remove custodial risk, although trading directly on the blockchain using DEXs' smart contracts requires advanced knowledge. If a user connects their cryptocurrency wallet to the exchange during a transaction, they will be able to engage in peer-to-peer trading without relying on any third party. This model provides you with full control over your assets, significantly reducing your exposure to platform manipulation or regulatory challenges that may affect centralised services.

But are they safe? Reputable platforms such as Uniswap, PancakeSwap, or SushiSwap, have certainly proved reliable thus far. However, make sure you are definitely on their official platforms, as mistakenly clicking a wrong link to a fraudulent impersonator would be disastrous and very costly. Scams are very common in this space. Also, DEXs are considered non-custodial, which means that there is no centralised authority holding user funds. This is important to understand as it means that users must maintain control over their private keys and assets at all times. Doing so competently can reduce the risk of losing funds from exchange hacks or mismanagement.

The regulatory challenges to CEXs, as discussed above, have also driven interest in DEXs, particularly in regions where governments have tried to restrict access to cryptocurrencies. For example, both the UK and China took action against exchanges in 2021, followed by many other countries over the last few years. China's 2021 crackdown on centralised exchanges forced platforms like Binance and Huobi to block access to users in mainland China. The Chinese government had previously imposed restrictions on crypto trading, but by 2021, it had banned everything. The effect was to make it illegal for foreign exchanges to provide any services to Chinese residents. "Virtual currency-related business activities are illegal financial activities", said the People's Bank of China, warning that this "seriously endangers the safety of people's assets". This left many traders few options, forcing them either to use offshore platforms with VPNs or move to DEXs, which were much harder to regulate and restrict. Additionally, because most DEXs do not require KYC or AML verification, they offer users greater privacy and the ability to continue using the technology even if bans have been put in place. In some cases, this pushed users who simply wanted to continue engaging with cryptocurrencies towards these platforms, often without the sufficient knowledge or experience to use them safely.

Nonetheless, decentralised exchanges do encounter a few challenges. Liquidity continues to be a significant issue, with centralised exchanges generally providing greater liquidity, prompting quicker trades and more favourable pricing. Although leading DEXs have advanced in this area, they continue to fall short compared with centralised counterparts. Usability is another frequent problem. DEXs often present a steeper learning curve, demanding that users grasp the intricacies of decentralised protocols, which can be overwhelming for those new to crypto.

Another key difference between centralised and decentralised exchanges is how they source liquidity. As we saw in the last chapter, these exchanges do not use traditional order books but instead rely on liquidity pools to facilitate trades. This is made possible with what are known as automated market maker (AMM) models. They work by allowing users to deposit pairs of cryptocurrencies to earn a yield and allow others to trade with their tokens, which is an attractive option for those looking to generate passive income. However, as stated previously, risks can occur if there are drastic price fluctuations, potentially leading to impermanent loss. These liquidity pools can also be vulnerable to hacks, where funds can be stolen, meaning that care is required when using them.

As you may recall from the last chapter, users should also be aware that the smart contracts that run on these decentralised platforms can themselves contain vulnerabilities. Any flaw could be exploited, leading to potential loss of funds. While established platforms undergo security audits, the risk of exploitation remains, particularly on newer or less-tested decentralised protocols. Also, any site pretending to be one of the familiar legitimate platforms can engineer conditions into their smart contracts that can drain your funds, so again, be 100% sure of what you are connecting to.

WALLETS

Having explored the various methods for trading and acquiring digital assets, the question is how to ensure that they are stored securely. Keeping your assets on centralised exchanges is an option, but it comes with the risk of counterparty exposure. These are the same types of risks you might be exposed to by keeping money in a traditional bank account, such as your account being compromised, often without the same protections. If the exchange fails, your funds can be in danger, just as a failing bank would use funds to pay off their own debts in a bail-in.

HARDWARE WALLETS

First of all, it is worth noting that alongside CEXs and DEXs, other types of crypto wallets can often facilitate buying, selling, and swapping of digital assets. One of the key reasons cryptocurrencies have gained such popularity is that they do not require you to trust someone else with your money. Many consider hardware wallets, also known as cold storage solutions, to offer the greatest security for your cryptocurrency holdings. This is because they keep your private keys offline, which significantly reduces the risk of hacking, as the device only connects to the internet briefly while it's in active use during a transaction.

A hardware wallet, such as the Ledger or Trezor, is a small physical device that securely stores your private and public keys without exposing them to your computer or the internet. As we may recall from Chapter 6, when you want to send cryptocurrency, you must sign the transaction directly through the device, which the wallet technology processes using elliptic curve cryptography. This eliminates the need to remember or manually enter the long hexadecimal private key. As long as you have access to the wallet, you have access to your private key. Since these wallets remain offline when not in use, they are immune to most types of malware, phishing attacks, and remote hacking attempts that commonly target software-based wallets.

I advise anyone holding significant amounts of cryptocurrency to use a hardware wallet, as they provide an extra layer of security by requiring physical confirmation. Every transaction must be manually approved by pressing a button on the device itself. Even if a hacker gains remote access to your computer, they cannot transfer your assets without your explicit approval on the hardware wallet. This crucial security feature massively reduces the risk of unauthorised transfers and makes it the safest way to store and transact with your crypto.

Setting up a hardware wallet might seem complicated at first, but the process is actually quite straightforward. Below is a step-by-step guide for first-time users to ensure your funds remain secure from the start:

- Ⓑ Purchase from a Trusted Source: I strongly advise buying your hardware wallet directly from the manufacturer or an authorised retailer to ensure your device has not been tampered with. Avoid buying from third-party sellers, including on Ebay or Amazon, since compromised devices may jeopardise your funds. If you receive a wallet that comes pre-configured with a seed phrase, steer clear of it, as this is a major red flag for a security breach.

- Ⓑ Connect the Wallet: Begin by connecting your hardware wallet to your computer with a USB cable or connect it to your mobile phone using the provided OTG cable or via Bluetooth, depending on the model. After connecting, simply follow the on-screen prompts from the device to start the set-up process.

- Ⓑ Initialise the Wallet: As you set your wallet up, it will create a random seed phrase, usually consisting of 12 to 24 words. Your seed phrase serves as a back-up if your device gets lost or damaged. It's this seed phrase that is used to create your private key cryptographically, and remember, this is what the device uses to derive your public key (see Chapter 6). Write your seed phrase down on paper and keep it in a safe place offline. Avoid taking photos or saving them in a digital format at all costs. If someone gains access to your seed phrase, they can take full control of your funds.

- Ⓑ Install the Wallet Software: Once your device is set up, install the applicable wallet management software, such as Ledger Live or Trezor Suite, on your computer. This will allow you to manage your cryptocurrency holdings, check balances, and send or receive transactions while keeping your private keys secure inside the hardware wallet.

- Ⓑ Set Up your Pin Code: You will also be prompted to choose a PIN code during the set-up process. This is important as it acts as your first line of defence if someone physically gets access to your wallet. The PIN must be entered each time you use the device or authorise a transaction. Some wallets, such as D'cent, use additional security features such as biometric fingerprint scanning. Theoretically, any type of face recognition or two-factor authentication could be used for this purpose. In any case, these are used mainly for convenience. If, for example, the fingerprint scan fails or is not recognised, the PIN still acts as a fallback, which is especially useful if the fingerprint sensor is damaged or unresponsive.

- Ⓑ Transfer Funds: Once your wallet is ready, you can transfer cryptocurrency to it for safekeeping. To receive funds, use your public wallet address, as provided by the wallet software. Remember, your wallet address, which is derived from your public key, can be shared, like giving out your email address, but your private key (in practice you will never really see this) and the seed phrase that grants access to your private key, must always remain secret. All outgoing transactions will require your physical confirmation on the device itself, adding an extra layer of security.

Ⓑ Keep Firmware Updated: Manufacturers consistently roll out firmware updates to enhance security and address vulnerabilities. It's crucial to keep your wallet updated to protect it from potential threats and maintain its security. Make sure to download updates straight from the official manufacturer's website to steer clear of phishing scams.

But what happens if you lose your PIN or even the cold wallet itself? What if it is stolen?

Most hardware wallets are designed to wipe themselves automatically after several failed PIN attempts. If this happens, you would then revert back to your seed phrase. If you just forgot the PIN, you would use the seed phrase on the same wallet to get set up again. If the device is damaged, lost, or stolen, then purchasing a new device would be necessary. In both cases, after inputting your seed phrase, you will be issued a new PIN. So, the seed phrase is the most important thing to ensure you can always access your funds. Store it securely offline and separately from the device itself.

SOFTWARE WALLETS

While hardware wallets offer the greatest security, they may not always be the most convenient option for daily transactions or quick access to your funds. In which case you may need a software wallet on occasion. Software wallets, commonly referred to as hot wallets, offer a perfect blend of convenience and security for users who require regular access to their assets. Usually set up on computers or mobile devices, they offer easy access to your cryptocurrency. However, using this system means that your private keys are encrypted on a device that is connected to the internet, making them more vulnerable to online threats. Consequently, software wallets are ideal for storing smaller amounts of crypto-currency for everyday transactions or trading activities.

Various software wallets exist, each offering unique levels of control and security. Desktop wallets like Exodus and Electrum are installed right on your computer, giving you the ability to manage your private keys locally. These offer enhanced security compared with storing funds on a centralised exchange, yet they remain susceptible to online attacks if your computer is compromised. Alternatively, mobile wallets like Trust Wallet and MetaMask are applications you can easily install on your smartphone and are popular among users who often engage with DeFi platforms or dApps. They offer a handy solution for managing crypto while on the move, yet like desktop wallets, they carry comparable vulner-abilities because of their ongoing internet connection.

Another type of mobile wallet is an exchange custodial wallet, which could be supplied by a centralised exchange, such as Coinbase Wallet. These function like standard mobile wallets but offer optional integration with your exchange account, allowing users to transfer assets between their self-custody wallet and the exchange when needed. As with the other software wallets, they too offer speed and convenience, but their continuous internet connection makes them more susceptible to cyber-attacks.

BEST PRACTICES FOR SECURING YOUR DIGITAL ASSETS

Regardless of which type of wallet, or combination thereof, you are using, it's crucial to adhere to these essential security practices to minimise risks and safeguard your funds from potential threats:

1. *Secure Your Private Keys*: Your private key is your most valuable asset. Never share or save it anywhere online. A good approach is to write your recovery seed phrase on two or three separate pieces of paper or cardboard, laminate them for durability, and store them in separate

secure locations. You could keep them in a safe, a fire-resistant lockable box, in a tamper-resistant location. Or there are metal wallets that are specifically designed for this purpose. Storing seed phrases in a fireproof and waterproof format offers an extra layer of protection, which is critical for both hot and cold wallets, as losing access to your seed phrase means losing access to your whole asset portfolio.

2. *Enable Two-Factor Authentication (2FA)*: Always turn on 2FA for your cryptocurrency accounts. SIM-swap attacks can compromise phone-based verification techniques, therefore use apps like Google Authenticator or Authy, instead of SMS-based authentication. While this mostly applies to hot wallets and exchange accounts, wallet management software that is linked to hardware wallets can provide an additional layer of security.

3. *Beware of Phishing*: Phishing scams often disguise themselves as legitimate services to trick users into revealing sensitive information or sending funds to the wrong place. Attackers may use fraudulent emails, fake websites, replace legitimate QR codes, or impersonate social media and messaging app accounts. If someone contacts you on an apps such as Telegram, which is full of crypto enthusiasts, exercise extreme caution. Crypto-related groups on these platforms are full of scammers who may initially appear friendly but later try to convince you to invest in fraudulent platforms or connect your wallets to malicious sites, from whence they can drain your funds. This poses a risk to both hot and cold wallet users, as scammers may attempt to access private keys or deceive them into connecting their wallet to a malicious dApp. To avoid being a victim of lookalike frauds, always verify URLs and email sources, and bookmark reliable websites. Never click on unsolicited links nor open dubious attachments.

4. *Use Secure Connections*: Only ever access your digital wallets using a secure internet connection. Public Wi-Fi networks can be exploited, making it easier for hackers to intercept sensitive data. A VPN (Virtual Private Network), such as NordVPN will provide an additional layer of security, particularly while using public or unprotected networks. While cold wallets remain offline, this step is still necessary when using wallet management software or carrying out transactions with a hardware wallet on a connected device.

5. *Risk of Browser-Based Wallet Exploitation*: Wallets that run in browsers can be vulnerable if your browser itself is compromised, especially through malicious plugins or unpatched exploits. Additionally, some malware replaces copied crypto addresses with the attacker's address, so users unknowingly send funds to the wrong wallet.

6. *Regular Back-Ups*: For software wallets, conducting regular back-ups and saving your recovery phrase in secure, offline locations is critical for recovering your assets if your phone or laptop is stolen, damaged, or compromised. The rules for hardware wallets are the same. If the device is lost, broken, or reset, the only method that will regain access is to enter the seed phrase. Keep your back-up in a separate location from your hardware wallet to avoid total loss in the event of theft or disaster.

7. *Risk of Outdated Wallet Software*: Using old wallet versions may leave you vulnerable to bugs or security flaws that have already been patched in newer updates.

I hear many people worrying about losing their funds, but if these rules are followed explicitly, then there really is more chance of your bank going under, or the government not fulfilling an FCSC (Financial Services Compensation Scheme) claim, for example, than losing your crypto assets.

CUSTODIAL VERSUS NON-CUSTODIAL WALLETS

We have spoken about different ways to store and manage cryptocurrency, so how can you choose what is right for you? One of the best ways to look at it is whether you want full control over your assets or whether you prefer someone else to manage them for you. In other words, do you want a custodial or a non-custodial wallet? This question is almost the same as choosing whether to use centralised exchanges or to secure your assets yourself. Before making your first crypto purchase, it is important to decide what will work best for you. Everyone is unique and we all have our particular goals, but choosing the right storage method depends on your security requirements, technical comfort, and anticipated frequency of use.

If convenience is a top priority and minimal technical knowledge is required, exchange-provided custodial wallets offer a straightforward option. Alternatively, if security is the essential consideration and you are willing to take full responsibility for managing your private keys, non-custodial wallets are the better option.

INSURANCE AND BACK-UP STRATEGIES

With the increasing popularity of cryptocurrencies, several exchanges have begun to offer insurance policies to protect users against potential losses. Platforms like Coinbase and Gemini provide insurance against hackers and breaches, securing funds held in their hot wallets. However, these do not protect against user errors such as forgetting passwords, losing private keys, or transferring money to the wrong address. Aside from exchange-provided coverage, third-party crypto insurance companies, including Nexus Mutual and Coincover, can provide policies to protect against smart contract failures, exchange hacks, and governance risks on DeFi systems. However, retail coverage is limited, with most insurance aimed at institutions. Even with insurance, the best method of protecting your assets is always to implement a strong security and back-up system.

We've now explored the vital components of successful crypto-currency management and the need to prioritise security measures. The foundation of a thriving crypto strategy is undoubtedly to understand the specific methods available and when and how to use each one. When you self-custody your assets, there is no protection as you would have with a traditional bank account. When approaching the technology in this way it is important to remember that only you are accountable when engaging with this exciting industry. Conversely, implementing measures such as 2FA and remaining cognisant of the risks associated with centralised platforms will allow you to interact with the crypto space with assurance and safety.

However, securing and protecting your assets is just the first step. The next big question is what impact the blockchain technology itself has on the world. In what ways might crypto reshape industries? What about the challenges to blockchain scalability? And can decentralised networks truly compete with traditional financial systems? Read on for a deep analysis to address these questions and explore blockchain's full potential.

Chapter 10

Advantages and Disadvantages

of Blockchain Technology

Blockchain has emerged as one of the most significant technological innovations in recent years, with applications that extend far beyond finance. We have come a long way since DigiCash developed its eCash system in the late 1990s in an early attempt to integrate cryptography into financial markets. Even though the first digital payments were designed to integrate with traditional banks in a centralised manner, the vision was always to create a system that could operate over the internet, independent of orthodox financial structures.

Online payment systems such as PayPal made digital payments easier, but they remained heavily reliant on banks and centralised financial networks. The challenge was not just to digitise payments, but to create a system where value could be transferred and stored without intermediaries. Projects like eCash introduced cryptographic privacy but still depended on a central authority. Others, such as Hashcash, introduced Proof of Work, but it was never fully developed into a working currency. The missing piece was a mechanism for trustless verification of transactions in an open, decentralised network.

But then Bitcoin arrived and changed everything. By combining blockchain technology with decentralised consensus and crypto-graphic proof, it finally achieved what no system before had, that is, creating a way to transfer and store digital value securely and verifiably without requiring permission from banks or governments. The breakthrough was not just in the technology, but in how the pieces fit perfectly together. For the first time, digital assets in an open system could be secure, scarce, and verifiable, creating entirely new possibilities.

While Bitcoin started as a solution for digital money, blockchain technology has since evolved into something much broader, unlocking new possibilities far beyond finance. However, like any technological breakthrough, it comes with strengths and challenges. While its potential seems vast, its long-term success depends on how well it adapts to real-world applications and the challenges that come with scaling an entirely new financial infrastructure.

By this point in the book, we have covered a lot. We've gone from the origins of Bitcoin, financial crises, and the evolution of money to the inner workings of cryptographic security, private keys, and mining. Along the way, we've also surveyed the ever-expanding landscape of alternative cryptocurrencies, from serious innovations to speculative experiments, including some that started as a joke. Dogecoin assumed a picture of a Shiba Inu dog as the face of the project, yet somehow gained a loyal following. There was also mention of the intricacies of network effects and the different ways cryptocurrencies are constructed, depending on their specific purpose and place in the market.

Just as various banks have different methods of management, confirming transactions, and recording financial data, so do digital assets. Whereas financial institutions operate under very different regulatory frameworks and risk models, in the case of cryptocurrencies they are all governed by different protocols, consensus mechanisms, and tokenomic structures. These all have a direct consequence on their respective efficiency and profitability. If this has felt like a crash course in economic history, computer science, and mathematics all at once, that is because, in many ways, it has been. Nonetheless, one fundamental question remains: What does it all mean for our future?

Chapter 9 discussed the practicalities of securing digital assets, so we need now to take a hard look at those assets. We need to ask what has potential to hold its value and if that value is likely to continue over time. It's vital that we critically examine both the advantages and limitations of blockchain technology to obtain a comprehensive view of its potential to transform global industries and indeed the world we live in. By the end of the chapter you will have a balanced perspective on the opportunities blockchain presents, the obstacles it faces, and how it might evolve as adoption continues to grow.

We'll start by examining whether Bitcoin's scarcity model can stand the test of time in a world of unpredictable economic cycles. Will its scalability, decentralisation, and security function cohesively or are there unavoidable trade-offs? And will alternative cryptocurrencies lead to an economic shift, or are we still awaiting blockchain's first truly indispensable use case beyond speculation?

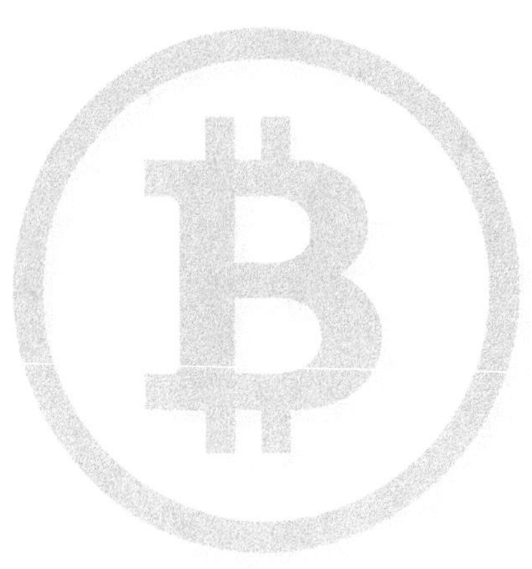

ADVANTAGES OF BLOCKCHAIN TECHNOLOGY

1. Control of Funds – Away from Failing Banks

As we've established, one of the most significant advantages that blockchain technology brings to the financial world is the ability to take full control of your own assets. Imagine controlling your finances without the lingering worry that your wealth could be taken away from you. As we have seen throughout history, for centuries the foundation of financial systems has involved banks, brokers, and governments. Time and time again, financial crises have shown how these systems can fail individuals.

Whether through bank collapses, frozen accounts, restrictive with-drawal limits, or even bail-ins with customer funds being used to stabilise struggling banks. Blockchain technology completely flips this relationship on its head and provides an alternative. With decentralised networks, you are no longer just an account holder; you can "be your own bank". In this system, you alone hold the keys to your wealth.

Possession of a private key means possession of the asset itself. It means access and control over that part of the database, which only you as the holder can use until you transfer it. There is no need to ask permission and no risk of censorship. And no third party stands between you and your money. Access to your funds depends neither on institutional policies nor political conditions, because ownership is absolute.

Nobody should have to deal with their money not being secure. In the twenty-first century, we have sent people into space, created a wealth of utility from the boundless information on the internet, and introduced AI. Yet people still have to navigate outdated financial systems. There is no question that markets should be advancing at the same pace as other technologies to provide greater security and access. But even as innovation accelerates, the financial system continues to expose people to the same risks today.

For those who have faced financial instability due to banking failures or lack of access, this concept is not just theoretical but deeply personal. Being locked out of your own funds, whether due to a failing bank or political uncertainty, is a critical reminder of the risks of centralised control. While this is a major concern even in developed countries, the issue is far more severe in regions where banking infrastructure is underdeveloped or unreliable, where basic survival is often the priority. In an age where technology allows global connectivity, financial access should not be a privilege but a right.

On a humanitarian level, the divide needs to be reduced. With the technology we have at our disposal, there should be limitless possibilities for all global citizens to be financially more independent. As cryptocurrencies mature, not only are they starting to help people living in poverty gain greater financial access, but on a national scale they could also level the playing field between institutions and the public.

Bitcoin and decentralised finance are shaping a world where individuals become the custodians of their own assets, significantly reducing their reliance on intermediaries. As highlighted at the beginning of Chapter 3, in traditional banking, a customer does not truly own the money they have deposited, as it exists within the bank's system and can be frozen, limited, or even confiscated in extreme cases. By contrast, Bitcoin and DeFi defines ownership with private keys and smart contracts, which if used correctly, ensure that assets cannot be altered, seized, or manipulated by external entities. The automation afforded by smart contracts helps to reduce the delays and manipulation that manual processing can bring about, adding efficiency and time savings to transactions.

And we no longer need to place our trust in third parties because the immutable and transparent nature of blockchain ensures that transactions are executed exactly as programmed. In this evolving financial landscape, users are no longer at the mercy of central institutions but can instead control their own financial destinies.

2. Security and Immutability

At this point, after learning that blockchain offers numerous benefits and control over your own assets, you might still ask, "But is it secure"? And rightly so. None of it matters if the technology itself isn't secure. Blockchain's reliability lies in its security and immutability, ensuring that once transactions are recorded, they cannot be altered or deleted. Specifically, Bitcoin's PoW consensus mechanism provides the greatest security in the blockchain space, making it virtually impossible to manipulate past transactions. Once a transaction is confirmed on the Bitcoin network, it becomes permanent, protected by thousands of independent nodes and immense computational power.

According to Bitnodes data from May 2025, there are approximately 63,000 Bitcoin nodes globally, each playing a role in verifying and securing the network. As each block is cryptographically linked to the previous one, any attempt to alter a past transaction would require recomputing the entire chain, which would demand a disproportionate amount of energy and resources. This level of security is important as it eliminates almost all risk of manipulation and fraud, making Bitcoin one of the most tamper-resistant financial systems ever created. A good way to think about this is like automation in artificial intelligence (AI). Just as the aim of AI is to eliminate human error with black-and-white decision-making, Bitcoin's mining process runs on autopilot, following the set cryptographic rules that, barring a colluding 51% attack, no single entity can override, ensuring that transactions remain secure and irreversible.

It's important to state that the other cryptocurrencies, most of which operate under some form of Proof-of-Stake consensus mechanism, are also highly secure and immutable. While PoS prioritises efficiency and scalability over energy-intensive mining, it still ensures the integrity and permanence of transactions. While the methods differ in their approach to confirmation, they still both use the fundamental method of elliptic curve cryptography to prevent fraud and ensure trustless verification of transactions.

Bitcoin's model is often misunderstood, with many dismissing it as an inefficient use of energy. Admittedly, Bitcoin mining is expensive, with the average cost of mining a single bitcoin in Q1 2025 estimated to be almost $85,000, depending on electricity prices, mining equipment, and network difficulty. However, this varies significantly by region and in February 2025 it could be as low as $1,000–$2,000 in countries such as Iran, where energy is subsidised, to over $300,000 in other regions. This disparity has an influence over where mining is concentrated but also plays a vital role in Bitcoin's self-adjusting difficulty model, which ensures consistent block production regardless of short-term profitability (see Chapter 6).

We've also established that Bitcoin self-regulates in real time, responding to shifts in network activity and miner participation. The Bitcoin protocol adjusts its mining difficulty every 2,016 blocks, which equates to roughly every two weeks. This mechanism was designed by Satoshi Nakamoto with the primary goal of ensuring that blocks are created on average every 10 minutes. If the network hashrate rises too much, blocks will be mined too quickly, causing the difficulty to increase. If they're being mined too slowly, the difficulty decreases. This automated recalibration helps maintain Bitcoin's predictable issuance schedule and makes it more resilient and is a foundational part of what makes the network so secure.

Now that we understand how the Bitcoin network regulates block production by adjusting the difficulty of solving puzzles every 2,016 blocks, it's important to look at why Satoshi Nakamoto chose a 10-minute interval in the first place. While it may seem a random choice, this was a carefully thought-out trade-off between usability, decentralisation, and network security. A faster block time might sound like a good idea at first. Why not process blocks every 2.5 minutes like Litecoin does? Or take it a step further and process them in seconds, like Solana and some other modern blockchains?

The problem with this is that if blocks are produced too quickly, it becomes harder for all nodes to stay in sync, especially with regard to PoW. The result would be instability because the chances of chain splits or forks would be higher, as described in my bees and honey analogy in Chapter 6. And when this happens it opens the door for potential 51% attacks to the network.

Additionally, fast block times favour miners with better connectivity and computer hardware, which leads to centralisation of mining power. This would go against Bitcoin's whole philosophy and reduce the security and resilience of the network.

On the other hand, setting block times too far apart would reduce the network's responsiveness. Transactions would take much longer to confirm, making the system less practical. Waiting an hour for confirmation might work for very large payments, but it's not ideal for daily use. Nakamoto chose 10 minutes as a compromise as it provides stability. At this pace, there is enough time to propagate each block around the world and it's still practical for transactions. Security is also protected because forks can't develop and it's harder for a small group of miners to dominate the network. When you think about it, waiting 10 minutes to securely send £20,000 to your family on the other side of the world for under a fiver doesn't sound that bad, does it?

But the consistent 10-minute block time doesn't just keep the network secure and decentralised in real time, it also plays an important role in Bitcoin's long-term pre-programmed monetary policy. Bitcoin was designed so that something crucial happens every 210,000 blocks: the block reward is cut in half. This halving cycle is one of the most important features of Bitcoin's fixed-supply model, which sets it apart from fiat currencies. This occurs roughly every four years and reduces the rate at which new bitcoins enter circulation. The first Bitcoin block reward was 50 BTC per block but through these halvings this has been systematically reduced over the years:

- ₿ **28 November 2012 (Block 210,000):** 50 → 25 BTC

- ₿ **9 July 2016 (Block 420,000):** 25 → 12.5 BTC

- ₿ **11 May 2020 (Block 630,000):** 12.5 → 6.25 BTC

- ₿ **20 April 2024 (Block 840,000):** 6.25 → 3.125 BTC

Neither the original White Paper nor any other document has stated why Nakamoto decided to create a Bitcoin halving every 210,000 blocks, leading to these four-year cycles. My view is that this wasn't chosen at random. One theory might be to mimic the process of gold mining, with new discoveries becoming increasingly scarce over time. This creates a gradual supply increase over time, which stabilises inflation between halvings and avoids abrupt shocks in miner income.

Not only this, it aligns closely with traditional economic cycles, which often span three to eight years. Business and investment cycles tend to follow a multi-year rhythm, with expansions and contractions occurring in roughly four-year intervals. In many countries, political terms, such as the U.S. presidential cycle, also follow this timeframe and have historically influenced monetary policy and inflation. Interestingly, this also aligns with earlier discussions regarding the multiple rounds of QE since 2008, with central bank liquidity being pumped into the system to create these roughly two-to-five-year cycles. This creates these artificial rolling over of government debt refinancing cycles, averaging around four years, as we discussed in Chapter 5.

Besides this, there may also be a psychological and behavioural element to Bitcoin's design. A four-year interval gives markets enough time to digest each halving, adapt to new supply dynamics, and reassess its valuation. This creates natural waves of speculation and consolidation, giving Bitcoin its own monetary heartbeat that gradually adjusts with time.

Figure: 10.1: Bitcoin Mining Difficulty

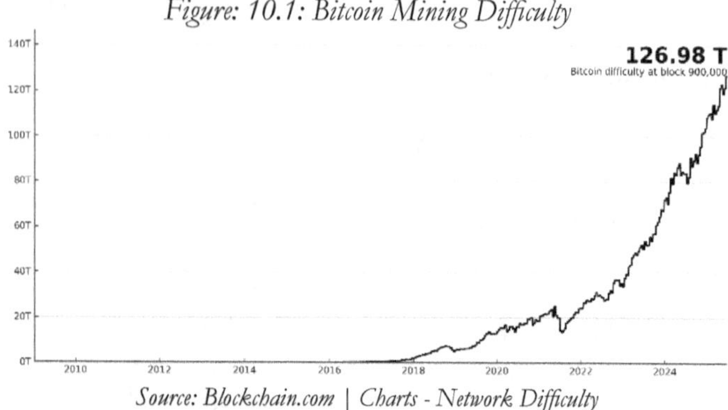

Source: Blockchain.com | Charts - Network Difficulty

Generally, if it costs more money to produce a bitcoin than its current price, miners will exit the network, lowering the hashrate. This triggers a reduction in the difficulty level, as there are fewer miners battling to find the next block. The opposite is also true, and as Bitcoin's price rises above its cost price in a particular region, it becomes financially viable for more miners from that country to participate, which in turn raises the hashrate, pushing the difficulty level upwards once again.

The increasing difficulty of mining Bitcoin is reflected in the growing computational power that miners are dedicating to secure the network. Miners worldwide collectively surpassed a network hashrate of over 1,113 exahashes per second (EH/s) on 13 April 2025. To put this into perspective, one exahash equals one quintillion (1,000,000,000,000,000,000) hashes per second. Investing this amount of computational energy is what sets the difficulty threshold and maintains the average 10-minute block time.

So, whether hashes are performed to create a Transaction ID on the way to computing a Merkle root, or to find the correct nonce that produces a valid block hash, giving it its digital fingerprint, they're happening at an astronomically high rate. This means that as more hashes are required to confirm blocks, more computational power must therefore be invested to run the network, and Bitcoin becomes increasingly secure, making it harder to alter, and hence the network becomes ever more resilient and tamper-proof.

3. Transparency and Trust

While benefits such as security and financial empowerment are highly important, it is also crucial that the technology can be trusted. That's why transactions need to be transparent. Later we'll see how the Yapese people in the Micronesian Island region of Oceana used a similar blockchain method back in 500 CE, for these very reasons. Whether global computers are verifying a network, or the inhabitants of a tiny island are storing a ledger system in their heads, it is this transparency and accountability that builds trust in any public ledger-based system.

As long as anyone can verify transactions in real time, then the whole system becomes trustworthy, which should eliminate manipulation or fraud. This is a very important quality for any open transactional method of trade, avoiding the hidden dealings of traditional finance that occur frequently behind closed doors. Cryptocurrency is often praised for its high level of transparency, and for good reason. Everybody can view every movement of each digital asset across their respective networks and this is imperative to build trust in the model.

This stands in vast contrast to what we saw in Chapter 2, where sleight of hand and deception were all too familiar. Too big to fail, they said. Reassurance after reassurance. But when the mighty Lehman Brothers caused the whole money machine to combust during the 2008 financial crisis, it revealed only opacity. High-risk subprime bets. Masked liabilities. Leveraged illusions. It proved that in traditional finance, no one was accountable. Heavy reliance on short-term funding sources and concealing its true financial condition meant that the extent of the distress only became apparent when it was far too late. That was not the first time. The financial fraud concealed by Enron in 2001 was another example of a corporate casualty which wouldn't have been possible in a system based on predefined and transparent rules that are embedded in its code.

Blockchain does not deal with illusions. When we pull back the curtain, transactions are final, records immutable, and publicly verifiable. There's no space for deceptive accounting or inadequate risk management. The risks associated with poor financial practices or human intervention disappear with trustless blockchain technology. It has redefined how financial transactions and data integrity are maintained in the digital age. Instead, by combining transparency and trust, blockchains of varying consensus mechanisms allow individuals to transact freely, without dependence on intermediaries.

These qualities are especially useful for blockchains like Ethereum, whose programmable features can track assets and automate verification in industries other than finance. Blockchain's transparency is already making a real-world impact in diamond tracking and supply-chain verification. Companies like De Beers and Everledger have integrated this technology to track diamonds from the moment they are mined to final sale. This ensures that the diamonds are ethically sourced, avoiding those mined in conflict zones that may have funded armed conflicts or involved exploitative practices. Verifying the origin of diamonds has traditionally been difficult, but blockchain changes that. When public ledgers are used, buyers can see goods' authenticity for themselves.

4. STORE OF VALUE

As highlighted throughout this book, Bitcoin is not just a means of exchange, it has also established itself as the strongest store of value in the cryptocurrency space. While some alternative cryptocurrencies share this trait, Bitcoin's scarcity stands apart due to its track record and predictable monetary policy.

If we compare progress over the last 15 years, it is hard to dispute Bitcoin's ability to preserve wealth over time. Alternative cryptocurrencies were created as extensions of Bitcoin's innovation, often aiming to improve upon aspects, such as transaction speed or smart contract functionality. Even though many of these projects are still in their early stages, the rapid pace of innovation means that some will no doubt evolve into long-term successes, driving new use cases and advances in blockchain technology.

However, investors in cryptocurrency must take a strategic long-term approach, because alternative cryptocurrencies tend to experience dramatic price fluctuations. The crypto space is still evolving, and it takes time for the market to determine which altcoins have true staying power.

On the other hand, Bitcoin's fixed capped supply ensures that it cannot experience hyperinflation or unpredictable levels of monetary expansion, unlike fiat currencies and even some alternative cryptocurrencies. We know that Bitcoin's inflation rate has been systematically decreasing since its inception, thanks to its pre-programmed monetary policy. And with each halving event, fewer new bitcoins enter circulation, making the existing supply even more valuable over time.

Figure 10.2: Bitcoin's Inflation Rate (2009-2040)

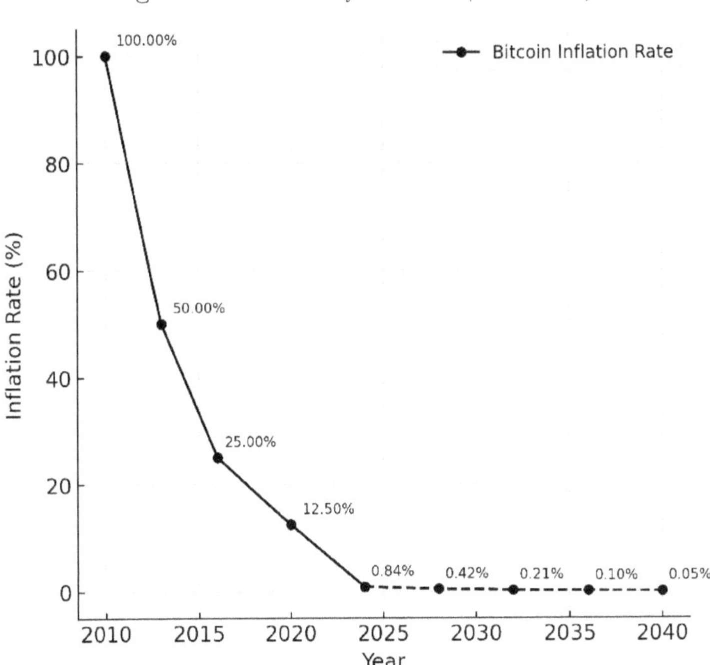

Figure 10.2 shows Bitcoin's inflation rate from the beginning. When no bitcoins were in circulation, and the block reward was 50 BTC, the effective inflation rate was 100%. Inflation in this context is calculated as the annual increase in supply relative to the total existing supply. Since Bitcoin's initial supply was zero, adding 50 BTC per block represented an extremely high inflation rate in the early days, but this has consistently declined over time, reinforcing both its scarcity and ability to store value.

Following the halving event in April 2024, Bitcoin's inflation rate stands at approximately 0.84%, 75% lower than U.S. inflation data from May 2024 and more than 70% lower than gold's annual issuance. By comparison, gold's annual inflation typically ranges from 1 to 3%, driven by a combination of newly mined gold and recycled supply. Recycled gold refers to gold repurposed from sources that include central bank reserves, industrial applications, and jewellery that has been melted down and reintroduced into circulation. With this latest halving event, at less than 1%, Bitcoin's inflation rate has now dropped below gold's lowest historical boundary for the first time.

To expand on this point, there are only around 1.14 million bitcoins left to be mined as of May 2025. Given that the difficulty of mining new coins is consistently increasing, the cost of doing so becomes ever more expensive. Added to this, the lack of supply due to built-in scarcity has also driven the price higher, all of which contributes to the deflationary nature of this asset. As the overall supply decreases, the intrinsic value of Bitcoin increases, and its purchasing power goes up. Another contributing factor is the fact that access to a number of bitcoins has been lost over the years, or more accurately put, they are inaccessible on the blockchain, meaning that there will never be as many as 21 million accessible coins in circulation.

Let's look at an example of Bitcoin's potential as a store of value. Consider the year 2009, when Bitcoin was worth only a fraction of a cent and a cup of coffee in an average U.S. coffee shop cost around $1.50.

Figure 10.3: Bitcoin's Increasing Purchasing Power

Year	Coffee Price (USD)	Bitcoin Price (USD)	Cost in Bitcoin (BTC)
2009	$1.50	$0.0007	2,142.86 BTC
2011	$2.08	$1.00	2.08 BTC
2012	$2.67	$5.00	0.53 BTC
2015	$3.25	$250.00	0.013 BTC
2018	$3.83	$6,500.00	0.00059 BTC
2021	$4.42	$50,000.00	0.0000884 BTC
2024	$5.00	$70,000.00	0.0000714 BTC

By 2024, the price of that coffee had risen to approximately $5, depending on location. Now, let's compare the purchasing power of Bitcoin over time.

- Ⓑ In 2009, buying a coffee for $1.50 would have cost over 2,000 BTC because Bitcoin had virtually no market value.

- Ⓑ By 2011, when Bitcoin had reached $1 per BTC, a coffee would have cost just over 2 BTC.

- Ⓑ By 2024, with Bitcoin valued at around $70,000, your cup of coffee would have cost just 0.0000714 BTC.

To put it another way, someone who bought just 1 BTC for $1 in 2011 could now buy over 70,000 cups of coffee at $5 each. In contrast, holding the $1 during that time would only provide enough money in 2025 to buy a few sips of coffee, if the coffee shop was being generous. In all seriousness, this shows the power of a scarce asset, which not only acts as an inflation hedge but truly preserves wealth.

Of course, the growth rate was much greater at the very beginning. But even looking at a more recent timeframe, the effect remains clear. Based on my data, in 2018, a cup of coffee cost £3.83, or 0.00059 BTC at the time. If you had bought $3.83 of Bitcoin and received 0.00059 BTC in return, by 2024 you could have bought nearly eight cups of coffee. In contrast, simply holding onto $3.83 in cash would no longer cover the cost of even one cup of coffee.

Bitcoin's ongoing ability to outpace inflation and preserve purchasing power remains one of its strongest advantages. Fig 10.4 illustrates this point clearly. As Bitcoin's value has increased, the amount needed to buy an equivalent coffee has gradually decreased to a tiny fraction of a single bitcoin, reflecting the currency's appreciation over time.

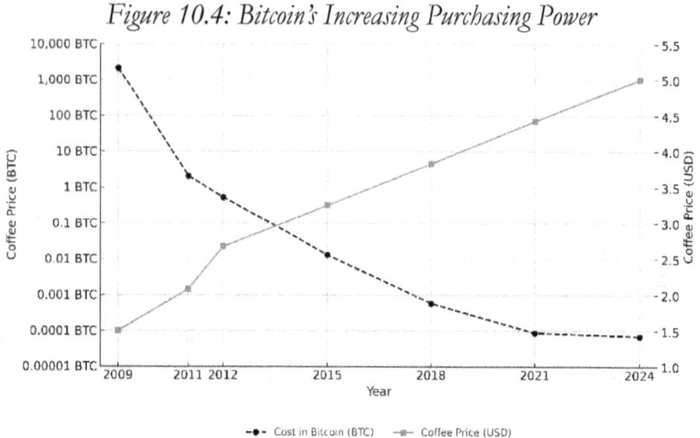

Figure 10.4: Bitcoin's Increasing Purchasing Power

We can now be in no doubt that Bitcoin's ability to store value has preserved and even multiplied its purchasing power compared with the decline of fiat currencies due to inflation and currency debasement. High inflationary events have decimated savings, forcing individuals to seek alternatives to protect their wealth. Bitcoin's fixed supply and deflationary design provides a compelling solution that can't be printed in unlimited amounts, due to inbuilt scarcity. The increasing value of Bitcoin has turned small early investments into significant purchasing power. Our example above showed how Bitcoin has outperformed the U.S. dollar for small purchases, but what about larger assets, like buying a house? People often say that purchasing a property is a good store of wealth and a solid investment, offering a way to preserve and grow purchasing power over time. Compared with simply holding onto national currency, real estate has historically provided long-term appreciation, shielding investors from inflation.

THE VALUE OF PROPERTY

Many people look at property price increases and assume they represent massive gains in real wealth. Take, for example, a three-bedroom terraced house in London in the mid-1980s, which could have been purchased for around £40,000. Today, if the same property were worth approximately £600,000, that would reflect a 1,400% increase over 40 years, or an uplift of £560,000. On the surface, this seems like an incredible investment, but when adjusted for inflation, the gain is less impressive.

Using inflation data from the Office for National Statistics, £40,000 in 1984 would need to be worth £176,000 today just to maintain the same purchasing power. This means that simply keeping pace with inflation required an average compound annual return of approximately 3.8%.

The actual price increase of the property (the nominal rate of return) amounts to an average compound return of 7% per year over the same period, which isn't astounding, but acceptable. However, more than half of this growth was simply keeping up with inflation, meaning the real rate of return was closer to a disappointing 3.2%. So, this means that the real price appreciation of this property over 40 years was around £424,000, which is the difference between £176,000 (current value of the initial £40,000) and £600,000. While it may seem an impressive increase in absolute terms on the initial investment, it is not quite as high as it looked at first glance. However, these opportunities are generally no longer present, as properties are now unaffordable for most people and excessive prices have constrained yields without the promise of price appreciation. To clarify:

$$\textbf{Real Rate of Return} = \textbf{Nominal Rate of Return} - \textbf{Rate of Inflation}$$

So, the real rate of return is simply the inflation-adjusted return. This illustrates a crucial point: it is not just about how much an asset increases in price, but how much it increases in real purchasing power.

THE ROLE OF RENTAL INCOME IN PROPERTY INVESTMENT

One major benefit of property as a store of value is that it also provides utility. You can live in it, meaning you do not need to rent accommodation from someone else, or you can rent it out for additional income. So, from an investment perspective, over a 40-year period if a property generated an average of £1,400 per month in rental income, you need to deduct an average of £400 per month for management, maintenance, and voids. The remaining £1,000 would be invested every month, say in low-risk bonds averaging 5%, for the 480 months on a compound basis, slightly skewing the data to take into account the fact that the rents would have been lowest at the start and highest at the end. By the end, this would have generated around £1 million in rental income. If we then add this to the £600,000 current valuation, we now arrive at a rough estimate of around £1.6 million, which also highlights the power of compound interest. Also consider that the 5% may not have been achievable over the whole period, and it doesn't consider tax or large renovation works, so the figure would have been closer to £1 million.

Either way, the point in fact is that property returns even in the golden period of property, produced significantly lower returns and more hassle than you would have achieved in gold or Bitcoin. Property offers stability and income generation, but its total long-term return lags more liquid and scarcer assets.

BITCOIN: A STORE OF VALUE VERSUS LARGER ASSETS AND OTHER INVESTMENTS

So, how do these assets compare with gold? Gold has long been considered a stable store of value, and property has been a go-to investment for wealth preservation. However, Bitcoin is now emerging as a strong competitor in this category.

Ⓑ In 1984, £40,000 could have bought around 1,250 ounces of gold at roughly $320 per ounce.

Ⓑ By 2024, that gold would have been worth just over £2.3 million at around $2,00 per ounce.

Now to make the comparison with Bitcoin fairer. Let's do a comparison from halfway between the start of Bitcoin's inception to the time of writing. Let's call it February 2017, when the Bitcoin price was approximately $1,000, and the gold price was approximately $1,500, and the property mentioned above was approximately £500,000 (converted at an approximate exchange rate of 1.25), making it $625,000, for a direct comparison. So, in February 2017, to buy this house it would have cost you 625 BTC, or 500 ounces of gold.

Fast forward to today with this property currently valued about £600,000, and then with the same logic as above, scaled up to approximately $1 million (taking into account rental income minus expenses and a current exchange rate of $1.35 to the £1). Now, the property including the generated rent, would be worth approximately 9.5 BTC (based on current price at the time of writing of $105,000) and 400 ounces of gold (based on the gold price of $2,500 at the time of writing). This is a clear indication that Bitcoin has dominated in this time frame.

Figure 10.5: Asset Price Increases (2017–2025)

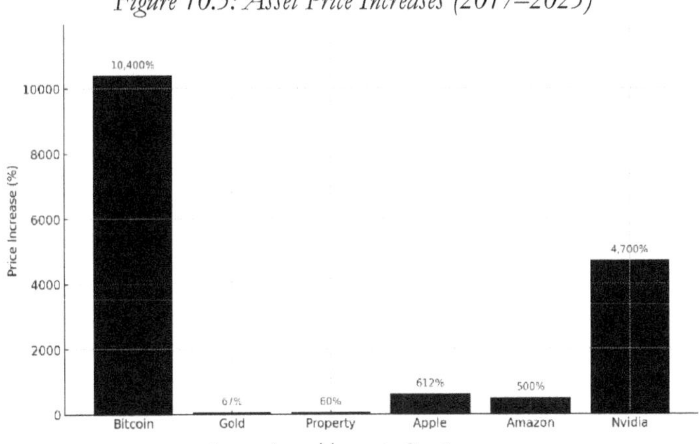

Source: https://www.tradingview.com

THE IMPACT OF CURRENCY DEBASEMENT ON WEALTH PRESERVATION

In recent years, excessive money printing and quantitative easing (QE) have further accelerated inflation. The result has been currency debasement, where fiat currencies lose their value not just due to supply / demand-driven inflation, but primarily because of aggressive monetary expansion by central banks, which we saw in Chapter 5.

In the last five years alone, the real inflation rate has exceeded 11% in many countries, meaning traditional investments have struggled to keep up. According to macro investor Raoul Pal, to truly preserve wealth, investors must now beat a hurdle rate of 8% (currency debasement) + 3% (structural inflation), which is a total of 11% per year. Property and bonds have largely failed to meet this hurdle. Granted, there are more advanced property strategies, and higher rates of return are possible, particularly in lucrative cities that could beat this threshold. Property has the advantage of leverage via mortgages, but on the whole struggles to reach double-figure returns. U.S. stock markets have generally performed better, particularly among tech stocks, as we can especially see in terms of Nvidia, but generally, even they face challenges from rising costs and interest rates.

Despite the issue of volatility, which we will focus on in the next section, this is undeniable evidence of Bitcoin's store-of-value properties, showing how holding Bitcoin over time has preserved and even multiplied purchasing power in a way that previous assets have never achieved.

While it is clear that the increasing price trajectory for Bitcoin is reducing, even if the per-annum gains of the last few years were reduced by more than 50%, it would still have performed better than all other asset classes.

While gold has provided steady returns and property has been a reliable investment, Bitcoin's scarcity, liquidity, and accessibility have combined to make it likely the strongest performing investment asset in recorded history. It's also a robust hedge against

214

inflation and currency debasement. Unlike property, Bitcoin is borderless, highly liquid, and requires no maintenance costs nor regulatory hurdles at the time of writing. Unlike gold, it can be instantly transferred and stored digitally without physical constraints.

Bitcoin has proven itself as an asset that not only preserves value but increases purchasing power over time. While property requires significant capital investment and maintenance, and gold relies on physical storage, Bitcoin is scarce, portable, and globally accessible. If you want to relocate to a different country, it could be problematic as you can't just pick up your property and move it across the world, just as holding gold creates similar problems and costs. History has shown us that a government can seize both property and money if it chooses. In 1972, Indians living in Uganda lost their properties, homes, and businesses and were forced to leave the country by then President Idi Amin. Everything was redistributed to Ugandans, who were often allies or military supporters of the president. Without a way to store your wealth away from a punitive regime, you could lose everything. While traditional assets still hold value, the clear portability and potential for long-term wealth preservation are making crypto assets extremely useful in the digital age, where wealth can travel with you if you decide or are forced to relocate.

AVERAGE WAGES AND USING DIGITAL ASSETS AS A RESERVE ASSET

It's not just that you might need to move assets swiftly in the event of a shock. With stagnating average wages, more and more people are falling into poverty due to currency debasement and inflation. In this case, blockchain investments could provide a way to help accumulate wealth over time. In the UK, the average salary stands at approximately £37,000, while in the U.S. it is around $66,000. Rising food and utilities prices, as well as for goods and services are making it extremely difficult for people to save money. Increased taxes across many countries has further impacted a global cost of living crisis. To amplify the problem, rising property prices are making it almost impossible for working people to get on the property ladder. For example, the average UK property price in 2024 was around £268,000, with homes in big cities like London often far surpassing £600,000. This is a staggering 16 times earnings, which is madness.

For those priced out of property in the short term, a carefully planned, slow and steady accumulation of assets, digital or otherwise, could present an alternative way to build wealth, and avoid falling into poverty. With a disciplined approach, individuals can gradually acquire digital assets over time, much like traditional savings or investment strategies, should they so choose. This gradual accumulation could also help to smooth out any volatility concerns, as averaging the purchase price out over months or years greatly reduces exposure to short-term price swings. In this way, by purchasing Bitcoin at a range of low and higher price points, it is possible to reduce the risks of market fluctuations while benefiting from long-term appreciation. The term "HODL" is used in the crypto community to describe just this. Buy and hold onto your Bitcoin. Have "diamond hands" and never sell.

Similarly, this method of building up and hoddling personal digital asset reserves can be applied to businesses and governments. As we will see in Chapter 13, Michael Saylor has strategically adopted this approach for his company, Strategy (formerly Microstrategy), and the government of El Salvador has begun a similar process. At the time of writing, the U.S. has announced plans to follow suit in 2025.

While Bitcoin's scarcity model and monetary policy make it a powerful long-term store of value, that's only part of the story. In today's fast-moving world, value also needs to move quickly. Whether it's businesses transferring capital, migrant workers sending money home, or simply paying for a coffee, speed and efficiency matter. So, how fast and efficiently can these networks operate, and what's it like to use them?

5. Speed and Efficiency

Bitcoin is widely regarded as the most secure cryptocurrency because of its transparency and highly decentralised characteristics. This makes it a reliable choice, particularly for high-value transfers, whether domestically or across borders, where maximum security is the priority. However, all cryptocurrencies are highly divisible, one of the qualities of sound money, meaning that they can be broken down into multiple decimal places. This can be useful for day-to-day transactions or smaller transfers, which are optimised for speed and efficiency. Networks such as Solana, Sui, Cardano and Avalanche, as well as many Layer 2 solutions built on Ethereum, like Arbitrum and Optimism, can process and settle payments in seconds, while maintaining a high standard of security.

Having been designed with speed in mind, these fast-settlement networks are ideal for a wide range of uses, from retail payments to high-frequency trading and near instant peer-to-peer transactions. In Chapter 8, we learned that Solana plus firedancer, as well as Cardano plus Hydra, could both become the fastest ever transaction processers in history, and by a wide margin. They could handle thousands of transactions every second, such that even over 1 million TPS is possible and with minimal fees. Ethereum's roll-up technologies also significantly reduce congestion and cost compared with Layer 1 execution, but generally not to the same extent as Solana, Cardano or Sui. Whichever cryptocurrency is used, the key advantage is that the underlying blockchain infrastructure can provide users with a high level of efficiency and much faster processing than traditional financial systems, and at a fraction of the cost.

6. Cross-Border Payments

As stated above, this applies across borders, and not just to transactions within a country. Borders define nations, but they have long been a barrier to moving money. Now, the borderless nature of blockchain technology has created a level of accessibility that is

breaking down financial barriers and making cross-border transactions faster, cheaper, and more efficient than ever before. The
fact that someone from Nigeria can send money to someone in
South Korea, or that someone in rural India can receive payments
from clients in New York using this technology, is making the
world much more interconnected.

Cryptocurrencies offer unparalleled efficiency and speed across
borders compared with traditional financial systems. For years,
the process of transferring money between countries with vastly
different economic sophistication could be slow and expensive.
The way the banking system works means that a payment from
Iceland to Indonesia, for example, would typically have to pass
through multiple third-party institutions such as SWIFT. This
entails counterparty and settlement risk if one of those intermediaries fails, not to mention than each one would take a percentage
of the transaction as fees.

7. TIME SAVING

But beyond the cost and risk, the time it takes for the payment
to clear is another significant issue. Due to differences in global
banking infrastructure, regulation, and time zones, international
transactions can take days to process. The period after the transaction that is required for it to settle is known as T + 1, or T
+ 2 and so on, depending on the anticipated number of extra
days. Payments must also pass AML checks and fraud screening,
further delaying the process. This system is neither cost-effective nor time-efficient for businesses or individuals who rely on
fast and affordable remittances. By contrast, all cryptocurrency
networks run 24 hours a day, and on weekends and bank holidays.
Without having to wait for banking hours, crypto transactions can
be executed and settled peer-to-peer in minutes or even seconds,
hugely benefitting business-to-business and retail transactions
alike. Eliminating T + 2 settlement periods for certain elements of
transactions in traditional markets also greatly improves liquidity
for businesses and individuals.

As we saw in Chapter 8, the cryptocurrencies from Ripple (XRP) and Stellar (XLM) are designed specifically for this purpose. They focus on speed and low transaction costs, making them suitable for frequent or lower-value international payments. Besides, both have high potential to scale to much higher volumes in the future. While Bitcoin transactions can take several minutes depending on network congestion, XRP and XLM transactions settle in seconds, providing a significant advantage for users who need quick and cost-effective transfers. This is why so many financial institutions have partnered with them as a complete upgrade for global payments via their outdated existing systems.

8. Cost Saving

Without intermediaries and regulatory barriers, Blockchain greatly reduces the infrastructure and compliance costs for payment providers. It is for this reason that many remittance start-ups are building their model with crypto from the outset. A good example of this is Bitso, a remittance-focused crypto exchange. Bitso uses blockchain networks and cryptocurrencies like XRP's RippleNet technology and its on-demand liquidity service to facilitate fast and low-cost transfers between countries that include the United States and Mexico. The company processes billions of dollars in remittances, offering a cheaper and faster alternative to traditional remittance services like Western Union. In 2024, Bitso's total transaction value exceeded $12 billion, with $6.5 billion of that attributed to U.S.–Mexico remittances alone, accounting for over 10% of the total remittance flow in this corridor. This marks a substantial increase from previous years, with $4.3 billion in 2023 and $3.3 billion in 2022.

And this infrastructure can be especially important for migrant workers, particularly those who need to send money home to support their families. Typically, these workers would have to pay between 5 and 10% of their total earnings to use traditional services, which can take several days to process a single transfer. Instead of paying $10–$20 in fees on a $200 transfer, a crypto transaction might cost less than a dollar and settle within minutes, even across continents. For workers earning modest incomes, these costs represent a significant burden that could otherwise go towards food, education, or healthcare for their loved ones. So, we can clearly see that both micropayments and large transfers can greatly benefit from the efficiency and cost-savings that cryptocurrencies provide.

9. FINANCIAL INCLUSION

"Blockchain can help address societal inequalities by providing access to financial services for all"

— Vitalik Buterin, Co-founder of Ethereum

So far in this chapter we have seen multiple benefits of blockchain technology. It is secure, efficient and can help with remittances, but how can it serve even more people around the world to help them become economically active?

With blockchain technology, financial services are no longer the preserve of richer nations. By lowering the barrier to entry, anyone with a smartphone and internet connection can participate, regardless of location and available banking infrastructure. The term "unbanked" refers to those without a bank account or access to financial services. Most unbanked individuals use only cash, and many have no insurance, pension, or other safety net, such as traditional retirement or savings accounts. According to the World Bank, 1.7 billion adults were unbanked in 2020 — down from 2 billion in 2014. With the emergence of the global financial technology (FinTech) industry, this number is finally trending sharply downward.

Building on the groundwork laid by FinTech, blockchain technology is positioned to assist in the next big movement of financial inclusion by bringing the numbers of unbanked people down even further. Bitcoin and other blockchain networks allow consumers to send and receive money securely, almost instantaneously, and at a fraction of the cost of a traditional bank. Apps like Bitpay and Circle Pay enable users to send funds with only a telephone number or email address, making it even easier to benefit from the technology. Alongside the effective cross-border remittance services we saw from XRP and XLM above, these methods can massively benefit people who could not otherwise have engaged in the global economy.

10. DeFi

And the benefits are not restricted to making transactions. Individuals and small businesses can now also utilise multiple financial services that would previously have been out of reach. Decentralised finance has created new financial opportunities for millions of people worldwide. For the first time in history, individuals can access financial services without needing a bank. As we saw in Chapter 8, the fact that programmable smart contracts from DeFi platforms are built on blockchain technology means that users can save, borrow, lend, and trade assets without centralised intermediaries.

This is even more important in regions where traditional banking is unstable or inaccessible, making DeFi a lifeline. Millions of people in developing countries lack access to a stable currency, compromising even basic living standards, let alone secure savings or access to fair lending options. DeFi bridges this gap by providing borderless financial tools that empower individuals to engage without the limitations of traditional finance.

Someone in Bolivia or Kenya, for example, can now access capital without a local bank. By using DeFi applications, they can start a new business, without borders or paperwork. With the divisibility advantages of the technology, even those with small amounts of savings can participate. Previously, this would have been extremely difficult and, in some cases, impossible.

With the ability to invest in cryptocurrencies and access decentralised lending platforms, new revenue streams are being created all the time. Even for highly developed countries, traditional banks have strict lending criteria, making it difficult for many to secure loans. However, with crypto-based lending, users can use their crypto assets as collateral and borrow against their holdings, in a secure smart contract on a reputable lending platform, whether in a fiat currency or another crypto asset. This ensures that funds cannot be manipulated or seized by a third party, providing a decentralised alternative to traditional loan systems.

Even in countries that suffer from hyperinflation or currency debasement, DeFi platforms provide access to stable assets that preserve value far better than local fiat currencies. Similarly, micro-lending through blockchain-based platforms enables small business owners to access capital without relying on restrictive banking systems. Self-custodied platforms, such as Compound and Aave use automated protocols to facilitate every element of the loan, from collateral to interest, and make them accessible to practically anyone at any time. This levels the playing field, granting financial freedom to people who had previously been excluded from the global economy.

11. NON-FINANCIAL APPLICATIONS

Aside from serving as an investment or transactional vehicle, blockchain technology is also unlocking entirely new business models and revenue streams. Picture a decentralised equivalent to platforms like Funding Circle, where blockchain technology could facilitate new forms of crowdfunding and peer-to-peer lending. It is not a huge stretch to imagine businesses and individuals relying on such alternative sources of funding, instead of traditional banks.

Another promising application is in supply chain management, where blockchain's transparent and immutable record-keeping can provide end-to-end traceability. In this way, businesses can track goods from point of origin to the final consumer, ensuring authenticity and quality, as well as ethical sourcing.

This is particularly valuable in industries like food and pharmaceuticals, where safety and regulatory compliance are critical. By leveraging blockchain, companies can also reduce fraud and improve inventory management. Examples include verifying organic certifications or as mentioned above, verifying that natural diamonds meet high ethical standards.

LOUIS VUITTON

With the rise of counterfeit products, particularly in the luxury goods market, blockchain provides a solution by offering verifiable proof of authenticity. To put this into context, it has been estimated that the cost to brands of the global counterfeit market in displaced economic activity was around $1.1 trillion in 2022. Now, by issuing digital product passports, brands can record a product's entire history on a decentralised ledger, ensuring that consumers can trace the provenance of high-end watches, designer handbags, and rare collectibles with complete confidence.

LMVH, the parent company of Louis Vuitton and many renowned luxury brands, has already embraced blockchain technology to combat counterfeiting and enhance product traceability. Through the Aura Blockchain Consortium, a platform developed in partnership with brands such as the Prada Group and Cartier, customers can verify the authenticity and ownership history of their purchases, with pseudonymity to protect their privacy. Even at this early stage of adoption, many companies are already implementing blockchain technology for these purposes, often without consumers even realising.

DOCUSIGN

In the past, contracts were always paper, whether for exchanging property, hiring employees, or agreeing legal terms. While these contracts served their purpose, they have always carried risks. Signatures can be forged and details can be altered. Then the internet arrived, making digital contracts easier to manage and store.

However, digital documents still have vulnerabilities. PDF files can be edited and electronic signatures, while widely accepted, rely on trust in centralised verification systems. This is where blockchain technology can step in. Contracts can be securely recorded and verified using cryptographic proof, ensuring that once an agreement is signed, it cannot be altered or manipulated.

> **"For customers that opt-in, DocuSign will compute a one-way cryptographic hash fingerprint for every completed transaction, and write the value to the Ethereum blockchain, the most popular blockchain for smart contracts in our view."**
>
> — Ron Hirson, chief product officer at DocuSign

In 2018, DocuSign began recording cryptographic hashes of agreements on the Ethereum blockchain, creating an immutable record of signed contracts. While the company has since explored alternative solutions with lower transaction costs than Ethereum, it remains actively invested in blockchain technology for secure contract management. In fact, DocuSign is just one of many businesses exploring private or hybrid blockchains to reduce costs while still benefiting from blockchain's security and transparency.

SOFT COMMODITIES

In the soft commodities sector, Covantis has been utilising the Ethereum blockchain to enhance post-trade processes in agricultural shipping transactions. Following its full production launch in 2020, Covantis is a collaboration by major agribusinesses, including Cargill and Viterra, that handled over 808 million metric tons of transactional volume in 2024. The platform leverages Ethereum's capabilities to digitalise and streamline operations, improving efficiency and transparency in the agricultural supply chain. Other blockchains like VeChain also support supply chain verification, allowing companies to track goods from production to sale.

These are just some examples of how companies are starting to use blockchain technology in day-to-day business operations. But it doesn't stop there. Blockchain can also transform digital identity verification by enabling individuals to securely store and share their personal data without relying on a centralised authority. This creates a self-sovereign identity model, where users control their own information, which is a key benefit of utilising web 3.0 technology. It's impossible to ignore how concerns of data mismanagement are becoming such a hot topic of conversation in this digital age, so these developments will bring comfort to many.

Large corporations and social media companies have so much access to people's data, as we discussed in Chapter 7, but blockchain and decentralisation could offer a remedy. Open-sourced data management means that no central authority will have access to personal information. This data is extremely valuable to large corporations, which can sell it to other companies for targeted advertising and promotions. Even worse, should this data get into the wrong hands, it could lead to fraud. At long last, blockchain technology might limit the extent of big corporations' access to personal data.

We saw earlier that blockchain has many other applications, such as streamlining Know Your Customer (KYC) processes in banking, improving online security, and providing access to services in under-served regions for people without traditional identity documents. With blockchain, identity verification becomes more secure and less prone to data breaches.

The benefits of the technology even extend to the heart of governance and democracy. Blockchain could create decentralised voting systems that would address the growing speculation about unfair voting practices. By adopting blockchain, votes could be recorded in an immutable and transparent ledger, making elections more secure and reducing the risk of fraud or tampering. If a voter could verify that their vote was counted without compromising their anonymity, it follows that their trust in the electoral process would increase. Blockchain-based voting can also make elections more accessible, enabling secure remote voting for people who are unable to visit polling stations.

We saw the advantages for gaming applications in Chapter 8. Real-world trading opportunities arise in the blockchain when in-game items, such as special swords, or in-game skins are moved from the game. Gamers are already taking advantage of this today and it's sure to gain more traction in the future. There is also huge potential to enhance transparency in the gambling sector with blockchain technology, including in lotteries, casinos, and sports betting, which is sure to disrupt many businesses operating in this sector. While in web 2.0, so-called trusted third parties are currently in control, blockchain and web 3.0 has the capabilities to perform these tasks with integrity and precision.

Across all these applications, blockchain has the potential to increase efficiency while reducing operational costs. As we've seen, it also improves transparency in a range of industries. As the technology continues to evolve and improve, it has the potential to transform the way we conduct financial transactions and interact with various industries.

DISADVANTAGES OF BLOCKCHAIN TECHNOLOGY

Despite the clear potential, blockchain's adoption and implementation still have a fair way to go. As we saw in Chapter 8, one of the biggest challenges is the complete lack of standardisation in the industry. There are so many different blockchain platforms, each with their own features and capabilities, but several that are very similar in design. So, how do we know which ones are worth using? How on earth can a business decide which ones will suit its needs? Then there is the steep learning curve. For both individuals and businesses, understanding and implementing blockchain certainly isn't straightforward. Not to mention the pressing questions of regulatory uncertainty and other fundamental risks that come with it.

1. Price Movements

So, let's first consider one of the most discussed disadvantages of cryptocurrencies, namely their susceptibility to extreme price volatility. "Bitcoin loses half of its value in two-day plunge." "Other cryptocurrencies also dropped this week. The world second largest digital currency, Ethereum, fell 46% this week while XRP lost nearly 40% of its value." Those were actual headlines from CNN on 13 March 2020, when the COVID-19 crash kicked in. We have all seen these stories, warning us about the risks and reporting wild price swings that make crypto seem as unpredictable as the first days of President Trump's second term in office.

Unlike stocks or fiat currencies, which tend to have relatively stable values over short periods, cryptocurrencies can experience explosive movements in a matter of hours or even minutes. This volatility creates uncertainty for users and businesses, particularly those considering crypto for everyday transactions or long-term investments. With prices constantly fluctuating, the risks are too great for many investors and routine transactions become impractical.

To put this into perspective, Bitcoin has experienced periods of both explosive growth and sharp decline. In 2017, it surged to nearly $20,000 before crashing to just over $3,000 a year later. Then, in the 2021 bull market, it hit a peak of over $68,000, only to lose more than three-quarters of its value within months during the subsequent market downturn. Price movements like these make it difficult for businesses to plan how best to accept cryptocurrency and for individuals to rely on it as a stable store of value. So, why have cryptocurrencies been so volatile?

There are several reasons. First, the relatively small market capitalisation of cryptocurrencies compared with traditional financial markets makes them more sensitive to large trades. Secondly, speculation plays a huge role, with prices often influenced by market sentiment and media coverage. Just as traditional markets respond to external events, regulatory announcements or macroeconomic shifts also have a big impact on cryptocurrencies. Remember, the crypto model is decentralised, so without the stabilising influence of central bank intervention, these fluctuations are only magnified. On top of that, speculative leverage trading adds even more fuel to an already burning fire.

Flash crashes. Liquidation events. Prices soaring or crashing in a matter of minutes. A short squeeze happens when the price of an asset rises sharply, forcing traders who bet against it (short sellers) to buy back their positions to limit their losses. This surge in buying pressure pushes the price even higher. On the flip side, a long squeeze occurs when an asset's price drops quickly, forcing traders who are long, i.e. they are betting on a price increase, to sell their positions to avoid further losses, or indeed a liquidation event, which drives the price down even further. This is gambling and greed is the main reason behind it. In a market that sees such big price appreciation and depreciation, why is leverage like this needed? It just adds another layer of volatility to an already unpredictable market. Engaging in this type of trading is not advised, and most people should avoid it unless they are highly experienced. The chances are high they will lose their shirt, their dignity, and possibly the money to pay their electricity bill as well.

The unfortunate reality is that too many people, especially young investors, see prices skyrocketing, jump into community chats, and get caught up in the hype. They see others posting huge leverage gains and think they can do the same. The problem is that no one brags about their losses. You will not see posts about the times they got liquidated or picked the wrong memecoin and watched it crash. In any market (crypto, FOREX, stocks, commodities), if you're using leverage, it means that you are borrowing funds to open a larger position than you could normally. Liquidation events have occurred as far back as the 1920s, where margin trading became popular. In 1929 many retail investors were liquidated from leveraged margin accounts during the Wall Street Crash, as we saw in Chapter 1. Liquidation happens when your losses hit a threshold where your collateral can no longer cover the position. Therefore, the exchange or broker automatically closes it to prevent further losses, and when leverage is high, it can completely wipe out your whole balance, or as known in the crypto community, get REKT. So, the reality is that people only share their wins, and that creates a false sense of success. It pushes others into risky trades they do not fully understand, often with money they cannot afford to lose.

With all this in mind, the question is, how can we manage price fluctuations? To mitigate the risks posed by volatility, several solutions have emerged. One term often used in the crypto community is applying a method of "dollar cost averaging". This means making periodic purchases of digital assets over the long-term to smooth out your average purchase price, as opposed to buying once at the peak and experiencing large unrealised losses should the price plunge. Additionally, stablecoins provide a more constant alternative for transactions. And financial tools like futures contracts, options, and other derivatives can help more experienced investors to hedge against market fluctuations. While these innovations address volatility to some extent, the underlying nature of cryptocurrencies as speculative assets means that price swings are likely to persist for the foreseeable future until the markets fully mature.

The high-risk, high-reward nature of cryptocurrency investments highlights the importance of education and risk management for anyone considering getting involved in the blockchain ecosystem. Without careful planning and understanding, users can find themselves exposed to significant financial losses, particularly during market downturns.

2. POTENTIAL LOSS OF FUNDS

As the last chapter emphasised, one significant risk of using blockchain technology is the potential to lose funds if access to private keys is lost. As we know, private keys are the cryptographic credentials that grant access to funds in a blockchain wallet. Unlike traditional banking, where lost credentials can be recovered, blockchain is decentralised and irreversible. Losing a private key means losing access to your funds, permanently. Many early Bitcoin users learned this the hard way, with some losing substantial amounts of cryptocurrency simply because they misplaced their keys or discarded the hardware that stored their wallets.

One of the most famous cases is James Howells, an IT worker from Newport, Wales, who accidentally threw away a hard drive containing the private keys to his Bitcoin wallet. Back in 2009, when Bitcoin was still in its infancy and had little monetary value, Howells mined around 8,000 BTC. He had stored the hard drive in a drawer but, during a reported clear-out in 2013, his ex-partner mistakenly threw it out, and it ended up in a local landfill site. By the time he realised his mistake, the value of the Bitcoin on the hard drive had soared. Despite his efforts to recover the drive, including proposing a full-scale excavation of the landfill, local authorities declined, citing logistical hurdles and the small matter of having to dig through tonnes of rubbish. At the time of writing, Howells' Bitcoin is valued at over $800 million, and his row on the spreadsheet will now show 8,000 BTC forever.

This example highlights the devastating risks of self-custody, especially in the early days when the need to secure private keys was not well understood. It reinforces the importance of secure storage and back-up strategies and shows the importance of proper education before engaging with the technology and risking any of your own money.

Fortunately, wallet technology and back-up strategies are continually being developed to address the challenge. Multi-signature wallets, for instance, require multiple private keys to access funds, reducing the risk of loss from a single misplaced key. We have already considered methods for storing seed phrases for hardware wallets and how custodial services can shift the responsibility away from users while balancing security with convenience. By preserving decentralised ownership while introducing practical safeguards, these advances help users manage blockchain's risks without compromising its core principles.

3. IRREVERSIBLE TRANSACTIONS

Not being able to reverse transactions is like a double-edged sword in blockchain technology. On one hand, irreversible transactions enhance security by preventing tampering. On the other, mistakes like sending funds to the wrong address or falling victim to scams cannot be undone. With no central authority to reverse transactions or recover lost funds, even a simple error can lead to permanent losses. So, double- or triple-check the details before making a transaction. Wallets and exchanges can save previous wallet addresses, and in some cases, these can be assigned names, making repeated transactions easier. However, when sending to a new wallet for the first time, it is always wise to do a test send with a small amount before transferring larger sums.

There are also times when the irreversible nature of blockchain transactions creates everyday challenges. Take online purchases, for example. If someone buys a product with cryptocurrency and the seller fails to send it, what happens then? Unlike traditional payments, there is no bank to step in and cancel or refund the transaction. You may recall we mentioned escrow services in Chapter 6, whereby funds can be held until receipt of the product is confirmed. In a similar way, smart contracts could also be programmed with terms that only release funds once delivery is verified. But how do you reliably feed that information into the smart contract? What if a buyer falsely claims they never received the item?

When purchasing physical goods, you are entirely reliant on the company's integrity to resolve disputes. Some businesses that accept crypto have sound reputations and customer service policies, but this is not always the case. Crypto transactions are final, meaning dishonest sellers could take advantage of buyers, leaving little recourse for complaints or refunds. Even large merchants using payment processors like BitPay or Coinbase Commerce have their own policies, and refunds are often left to their discretion. If there were a way to record which companies are reputable and to verify reviews on the blockchain, this could really build trust among buyers.

Fortunately, digital purchases are far less affected, such as for pay-per-view events or digital artwork, since these can be transferred through a smart contract instantly. But for physical goods and real-world assets, uncertainty needs to be addressed if it is ever going to achieve widespread use.

Credit and debit cards were never designed to be used over the internet. Similar concerns arose during the early days of internet commerce, when slow processes and fears over stolen bank details led to projects like DigiCash, aiming to let users pay online without exposing sensitive financial information. We look at a few potential solutions in the final chapter, but for now, it's enough to just understand that many questions are still unanswered.

4. Hacks and Security Vulnerabilities

The storage solutions we have discussed so far have focused on keeping private keys secure for hardware or software wallets and being cautious when holding funds on exchanges. But as we saw in the last chapter, hacks and security vulnerabilities remain a significant issue in the cryptocurrency and blockchain space. While Bitcoin itself has never been hacked, many altcoins and blockchain platforms with smaller networks or based on newer technologies have proven more vulnerable. This is especially true for platforms that rely heavily on smart contracts, DeFi protocols, and exchanges.

More programmable blockchains which facilitate smart contracts often introduce additional security risks, and history has shown that vulnerabilities can be exploited with devastating consequences. An infamous example is the DAO hack of 2016, when a flaw in the DAO's smart contract allowed an attacker to drain approximately $60 million worth of Ether. The impact was so severe that it led to a controversial hard fork, splitting the network into Ethereum (ETH) and Ethereum Classic (ETC). This meant that a large proportion of the miners and developers collectively agreed to redo a new version of the chain, by working on the block before the hack, to bypass the lost funds. And the remaining miners and developers continued operating on the original hacked chain. This effectively split the chain into two branches, leaving the hacked funds associated with the new ETC chain, thereby reversing the losses on ETH.

Five years later in 2021, the Poly Network Hack involved an attacker exploiting weaknesses in a cross-chain protocol, stealing over $600 million in cryptocurrencies. In a strange turn of events, most of the funds were later returned, but the breach exposed serious risks in blockchain interoperability and smart contract security.

Centralised exchanges, which hold large amounts of cryptocurrency on behalf of users, have long been prime targets for hackers. The Mt. Gox hack, where 850,000 BTC was reported stolen between 2011 and 2014, saw some later recovered from a cold storage wallet, leaving approximately 647,000 BTC still missing. It remains one of the largest losses in cryptocurrency history. More recent examples, such as the 2022 FTX hack, continue to highlight these risks and remind us how easily investor confidence can be undermined.

Even in early 2025, ByBit, a Dubai-based exchange, was hit by what has been described as the worst crypto hack in history, with close to $1.5 billion in cryptocurrency stolen. The company, which claims client assets are backed 1:1, has since assured users it would cover all losses. Nonetheless, the fact that hackers were able to breach the Ethereum wallet of one of the largest exchanges despite its extensive security measures, raises grave concerns.

Figure 10.6: Largest Crypto Hacks by Value (as of Feb 2025)

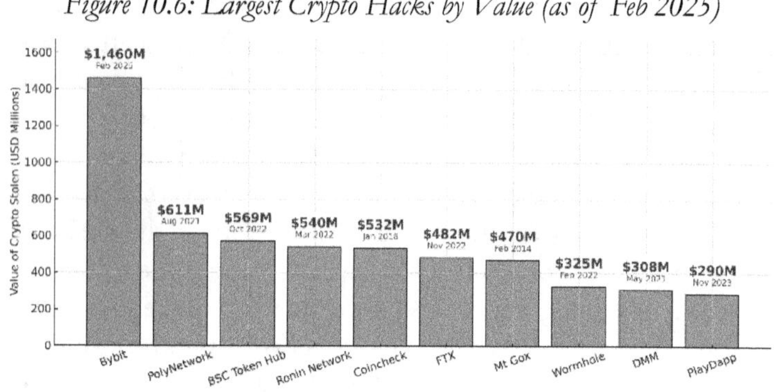

Source: The largest theft in history - following the money trail from the Bybit Hack

Investigators have attributed the cause of the hack to malware which tricked the platform into approving unauthorised transactions and sending the funds to the attacker. But, in many cases, criminals seem to be able to bypass firewalls and advanced security systems, often targeting employees through social engineering or phishing attacks rather than attacking the technology directly, however, this isn't always the case. Either way, it begs the question whether these platforms need to tighten up their internal security and compliance, as well as HR policies, with improved training to help address these issues.

In 2018, Bitcoin Gold (BTG), established in 2017 as a hard fork of Bitcoin (with the chain split into two branches, similar to the ETC/ETH example above), experienced an actual protocol-level hack, with a 51% attack occurring within the network. Ironically, the original decision to fork into Bitcoin Gold was because a proportion of the developers wanted to make the new chain less centralised than Bitcoin, but the lack of hashing power on the network enabled attackers to gain control of the majority of the network, reversing transactions and stealing over $18 million. Also in 2018, attackers targeted Verge Network (XVG), exploiting a flaw in their PoW algorithm, causing timestamp manipulation. This allowed the attackers to mine blocks quickly and steal 35 million XVG tokens, highlighting another protocol-level attack, which reminds us that these can occur.

But returning to the central discussion, the number of exchange-related hacks has never been higher. According to blockchain analysts Chainalysis, there were 303 hacking incidents in 2024, with $2.2 billion in stolen assets. This reinforces the importance of being cautious when storing large amounts of cryptocurrency on centralised exchanges.

To address these vulnerabilities, the blockchain industry continues to develop stronger security measures. Smart contract auditing has become standard, whereby independent firms review code to detect vulnerabilities before deployment. Enhanced security protocols, such as multi-signature wallets, cold storage, and decentralised exchange designs that reduce custody risks are being implemented to protect against theft. As we saw in Chapter 9, decentralised insurance platforms are increasingly providing users with a safety net, offering coverage for losses due to hacks. These advances reflect a growing awareness of the importance of security in the blockchain ecosystem.

However, it's important to put this into perspective. Fraud still plagues established banks and lenders. In the U.S. alone, over $10 billion was lost to financial fraud in 2023, spanning identity theft, unauthorised bank transfers, credit card fraud, scams, and more. So, while no system is entirely risk-free, it's clear that financial fraud is not confined to cryptocurrency. What matters is how both industries continue to tighten their security measures. In the crypto space, ongoing innovations in security are helping to mitigate vulnerabilities and build trust, just as traditional financial institutions work to strengthen their own defences.

5. Regulatory Uncertainty: lack of legal protections, and illegal activities

Nor is it solely security concerns that stand in the way of mainstream adoption. A lack of clear government regulation is also one of the biggest obstacles. While blockchain offers freedom and innovation, it also introduces significant risks, so without consistent rules, concerns around financial crime and money laundering grow unchecked. This lack of oversight increases the risk of fraud, scams, and market manipulation, as the protections for consumers are limited. At the same time, until governments fully address tax evasion and illicit activities, the absence of clear oversight leads would-be investors to hesitate over fully embracing the technology.

While such cases represent only a small fraction of blockchain transactions, scrutiny has increased, as regulators aim to encourage innovation while preventing misuse. In Bitcoin's early days, transactions took place on Silk Road, a dark web marketplace that facilitated the sale of illegal substances, firearms, and other illicit goods. Although authorities cracked down on platforms like this and Silk Road was shut down in 2013, with its successor, Silk Road 2.0, later closed down by authorities in 2015, citing growing concerns over cryptocurrency's use in financial crime.

But it is not just illicit activity that raises concerns. Without clear legal protections, in a decentralised model individuals have nowhere to turn when things go wrong. A shocking example was the collapse of FTX, once one of the largest cryptocurrency exchanges in the world.

In late 2022, it was revealed that FTX had misused billions in customer funds to cover losses in its sister company, Alameda Research, a quantitative trading firm. Rather than leaving them untouched, customers' funds were secretly funnelled into high-risk trading by Alameda. The mastermind behind both companies, Sam Bankman-Fried, had positioned himself as a rising star in crypto, attracting major investments from both Silicon Valley and Wall Street. Under his leadership, FTX had grown into the third-largest cryptocurrency exchange for derivatives trading.

Then, in November 2022, everything unravelled in just three days. The collapse wiped out $150 billion in market capitalisation from the top 15 cryptocurrencies. The value of the exchanges' native FTX token (FTT) plummeted and created a liquidity crisis that sent customers rushing to withdraw their funds. As panic set in, shockwaves were felt throughout the crypto industry, shaking market stability and fuelling calls for stricter regulation.

When the full extent of the mismanagement was exposed, both FTX and Alameda Research filed for bankruptcy, leaving millions of customers unable to access their funds. It became the largest bankruptcy in cryptocurrency history to date, wiping out billions and further undermining trust in the broader crypto ecosystem. Bankman-Fried was later sentenced to 25 years in federal prison on 28 March 2024 for orchestrating the multiple fraudulent schemes, and it has taken until May 2025 for creditors to start to receive payouts from the former exchange. What had once been a powerhouse of the crypto industry turned into one of its greatest scandals, highlighting the risks of an unregulated market.

To make matters worse, another platform experienced difficulties due to the FTX disaster. BlockFi was a centralised platform that had financial exposure to both FTX and Alameda Research. It promised to provide yield for holding cryptocurrencies, including Bitcoin and Litecoin. Although its bankruptcy may not have been solely due to mismanagement or bad intentions, the fact that it offered yield on PoW assets, in hindsight, was questionable.

Platforms paying yield on PoS cryptocurrencies, like Ether, make more sense, as those assets are pooled and staked to earn native rewards. As we know, PoW chains instead have miners, so they don't generate yield on their own. So, how did platforms like BlockFi pay out returns on Bitcoin and Litecoin? The likely answer is through lending out the cryptocurrency or in some cases, wrapping these assets, such as wrapped Bitcoin (wBTC) and deploying them into DeFi protocols, as discussed in Chapter 8.

In BlockFi's case, much of the yield was generated by lending customer funds to derivative platforms like Alameda Research and concentrating risk in a way many users didn't fully understand. This ultimately contributed to BlockFi's bankruptcy, although around 50–60% of lost funds were eventually returned to users after a lengthy court unwinding of the company. Either way, the cautionary tale is clear: be wary of putting cryptocurrencies on centralised platforms to generate yield. Regardless of their intentions, the added counterparty risk can lead to significant losses.

But the chaos did not end with BlockFi or FTX. Another high-profile case involved Changpeng Zhao, better known as "CZ", the founder and former CEO of Binance, the world's largest cryptocurrency exchange. In November 2023, Zhao pleaded guilty to violating U.S. anti-money laundering laws, specifically the Bank Secrecy Act, by failing to prevent illicit activities on the Binance platform. As part of a plea agreement, he resigned as CEO and was sentenced to four months in prison in April 2024. Binance also agreed to pay a $4.3 billion fine to settle related charges. At the time of writing, Zhao has nonetheless sought a presidential pardon from President Trump of the U.S., following the full and unconditional pardon issued to Silk Road founder, Ross Ulbricht in January 2025. Sam Bankman-Fried has also been open in his quest to also have his sentence revoked.

These all raise questions about whether major financial crimes in the crypto space are being taken as seriously as they should be. While the picture regarding oversight has been recently blurred, these examples expose how the absence of regulation leaves investors vulnerable, reinforcing the need for clear legal frameworks to establish safeguards. How else can legitimate businesses find a level playing field using cryptocurrency? Indeed, how would institutional investors enter this market without clear guidelines? We will explore this topic in greater depth in Chapter 13, but for now, it is important to understand that if we want the industry to evolve, establishing clear rules and protections is essential for attracting broader participation.

6. Limited Adoption and Complexity

Another issue is resistance from traditional financial institutions, for whom blockchain seems a disruptive threat to the systems they have relied on for decades. These institutions operate with entrenched processes and legacy infrastructure that make integrating blockchain solutions difficult. We have spoken about the lack of regulatory clarity, but it's not just institutions that face challenges.

Complexity for users is another major issue. Understanding wallets, private keys, and blockchain networks can feel overwhelming, especially for beginners. This complexity often leads to costly mistakes, resulting in the permanent loss of assets. Despite its potential, and unless there aren't any other options, blockchain remains largely inaccessible to the average person. The steep learning curve creates a gap between what the technology can offer and ease of using it. For blockchain truly to go mainstream, simplifying the user experience is essential.

Businesses also face their own challenges. It takes a considerable level of technical expertise to implement blockchain technology, which many companies simply do not have. Developing and maintaining a blockchain network is not as straightforward as adopting standard software solutions, so education and awareness will play a key role in making blockchain more accessible.

Despite being over 15 years old and having achieved mainstream recognition, Bitcoin still struggles as a medium of exchange. We've seen that it has proven itself as a store of value and an investment vehicle, so why are everyday purchases still impractical? Transaction speed, network fees, and price volatility all make routine transactions like buying a coffee or groceries difficult with Bitcoin. While solutions like the Lightning Network are designed to address these issues, the reality is that Bitcoin is still a long way from replacing traditional payment methods in daily life.

Despite gaining popularity in recent years, most businesses and individuals still do not accept cryptocurrencies and blockchain as a form of payment. With limited current real-world use cases, they are unlikely to become a mainstream alternative to traditional financial systems any time soon. Even among the businesses that do accept Bitcoin, many immediately convert it back into fiat currency after a transaction, to avoid holding or using Bitcoin directly. Bitcoin's role as a true currency is thus weakened, highlighting the broader challenges of integrating blockchain-based systems for general use.

Overcoming these hurdles will require a combination of improved accessibility and regulatory clarity, as well as user-friendly interfaces to increase trust in the technology. However, until industry innovations achieve widespread adoption, the gap between blockchain's potential and its everyday adoption will remain.

7. The Ultimate Trade-Off

We have already extensively reviewed why security and decentralisation are so fundamental to blockchain networks. Without strong security, there would be little reason to adopt the technology. It would simply be safer to stick with fiat currencies. Trust and adoption depend on security, and as we have seen with cryptographic proofs in Chapter 6, particularly elliptic curve cryptography, make blockchain networks virtually impossible to hack. Just to be clear, the hacks detailed in this chapter instead usually exploited weaknesses in key management or employee awareness at exchanges, and vulnerabilities in smart contracts. Therefore, it is important to fully distinguish between the two.

Decentralisation is just as important. Bitcoin has set the standard, proving that a system without central control can function securely and independently. The whole point of cryptocurrency is to move away from traditional financial structures, where central authorities have historically controlled the supply of money, leaving them open to manipulation and currency debasement. However, not all cryptocurrencies are equally decentralised. If control over a network is concentrated among a small number of users or a limited group of validators, it risks shifting back towards traditional systems. XRP, for example, has faced criticism for relying on a select group of validators, leading some to argue that it leans too close to centralisation, despite being marketed as a decentralised network.

THE BLOCKCHAIN TRILEMMA

This brings us to one of the most debated challenges in blockchain technology: the Blockchain Trilemma. This refers to the trade-off between three essential aspects of blockchain networks: security, scalability, and decentralisation. The question is, can a blockchain truly optimise all three at once, or does prioritising one always come at the cost of another? Does increasing scalability inevitably lead to more centralisation? And do the most secure and decentralised networks struggle to scale efficiently? This debate is ongoing, and it lies at the heart of blockchain development, as projects attempt to achieve perfect balance.

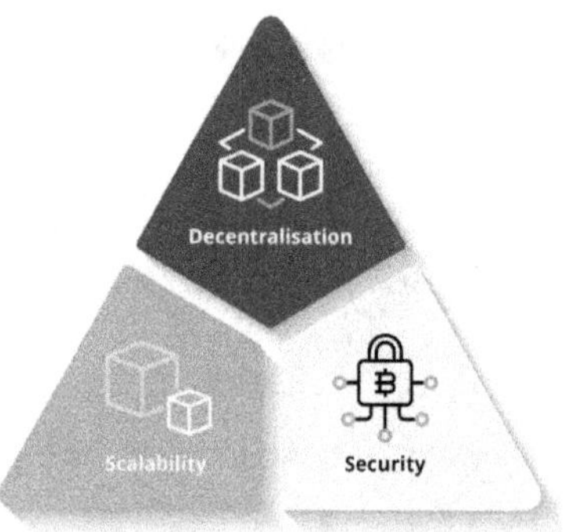

SCALABILITY

Scalability has long been one of blockchain's biggest challenges. As we have extensively discussed, networks like Bitcoin and Ethereum can only process a limited number of transactions per second, leading to congestion and delays when demand is high. This not only slows down transaction times but also drives up fees, making networks less efficient and more expensive to use.

Some blockchains, however, prioritise speed and scalability over decentralisation. XRP, for example, is highly scalable, capable of handling a large number of transactions quickly and efficiently, though its centralised structure remains in question.

Balancing decentralisation and scalability is crucial, especially when comparing blockchain with traditional payment systems like Visa and Mastercard, which have been claimed to process approximately 24,000 and 5,000 transactions per second (TPS), respectively. Although Solana has surpassed these figures in tests, if blockchain payment systems are ever going to see widespread adoption, solving scalability issues will be critical. Without significant improvements, blockchain networks will struggle to handle global payments, DeFi, and other large-scale applications effectively.

Transaction Costs

One of the biggest drawbacks of some blockchain networks is high transaction fees, especially during times of heavy demand. On networks like Ethereum, fees can skyrocket during congestion, pushing up the cost of sending funds or interacting with dApps. These high fees can discourage smaller users, limiting blockchain's accessibility for everyday transactions. If the technology is to achieve mainstream adoption, transaction fees must be more affordable and predictable. For example, when Bitcoin block rewards reduce in future halvings, a concern is that the fees would need to increase considerably to maintain miner profitability and sustain the network.

Scalability solutions will be key to reducing costs and making the blockchain a viable alternative to traditional financial systems. As we saw with the example of DocuSign, high fees for Ethereum made contract hashes on the network expensive, so the company had to explore other blockchain solutions.

Bitcoin operates on a blockchain that prioritises decentralisation and security. As we have seen, it remains the most secure network, thanks to its PoW consensus mechanism and the thousands of nodes worldwide that verify transactions. While its transaction speed is low compared with traditional payment systems, Bitcoin still allows a significant global user base to transact daily.

Layer 2 Solutions

Nevertheless, Bitcoin's processing capacity is a major limitation. The Lightning Network speeds things up, particularly for microtransactions, but does not yet provide the scalability needed to function as a standalone global currency. One of the leading firms advancing Lightning infrastructure is Blockstream, co-founded by Adam Back, who helped lay the foundation for Bitcoin itself. However, the concentration of development, funding, and infrastructure in the hands of a few entities has raised questions about the network's decentralisation. In theory, the Lightning Network was meant to be a permissionless, peer-to-peer solution. However, in practice it has meant that liquidity and channel management often favour larger operators, making it harder for smaller participants to compete, which goes against the whole philosophy of Bitcoin.

SCALABILITY VERSUS SECURITY TRADE-OFF

While it is generally accepted that a public blockchain can only optimise two out of the three key elements of the blockchain trilemma at any given time, efforts to overcome this are ongoing. Solana and Sui aim to prioritise both scalability and speed within their networks. By using variations of PoS and parallel consensus mechanisms, they achieve thousands of TPS, bypassing the more secure but slower PoW model. The inevitable sacrifice, however, is security and decentralisation relative to Bitcoin. This raises one of the biggest questions in blockchain development: Which consensus mechanism is best, PoW or PoS? Each has clear advantages, but striking the right balance remains an ongoing challenge.

PoW

PoW has established itself as a highly secure way to validate blockchain transactions, and Bitcoin is its most successful implementation. Its strength lies in being tamper-resistant, thanks to a decentralised network of miners competing to validate transactions.

However, as we've seen above, PoW struggles with scalability. Bitcoin's maximum capacity of around 7 TPS makes it inefficient compared with Visa and other traditional payment systems.

This lack of scalability limits PoW's practicality as a global payments system. Should PoW systems remain primarily a store of value rather than a medium of exchange? The slow transaction speeds indicate that solutions such as Layer 2 protocols are necessary for PoW networks to become competitive for everyday transactions. Other PoW-based chains, like Litecoin with 56 TPS and Dogecoin with around 33 TPS, offer slightly better performance. However, these are still far below the capabilities of traditional banking systems and significantly lower than many PoS-based blockchains.

PoS

PoS was developed for enhanced scalability and efficiency, enabling faster transactions and at lower costs. Unlike PoW, which requires expensive mining equipment, PoS simply requires users to stake cryptocurrency to help secure the network, lowering the barriers to entry. But this still could lead to the risk of validators with larger stakes holding too much influence over the network. If a small group of people control a network's cryptocurrency supply, PoS chains risk becoming significantly more centralised than Bitcoin. While hybrid models like Polkadot's Nominated Proof of Stake (nPoS) attempt to balance decentralisation with efficiency, concerns remain about whether these systems can match PoW's long-term security and resilience.

HOW DO THESE CONSENSUS MECHANISMS COMPARE?

PoW chains generally lack advanced smart contract functionality, as they were designed primarily for security, decentralisation, and reliability as peer-to-peer payment networks. Bitcoin's scripting language, for example, is intentionally limited, supporting only basic functions for simple transactions. This reduces potential vulnerabilities but also limits programmability. PoS-based networks, by contrast, often prioritise smart contract execution, facilitating more complex applications while adding security risks.

Imagine you're hosting a large dinner party. To serve everyone efficiently, you set up multiple food stations, with different sections handling starters, main courses, and desserts. This is similar to PoS, where transactions can be processed in parallel to improve speed. However, if too many guests gather at one station or food runs out, maintaining oversight becomes difficult.

Now, consider a single serving station where all the food is distributed from one place. It might take longer, but you have full control over the process and can ensure nothing is overlooked. This is like PoW, which is less scalable but highly reliable and secure. The choice between these models depends on the specific needs of each blockchain network.

SOLVING THE TRILEMMA

New blockchain projects are constantly emerging, each aiming to address the challenges we've discussed. One of the first decisions they face is how to distribute tokens because managing issuance and supply plays a critical role in long-term sustainability and economic function. This is why understanding tokenomics is essential before investing in or using any digital asset.

In many cases, seed investors and project creators hold a significant portion of the total supply, releasing only a small percentage to the open market. This concentrated ownership raises concerns about centralisation and market impact. For example, in the case of Sui, more than 70% of its total supply is still held by early investors and developers. As these tokens are gradually unlocked and sold, they can dilute existing holdings and drive down prices, much like what happens when a company issues new shares. To make matters worse, these token-unlocks often happen in increments, so as more tokens enter circulation, the value of each token decreases. This is akin to currency debasement, where elevated money supply reduces purchasing power.

Understanding the difference between circulating supply and fully diluted market capitalisation is crucial when investing in cryptocurrency. Circulating supply refers to the number of tokens currently available on the market, similar to the number of shares actively traded on a stock exchange. In contrast, fully diluted market capitalisation accounts for all the potential tokens that could enter circulation, including those still held by early investors or project teams. If a significant percentage of a token's total supply has yet to be released, new investors risk being diluted when these holdings enter the market. When these unlocks do occur, early investors or large holders may choose to sell their tokens, flooding the market and putting downward pressure on price.

However, unlike currency debasement or newly issued company shares, which have no fixed limit, a fully diluted market capitalisation represents the maximum number of tokens that can ever exist. This means that once all tokens are released, no further dilution can occur. For long-term sustainability, token distribution should be as decentralised as possible, allowing individual users to stake their holdings and contribute to network security as validators.

CHOOSING THE RIGHT BLOCKCHAIN FOR THE RIGHT USE CASE

At this stage in blockchain development, choosing the right network depends on a user's priorities. If security is the most important factor, Bitcoin might be the best choice, just as large bank transfers come with additional security measures and fees. For high-frequency transactions or smart contract functionality, networks like Solana and Sui may be more suitable. If the goal is fast and low-cost cross-border payments, XRP or XLM might be the preferred option. As the technology evolves, users will have more flexibility in choosing the right blockchain solution for their needs.

It is also important to acknowledge that as of 2025, there are over 10,000 cryptocurrencies in existence. This number will only rise with platforms like pump.fun and similar tools on Solana, Ethereum, or Base that allow anyone to launch a token with minimal technical knowledge. Many of these tokens are meme-coins or purely speculative, without any utility. Fewer than 500 of them demonstrate any meaningful utility or active development engagement. Of these, any that have strong active communities can nonetheless have value, as we saw in Chapter 8. Popular plat-forms, such as Coin Market Cap or CoinGecko have an extensive list of cryptocurrencies on the market and as of May 2025, the 500th spot holds a valuation of around $50 million, going all the way up to Bitcoin at number one, valued at over $2 trillion.

As opposed to stock valuations, which have fundamental revenues and operating profits, the crypto valuation is basically a vote of confidence from the market, and it reflects the level of adoption of each project. For new users, the vast number of these projects and their saturation, is clearly very fragmented and confusing. While innovation should be encouraged, most of these cryptocurrencies will most likely become worthless in the coming years. Unfortunately, hyped or fun tokens often divert attention from projects that are genuinely solving problems or building meaningful infrastructure layers that will benefit blockchain for many years to come.

8. Fragmented Ecosystem and Interoperability Issues

The question then is, if there are so many cryptocurrencies avail-able, how do we know which will stand the test of time? Which will enable the technology to reach its full potential? At this stage we can only go by the available information on each project in terms of which seem to have the most potential. We must decide which ones solve real-world problems and have unique use cases, as well as how much developer adoption there is, and consider the transactional volume that a particular chain can process every day.

But aside from valuations, the projects that survive need to be surrounded with a more seamless and interconnected system.

Right now, the ecosystem is so highly fragmented that these different cryptocurrencies and blockchain networks struggle to communicate with one another. This lack of standardisation and interoperability creates barriers, making it difficult to transfer assets or data across platforms efficiently.

Although Layer 0 solutions like Polkadot and Cosmos are working to bridge these gaps, a fully integrated system is still a long way off. It's as if there were multiple banks, but no easy way to send money between them. The infrastructure is not yet sufficiently developed to allow smooth, automated interactions between blockchains. It's true that blockchain bridges are currently being developed to enable cross-chain transactions, but as yet they are still limited and insecure. For blockchain to function as a truly connected ecosystem, sending Bitcoin to a Solana-based protocol should be as simple as sending an email. This would require stronger Layer 0 infrastructure, allowing different blockchains to interact without friction.

Besides interoperability, a seamless user experience is also crucial. Ideally, users should only need to connect their wallet to an interface, while the underlying blockchain infrastructure handles the complexities in the background. Making cross-chain transactions as secure, automated, and user-friendly as possible will be key to blockchain's widespread adoption.

9. Bitcoin Energy Consumption

Stepping back from infrastructure layers, one of the most widely debated topics in blockchain is energy consumption. We have all seen the headlines regarding PoW networks like Bitcoin, which require intensive computational work to validate transactions, this makes them highly secure but also energy intensive. The difficulty level rises as more miners join the network, which enhances security but also drives up electricity consumption. This has led to criticism, especially in a world striving for more environmentally friendly solutions.

PoS, on the other hand, eliminates the need for mining, relying instead on token holders to secure the network. This dramatically reduces energy consumption but can come at the cost of security and decentralisation. Ethereum's transition to PoS illustrates how a blockchain can move towards energy efficiency while balancing security. But Bitcoin mining remains a controversial topic. Critics argue that its energy use is excessive, while supporters highlight its increased reliance on renewable energy and its role in securing an alternative and potentially fairer financial system.

In 2025, estimates from Statista, suggest that Bitcoin is set to consume roughly 176 terawatt-hours (TWh) of electricity. This equates to approximately 0.5% of total global electricity consumption. This is comparable to Poland and its carbon footprint is comparable to that of Qatar, using approximately 98 megatons of CO2 per year, according to digieconomist. Furthermore, just over 800,000 visa transactions (1198kWh) and just over 1.4 million visa transactions (668kgCO2) each equate to the same energy use and carbon footprint of a single Bitcoin transaction, which is shocking in comparison.

The energy consumption for a single Bitcoin transaction of 1,198 KW/h of electricity could power an average U.S. household for roughly 41 days. On the face of it, it certainly doesn't make for pleasant reading. However, without bypassing it as an excuse or justification, it is worth noting that worldwide banking is estimated to consume around 258 TW/h of energy annually. Therefore, it is at least worth considering the broader context.

PUTTING BITCOIN'S ENERGY USE INTO PERSPECTIVE

Many industries consume vast amounts of energy yet are rarely subject to the same scrutiny as Bitcoin mining. Traditional banking systems, with their branches, ATMs, and data centres, still require significant energy to operate. Gold mining, another store of value, demands immense resources for extraction, processing, and transportation, albeit nowhere near that of Bitcoin. Large corporations, including tech giants like Amazon and Google, maintain energy-intensive data centres, while manufacturing and global logistics networks also have substantial carbon footprints. ChatGPT and zoom have also recently received attention for their respective high consumption of energy. Even city-based office spaces consume huge amounts of electricity. Think of all the electricity used for lighting and computing, as well as heating and air-conditioning that is required for these businesses to function. The real debate should focus on whether Bitcoin's benefits justify its energy use, and how efficiently that energy is sourced.

RENEWABLE ENERGY IN BITCOIN MINING

To address environmental concerns, Bitcoin miners are increasingly turning to renewable energy sources, including hydroelectric, solar, wind, and geothermal power. Many operations seek out areas with surplus renewable energy, ensuring that excess electricity that might otherwise go unused is put to productive use. For example, Iceland and Northern Scandinavia have vast reserves of geothermal and hydroelectric energy. Bitcoin miners, such as Genesis Mining and Bitfury, have established data centres there to take advantage of this surplus energy. Additionally, the lower temperatures in these regions reduce the hardware cooling costs, showing how harnessing underutilised energy can be positive for bitcoin mining operations.

Some mining companies are also investing in carbon offset initiatives, with the aim of neutralising their emissions. Meanwhile, advances in crypto mining hardware and cooling technologies are continually reducing the energy footprint per transaction. While concerns over energy consumption are valid, ongoing technological innovations and sustainability efforts are contributing to a more energy-conscious blockchain ecosystem.

WHERE DOES BLOCKCHAIN GO FROM HERE?

What's clear is that blockchain is no longer just an emerging trend. It is becoming a major force in financial technology, offering borderless transactions, decentralised finance, and new ways to store and transfer wealth. For the first time, you can send value anywhere in the world without relying on a bank. Stablecoins offer alternatives in inflation-hit economies, while blockchains like XRP and Solana have made sending funds faster and cheaper. And Bitcoin is continuing to establish itself as a real store-of-value asset, one that rivals gold. As the technology continues to evolve and improve, it has the potential to transform the way we conduct financial transactions. Supply chains are becoming more transparent, allowing businesses and consumers to track products from production to delivery. And we're only really getting started.

Despite all this progress, challenges remain. Scalability, regulation, and energy consumption continue to pepper the conversation. The blockchain trilemma is still an issue, though Layer 2 solutions and PoS-based networks are making transactions faster. Concerns about PoW's energy use are being tackled through renewable mining initiatives and improved efficiency.

So, what's next for blockchain? Will governments manage to regulate crypto without holding back innovation? Can blockchain transactions ever become as seamless as using a credit card? And as businesses quietly integrate blockchain behind the scenes, will people even realise they are using it at all? As industries evolve, blockchain is becoming more than just a financial tool. It is laying the foundation for new business models and digital ownership as we know it.

This brings us to one of blockchain's most talked about and unpredictable applications, NFTs, or Non-Fungible Tokens. Some call them a revolution. Others say they are a bubble, a fad, or the future of digital ownership, depending on who you ask. For some, they are a way to give artists and creators more control, while others just see them as overpriced JPEGs. The reality? Most probably somewhere in between. After all, a few years ago, who would have thought people would be spending six figures on pixelated punks, cartoon apes, and digital sneakers they can't even wear?

What if NFTs are more than that? What if they redefine ownership, creativity, and value itself? Could they change the way we buy, sell, and interact with digital assets? And if we are already seeing luxury brands, musicians, and even real estate projects experimenting with NFTs, where does this all lead?

In the next chapter, we explore how NFTs are pushing the boundaries of blockchain technology and challenging everything we thought we knew about digital ownership.

Chapter 11

NFTs and Their Use Cases

> *"A way to almost cut out the middle man a little bit more for artists, directly sharing art with our fans and hopefully artists make more money."*
>
> — Jared Followill, Kings of Leon

Thus far, we've explored a variety of crypto use cases, including briefly touching on NFTs in Chapter 8, but we need to go further to understand how they function and fit into the cryptocurrency ecosystem.

In recent years, Non-Fungible Tokens, or NFTs, have emerged as one of the most innovative and disruptive applications of blockchain technology. As we know, unlike Bitcoin, Ether, or traditional forms of currency, NFTs are not interchangeable; each one is unique. This non-fungible quality makes them ideal for representing rare, one-of-a-kind digital items, such as artwork or collectibles or even property in virtual worlds.

So, what are NFTs? Essentially they are digital assets powered by the same blockchain technology that underlies cryptocurrencies. But instead of serving as a medium of exchange, NFTs authenticate ownership of various types of content. The blockchain keeps a record of who owns what, ensuring that each NFT is singular, trackable, and verified by the network. This brings the new dimensions of scarcity and originality to digital assets. Dimensions that had only previously been possible with physical items.

NFTs are making a significant impact across multiple industries, from art and entertainment to real estate and gaming, enabling creators and collectors to engage in a global digital economy. As we delve deeper, we'll explore the mechanics of NFTs, their major use cases, and how they might shape the future of ownership and identity in an increasingly digital world.

HOW NFTS WORK: THE TECHNICAL FOUNDATION

The foundation of NFTs lies in blockchain technology, with its transparent, secure records of ownership. It's this uniqueness that sets NFTs apart. From early origins on the Ethereum blockchain, now other networks, such as BNB Chain and Solana also support NFTs. Each one exists as a token created through a smart contract that outlines an NFT's ownership details and links it to the specific content it represents. This content can include audio files (like music), video clips, images, graphics, or even interactive media and documents.

NFTs are most commonly developed using Ethereum's ERC-721 standard, specifically designed to make unique, indivisible tokens. In contrast to standard ERC-20 tokens, which are fungible and interchangeable, ERC-721 tokens add all-important uniqueness to each NFT. These are joined by ERC-1155, an emerging standard that allows both fungible and non-fungible tokens to be made within a single smart contract, which can be useful in applications such as gaming where a mix of unique and common items exists. For example, in-game items might equally include a general token exchange and specific artefacts.

The process of minting an NFT involves linking the asset to a blockchain entry. This entry contains metadata that points to the asset's location, often stored off-chain on services like IPFS (InterPlanetary File System) due to the high storage costs on blockchain networks. Once minted, NFTs can be traded on dedicated marketplaces including OpenSea, Rarible, and Foundation, where each transaction is recorded on the blockchain. This provides a public, tamper-proof history of ownership.

NFTs essentially redefine ownership by allowing anyone to verify or trade a digital asset as they would a physical one. The technology supports a broad range of applications that empower artists, musicians, and gamers with new ways to create and capture value.

EXISTING NFT USE CASES

From its original digital art roots, NFTs have now leveraged blockchain technology to transform digital ownership and access. By linking digital items to unique tokens, NFTs can establish authenticity in exciting ways across many industries. By verifying ownership, this opens up fresh new revenue streams and business models.

NFTs initially became popular in the art world, by enabling artists to sell digital works with verified ownership, thereby reassuring buyers of their exclusivity. Artists can now mint and sell their creations, often incorporating programmable royalties that provide them with a share of resale profits as well. This new model has changed how art is bought and sold, creating opportunities for artists to reach global audiences directly.

In the gaming sector, NFTs offer a way to own and trade in-game assets, such as character skins, weapons, and other collectibles. This ownership is unique to the player and often transferable between games or platforms. Games like Axie Infinity, Decentraland, and The Sandbox go even further by allowing players to trade the assets they hold with real-world value.

This means gamers can profit from their gameplay efforts by adding an economic layer that traditional gaming lacks.

Since 2021, musicians and content creators have been exploring ways to distribute exclusive content directly to fans using NFTs, harnessing their ability to function like certificates of ownership on a blockchain. In this sector, NFTs can represent music tracks, albums, concert tickets, or even interactive experiences, bypassing traditional distribution channels and giving artists greater control over their work. Artists such as Kings of Leon and Grimes have led the way in releasing albums as NFTs, providing fans with collectible music experiences, often including special perks.

You might then ask how multiple copies of the same album can be sold as NFTs and still be unique? Although they are non-fungible, artists can release multiple NFTs that represent the same album or track by creating various editions of the content. This means that each NFT within an edition is still unique on the blockchain, even though it represents the same content. Therefore, the artist can create 1,000 or 10,000 copies of the same musical content, each with a unique identifier on the blockchain. This differs from traditional digital files, which can be infinitely copied. This is an important distinction, as each version of the content is stored on the blockchain, confirming its authenticity and scarcity.

For example, when Kings of Leon released their album as an NFT, the band offered versions that included not only the music but also genuinely valuable perks — such as the standard album NFT (with bonus content), exclusive audiovisual and digital artwork, VIP concert passes and even golden tickets granting lifetime front-row seats. These weren't just digital gimmicks; they offered real-world experiences fans could actually use.

After COVID-19, this model became especially beneficial, as it allowed artists to monetise their work even without touring, which has become difficult with the rise of music streaming on platforms like Spotify and Apple music. Traditionally, intermediaries that include record labels and streaming platforms usually take the lion's share of their profits. By using NFTs, artists can sell directly to fans and build a unique relationship with them, and as mentioned above, earn royalties whenever the asset is traded in the future; a feature that historically hasn't been possible with physical CDs or cassettes. This gives artists more control over their creative and financial arrangements while providing fans with ownership of limited-edition content.

NFTs are also changing the concept of ownership in virtual spaces, where users can buy, sell, and build on digital land. Platforms like Decentraland and The Sandbox have created metaverse worlds where virtual land can be bought and used for various purposes — whether that be for setting up businesses or hosting events. Unlike earlier platforms like Second Life, a virtual world launched in 2003 by Linden Lab, where users built digital spaces without true ownership, NFTs enable verifiable, tradeable property rights. Virtual land has become an investment opportunity, offering the potential for users to rent or sell digital properties at a profit, and this works because ownership can now be secured on the blockchain.

For example, each parcel of virtual land can be customised to host unique experiences, such as digital storefronts or immersive art galleries, where users can purchase items or pay to view the exclusive content. These are essentially virtual shopping districts, full of digital stores selling items like clothes or trainers. In the metaverse you can even see in 3D how certain items look from all angles. Not only could you purchase them for your avatar in the virtual world, but also as real-world products linked through e-commerce integrations. The benefits for retailers from digital traffic mean that real-world revenue could be generated through direct sales and advertising. Just like prime real estate in the physical world, high-traffic, desirable locations in the metaverse would also hold greater value and so attract higher investment.

Retail is not the only potential beneficiary. Owners of virtual land can also generate profits by leasing their spaces to other users or businesses, or by re-selling their land for profit when the value increases alongside rising platform adoption and limited supply. Only time will tell which platforms will be most favoured moving forward.

Ticketing companies are beginning to integrate NFTs to offer secure, verifiable tickets for live events. Event organisers can minimise fraud and ensure authenticity with NFTs, since each ticket can be traced back to its original source. For companies like Ticketmaster, NFT-based ticketing systems provide a way to simplify ticket verification as well as giving fans a collectible item and a treasured record of attendance.

In 2022 the company collaborated with the Flow blockchain to enable event organisers to issue NFTs tied to tickets. This began with the distribution of over 70,000 unique commemorative NFTs to attendees of Super Bowl LVI, each reflecting the holder's specific seat location. Building on this, Ticketmaster extended its partnership with the NFL for the 2022 season, offering NFTs to attendees at 101 select games, including at least three home games for all 32 teams. By August of that year, Ticketmaster had minted over 5 million NFTs on the Flow blockchain through various events.

In March 2023, Ticketmaster introduced a feature allowing artists to provide NFT holders with special access to events. This "token-gated ticket sales" system was piloted with heavy metal band Avenged Sevenfold, enabling holders of their Deathbats Club NFTs to access exclusive concert experiences. The band reported NFT sales of around 1,000, creating a social media buzz at the time and a cohort of very happy fans.

Eventually, the intention is that an NFT would serve as the digital ticket, granting entry to an event. It would be stored in a digital wallet and scanned at the venue for access, much like QR codes or e-tickets. However, venues and event organisers currently need significant technology upgrades to scan and verify NFT tickets successfully. Many attendees are also not yet familiar with

NFTs or digital wallets, making a full transition impractical for now. That said, I hope this book helps demystify this concept and as Linkin Park would say, brings us "one step closer" to a world where digital NFT tickets are the norm.

THE ADVANTAGES OF NFTS

NFTs are redefining the concept of digital ownership, introducing unique features and opportunities that extend beyond traditional digital assets. By leveraging blockchain technology, creators, businesses, and consumers can use NFTs to establish authority and ownership, both in traditional and digital industries. These innovations open up once-unimaginable possibilities, offering a glimpse into how NFTs might further integrate into our digital lives and add value across various sectors.

VERIFIABLE OWNERSHIP AND AUTHENTICITY

NFTs' ability to establish verifiable ownership and authenticity of digital items is particularly important in preventing forgeries of collectible and unique items. Unique items often need verification or marking to indicate authenticity. Problems can arise, however, as hallmarks and signatures can be forged, and professionals can often also be dealers. Ulterior motives, such as angling for a lower price to flip it for a higher profit, mean that there also needs to be a level of trust. This might come across as cynical, but unless you personally know the professional or the exact provenance of an item, your only option is simply to trust them. By contrast, NFTs are unique and are recorded on the blockchain, so have built-in verification, therefore creating a trustless system, as with Bitcoin and other cryptocurrencies. Buyers and collectors can confirm the origin and authenticity of an NFT-backed item, which reduces the risks of forgery or duplication often seen in traditional markets.

Empowering Creators with Direct Access to Markets

Currently creators rely on intermediaries like galleries, record labels, or publishers to reach their audience. NFTs, however, allow them to retain greater control over their work, by being able to set their own prices on platforms like OpenSea and Foundation. There, creators can showcase and sell their NFTs independently, ensuring they keep the majority of profits, unlike traditional models where intermediaries take significant cuts.

Programmable Royalties for Ongoing Revenue

With built-in programmability, creators can also embed royalties directly into their NFTs. This earns creators a percentage every time their NFT changes hands in the secondary market. This mechanism, facilitated by smart contracts, ensures creators continue to benefit from the increasing value of their assets, a feature that isn't easily achievable in traditional art and collectibles markets. For example, an artist can earn a recurring 10% royalty on every re-sale of their work. When *Sabado Noche* by Jean-Michel Basquiat was sold for $14.5 million in March 2025, that would have earned his estate $1,450,000, on top of the $1,070,000 the same work's sale would have realised on its hammer price of $10.7 million in 2019.

Enhanced Utility in Virtual and Real Worlds

NFTs go beyond static assets because they can represent a wide array of digital and physical experiences. When used to trade digital land parcels in the metaverse, this creates exciting economic ecosystems within digital space. And as we've seen, NFTs are even useful for event ticketing, where they ensure authenticity and enable a collectible record for attendees. This versatility allows NFTs to blend digital and tangible experiences, offering a unique bridge between the two realms.

INCREASED PRIVACY AND OWNERSHIP CONTROL

Unlike assets managed by centralised entities, NFTs give owners direct control of their assets. This gives NFT holders greater privacy and independence, as they need no authentication or security from mainstream institutions. The self-custody aspect of NFTs resonates with the broader ethos of decentralised finance, enabling users to manage and secure their assets personally.

A NEW PARADIGM FOR COLLECTIBLES AND INVESTMENT

For collectors and investors, NFTs offer an innovative approach to diversifying their portfolios by owning digital assets whose value can appreciate. High-profile sales of NFTs, particularly in digital art and virtual real estate, have attracted investors looking to own unique pieces of the digital world.

DISADVANTAGES AND CHALLENGES IN THE NFT ECOSYSTEM

Despite their clear benefits, NFTs face significant challenges that impact the broader digital asset ecosystem. Addressing them is crucial for NFTs to fully realise their full potential in the digital economy.

SECURITY AND INTELLECTUAL PROPERTY RISKS

First, unauthorised minting of copyrighted or stolen content remains a big concern. This complicates the legitimacy and enforceability of ownership rights. In response, clearer intellectual property (IP) protections and security protocols are essential if we want to build trust and verify the authenticity of NFTs.

NFTs REPRESENTING REAL-WORLD COLLECTABLES

NFTs can create a digital certificate of ownership for a physical item, such as an antique. This process creates a digital twin through high-quality images or 3D scans, which can be minted on the blockchain. The NFT stores metadata that details the item's history and authenticity, helping to verify its origin. This allows the NFT to be traded digitally, without moving the physical item until necessary.

However, limitations of the current technology mean that care is required to ensure the authenticity of the antique and the reliability of the seller. While NFTs can verify digital ownership, they don't guarantee that the physical antique is genuine, as independent verification or professional appraisal would still be necessary. Additionally, trust mechanisms are essential after purchase to confirm that the seller will indeed ship the antique to the buyer. To alleviate concerns, platforms are developing processes like escrow services and smart contract terms, to hold funds until the item's delivery has been verified. While these steps do add protection, further development is needed to create a fully secure and seamless system for physical-to-digital asset trading.

MARKET VOLATILITY AND SPECULATION

It's no secret that the NFT market has also faced significant price swings and speculative buying. While high-profile sales and skyrocketing valuations have attracted mainstream attention, they have also led to rapid and often unsustainable price inflation. This volatility can raise the barrier to entry, deterring long-term collectors and prompting concerns about the stability of NFTs as an asset class. The speculative nature of NFTs has also caused scepticism about their intrinsic value, with some expecting the bubble to eventually burst.

There was an actual NFT bubble in 2021, when projects like Bored Ape Yacht Club (BAYC) became massively popular, with celebrities paying exorbitant amounts for these digital collectibles. Justin Bieber purchased a Bored Ape for $1.3 million, significantly above its market value, while Jimmy Fallon and Madonna spent $216,000 and $570,000, respectively, on their apes. Snoop Dogg also invested heavily, incorporating NFTs into his online identity. The highpoint was reached in December 2021, when a work titled *The Merge* by an artist named Pak was sold for $91.8 million. While these high-profile purchases boosted NFTs' visibility, the market's speculative nature became apparent as by 2022 many had lost significant value. To put this into context, as of May 2025, *The Merge* is now worth in the region of three and a half million dollars, which is a monumental collapse of over 96%.

PLATFORM SECURITY RISK

Market volatility aside, the decentralised and often anonymous nature of NFT platforms can expose users to security risks, including hacks and vulnerabilities lurking in smart contracts. If a platform is compromised, assets stored in wallets connected to that platform could be at risk, leading to potentially irreversible losses. Additionally, IP issues are posing a complex problem in the NFT space. Just as you would with fungible tokens, a remedy for this would be to disconnect your wallet from the platform and transfer the NFT to a cold storage solution like Ledger, before disconnecting it from the internet as protection from hacks.

LIMITED ADOPTION

The limited adoption of blockchain wallets becomes clear when you compare them to, say, Apple Wallet, which most people already know and trust. While both are called wallets, don't be confused about the different purposes they serve. Apple Wallet is all about digitising everyday things like credit cards, boarding passes, and event tickets, making them easy to manage in one place. It's built to fit seamlessly into the traditional financial system that we all use every day. MetaMask or Trust Wallet, on the other hand, are focused on web 3.0 technology and blockchain-based assets, encompassing cryptocurrencies, NFTs, and decentralised apps. The key difference is that Apple Wallet relies on centralised systems, while MetaMask uses decentralised networks to give users more control and transparency. For the more complex, blockchain-based approach of wallets like MetaMask to become mainstream for everyday transactions, broader understanding and adoption of NFTs still has some way to go.

Addressing these disadvantages is essential for NFTs to grow sustainably and to be accepted as a transformative digital asset class. Solving these challenges will require ongoing improvements in blockchain technology, the establishment of regulatory guidelines, and broader industry efforts to create a secure, equitable, and climate-conscious NFT ecosystem.

HOW TO BUY, SELL, AND MINT NFTS

For anyone interested in participating in the NFT market, understanding the basics of buying, selling, and minting NFTs is essential. Whether you're a creator looking to mint your work as NFTs or a collector considering adding digital assets to your portfolio, engaging with NFTs typically involves some foundational steps, including setting up a cryptocurrency wallet, choosing a platform, and navigating marketplace fees.

SETTING UP A WALLET AND BUYING CRYPTOCURRENCY

To interact with NFTs, you'll first need a cryptocurrency wallet compatible with NFT marketplaces, as most transactions involve blockchain-based tokens. Wallets like MetaMask, Trust Wallet, and Coinbase Wallet are popular choices that support Ethereum and the other cryptocurrencies commonly used for NFTs. Once your wallet is set up, you'll need to buy some cryptocurrency (often Ether, or ETH, for Ethereum-based platforms) for transactions and paying associated gas fees on NFT marketplaces. You can purchase ETH or other cryptocurrencies from exchanges like Coinbase, Binance, or Kraken, then transfer it to your wallet. And just like that, you will be ready to dive into the world of NFTs, whether that means collecting digital art, picking up a piece of virtual land, or even securing a cartoon monkey of your very own.

CHOOSING AN NFT MARKETPLACE

There are several NFT marketplaces to explore, each with unique characteristics that cater to different types of NFTs and audiences:

- Ⓑ **OpenSea**: One of the largest and most versatile marketplaces, OpenSea hosts a wide range of NFTs, including art, music, virtual land, and collectibles.
- Ⓑ **Rarible**: A community-driven platform that allows users to create, buy, and sell NFTs. Rarible offers a similar range of NFTs as OpenSea but emphasises community participation and user governance.
- Ⓑ **Foundation**: This marketplace primarily focuses on digital art and provides a curated experience for artists and collectors, creating a gallery-like atmosphere for high-quality works.
- Ⓑ **SuperRare**: A more exclusive platform, SuperRare curates its digital art collection carefully, showcasing works from established digital artists.

Each of these platforms has its own listing and gas fees for processing transactions.

BUYING AND SELLING NFTS

Once you've chosen a platform, the buying process is straight-forward. You can browse the available NFTs and either bid for items in an auction format or purchase them at a fixed price if the seller has set one. After completing the transaction, the NFT will appear in your wallet, as well as being on view in the marketplace or from a compatible NFT wallet.

Should you decide to sell an NFT, you can list it for auction or set a fixed price. If you are the creator, you can then decide whether to set royalties, giving you a percentage of future sales if your NFT is re-sold. When someone purchases your NFT, the funds (minus platform and gas fees) are transferred to your wallet. Future sales earning royalties are taken as a percentage of the sale price after gas and platform fees have been deducted.

Minting Your Own NFTs

So, having examined how to trade NFTs, what about minting your own? Minting an NFT involves creating a new token on the blockchain to represent your digital asset. This is done directly through NFT marketplaces, where creators can upload their work (such as an image, audio, or video file) and mint it as a unique NFT.

Here's a simplified overview of the minting process:

1. *Choose a Platform*: Select a marketplace that supports minting, such as OpenSea, Rarible, or Foundation.

2. *Prepare Your Content*: Ensure the file you're minting meets the platform's specifications in terms of file size, format, and quality.

3. *Upload and Mint*: Follow the platform's instructions to upload the file, add metadata (such as title, description, and properties), and set royalty options if desired. Once you confirm, the marketplace will process the transaction, deducting any required gas fees so it is ready to list for sale.

Security and Best Practice

When engaging with NFTs, security is essential. Always use strong passwords for your wallet and enable two-factor authentication (2FA) where available. Avoid clicking on unfamiliar links and only use verified platforms to prevent phishing attacks. Additionally, be mindful of gas fees when buying, selling, or minting, as fees can vary and the cost of transactions can mount up.

By understanding how to navigate the NFT ecosystem, you can actively participate in this growing digital economy, whether as a creator, collector, or investor. As with all investments, careful research and secure practices are key to maximising your experience and success in the NFT space.

THE START OF THE NFT JOURNEY

The future of NFTs holds tremendous potential, shaping not only digital art and collectibles but many other sectors as they discover new ways to leverage this technology. Whether it produces advances in utility-focused NFTs to more real-world blockchain solutions, the next phase of NFT development will address the limitations listed above, while pushing boundaries in areas far beyond art and gaming.

UTILITY AND REAL-WORLD APPLICATIONS

As NFTs evolve, there's growing interest in their utility beyond static digital assets. Their capacity to grant exclusive access, privileges, or real-world benefits to holders is increasingly in demand. For example, NFTs that are tied to membership programmes can provide access to events, communities, or experiences exclusively to token holders. This emerging use case, seen in projects like Gary Vaynerchuk's VeeFriends, allows NFTs to serve as tickets that unlock both digital and physical experiences, adding a practical layer to owning them.

Alongside entertainment, NFTs are finding applications in sectors such as real estate and logistics. Real estate NFTs aim to represent the ownership of physical properties, to make real estate transactions more transparent and efficient. The benefits of doing this are clear for someone wanting to get into the property market but who can't afford a full property.

However, if 100 tokens represented ownership of a property, without any special rights, or distinction between each token, then these would be fungible and classed as the real-world asset (RWA) tokens that we discussed in Chapter 8. By contrast, if each token represented a distinct aspect of the property — such as a particular room (like a hotel room) or a whole floor in a property, which had specific rights, then it could be structured as an NFT, since each would carry unique attributes.

These both differ from a property fund like a REIT that manages disparate property interests on trust, whereas buying a property NFT or a RWA would mean becoming a part owner in a particular property. Over time, it would be feasible to increase ownership in that property. In the way that properties are listed on the Land Registry in the UK, this could be listed on an immutable, decentralised blockchain.

In the case of logistics, NFTs act as digital certificates that track the origin, movement, and authenticity, as we discussed in the last chapter, in terms of luxury goods or diamonds. They can be used in supply chain management to ensure transparency and accountability for consumers and stakeholders at every stage.

NFTs also have the potential to transform identity verification in the decentralised digital domain. By representing unique, verifiable credentials on the blockchain, NFTs could serve as proof of identity, certifications, or qualifications, giving individuals full control over their digital identity. When hiring employees or evaluating students, it would make verifying an applicant's credentials so much quicker and easier, removing the need to double check every detail at source, and cutting down identity fraud. This shift towards decentralised identity management, which companies like Microsoft are exploring, could revolutionise industries such as education, employment, and personal data privacy. Again, as with all other blockchain-based personal details, these credentials will need careful management to avoid security risks from smart contract vulnerabilities.

INTEROPERABILITY AND CROSS-CHAIN SOLUTIONS

The demand for interoperability between different blockchain networks is driving the development of cross-chain NFT solutions. As with traditional cryptocurrencies, the goal is to enable NFTs to move seamlessly across multiple blockchains, expanding their utility across platforms. As we know, protocols such as Polkadot and Cosmos were designed to facilitate interoperability, creating a more unified blockchain ecosystem where NFTs and other assets can exist across different chains. However, tighter cross-chain security is needed, which will not only broaden the use cases of NFTs but also promote a more connected digital ecosystem, where assets, identities, and experiences can be fully portable. Indeed, they may hold the key to the widescale uptake of blockchain networks by securely breaking down the silos between them.

REGULATION AND CONSUMER PROTECTION

With the rapid expansion of the NFT market, regulatory bodies worldwide are beginning to pay closer attention. Issues around intellectual property rights, consumer protection, taxation, and financial regulations are all being explored to prevent fraud and protect investors. As governments and regulatory bodies examine the potential risks, clearer guidelines are likely to emerge, shaping the legal and regulatory landscape for NFT transactions. Regulation could help legitimise the space, offering safeguards that encourage mainstream adoption while mitigating the associated risks.

EMERGING TRENDS FOR NFTS

NFTs have already made a significant impact on digital ownership. However, their full potential is still emerging so what could the future hold for NFTs? By integrating NFTs more deeply into both digital and real-world economies, they could revolutionise every aspect of our daily lives. It's important to remember that the utility of NFTs in sectors like real estate is only just becoming apparent. Yes, virtual land sales are already taking place in the metaverse, but there's such great potential for NFTs to redefine ownership in real-world property transactions.

Think about how we buy and invest in property today. It's long, stressful, and packed with paperwork, but blockchain could revolutionise all of that. With properties securely recorded on a distributed ledger, the process could become seamless and secure. Imagine surveyor reports, property checks, and the other essentials being locked into smart contracts. Not only would this be more efficient, you would instantly know exactly what you're buying, instead of waiting on solicitors for every step.

Stay with me a little longer. Imagine automated, secure blockchain systems to which conveyancers could upload property searches or title deeds directly. This would all be verified and transparent. It would also be a much faster and smarter process with automated tasks, reduced workloads, and timely completion of processes. Property buying could move from being an ordeal lasting several months to a smooth, efficient transaction featuring greater security, fewer errors, fewer intermediaries, and more trust. Tokenising property and recording transactions on the blockchain could result in a faster process which is far less prone to fraud and be especially useful in complex cross-border global property transactions.

Supply chains are another area where NFTs may offer further transformative solutions. If customers could clearly see the origin and authenticity of their purchases, it could bring a whole new level of transparency, especially in industries where authenticity really matters, like one-of-a-kind artwork or luxury goods. Of course, for NFTs to reach their full potential, the infrastructure needs to scale. Right now, platforms like Ethereum 2.0 and Solana are working on more efficient systems to reduce costs and transaction fees, which could make NFTs far more accessible. Other blockchains like Flow and Polygon are also addressing scalability challenges, making it easier for creators and collectors to engage with NFTs in an affordable way.

As the NFT market continues to grow, there's no denying that regulation will play a huge role in shaping where it goes next, addressing intellectual property and consumer protections in particular. As platforms become more user-friendly, the potential for NFTs to reach mainstream adoption and reshape industries feels closer than ever. NFTs have completely changed how we think about value in the digital age, offering new ways to own and interact with assets. But it is important to recognise that value isn't just about digital art or collectibles. It's about something that touches every part of our lives through the financial systems we rely on every day. So, what happens when those systems start to fail? When trust in money itself falters, and the currencies we depend on lose their worth? These questions take us beyond the digital landscape and back to the crises that in recent times have reshaped economies and livelihoods around the world. And as we've partly explored previously, they might hold the key to why decentralised technologies matter now more than ever. As we come full circle, we're left with a pressing question, what happens when money itself loses its meaning?

Chapter 12

Hyperinflation Crises:

Case Studies and Wealth Preservation

What happens when the value of money diminishes before your very eyes? When it happens, hyperinflation is a financial catastrophe that devastates nations and upends the lives of millions. In this chapter we confront the harsh reality of hyperinflation and currency collapse in the modern era, exploring how nations have spiralled into economic chaos when their currencies became almost worthless. These are not mere history lessons, they're warnings of what happens when inflation runs unchecked, tearing through economies and leaving ordinary people to face the devastating consequences.

Could your entire savings really be wiped out overnight? Your pension become meaningless? Were people in the recent past truly left scrambling for basic necessities? These questions remain as relevant as ever today. Inflationary pressures are still brewing across all major economies, from Turkey to the UK, and even the U.S., reminding us of the fragility of financial systems and the impact such instability can have on people's lives. When a currency loses its value, the effects ripple far beyond numbers on a screen.

Historically, inflation referred to an expansion of the money supply, not just rising prices. Over time — particularly from the 1960s onwards — mainstream economics redefined it as a general increase in consumer prices (CPI). As Henry Hazlitt put it, "Inflation is an increase in the quantity of money and credit. Its chief consequence is soaring prices." This shift has helped obscure the true cause behind many economic crises, with unchecked monetary expansion. This reinforces our analysis of the failures of so many empires throughout history.

Savings disappear. Everyday essentials become unaffordable. Entire communities are left struggling to meet their basic needs. Hyperinflation isn't just an economic phenomenon, it's a human one. For those living through it, it means watching the value of their money erode at an unimaginable pace, erasing trust in the very systems meant to provide stability. And yet, the conditions that create these crises are not as distant or rare as we might think.

As economist Murray Rothbard warned, "The state is the only institution in society that can legally counterfeit money — and plunder society in the process."

As we delve into the case studies that follow, we'll explore why having a stable store of value is critical during times of economic distress. Stable currencies aren't just convenient, they're essential for maintaining confidence in a country's financial system. A faltering currency touches every aspect of life, undermining investments and eroding trust in governments and institutions.

We'll also examine how alternatives like gold have historically safeguarded wealth during periods of high inflation. And could new technologies hold the key to protecting wealth in a world where money itself is at risk of losing its meaning?

STABLE CURRENCY

As we have seen in earlier chapters, a stable currency forms the backbone of a thriving economy. This isn't only about consistent prices; it reflects trust and confidence in a nation's financial system. It helps keep prices steady, which is essential for economic growth and prosperity. When prices remain relatively constant over time, consumers and businesses can make informed decisions about spending, investment, and production, which in turn reduces uncertainty and encourages economic activity.

A stable currency also smooths the path for international trade. Foreign investors and trading partners are more likely to do business with countries that have stable currencies because it reduces the risk of currency fluctuations affecting the value of transactions. Stable currencies also promote confidence in a country's economy, thereby attracting foreign investment and stimulating export growth. This confidence is important to stimulate economic growth, create jobs, and improve living standards.

Not only this, but a stable currency supports central banks' efforts to control inflation by providing a reliable benchmark against which to set interest rates and monetary policy. By keeping inflation in check, a central bank can in theory preserve the purchasing power of the currency and promote long-term economic stability. In a virtuous cycle, this then greatly contributes to social stability by reducing the risk of financial crises and income inequality. When people have confidence in the value of their own currency, they are more likely to save, invest, and participate in the economy, leading to overall prosperity and well-being.

Currency Instability

Equally, the absence of stability can have catastrophic consequences. Hyperinflation, at the extreme end of currency instability, is one of the most devastating economic scenarios a nation can face. It's not just about skyrocketing prices, it's about the collapse of trust, savings, and livelihoods.

Two notable examples of hyperinflation, Zimbabwe in 2007–2008 and Venezuela in 2017–2018, offer stark reminders of how quickly entire economies can crumble when stability is lost. Let's look at how not having a stable currency has caused devastation and why alternative assets are increasingly seen as lifelines in times of economic distress. The question we must ask is this: what happens when money itself can no longer fulfil its purpose?

Case Study: Zimbabwe 2007–2008

In the early 2000s, Zimbabwe had already been grappling with economic instability, but the situation began to intensify by mid-decade. In the face of mounting deficits, the government's response was to increase the supply of money. As already established, a central bank will typically print money to help the economy during a crisis. In the old days, this literally meant printing new physical cash, but now it is mostly done digitally. The central bank simply adds digits to its balance sheet and adds money to the economy by buying government bonds or other assets.

At first, the impact on Zimbabwe seemed manageable, but it didn't take long for inflation to creep into everyday life. With borrowing suddenly cheaper, people felt encouraged to spend. As the supply of goods and services couldn't keep up with the additional demand this had created, prices for basic goods steadily began to rise, leaving households struggling as wages failed to keep up with the cost of living.

At the heart of the crisis was the government's reliance on excessive money printing to cover ballooning fiscal deficits. Facing dwindling tax revenues and mounting public spending, the Reserve Bank of Zimbabwe began creating vast amounts of new money to fund state operations. This strategy, known as monetising the deficit, flooded the economy with cash far in excess of what it could absorb. The surplus money eroded the currency's purchasing power, driving prices up ever faster. What initially seemed like a short-term solution quickly spiralled into economic catastrophe.

To add to the problem, Zimbabwe's agricultural backbone was severely weakened by controversial land reforms. Once celebrated as the breadbasket of Africa, Zimbabwe's commercial farms were forcibly seized and redistributed under the then government's Fast Track Land Reform Programme (FTLRP). While the aim was to address historical land inequalities, it disrupted agricultural production on a massive scale. Experienced farmers were replaced by less-skilled workers and crop yields plummeted. Food was in short supply, driving up prices for essentials like maize and wheat. For many families, finding enough to eat became a daily struggle, and in rural areas bartering replaced cash transactions.

As inflation accelerated, the government took increasingly desperate measures to address the crisis. In an attempt to stabilise the cost of goods, price controls were introduced. However, this backfired spectacularly, as businesses were unable to sell goods at a loss, so they began hoarding or withdrawing products from the market entirely. Shelves in grocery stores stood empty, exacerbating the shortages and fuelling further public frustration.

By 2007, hyperinflation had taken hold entirely. Prices were doubling almost daily, and the Zimbabwean dollar's value fell so rapidly that savings and pensions became meaningless. With no alternative, the central bank began printing larger denominations of currency, culminating in the now infamous one hundred trillion Zimbabwean dollar note. The note became a symbol of the crisis and sadly it was little more than a last-ditch measure. No amount of printing could keep up with the skyrocketing prices. A loaf of bread could cost millions in the morning and trillions by nightfall, making the currency effectively unusable.

The impact on everyday life was so severe that keyworkers including teachers and nurses were forced to abandon their jobs because their wages could no longer cover even basic transportation costs. Hospitals ran out of essential medicines. Schools shut their doors. Businesses closed. People queued for bread for hours, and even those who managed to secure food found themselves struggling to pay for it. For many, survival meant relying on remittances from family members abroad or turning to foreign currencies like the U.S. dollar and the South African rand.

The sad fact is that the Zimbabwean government had had several options that would have prevented, or at least mitigated, the crisis. These solutions would have required a mix of fiscal discipline, monetary restraint, and structural reforms. Instead of resorting to printing money, the government could have focused on cutting unnecessary public spending and reallocating funds to critical areas like agriculture and infrastructure. Rather than imposing price controls, the government could have offered subsidies or tax incentives to producers to stabilise supply chains and keep goods on the market. Letting prices adjust naturally, while focusing on improving supply, might have prevented the shortages and black-market activity that aggravated the crisis.

Had they enacted transparency and anti-corruption measures, the government could also have reassured investors and international partners, creating a more stable environment for investment. Strong property rights and incentives for investment, might also have encouraged long-term economic growth, instead of deterring foreign investors through land seizures and instability.

By 2009, the country had no choice but to abandon the Zimbabwean dollar in favour of the U.S. dollar and a basket of other currencies. Opportunities to negotiate a stabilisation programme with international institutions were missed, that could have provided funding and policy guidance to address the crisis. Rebuilding relationships with key trading partners and donors could have opened up financial and technical assistance. And investing in industries beyond agriculture, such as manufacturing or mining, could have provided additional sources of income and employment, while supporting entrepreneurship and SMEs, thus boosting economic resilience.

Sometimes, it isn't only a government's bad decisions and policies that can cause economic turmoil. External factors can also trigger a crisis. Only a few years after the Zimbabwe hyperinflation crisis, Venezuela was hit by extreme financial hardship in 2018.

A Tale from Venezuela: Carlos and the Vanishing Savings (2017–2018)

Carlos, a small business owner in Caracas, prided himself on running his family bakery, a legacy that had been passed down for two generations. Over the years he had carefully saved the equivalent of $10,000, a safety net to secure his daughters' education and protect his family's future. But by 2017, the whispers of economic instability had turned into a full-blown crisis.

The Venezuelan bolívar, once a symbol of national pride, was spiralling into worthlessness. Each day brought news of rising prices, and Carlos noticed it acutely in his bakery. A bag of flour that had cost 1,000 bolívars a month ago now cost 10,000. Bread, the staple of his livelihood, had to be sold at prices that changed daily, sometimes even hourly, just to keep up with skyrocketing costs.

At first, Carlos thought his savings would shield his family from the chaos. But as hyperinflation worsened, he quickly realised how wrong he was. The bolívars he had squirrelled away were losing value at an alarming rate. What could once have bought a year's worth of groceries could, by 2017, barely covered a week's supply of bread. Every time he visited the market, prices had doubled or tripled since the last foray. A loaf of bread costing 1,000 bolívars on Monday could cost 5,000 by Friday.

Carlos's story reflects what millions of Venezuelans endured as hyperinflation gripped the economy. By 2018, the annual inflation rate had reached an unfathomable 1,700,000%, rendering the bolívar practically worthless and forcing families to adopt desperate measures for survival.

THE ROLE OF OIL DEPENDENCE AND ECONOMIC MISMANAGEMENT

The roots of Venezuela's crisis lay in years of economic mismanagement, over-reliance on oil revenues, and political instability. The collapse of oil prices in 2014 exposed the fragility of an economy where over 90% of revenue depended on oil exports. For Carlos, this meant his already struggling bakery faced even greater challenges, as public spending cuts and dwindling consumer confidence impacted his business.

Instead of adapting to this new reality, President Nicolás Maduro's government doubled down on unsustainable populist policies, including heavy subsidies for food, fuel, and public services. To cover the growing fiscal deficit, the Central Bank of Venezuela began printing money at an unprecedented rate. This flood of newly created bolívars far exceeded the productive capacity of the economy, devaluing the currency and triggering runaway inflation. For Carlos, the bolívar that once represented security became a source of anxiety. Every time he withdrew money from his savings account, he knew its value would erode within days, sometimes even hours.

Compounding the crisis were strict currency controls that created a thriving black market for U.S. dollars. The official exchange rate became meaningless, and like many other small business owners, Carlos was forced to accept payments in foreign currency or barter goods with his customers. Even these measures barely kept his bakery afloat.

HUMAN IMPACT: DAILY SURVIVAL AMID ECONOMIC COLLAPSE

The human cost of Venezuela's hyperinflation was devastating. Necessities like food and medicine became unattainable for families like Carlos's. By 2018, a kilogramme of rice could cost more than a month's minimum wage. Grocery store shelves were barren. Carlos, once proud of his ability to feed his community, found himself standing in long queues to buy bread, which he had previously baked himself.

Malnutrition surged as families skipped meals to stretch their dwindling resources. Hospitals, overwhelmed by shortages of critical supplies, could no longer provide adequate care. For Carlos's family, the fear of getting sick was constant. "If one of us ends up in a hospital," he thought, "how will we afford the medicine?"

Many Venezuelans turned to alternative methods of survival. Carlos started accepting payment in eggs, flour, and other goods, as bolívars became worthless. Others relied on remittances from abroad, using U.S. dollars or cryptocurrencies like Bitcoin to buy what little remained in the markets. For millions, these coping strategies were not enough. Carlos's daughters, once dreaming of attending university, began looking for ways to emigrate. Like many Venezuelans, they saw no future in their homeland.

THE TRAGEDY OF HYPERINFLATION

By 2018, Venezuela's hyperinflation reached a crescendo. The government printed more and more money but it only further devalued the currency. These astronomical sums were no match for the soaring prices. Carlos's life savings, once equivalent to $10,000, had become virtually worthless, leaving him with sacks of bolívar notes that couldn't buy enough food to feed his family for a week. His bakery, the legacy he had fought to preserve, was forced to close its doors.

For Carlos and millions of Venezuelans, the collapse of the bolívar wasn't just an economic event, it was the unravelling of a way of life. Trust in the financial system destroyed, while a nation grappled with poverty, uncertainty, and fractured communities.

Venezuela, like Zimbabwe, raised the question of whether different policies could have averted the collapse. While the dramatic fall in oil prices was beyond the government's control, measures could still have been put in place to mitigate the crisis. Relying almost exclusively on oil revenues left Venezuela vulnerable to external shocks. By diversifying the economy and investing in other sectors, such as manufacturing, agriculture or tourism, a more balanced economic foundation could have been established.

Here too, limiting the supply of money and not printing so much of it would have reduced the inflationary pressures. Seeking international loans or imposing austerity measures are painful but much less so than hyperinflation. Measures such as addressing corruption and enforcing transparency would have gained trust in public institutions as well as encouraged domestic and foreign investment. Attempting to peg the bolívar to a stable foreign currency like the U.S. dollar could also have helped. Lastly, engaging with international organisations like the International Monetary Fund (IMF), could have stabilised the economy with financial support and technical expertise.

The parallels between Venezuela and Zimbabwe are evident. Exuberant money printing and political instability played central roles in both crises. For Venezuela, the collapse of the bolívar was more than an economic failure, it was a humanitarian disaster. Families went hungry. Healthcare systems crumbled. And millions were forced to flee their homeland. It's a stark reminder of the importance of sound monetary policy, economic diversification, and the role of trust in maintaining financial stability. As we compare these two case studies, we must ask: Are these failures unique to Zimbabwe and Venezuela, or could other nations face similar challenges under the right conditions? Can assets like gold, Bitcoin, or even emerging technologies like decentralised finance offer a hedge against such catastrophes?

LESSONS FROM TURKEY

In recent years, Turkey has also encountered economic turbulence, marked by a rapidly devaluing lira and spiralling inflation. Domestically, political instability and economic mismanagement have demoralised investors, while unsustainable fiscal policies, including loose monetary policy and significant government spending, have weakened the lira. The COVID-19 pandemic amplified these issues, further straining Turkey's economy by necessitating increased public spending and driving up the budget deficit.

Nor were Turkey's challenges all domestic. Rising global commodity prices and ongoing geopolitical tensions placed additional pressure on the lira, contributing to an inflationary surge. As prices for goods and services soared, Turkish citizens found their purchasing power diminished, which fuelled economic uncertainty and public frustration. The result was an uphill battle for the Turkish government to establish effective monetary and fiscal policies that could stabilise the lira and restore public and investor confidence in the economy.

LESSONS FROM GREECE AND CYPRUS

Greece and Cyprus have also faced severe financial crises, highlighting the risks associated with high levels of debt and economic mismanagement. In the early 2010s, the banking sector in Cyprus was heavily exposed to Greek debt. It had no defence therefore when Greece's debt crisis escalated, prompting a severe Cypriot banking crisis in 2012.

CYPRUS: THE STORY OF ANDREAS

Early one Monday morning, in Nicosia, the bustling capital of Cyprus, Andreas woke early, ready to start the week. He had a routine of grabbing a coffee, heading to the office, and withdrawing a little cash from the ATM to cover the week's expenses. But this Monday morning in March 2013 was different.

When Andreas reached his local ATM, a small group of people were huddled around it, frustration etched on their faces. "Out of cash", one man muttered as he walked away. Puzzled, Andreas checked his phone. The news was everywhere; the government had imposed capital controls overnight.

Andreas felt a knot tighten in his stomach as he read on. Daily ATM withdrawals were now capped at €100, regardless of how much people had in their accounts. Worse, some machines had already run dry, leaving countless families unable to access even this limited amount. He hurried to another ATM, hoping to beat the rush, only to find a long queue snaking out the door of a nearby bank.

As the hours passed the chaos spread. Andreas overheard an elderly woman in line pleading with a bank teller to release more money so she could pay for her husband's medicine.

A small business owner behind him grumbled about being unable to pay his suppliers. The once-trustworthy banking system now seemed a distant memory, replaced by fear and uncertainty.

For Andreas, the real shock would come later that week when the government announced a bail-in. It was announced that depositors with more than €100,000 in their accounts would lose a portion of their savings to help stabilise the country's failing banks. Andreas didn't fall into that category, but many of his friends and colleagues did. Years of careful saving and hard work were wiped out overnight, sacrificed to rescue a financial system that had failed them.

At home that evening, Andreas sat with his family, trying to make sense of the situation. "How did it come to this?" he wondered aloud. The crisis wasn't just about money, it was about trust, about the promises banks made to safeguard people's savings. And now, that trust had been shattered.

The experience left a mark on Andreas and many others in Cyprus. It was a painful reminder of how fragile financial systems could be and how quickly life could change when stability faltered. For Andreas, it was also a turning point, a moment that made him rethink where and how he stored his wealth, and whether the old system could ever truly be relied upon again.

To stabilise its economy, Cyprus sought a bailout from the European Union and the International Monetary Fund (IMF). The assistance the country received was contingent upon implementing strict austerity measures, including significant budget cuts, tax increases, and structural reforms within the banking sector.

The bailout also imposed losses on uninsured bank deposits, marking the first instance in the Eurozone crisis where depositors would bear a share of the burden. The subsequent economic contraction led to a prolonged recession, higher unemployment, and social hardship, underscoring the challenges of recovering from financial instability. Over time, Cyprus implemented reforms that gradually restored economic stability, though the impact of the crisis lingers.

The inflation crises described above have occurred in so many countries over the last few years. The effects are disastrous, not only economically but on the humanitarian level. In a world that is so technologically advanced, it is very hard to comprehend. And high inflation does not only affect smaller or less developed economies. Over the last 30 years many larger, developed economies have had their share.

INFLATION IN DEVELOPED COUNTRIES AND QE

Notably, Japan's quantitative easing (QE) strategy during the "Lost Decades" illustrates a more controlled yet ultimately problematic form of monetary expansion. Quantitative easing was a response to stagnation, deflation, and low growth following the bursting of a major asset bubble in the 1990s. The practice shares similarities with the money printing we have seen above in countries like Venezuela and Zimbabwe, but there are some key differences. While money printing involves creating currency to finance government spending, QE is less direct.

As we saw in Chapters 2 and 5, central banks create money to buy financial assets, such as government bonds, from banks and other institutions. This increases liquidity in the financial system and reduces the cost of borrowing. The aim is to encourage lending and investment. Unlike simply printing money, QE is designed to stimulate economic growth without immediately flooding the broader economy with cash, as happened for Venezuela and Zimbabwe. However, prolonged or excessive QE can still have inflationary effects, particularly if it inflates asset prices or contributes to inequality by concentrating wealth in financial markets and among the wealthy. This is what has occurred in Japan since the 1990s. By expanding the money supply through government bond purchases, the Bank of Japan sought to stimulate lending, spending, and economic recovery.

This intervention has wrecked the economy, with what initially was meant to be a short-term intervention leading to a dependence on central bank intervention. After decades of ultra-low interest rates and government stimulus, Japan has a staggering amount of public debt, leading to stagnant wage growth and deflationary pressures. To make matters worse, in 2016, Japan's central bank (BoJ) introduced Yield Curve Control (YCC), focusing on the price of the bonds bought by the central bank, or rather, the interest rate and yield of those bonds. The effect was to keep the 10-year yield, as in long term interest rates, at near zero or even negative. This was done to encourage businesses to invest and households to spend to alleviate fears of deflation, but the long-term side effects of this have only distorted asset prices and increased wealth inequality.

The Japanese constant low interest rate has also led to what is known as the yen carry trade, where foreign investors borrow yen at the low interest rate and earn a higher yield elsewhere. But like what happened in early 2025, if there is doubt about the rates staying low, investors will dump their investments on the market to buy the yen back, causing major stress in the financial system. It's clear that QE did not produce the desired effect, causing asset prices to rise without the anticipated economic growth. What it did produce was ongoing concerns over speculative bubbles, currency depreciation, and long-term fiscal risks.

Modern Inflation: The UK and America

Despite witnessing Japan's unsuccessful attempts at using QE to revive their economy, it seems surprising that Western economies adopted the same technique from 2008. As covered previously with the example of QE1, further rounds of monetary expansions occurred in the subsequent years —QE2 (2010-2011), then QE3(2012-2014) — fuelling astronomical house price growth. Then came Brexit in the UK in 2016, prompting another wave of monetary easing. Repo injections followed in 2019, as short-term lending markets between banks and institutions began to freeze. Liquidity dried up. Financial stress ensued.

The problems weren't just limited to traditional banks. Shadow banking institutions like hedge funds and money market funds also relied on short-term liquidity, and the 2019 repo crisis revealed these hidden vulnerabilities. By early 2020, interest rates began rising, after a decade at near zero. Could it have finally been a signal to regain control of public debt and begin winding down these two to five-year debt refinancing cycles? But before this tightening could take hold, the COVID-19 pandemic hit, and everything changed. A black swan event. Rare. Unpredictable. But with massive global impact. The whole economy was forced to shut down across the world.

In March 2020, global markets crashed. The S&P 500 dropped over 30% in weeks. The FTSE100 fell by about 25% that quarter and Bitcoin sharply plunged by around 50% in just two days.

Desperate governments stepped in once again. Interest rates slashed to near zero. Previous QT efforts reversed. Furlough payments. Stimulus cheques. Once again, rapid QE began with central bank liquidity flooding into the global economy to weather the storm of the pandemic.

The Bank of England expanded QE by £450 billion between 2020 and 2021, bringing total asset holdings to £895 billion by late 2021.

The Federal Reserve's balance sheet expanded by $5 trillion, reaching nearly $9 trillion by 2022, reflecting massive QE during COVID-19.

This liquidity injection ignited asset prices, and an extreme bull market ensued. Initially, it appeared a skilful move to prevent another Great Depression, but the true pain was yet to be seen.

By 2022, reported inflation surged to 11.1% in the UK and 9.1% in the U.S., though the real figures are likely higher. Savings eroded. Fiat currencies debased. Wealth inequality increased. The central banks response? To aggressively hike interest rates to around 5% to contain inflation. However, in doing so, debt servicing became significantly more expensive. Sovereign bond markets began showing signs of stress. UK gilts wobbled in late 2022. Japanese yields came under pressure despite years of YCC.

Could the substantial increase in global central bank balance sheets through years of liquidity injections eventually take their toll? With all these macroeconomic risks in mind, the need to preserve wealth has never been more important.

While QE did offer temporary relief, it also inflated asset prices, which meant that the wealthy who held scarce assets got richer, deepening wealth inequality. It raised serious concerns over long-term fiscal sustainability. The substantial expansion in central bank balance sheets that followed highlights the inherent limitations of fiat currency systems and even more acutely, the serious risks associated with large-scale central bank interventions.

PRESERVING WEALTH WITH HARD ASSETS

"The gold standard alone makes the determination of money's purchasing power independent of the ambitions and machinations of governments, dictators, and political parties."

— Ludwig von Mises, *The Theory of Money and Credit* (1912), Austrian School of Economics

Gold has long provided a safe haven, prized for its scarcity and durability. It has industrial uses in electronics and aerospace, and is also used in precision medical instruments. Its applications even extend to nanotechnology, advanced sensors, and of course, jewellery. Its role as a stable store of value for hundreds of years is unquestionable, enduring multiple periods of economic instability. This hard asset has historically offered investors a defence against inflation and currency devaluation, thanks to its intrinsic properties and broad acceptance worldwide. Bitcoin, often termed "digital gold", has emerged with many comparable hard asset qualities, combining digital sophistication and enforced scarcity. With its capped supply of 21 million coins, its ability to be transferred across borders at minimal cost, and its superior portability and divisibility, Bitcoin offers clear advantages over traditional money.

While Bitcoin and gold are sometimes seen as competitors, they are very much complementary. While gold remains a physical, tangible store of value, Bitcoin capitalises on the advantages of digital transactions, offering a modern solution to currency instability and inflation. Bitcoin's accessibility positions it as a financial tool in countries where national currencies have become worthless. For some of these countries, rather than adopting a more stable currency like the U.S. dollar, holding gold and Bitcoin provide a great hedge against fiat currency inflation. Like we saw with Gresham's Law in Chapter 5, holding superior store-of-value assets enables people worldwide to securely preserve their wealth.

LESSONS FOR ECONOMIC STABILITY

As we have explored through these case studies, we can see that currency instability can have devastating economic and social consequences. From hyperinflation eroding savings and wealth to political uncertainty and mass emigration, the lessons are clear: reliance on fiat currencies without proper economic safeguards can be catastrophic. These examples serve as clear reminders of the importance of wealth preservation in times of monetary uncertainty.

The common trend across these crises is a loss of trust in the national currency and the government's inability to manage the economy competently. As confidence erodes, people seek hard assets such as gold, real estate, and increasingly, Bitcoin.

Looking to the future, digital assets are likely to play an integral role in economic systems, especially as nations grapple with further inflation and currency erosion. The way that value is stored and transferred is evolving on a global scale. As nations tackle these challenges, the use of digital assets in the global economy could become even more critical. In the next chapter, we examine how governments and institutions are responding to this shift.

Chapter 13

Governmental Regulation

and Institutional Adoption

"Bitcoin is a path to financial inclusion for millions around the world, but it challenges traditional systems of control."

— Nayib Bukele, President of El Salvador

The rise of cryptocurrencies, led by Bitcoin, has taken the world by storm, sparking a wave of economic and financial transformation. What began as a unique concept among tech enthusiasts quickly turned into a worldwide sensation, capturing the interest of governments and institutions alike. National responses to the technology are varied, however. Some are fully embracing it, seeing it as a tool for financial empowerment and economic innovation, while others perceive it as a threat to financial control.

As governments consider their approaches, major financial players such as banks and asset managers have stepped in, giving digital assets a new level of credibility. But with this credibility brings regulatory attention, as decentralised systems are boldly pushing the boundaries of traditional structures. This chapter uncovers the ways that governments and institutions are reacting to the crypto boom and what it could mean for the future of global finance.

CASE STUDY: EL SALVADOR'S BITCOIN EXPERIMENT

In June 2021, El Salvador made history by adopting Bitcoin as legal tender, marking an exciting shift from traditional monetary policy. President Nayib Bukele led the initiative, envisioning Bitcoin as a tool to assist financial inclusion in the country. It was also seen as a way to improve the efficiency of remittances and bolster the economy. In a nation where a significant proportion of the population faced challenges accessing traditional bank accounts, Bitcoin opened up exciting new financial opportunities, enabling individuals to engage more actively in the economy.

To facilitate Bitcoin adoption, the government launched the "Chivo Wallet", a state-backed digital wallet preloaded with $30 worth of Bitcoin for each citizen. This custodial hot wallet allowed Salvadorans to make purchases, pay bills, and send remittances while avoiding the hefty fees typically associated with traditional money transfers. Despite these benefits, reactions were mixed. Some Salvadorans expressed concerns about Bitcoin's volatility and its potential impact on the stability of their currency, fearing it might provoke more economic uncertainty. El Salvador's Bitcoin experiment sparked a global debate on cryptocurrency's role in emerging economies, especially those with limited access to banking and high reliance on remittances.

In the bustling markets of San Salvador, where vendors call out over the hum of traffic and the mouthwatering aroma of sizzling street food fills the air, some merchants eagerly embraced the change. Vibrant handwritten signs that read, "We accept Bitcoin" hung beside more familiar cash prices on colourful stalls brimming with fruit, textiles, and electronics. Others were less comfortable with the new system. Here was an invisible currency that was linked to technology many had never used before, in a country predominately focused on cash and where digital infrastructure was still catching up.

Take María, a single mother living in a rural village, who used the $30 Bitcoin incentive provided by the Chivo Wallet to purchase groceries for her family. This was María's first experience with digital money, and it was thrillingly empowering. Without access to a traditional bank account, she could now conduct transactions, save money, and even send funds to her sister in the United States using only her phone, avoiding the high remittance fees that used to consume a portion of every dollar.

In urban areas, entrepreneurs began to recognise the incredible potential of Bitcoin for their businesses. Small café owners and food vendors equipped themselves with QR codes, enabling customers to make direct Bitcoin payments through the Chivo Wallet. The transition wasn't always seamless; connectivity issues and technical glitches occasionally led to delays, which understandably left customers and vendors feeling a bit frustrated. Yet, for those who persisted, embracing digital payments unlocked exciting new opportunities, particularly as international Bitcoin enthusiasts were drawn to the country to experience this bold experiment firsthand.

Among these were crypto investors and entrepreneurs who were captivated by El Salvador's innovative policies. In late 2023, the government introduced the Freedom Visa Programme, offering lifelong residency and a pathway to citizenship for those who contribute a minimum of $1 million in Bitcoin or U.S. dollars to the country. Capped at 1,000 applicants per year, the initiative is designed to attract high-net-worth individuals who align with El Salvador's Bitcoin vision. While official participation numbers have not yet been released, the programme has gained global interest, especially among Bitcoin advocates seeking a tax-friendly jurisdiction and a stake in the world's first country to adopt Bitcoin as legal tender. The government claims the proceeds will support economic and social development, framing the visa not only as a relocation opportunity, but a contribution to the country's digital and economic transformation.

However, aside from all these positives, some Salvadorans were more sceptical. Take Antonio, a bus driver from Santa Ana, who admitted to cashing out the value of his Bitcoin wallet immediately, fearing the price volatility. "One day it's up, and the next it's down. I don't want to lose what little I have", he explained. For many like him, trust in the new system was not straightforward. With Bitcoin's value fluctuating often, it felt risky compared with the stability of holding cash.

Despite some initial reservations, reports of early successes began to emerge. Remittances, a lifeline for more than 20% of the population, had now become cheaper and faster thanks to Bitcoin. Families who had previously waited days for international transfers now received funds instantly, directly into their Chivo Wallets. For Salvadorans living abroad, this meant they could send money home without having to pay the high fees, a welcome relief for families who were already struggling.

Generally, large retailers and tech-savvy businesses were swift to adapt, but in rural areas with limited internet access and significant gaps in financial literacy, the transition was slower. For this reason, the government pressed forward with educational campaigns and incentives to encourage adoption, giving examples of people who had successfully integrated Bitcoin into their daily lives. For many, this was not just a monetary change; it was a step into a new digital economy and an opportunity to envision what financial inclusion might truly feel like.

In January 2025, under pressure from the IMF, regarding a new $1.4 billion financial assistance programme granted to the country, the government has removed Bitcoin as legal tender, limiting it to voluntary use in the private sector. This means that no longer can taxes be paid in Bitcoin, but transactions such as purchasing property, which has become popular in El Salvador, still occur as long as the agent or seller will accept them.

Nonetheless, El Salvador holds over 6,000 BTC on its balance sheet and is consistently adding more to its state holdings, highlighting its commitment to the technology. At current prices, at around $109,000, El Salvador currently has over $350,000 in unrealised profits from its Bitcoin investment.

CHINA'S CRYPTOCURRENCY BAN

While El Salvador has welcomed Bitcoin, other countries, such as China, are taking a far stricter stance. China imposed a total ban on cryptocurrency trading and mining in 2021 to prevent its widespread adoption, citing fears about capital flight. Some argue that this has been more motivated by a strong desire to retain control over monetary systems in the country. More to the point perhaps, is that at the time of the ban China was launching its own central bank digital currency (CBDC), the digital yuan, with the aim of removing competition from decentralised alternatives. Equally, Bitcoin mining had become another point of contention, with authorities arguing that the energy-intensive process conflicted with China's carbon reduction goals.

This crackdown led crypto mining operations to migrate to countries that included the United States, Kazakhstan, and Canada, where policies were more favourable and energy costs often lower. As a result, China's dominance in Bitcoin mining fell, dispersing the network of miners more widely around the world, which possibly wasn't a bad thing at all. Despite its position, the Chinese government still retains close to 200,000 BTC, worth roughly $21 billion at the time of writing.

US ABOUT-FACE

While the US started to expand its mining operations in 2021 and 2022, increasing its share of the Bitcoin network, until recently the government and regulatory bodies' openness to embrace the technology had remained uncertain. Regulatory agencies like the Securities and Exchange Commission (SEC), have targeted platforms like Coinbase and most notably, Ripple Labs with legal action, demonstrating the difficulty of balancing innovation and financial stability. Until late 2024, Crypto had increasingly been viewed as a challenge to the dominance of the U.S. dollar, leading to a cautious and often hostile regulatory environment. Interestingly, former SEC Chairman Gary Gensler, who is also Professor at MIT teaching courses on cryptocurrency and digital assets, was among the most vocal critics of risky practices in the industry. His approach led to great anguish from the crypto community since he was sworn into office on 17 April 2021.

The SEC's legal battle with Ripple Labs commenced in December 2020 over Ripple's issuance of XRP. It claimed that XRP was a security and accused Ripple of conducting unregistered securities offerings by selling XRP, raising $1.3 billion without proper registration. The legal battle lasted over four years and had a detrimental impact on the crypto market and XRP's price over the course of the legal proceedings. Unlike Bitcoin and Ethereum, which the SEC did not classify as securities, Ripple's business model and the way XRP was marketed and sold raised concerns about its compliance with securities regulations.

On 13 July 2023, U.S. District Judge Analisa Torres delivered a mixed ruling in the case, but with a partial victory to Ripple Labs. After lengthy appeals from the SEC, Ripple explained in a statement on 19 March 2025 that the SEC had decided to drop the lawsuit against it. CEO Brad Garlinghouse claimed it as a "victory for the industry". In the July 2023 ruling Ripple's secondary market sales of XRP were not found to be securities transactions.

The court did find, however, that the sales to institutional investors qualified as securities, resulting in an initial $125 million fine. However, pending the official lifting of the injunction, and what seems an agreement between the two parties, this could be reduced to $50 million.

If as is looking likely, the injunction is lifted, it will mark a positive shift towards the industry, following Donald Trump's 2024 election campaign and subsequent second term in office, during which he has embraced Bitcoin and cryptocurrencies generally. However, this positive stance has not always been the case.

On the back of news of El Salvador's plans to make Bitcoin legal tender in 2021, the then former U.S. President Trump stated: "Bitcoin, it just seems like a scam", and "I don't like it because it's another currency competing against the dollar". He added that he wanted the dollar to be "the currency of the world". Taking his previous comments into account, he would seem the unlikeliest person to speak at a Bitcoin conference. It was even reported on CNN that, when Donald Trump was in his first term in office, he declared bitcoin was "not money" and criticised it as "highly volatile and based on thin air", while implying that crypto assets helped facilitate illegal underground markets.

However, he fully changed his narrative during a notable presidential rally in Charlotte, North Carolina on 24 July 2024. Three days later, he went on to speak at the largest and most prestigious gathering of the Bitcoin industry, Bitcoin 2024 Conference in Nashville, Tennessee. During the conference he further emphasised that he wanted to make the United States the centre of the cryptocurrency space. And he also expressed some ambitious plans for crypto if re-elected, stating, "on day one, I will fire Gary Gensler". He went on to say, "I will appoint a new SEC chairman who believes that America should build the future, not block the future."

Trump went on to be elected as President, being inaugurated on 20 January 2025. After Trump's victory, on 21 November 2024, Gary Gensler announced he would step down from his position on Inauguration Day, surely to avoid embarrassment. President Trump is staying true to his word and making the U.S. a global hub for cryptocurrency innovation, overseeing a boom in crypto mining companies setting up to take advantage of the favourable conditions. There has been speculation over exempting U.S.-based cryptocurrencies from capital gains tax and aiming to attract blockchain businesses and investment into the country. Additionally, as expressed during the Bitcoin conference speech, President Trump issued an Executive Order on 6 March 2025, stating that the United States will establish a strategic crypto reserve, in a complete game-changer for the industry and mass adoption more generally. With the U.S. government currently holding over 200,000 BTC, mainly from seizures connected to illicit activity, the aim is to convert this into a ready base for the reserve. In addition, the Order included details of the formation of the digital asset stockpile, which will include Ethereum (ETH), Solana (SOL), XRP (XRP), and Cardano (ADA).

These reserves and stockpiles can help provide decentralisation, diversification, and financial sovereignty, while attracting technological investment and innovation in digital finance. They have been carefully selected due to their market relevance and technical utility in the space. As discussed in Chapter 8, Ethereum, Solana, and Cardano are all prominent Layer 1 blockchains that facilitate smart contracts, so they provide all of the DeFi use cases. The list includes XRP for the benefits of cross-border settlement, which would allow the major financial institutions to partner up and use the technology. This could be especially relevant as it all but appears the regulatory clarity is now in place for XRP. The rationale, as outlined in a White House briefing, is to ensure the United States maintains influence and optionality in the emerging blockchain ecosystems that show technical resilience and longevity, while encouraging domestic innovation.

The concept of strategic reserves has existed for centuries. Governments have traditionally stockpiled critical assets such as oil and gold to safeguard national interests. These funds can bolster a country's economic resilience, particularly amid uncertainties in the global financial system. For example, government officials might respond to oil shortages with the Strategic Petroleum Reserve. The formation of a crypto strategic reserve draws many parallels with the historical gold reserves that once backed the U.S. financial system before 1971, reflecting a growing recognition that block-chain and cryptocurrencies are not just disruptive technologies, but pillars of future financial infrastructure. It seems likely that many other countries will follow suit.

CRYPTO FRIENDLY VERSUS CRYPTO CAUTIOUS

There are other countries attempting to achieve a balance between regulation and innovation and position themselves as global hubs for cryptocurrency. Consider Switzerland, where locations such as the Canton of Zug have become known as "Crypto Valley". Clear, supportive legal frameworks make it a hub for blockchain and cryptocurrency projects. In Zug, you can even pay your taxes in Bitcoin and Ether, all of which has helped Switzerland to achieve growth and innovation in the sector. In the context of cryptocurrency projects, a Foundation is usually a non-profit organisation that helps guide, support, and fund the development and promotion of a blockchain ecosystem. Zug hosts the headquarters of the Foundations of Solana, Cardano, and Ethereum in support of these goals. So, it's no surprise that major blockchain companies and start-ups are thriving in this positive environment.

Singapore has also emerged as a leading destination for crypto innovation. Well-known for its fintech-friendly legislation, it has developed regulations that stimulate innovation while protecting investors. It is home to Crypto.com, a well-known cryptocurrency exchange, as well as the Tron Layer 1 blockchain Foundation and other fascinating projects and crypto companies. Singapore's clear legal frameworks, cheap taxes, and extensive support structure for blockchain entrepreneurs make it an attractive destination for crypto enterprises.

Similarly, Portugal has long been a popular destination due to its tax advantages on individual crypto earnings. That changed in 2023, when Portugal imposed a 28% tax on short-term cryptocurrency gains (assets held for less than a year), while long-term holdings and cryptocurrency transactions remain tax-free. With a crypto-friendly government, a growing community, and a low cost of living, Portugal has emerged as a popular destination for enthusiasts seeking to embrace digital assets.

Malta, also known as the "Blockchain Island", has established a complete regulatory framework for blockchain and cryptocurrency companies. With government-backed blockchain efforts and robust legal protections, it continues to attract cryptocurrency entrepreneurs, resulting in a thriving ecosystem.

Another crypto-friendly nation is Estonia, which has long been a leader in digital innovation.

Its expedited process for founding cryptocurrency-related firms, as well as its e-residency programme for entrepreneurs have helped it stand out. The way that the government has incorporated blockchain into public services, combined with a tech-savvy population, further adds to its appeal. However, taxation applies to short-term holdings and commercial trading operations.

With notable pragmatism, Germany has recognised cryptocurrencies as prominent legal financial instruments. Long-term holders can, at the time of writing, enjoy tax exemptions on crypto gains after one year, however, Germany, along with several other European countries, is reviewing its current tax regime concerning cryptocurrencies. In contrast to U.S. government plans to hold cryptocurrency in a strategic reserve, nearly 50,000 BTC seized by the German government from piracy website Movie2k.to were sold off in June and July 2024, at an average price of just under

$58,000. Needless to say, that would have been considerably more had the sale been deferred until mid-2025. That said, with strong regulatory clarity and growing institutional adoption, Germany is paving the way for a crypto-friendly future for users and investors.

Next let's consider the efforts of the UAE, especially Dubai, to become one of the most crypto-friendly cities globally. The Dubai Virtual Assets Regulatory Authority (VARA) is at the heart of this exciting development. Established in 2022, it aims to offer clear and comprehensive guidelines for crypto exchanges, token issuers, and service providers. This regulatory clarity has drawn interest from major exchanges like Binance and Crypto.com, enhancing confidence and stability in the sector.

Dubai's Blockchain Strategy aims not only to leverage block-chain technology, but to streamline its use cases for public services and enhanced transparency. This, combined with tax-friendly policies that do not levy personal income or capital gains tax, has made the city a favourable location for crypto investors and start-ups. Its strategic geographical location also enhances its status as a vibrant global crypto hub, in which major events, such as the World Blockchain Summit, are testament to Dubai's dedication to the sector. With its supportive environment and innovative policies, Dubai has truly established itself as a leading host to the crypto industry.

In contrast, even though the UK is home to a growing community of cryptocurrency enthusiasts, in my experience, the regulatory environment has thus far made it difficult for the industry to thrive.

The Financial Conduct Authority (FCA) has taken a cautious approach, banning Binance from offering regulated services in the country, for instance. Opinion is divided on this front. In the U.S., authorities view the Binance platform as being used for money laundering without the appropriate oversight, and the platform has gained a reputation for not cooperating with regulators. Additionally, Binance has offered leveraged trading without sufficient investor guidance, leading some to engage in risky practices without being fully aware of the risks. Compare Coinbase in the UK for example, which provides leverage trading within its app, but restricts this functionality for UK residents. So, while aiming to protect consumers from the risks of fraud and volatility, the FCA has also created significant barriers for businesses and investors. Indeed, as of October 2024, only 48 crypto firms offering exchange services had been approved out of approximately 500 applicants, which is around a 10% approval rate, using a slow and methodical approach. There are also stricter advertising regulations and enhanced compliance requirements, which have further added to the challenges, discouraging smaller crypto firms from operating in the UK.

Being UK-based, I am witnessing the regulatory challenges faced by new crypto -based companies to get off the ground. However, I am hopeful the environment is starting to evolve. Cointelegraph suggested in September 2024 that CryptoUK, a self-regulatory trade association for the UK crypto industry, said some of its members "have expressed reluctance about the process" under the scrutiny of the Financial Conduct Authority (FCA). The implication is that the FCA is acting as a deterrent to the crypto industry.

At the same time, a Scottish private school in Helensburgh has announced it will be the first in Britain to let parents pay their fees in Bitcoin: "Boarding school is first in UK to accept bitcoin for fees" — *The Times*, 11 April 2025. The school did stress, however, "that it had strict anti-money laundering procedures in place for when it started accepting the cryptocurrency for the autumn term". This shows that when using the technology wisely with sufficient oversight, anyone can accept digital assets. Despite its relatively slow start, the UK government has begun to show interest in the potential of blockchain technology and digital assets. Recent proposals aim to create a clearer regulatory framework, focusing on AML and KYC standards to bring more legitimacy to the space. Nonetheless, many residents feel the restrictions hinder innovation and limit their access to global platforms, leaving the UK trailing more crypto-friendly countries. Like China, the UK has also floated the idea of a CBDC, often referred to as "Britcoin", signalling a willingness to engage with digital technologies, but on its own terms. We explore CBDCs in the next chapter to see whether they strike the balance between promoting innovation and providing financial stability.

Aside from experimenting with CBDCs, governments have primarily focused on holding digital assets as strategic reserves and / or regulating their use. It's worth noting that the active use of cryptocurrencies by governments is still extremely limited. Aside from El Salvador's integration of Bitcoin for remittances and everyday payments, most nations are not yet using crypto for transactions, nor DeFi and smart contract applications. However, small-scale experiments are emerging. For example, Palau, part of the Micronesian Island region in Oceania, has trialled USDC for digital citizen payments, and countries like Argentina have considered crypto-based trade settlements as alternatives to foreign exchange shortages. Although early, these initiatives suggest that government usage may follow once the regulatory and technical foundations have matured.

INSTITUTIONAL ADOPTION OF CRYPTOCURRENCIES

So, having highlighted how some governments are approaching the technology, what do national and international institutions think about the crypto industry? Once seen as a fringe technology, cryptocurrencies have attracted significant interest from institutional investors seeking new ways to diversify their clients' portfolios. Leading financial institutions like Goldman Sachs and J.P.Morgan have introduced crypto services, highlighting the growing legitimacy of digital assets. This marks a shift from early doubt to acceptance, driven by Bitcoin's unique value proposition as an alternative hedge against inflation.

In February 2021, Canada launched the first Bitcoin spot exchange-traded fund (ETF), giving investors direct access to the cryptocurrency for the first time without requiring them to hold it themselves. Not long after that, the first U.S. Bitcoin futures ETF was launched by ProShares on 19 October 2021, following multiple rejections of similar schemes in the U.S. Strangely, the approved fund is arguably riskier than rejected predecessors, as it tracks contracts tied to Bitcoin's future price, not the actual asset itself.

After several more spot Bitcoin ETF applications, a notable step forward took place on 10 January 2024, when the SEC approved 11 Bitcoin spot ETFs, sending the crypto markets soaring. Financial giants such as BlackRock (ishares Bitcoin Trust), Fidelity (Wise Origin Bitcoin Fund), and Grayscale (Grayscale Bitcoin Trust) were some of the highest profile institutions to launch these products. This not only offered U.S. retail investors a convenient entry point into the crypto market, it also enabled financial institutions to invest in these products on behalf of their clients. Using ETFs enables them to avoid many of the stringent regulatory and compliance hurdles that would otherwise apply if investing directly in Bitcoin. The launch was so popular that $4.6 billion in Bitcoin ETFs was traded on the first day. Six months later, the first U.S. spot Ethereum ETFs were approved and launched on 23 July 2024, marking another milestone for institutional access to cryptocurrency. The enthusiasm has raised anticipation for new U.S. spot crypto ETFs that include assets such as Solana and XRP in the near term.

In countries without a locally approved Bitcoin or Ethereum spot ETF, investors may still gain exposure through international brokerages, provided domestic regulations permit access to foreign-listed products. However, some countries are not there yet. In the UK for example, retail access to crypto-based ETFs, including those listed overseas, is restricted by the Financial Conduct Authority (FCA). I believe that this area is ripe for reassessment. Although not ideal, a workaround for UK investors, should they so choose, is to gain indirect exposure through ETFs such as the VanEck Crypto and Blockchain Innovators, with ticker DAGB, which holds companies like MicroStrategy (now Strategy), Coinbase, and major Bitcoin mining firms.

ETFs are not the only way to hold cryptocurrencies indirectly. Payment giants such as PayPal, Visa, and Mastercard have also accelerated crypto adoption by integrating digital assets into their platforms. PayPal enables users to buy, hold, and spend cryptocurrencies, while Visa and Mastercard have partnered with crypto companies to issue crypto-backed payment cards. Revolut, a rising fintech company, has also integrated cryptocurrency into its online banking platform to make the process of holding the asset much easier. All this has enabled investors to gain exposure to cryptocurrency through regulated financial products, eliminating the need to directly manage wallets or private keys that enable daily transactions and long-term holding. It signals another step towards mainstream acceptance as a legitimate asset class and sets the stage for further institutional involvement in the years ahead.

Naturally, premier financial institutions such as Goldman Sachs and Morgan Stanley have now invested in these ETFs, as either financial instruments for trading or client offerings. However, it is important to understand that corporate adoption of crypto as long-term reserve assets is some way off. This is largely due to regulatory and compliance restrictions that limit how financial institutions can hold or treat digital assets on their balance sheets. Consequently, while ETFs have expanded institutional access, they have not meaningfully changed the number of companies holding crypto directly as part of their treasury strategy.

Aside from financial institutions, other, less tightly regulated, organisations have decided to hold Bitcoin directly as part of their corporate reserves. Elon Musk's Tesla made headlines in early 2021 when it added Bitcoin to its balance sheet. This signalled early interest from the tech and innovation sector, citing its potential to hedge against inflation and diversify corporate holdings, with over 11,000 BTC, as of Q1 2025. The standout example, however, must be Strategy (formerly MicroStrategy), which has taken the lead by first purchasing Bitcoin in August 2020. Executive Chairman Michael Saylor has been instrumental in positioning Bitcoin as a digital gold alternative to traditional cash reserves.

Saylor's conviction in Bitcoin has truly influenced the company's business plan, issuing convertible notes and corporate bonds to raise capital with the specific goal of acquiring even more Bitcoin. Some would certainly deem this approach controversial or even utter madness, however, it has enabled the company to significantly expand its holdings, making it the largest corporate holder of Bitcoin by a wide margin. As of early 2025, Strategy holds almost 580,000 BTC, worth over $64 billion, which represents around 2.7% of the total supply and gives the company close to $10 billion of unrealised profits.

Saylor views Bitcoin as digital property and believes it will be adopted as a store of value in nations that allow private property ownership. He asserts that Bitcoin is more efficient than gold, fiat money, and even real estate investments, describing it as "the most efficient energy system". Pointing to the way Bitcoin is setting itself apart from other cryptocurrencies, Saylor describes it as the preferred choice for institutional investors seeking scarce digital property that serves as a reliable store of value. Over 130 companies around the world currently hold BTC as part of their reserves. This corporate adoption means cryptocurrencies are no longer viewed as simply speculative assets, but as a crucial element of a long-term financial strategy in the face of fiat currency debasement.

This growing institutional adoption across ETFs, payment platforms, and corporate treasuries, makes secure and scalable custody solutions non-negotiable. In response, institutional crypto custody solutions have been developed by companies like Coinbase Custody, Fidelity Digital Assets, and Bakkt. These services provide the robust infrastructure institutions need to manage large crypto holdings confidently and in compliance with regulatory standards.

MOVING FROM INVESTMENT TO REAL ADOPTION

Despite increasing exposure to digital assets, most institutions are not yet using cryptocurrencies for payments or DeFi protocols in their day-to-day operations. I would love to say that the technology is starting to be used extensively by companies as well as governments, but the fact is, adoption is still extremely early. For now, the focus remains on holding cryptocurrency for investment purposes to gain early exposure as well as custody for clients, so that as adoption increases, holding the infrastructure will be lucrative when things really take off. That said, a few early private-chain experiments by institutions somewhat mirror CBDCs, but on a corporate level. For example, J.P.Morgan has developed its own Kinexys (formerly Onyx) blockchain platform and uses its own digital payments system for internal transfers between institutional clients. There have also been trials with DeFi platforms being used as a bridge between decentralised finance and regulatory compliance, again at a really early stage, but functional usage should eventually accompany asset exposure.

J.P.Morgan has also been testing the technology with international payments. As in the example of El Salvador, offering crypto as a faster and cheaper alternative to traditional cross-border payments can be revolutionary. On an institutional level, Ripple's XRP is in active use in financial infrastructure by Ripple's XRP Ledger and the RippleNet for ODL services. This system has already been adopted by banks and payment service providers in Asia, the Middle East, and Latin America, offering a faster and cheaper alternative to traditional SWIFT-based transfers. These institutions include Santander, Tranglo, SBI Remit, and Banco Rendimento.

Even if direct institutional usage is still limited, interest is growing in the tokenisation of real-world assets. We've seen how traditional assets, such as real estate, stocks, or bonds, can be listed and traded on the blockchain. This is where the institutions are getting excited about how they could monetise the gap between crypto and traditional finance. While platforms like Polygon and Ethereum have been used to create tokenised financial products, there is still some way to go. But it would allow fractional ownership and greater liquidity, rather than an individual having to buy a whole asset themselves. In this way, institutions could modernise asset trading and broaden access to investments, while making a profit from providing a more efficient system.

You may recall in Chapter 10 we discussed commodity companies and companies like DocuSign experimenting with the technology, as well as applications in identity documents or graduate qualifications, but all are currently either limited or in experimental stages.

REGULATION: PROTECTING INVESTORS AND ENHANCING STABILITY

As cryptocurrency markets evolve, what is clear is that adoption from governments and institutions as well as individuals is increasing all the time. As it grows, so too does the need for regulatory oversight to protect investors and ensure stability. We need measures to prevent fraud and guard against market manipulation, as well as needing to mitigate the risks of leveraged trading, which is an area of particular concern. As mentioned previously, allowing traders to borrow funds to increase their exposure to crypto assets adds risk to an already volatile market. Regulators across the board are pushing for greater oversight in this area, aiming to safeguard retail investors from the potential dangers of high-risk trading practices. This is certainly a positive move, and from first-hand experience, one that needs strict controls, as most crypto users aren't typical investors and need education before engaging in such risky practices.

The QuadrigaCX fraud case perfectly illustrates what can go wrong. When Gerald Cotten, co-founder of Canada's largest crypto exchange at the time, reportedly died in India in 2018, he took with him the passwords to cold wallets holding more than $190 million in user funds. It was made into Netflix documentary *Trust No One: The Hunt for the Crypto King* which features Tong Zou, who lost $560,000 CAD after depositing his life savings into QuadrigaCX. As there was no proper oversight or protection, there was no recourse. Sadly, it would only be another three years before FTX would collapse for very similar reasons. The fall-out from these events re-ignited global calls for regulation and shows just how vulnerable retail investors are in the absence of legal protections, and why decentralised custody of assets is essential.

But stepping aside from the regulatory and compliance issues towards exchanges, as well as the fraudulent activities as we have seen from the Quadriga and FTX exchanges, actual criminal activity on-chain are a concern for regulators.

As we saw in Chapter 3, one of the earliest examples of criminal activity in the crypto space was with the Silk Road marketplace in 2011, which operated on the dark web, and relied on Bitcoin as the primary payment method. While the FBI closed the site down in 2013, and its founder, Ross Ulbricht was sentenced to life in prison, it showed that pseudonymity, rather than full anonymity, could still hinder the efforts of early law enforcement crackdowns.

Since then, the landscape of crypto-related crime has evolved significantly. Ransomware attacks frequently demand payment in Bitcoin or privacy coin Monero. In 2021, the Colonial Pipeline breach highlighted just how critical infrastructure can be held hostage through encrypted extortion.

DeFi protocols have also become a major target for exploitation. Smart contract vulnerabilities. Flash loan attacks. Oracle manipulation. These have all resulted in billions of dollars being drained from decentralised systems, often without a clear path to recovery.

Then we come to smaller scale schemes such as what are known as pump-and-dump scams and rug pulls. As it is now so easy to create cryptocurrency tokens and promote them online and on social media, influencers are often lured with financial incentives or otherwise, with the intention of artificially inflating their price. Once investor hype has been driven, the development team sells all their tokens at the inflated price, leaving investors left with worthless tokens. Two notable examples spring to mind. Remember when the popular series called Squid Game was released on Netflix in 2021? Well, a crypto token was created soon after, and its price shot up like a rocket. A few investors, by luck more than judgement, managed to get out making life-changing gains, but the majority were left losing everything, and in some cases, their life savings. Only the development team departed with a massive pay day.

Rug pulls like this are commonplace for new speculative memecoins created with low market capitalisations, however, pump-and-dump methods have happened to even the most established of coins. Take XRP for example. which I witnessed playing out. In a community chat on social messaging platform Telegram, within an XRP group, there was a collective that promoted a massive push in the price of XRP at a specified day and time. They built hype all over social media and in various social messaging groups. Anticipation was building. When the day arrived on 1 February 2021, the price of XRP opened at around 49c, having risen from about 24c in anticipation of the event four days prior. At the appointed time, the price of XRP shot up, with volatility moving the price violently in all directions. Next it was at 60c then back down to 55c, then up to around 65c, surpassing the previous high.

It eventually peaked at just over 75c before the colluding pump-and-dump initiators presumably dumped their tokens onto the market, causing the price to crash all the way down to 37c. The historic price chart shows a large red candle spike on this day, recording one of XRP's highest daily trading volumes.

Similar things have occasionally happened in traditional markets, such as with GameStop in 2021, so it is not unique to cryptocurrencies, but it is certainly most prominent there by a long way. These kinds of schemes surged during the 2021 bull run, particularly for memecoins and in the NFT market. Phishing and impersonation attacks, with criminals creating fake wallets, airdrops, and support teams on social media to deceive unsuspecting users into handing over access to their funds.

While I may have just laid out the worst that crypto has to offer, in terms of the variety and scale of some of these criminal activities, it's important to recognise that the traceability of blockchain transactions as well as the advancements of crypto analysis tools are steadily improving enforcement outcomes. According to Chainalysis, illicit crypto transactions reached over $20 billion in 2022, but this only represented about 0.24% of all crypto activity.

Nor are the authorities entirely defenceless. Advancements of blockchain forensic tools such as AI-based wallet clustering, which can track patterns and inter-agency cooperation now mean that funds can be tracked with increasing accuracy. A good example of this was the recovery of $3.6 billion worth of Bitcoin by U.S. authorities in 2022, where the funds were originally stolen from the Bitfinex exchange in 2016. Even if it may take time to uncover, the transparent nature of the blockchain makes it possible to identify criminality eventually.

I would say that with the advancement of these new tools, as well as governments tracking the ownership ID credentials of exchange wallets through KYC, it is becoming more and more difficult for criminals to bypass the transparency of the blockchain space.

While many crypto users have good intentions and see the industry as a way to break away from the control and oversight of traditional systems, the reality is that without appropriate regulation, they are at financial risk. With all this in mind, a careful approach is needed to ensure users are protected, but at the same time innovation is not stifled.

The EU have already initiated what is looking like the most comprehensive largescale and unified multi-country framework using their MiCa (Markets in Crypto-Asset) regulation. This encompasses stablecoins, exchanges, and licensing across all EU member states, but leaves individual tax treatments up to the discretion of each government.

The implementation of frameworks worldwide will make the crypto markets much safer. In the UK, Japan, and Australia, new regulations are addressing issues like security breaches, money laundering, and consumer protection, emphasising the need for robust oversight in a fast-growing industry. Other countries will need to follow suit. Instead of simply banning the technology, they must start by understanding how it works, its potential, and how it can be used safely and efficiently moving forward.

REGULATION AND INNOVATION MUST CO-EXIST

The rise of cryptocurrencies is forcing governments and institutions to rethink their approach to money. Governments face the delicate task of embracing innovation while protecting monetary systems that have existed for centuries. Nobody doubts the potential of blockchain and digital assets, but it is complicated by the geopolitical implications of decentralised currencies. As detailed above, some institutions are moving swiftly to integrate Bitcoin and other digital assets into their portfolios, while others remain hesitant.

Will crypto become a global store of value, or will governments and central banks find ways to contain its influence? Perhaps governments will step in more aggressively, ensuring that digital assets can only really exist on their terms.

Regulation is tightening, but innovation isn't slowing down. Decentralised finance is offering alternatives to traditional banking, and institutions are steadily increasing their exposure.

But where is the line between adoption and control? Control is a key aspect of blockchain technology, and ironically, the same technology that was designed to be decentralised is now being explored by governments as a tool for financial oversight and taxation. Governments don't want to be left behind, but they also can't risk losing control. This is why many are looking beyond existing cryptocurrencies and working on their own digital assets instead.

How much influence will crypto have before governments step in more aggressively? This brings us to one of the most significant developments in digital finance, Central Bank Digital Currencies (CBDCs). Unlike Bitcoin, which operates outside the control of any government, CBDCs are state-issued digital currencies designed to bring efficiency to the financial system while keeping monetary policy firmly in the hands of central banks.

But what does this mean for financial freedom? Can CBDCs coexist with decentralised cryptocurrencies? Will they give governments more control over spending and transactions, or will they simply be a modernised version of the money we already use? Will they represent progress or a step towards a more centralised and controlled monetary future? Moving into Chapter 14, we explore how CBDCs could reshape the financial system.

Chapter 14

Central Bank Digital Currencies

As cryptocurrencies are making strides to reshape the financial landscape, Central Bank Digital Currencies (CBDCs) have surfaced as a groundbreaking response from central banks worldwide. They mark a distinct shift from the current traditional financial systems by embracing blockchain technology. Unlike decentralised cryptocurrencies such as Bitcoin, CBDCs are government-issued digital forms of national currency, offering a new digital paradigm for managing national economies. The motivations for creating CBDCs are as complex as they are diverse, ranging from boosting financial inclusion and streamlining payments to reinforcing government influence over money in an increasingly digital economy.

This chapter builds on what we've learned about the uses and applications of cryptocurrencies to uncover the development of CBDCs, the pros and cons of their adoption, and how some countries are more actively engaged than others in driving their own projects forward. But will CBDCs support economic stability or just introduce new layers of financial surveillance and control?

By analysing CBDCs' design and goals, we can get to grips with their potential to bridge traditional finance with the digital age, as well as the challenges they present.

A NEW CHAPTER IN DIGITAL ASSETS: CBDCS

A CBDC is a digital token issued by a nation's central bank, whose value is pegged to that country's fiat currency. As such, it is designed to serve as a new digital form of legal tender. It bears similarities to a cryptocurrency as it is based on blockchain technology, which as we know, allows all users to hold a copy of transaction history so that it is distributed and not under the control of just one entity. However, depending on the way the technology is used, this can influence the level of centralisation that is implemented, just as different consensus mechanisms and cryptocurrency structures can create different degrees of decentralisation.

CBDCs are essentially a hybrid of cryptocurrencies and government-issued fiat currencies. In contrast to Bitcoin or Ethereum, which depend on decentralisation and open networks, CBDCs are centralised and influenced by government institutions. They typically employ a private ledger blockchain system that allows exclusive access to authorised parties.

Most of us already have a digital wallet on our phones, so it's not a stretch to imagine the crypto wallets we discussed in Chapter 9, that can hold digital currency directly from the central bank. This is the fundamental idea behind CBDCs. For example, if the UK issued a "Britcoin" CBDC denomination to the value of £10 sterling, each digital coin would be worth the same as a physical £10 note and could be used for transactions. This approach would enable central banks to supervise and oversee transactions directly, simplifying electronic payments and reducing reliance on physical cash, especially in regions that still rely heavily on it.

Traditionally, a central bank offers physical money in the form of banknotes, which are then used to make various payments.

A CBDC would be issued by the central bank, and it would represent electronic money which can then be used by businesses and households via the blockchain, albeit with some distinctions which we will shortly see. As a result, anyone could make electronic payments with central bank money.

The function of a central bank is to ensure monetary and market stability, and CBDCs are designed to promote these goals. Their intention at this stage is believed to be to supplement a country's monetary system, rather than replacing it, by providing a secure, regulated digital payment option. However, what distinguishes central bank digital currencies from the digital money that we use today to make payments and receive our salaries?

THE EVOLUTION OF DIGITAL CURRENCIES

The rise of CBDCs and their evolution can be traced back to centuries-old shifts in monetary systems. After the bartering systems in around 10000–3000 BCE that we looked at in Chapter 4, there are four types of money that have either been used throughout history or are known and could be used in the future.

COMMODITY MONEY

First let's revisit the concept of commodity money from Chapters 4 and 5. This refers to the traditional form of money which has operated for thousands of years. These forms of money included cowrie shells, obsidian, or gold and silver coins, where the commodity is the money. As we have seen, this type of money holds the intrinsic value of the material itself.

COMMODITY-BACKED MONEY

In relatively recent times, to make a currency more divisible, commodity-backed money emerged, where currency represents a claim on commodities held by governments, such as gold reserves. The bank stores gold or other commodities in a secure vault and issues a piece of paper that you can use to trade. This piece of paper allows you to claim the stored commodity any time by exchanging it back at the bank. So, instead of trading the actual commodity, the paper bank note is used to represent an amount of the underlying commodity. This was an extremely convenient and popular method of trade.

However, as we know from Chapter 5, in 1971, the U.S. government abandoned the gold standard, ending the Bretton Woods system. This meant that all the paper currency the government had issued and was circulating around the world was no longer redeemable for the gold that had once backed it. The paper became the money itself, creating a hybrid system over the last 50 years, somewhere between commodity money and commodity-backed money. But instead of gold being the underlying commodity, debt became the commodity. Debt in the form of U.S. government treasuries and bonds served as the foundation for printing dollars. As we have seen, the adoption of fiat currency, backed solely by government assurances, has contributed to numerous global financial crises, sovereign debt defaults, and, as we explored in detail, hyperinflation.

Public Ledger

Next, let's look at public ledger money, a system where everyone has access to all the transactional data. A historical example of this goes back to 500 CE, to the Micronesian Island region of Oceana. We've seen how Palau is currently trialling USDC and coincidentally, over 1,500 years ago, it was this island that predominantly quarried large 8–10 ft Rai stones and transported them to nearby, Yap Island, where this part of the story begins. The Yapese used these large limestone disks as currency. Each stone represented its owner and was placed in a public location on the island. To spend a disk, the owner would announce the change in ownership to the community, who would then record it by updating their ledgers.

This differed from commodity money in that the disks were too heavy to move, meaning they couldn't be physically exchanged in transactions. Instead, ownership was transferred through a mental public ledger system, with the community acknowledging and recording each new owner.

If Peter owned a Rai stone and wanted to buy a cow from Jim, they would both announce the trade to the entire island. Peter would declare that he was transferring ownership of his stone to Jim, while Jim would confirm that he was transferring ownership of his cow to Peter. Now that the whole community had acknowledged the exchange, everyone knew that Peter owned the cow, and Jim owned the Rai stone. This meant that theft of money was virtually impossible because of this public ledger system.

This example shows that, as long as everyone follows the agreed rules, a public ledger system can't lead to theft and manipulation. When I talk about rules, it's less about strict enforcement and more about collective agreement. If the majority acknowledges a transfer, that decision stands. This is similar to Bitcoin, where only a 51% attack could override the network's consensus. Additionally, the Rai stones couldn't be stolen or easily moved, and the fact that they had to be imported from Palau reinforced their effectiveness as a stable and trusted monetary system. However, what happens when this type of approach is applied to more transferable or portable commodities?

As the digital era progressed, banks began recording transactions electronically, but these records remained private and controlled within the centralised banking system. The emergence of cryptocurrencies like Bitcoin has reintroduced the concept of a public ledger system, where transaction records are stored on decentralised networks and made accessible to anyone. It is considered public because everyone is aware of it at the same time. This shift brought back transparency and trust that didn't rely on a central authority, echoing the principles of the Rai stone system but on a global scale.

PRIVATE LEDGER

In contrast, CBDCs more closely resemble a private ledger, functioning as a digital extension of fiat currency that is fully controlled by central banks. They have emerged in response to the growing demand for digital transactions and the power of blockchain technology, as well as an appetite for modernising monetary systems in a way that retains regulatory control within existing financial institutions.

Private ledger monetary systems are the opposite of public ledger systems in that transaction data is not visible to the community. Imagine an Excel spreadsheet where each row represents a person in the country, showing their balance and the transactions that have taken place between any rows. However, unlike traditional cryptocurrency public ledgers, which everyone can see, and miners or validators verify transactions, only the central bank has access to the spreadsheet.

Not only can the central bank view it, but they also have full control over it, meaning they could in theory edit balances and transactions, just as they can currently increase the money supply by updating their systems with new virtual money. This means the public would not be able to foresee changes to the spreadsheet until after they had occurred, and the issues of high inflation and currency debasement would still be present. The benefit of cryptocurrencies like Bitcoin is that you can't alter the currency as it is based on cryptographic and mathematical proofs. That is why they are becoming so popular, as they can't be manipulated, something that governments and central banks throughout history made a habit of doing.

> *"We don't know who's using a $100 bill today and wedon't know who's using a 1,000 peso bill today. The key difference with a CBDC is the central bank will have absolute control on the rules and regulations that will determine the use of that expression of central bank liability — and also we will have the technology to enforce that."*
>
> — Agustín Carstens, BIS, 2020

This quotation is powerful because it comes from an advocate of CBDCs, yet one who has unintentionally confirmed the concerns of many critics.

How CBDCs Differ from Cryptocurrencies

As we can see this is very different to a public ledger where no individual can easily control or hack the underlying protocol. With Bitcoin, for instance, the miners, the software, and the value within the network can't be manipulated in such a way.

By contrast, CBDCs operate on permissioned or private blockchains that are tightly controlled by central banks. A private ledger centralises control over the excel spreadsheet, as in the example above, long with any accounts via credits and debits. Only designated entities, such as government institutions or authorised financial intermediaries, would be able to access and verify the network, centralising control. As a result, while both CBDCs and cryptocurrencies operate digitally and use blockchain or comparable ledger technologies, they differ dramatically in purpose and control.

Another key distinction and benefit as a transactional currency, is bypassing volatility. CBDCs are pegged to a fiat currency, so they more closely resemble stable coins like USDT, which is pegged 1:1 with the U.S. dollar, rather than traditional cryptocurrencies such as Bitcoin. CBDCs provide a controlled, reliable alternative to traditional fiat currency, and can aim to reduce the operational costs if their model is designed to completely bypass commercial banks, directly to the consumer, but more on this shortly.

CBDCs generally fall into two categories: wholesale and retail. Wholesale CBDCs are designed for use by commercial banks and financial institutions to streamline high-value interbank settlements and improve the efficiency of financial infrastructure. An example used in the previous chapter was the digital payments system issued by J.P. Morgan Chase. This acts like wholesale CBDCs, but as it is privately issued by J.P. Morgan and not the central bank, it's exclusively used by the bank's institutional clients and pegged 1:1 with the U.S. dollar in the style of a stable coin. It supports instant settlements by improving speed and reducing reliance on traditional clearing methods. Retail CBDCs, on the other hand, are intended for the general public and function as a digital alternative to physical cash and traditional digital bank deposits, thereby enabling users to make routine payments. While both forms have strategic importance, it is the retail CBDC that has received the most attention globally, so that is the primary focus here.

MOTIVATION, FUNCTION, AND THE CONSUMER STANDPOINT

The first question to consider when exploring retail CBDCs is what are the main motivations for implementing this technology? With the emergence of digital assets and stablecoins, including CBDCs elsewhere, central banks want to maintain influence over the national currencies that they issue. Not only do they want to avoid losing control, but they also don't want to fall behind in terms of technology. China, for example, is embracing blockchain technology in a big way, but wants to implement it on its own terms.

By introducing a centralised, digital currency China hopes to regain any lost public trust so that CBDCs become the go-to instruments in the digital economy. The aim is to use the technology to enhance the effectiveness of monetary policy and ensure that financial flows stay within formal regulated systems, meaning that they would be traceable. Importantly, this would place the national currency squarely at the centre of daily economic activity.

Another key incentive is due to the declining use of physical cash. In an increasingly digital world, governments see CBDCs as an alternative way to preserve public access to central bank currency.

A government-provided digital wallet would presumably resemble those that we saw in Chapter 9, which would contain the balance of your CBDC account. To work inclusively, and to fully replace cash, everyone would need to have a sufficiently charged mobile phone, which isn't guaranteed for all segments of the community. Clearly, much work is required to determine how benefit payments would be made into wallets, as well as salaries, and how that would integrate with existing bank accounts.

For central banks, CBDCs could provide real-time transactional data and money flows. As well as oversight, policy makers would be better equipped to implement interest rate and other monetary adjustments, which would be extremely beneficial for the speed and impact of their implementation. They also offer governments a direct way to distribute stimulus and manage the money supply to preserve economic stability.

Consumers also stand to benefit from the introduction of CBDCs. This digital form of money is designed to improve payment efficiency and reduce transaction costs. It is being positioned as a way to expand access to the financial system by providing secure, digital payment options to the unbanked, who would no longer require a traditional bank account. Although this would be more relevant to the Global South, it can't be ignored that these issues are still present in the Western world, albeit to a lesser degree. So, as well as domestic payments, they could also optimise how cross-border payments are conducted. However, governments need to be certain that this need is not already filled with decentralised options such as Bitcoin or XRP.

THE EXAMPLE OF CHINA

Countries like China, Sweden, and The Bahamas are leading the way in implementing or piloting CBDCs. Each has its own unique goals, such as promoting financial access by enhancing payment efficiency, or improving transaction transparency. The digital yuan, one of the most advanced CBDC projects, aims to bolster China's monetary control and expand financial reach domestically. Through widespread trials, the People's Bank of China has integrated the digital yuan into various retail applications, with plans for broader adoption. China uses a two-tier model, where the central bank issues e-CNY to commercial banks and payment providers, which then distribute it to consumers.

In June 2021, Chengdu became the first Chinese city to fully integrate the digital yuan into its public transportation system, allowing passengers to pay fares on buses and subways using e-CNY. This was part of broader pilot programmes to test the currency's feasibility in everyday transactions. The digital yuan has also been accepted by major retailers and online platforms, including JD.com, where consumers could use e-CNY to make purchases, demonstrating its potential for widespread retail adoption.

THE BAHAMAS

Known as the "Sand Dollar", the Bahamian CBDC was one of the first fully deployed CBDCs. Its purpose is to enhance financial inclusion by providing a reliable payment option, especially for residents on remote islands with limited access to physical banking infrastructure. In 2021, Bahama Eats, a food delivery company, began paying its employees using the Sand Dollar. Employees who downloaded the Island Pay digital wallet could receive their salaries in the digital currency, showcasing its practical use in payroll operations. It also offers a resilient payment solution during natural disasters when traditional cash distribution might be disrupted, which is particularly important in hurricane-prone Caribbean nations. The Sand Dollar uses a one-tier model, meaning the central bank issues the digital currency directly to consumers through authorised digital wallet providers, without relying on commercial banks.

SWEDEN

The Swedish Riksbank's e-krona project is another good example. Still in its pilot phase, it aims to ensure Swedish residents retain access to central bank-backed currency as cash use declines, reducing the risk of an entirely privatised or alternative cryptocurrency digital payment landscape. This CBDC reflects how digital money can support financial accessibility and adapt to evolving economic trends while providing a secure government-backed currency. Like China, Sweden is exploring a two-tier model, where the central bank would issue the e-krona to intermediaries such as commercial banks, which would then distribute it to the public.

INFRASTRUCTURE DESIGN AND IDENTITY

As touched upon earlier, a fundamental decision for CBDC design is choosing the infrastructure on which it will operate. Centralised databases are the standard approach, offering high efficiency, quick transaction speeds, and robust control for central banks. In a centralised system, a single entity manages the ledger, making it easier to implement regulations and oversee compliance. However, this can reduce transparency and introduces the risk of single points of failure, which can impact the system's resilience.

Alternatively, blockchain-based systems provide a distributed ledger, enhancing transparency and resilience by recording transactions across multiple centrally controlled nodes. While central banks often prefer private, or permissioned blockchains, which restrict access to authorised participants only, this design still allows for decentralised validation and can improve system security. Blockchains can be slower than centralised databases due to consensus mechanisms, which take longer to process transactions, but they enhance transparency and trust within the system. This means that no individual at the central bank would have full control over transaction verification, reducing the potential for misuse.

Most central banks exploring blockchain infrastructure lean towards permissioned blockchains, allowing them to retain control while benefiting from aspects of distributed ledger technology. These blockchains strike a balance between transparency and efficiency, so that central authorities can still regulate and manage the currency while enabling the multi-node verification that increases data integrity. This transparency at the infrastructure level is often framed by policymakers as positive because it supports auditing and real-time insight into financial flows. However, it also begins to open up the conversation around potential surveillance.

DIGITAL IDENTITY AND AUTHENTICATION MECHANISMS

A secure digital identity framework is critical to any CBDC rollout. For the general public to use CBDCs safely, central banks must be able to verify user authentication as well as offer privacy. They also need to be able to effectively manage access and prevent fraud within the system to control access effectively and ensure that transactions are secure. To achieve all these goals, digital identities would need to function much like a digital passport and may have to be tied to existing national ID systems, as well as tax records or social security data.

Some of these projects also propose pseudonymity. This would allow transactions to be traceable without revealing the identity of the user immediately unless legally required. This hybrid model aims to balance user privacy with regulatory oversight. Striking a balance between secure authentication and user privacy is key, particularly in an era where public concern often focuses on data misuse by private companies, rather than primarily by governments.

LEGAL, REGULATORY, AND INTEROPERABILITY FRAMEWORKS

For CBDCs to function effectively in a globalised world, new, shared regulatory standards and international cooperation will be essential. Unlike traditional currencies, CBDCs have unique cross-border implications that could affect everything from foreign exchange to international trade and remittance flows. To facilitate smooth global transactions and uphold financial stability, central banks and regulatory bodies need to align on interoperability frameworks to ensure that national CBDC networks can communicate with each other, much like the Layer 0 protocols do in the decentralised cryptocurrency space. Cooperation on policies such as cybersecurity and AML measures will also be needed to ensure the systems work seamlessly together.

Cooperating also involves addressing data privacy standards across countries with different regulations without compromising financial sovereignty. Ensuring compatibility with existing systems and other CBDCs would prevent fragmentation and enhance trust across markets. Clearly, none of this is going to be easy. Speculation has been increasing that XRP could serve as an intermediate solution, forming a bridge currency to integrate various CBDCs, on a remittance basis. By so doing, it could bypass some of the potential regulatory disparities and be incorporated into a global CBDC international cross-border payment network.

IMPACT ON MONETARY POLICY AND FINANCIAL STABILITY

Given recent economic turbulence, CBDCs could transform financial stability by providing central banks with greater oversight of deposits and money flows. Unlike traditional systems, where commercial banks are the primary custodians of deposits, CBDCs would enable individuals to hold digital currency directly with the central bank. This set-up would offer central banks real-time visibility over deposits and transactions, giving policymakers a clearer picture of economic activity and the ability to respond to financial stress faster. The transparent nature of CBDCs could allow governments to monitor risks more effectively and even prevent bank runs, since these digital deposits would be backed directly by the central bank.

As CBDCs mature, their programmable features could significantly influence the way that central banks implement monetary policy.

In theory, governments could introduce built-in parameters to encourage or restrict certain types of spending, allowing for faster and more targeted economic interventions.

This opens the door to concepts like direct-to-consumer stimulus payments, sometimes referred to as helicopter money, where funds could be deposited directly into digital wallets, bypassing traditional banking, and accelerating policy impact.

While such mechanisms remain largely theoretical, institutions like the IMF and BIS have acknowledged the potential for CBDCs to improve policy efficiently in times of economic stress.

As seen during COVID-19, such tools could give central banks a more agile response to crises. But they also raise important questions about privacy, fairness, and the risk of monetary overreach. The hope is that these systems would truly serve the public interest, rather than obscure unsound policy decisions.

CBDCs could also make negative interest rates more feasible to implement. Unlike physical cash, which retains its face value (inflation aside), regardless of policy decisions, CBDCs can be programmed to depreciate over time and at a specified rate. Doing this could encourage spending and investment during economic downturns. In this way, CBDCs offer a more direct and flexible tool for managing consumption, inflation, and liquidity within the economy.

What's evident is that any direct relationship between central banks and consumers, as in the one-tier model used by the Bahamian Sand Dollar, could pose risks to commercial banks. If, for example, too many people migrated to these CBDC accounts, commercial banks would see reduced reserves. The Polish National bank, for example, has previously expressed concerns over CBDCs for this reason.

In traditional systems, commercial banks are the primarily custodians of deposits, and the flow of funds from these deposits fuels their lending, just as the Medici family did in 1397. Lower reserves could impact banks' ability to lend, especially during times of crisis, which could reshape the entire banking system. It raises questions about how these two will function together and coexist once CBDCs are fully launched.

PUBLIC PERCEPTION, ADOPTION, AND USER EXPERIENCE

To encourage consumer trust and CBDC adoption, central banks must ensure the user experience is intuitive and accessible. CBDCs need to be as easy to use as cash or existing payment apps to smooth the transition. Comprehensive public education will also be essential, both to explain how CBDCs work and to address common concerns.

One of the most significant concerns relates to privacy. While many already share financial data with commercial banks, CBDCs centralise that data under direct governmental control. This could give central banks unprecedented visibility into every transaction and raises questions around surveillance and data security. This isn't to suggest that the public are trying to disguise or obscure the financial transactions they are making, and more a case of protecting their personal financial autonomy. A 2023 survey conducted by the Chartered Financial Analyst (CFA) Institute found that 63% of respondents were concerned about CBDC-related privacy risks. Additionally, a 2022 Cato Institute poll showed that 76% of Americans opposed CBDCs due to fears of governmental control and monitoring.

From the authorities' perspective, some governments and leaders have expressed opposition to CBDCs. In the U.S., President Trump has been a vocal critic of the technology. In January 2025, he issued an Executive Order, titled "Strengthening American Leadership in Digital Financial Technology", which prohibits federal agencies from establishing, issuing, or promoting a U.S. CBDC. The Order expresses many of the criticisms discussed above, such as concerns over financial stability and national sovereignty. President Trump has described a digital dollar as "very dangerous", arguing that it could enable the government to monitor and control individual's financial transactions. Other politicians such as Nigel Farage, of the UK Reform Party, have also expressed scepticism. He similarly emphasises a pledge to spearhead a "crypto revolution" in Britain.

Either way, CBDCs are still being positioned by many countries as the future of government-issued money, a digital replacement for cash that promises lower fees, improved efficiency, and enhanced financial inclusion. But the question remains: at what cost? Behind the promises may lurk a motive of control. Many governments, including China, seem to want real-time visibility over financial activity to maintain the hegemony of digital fiat currencies. This isn't necessarily surprising given that throughout history, the evolution of money has often been driven not just by innovation, but by power. As new technologies emerge, including cryptocurrencies and AI, eventually those in power will try to harness them. So, why should CBDCs be any different?

The issue of control over individuals' finances is indeed a significant part of the debate. As CBDCs allow every transaction to be monitored, logged, and analysed by the authorities, it creates an unprecedented level of oversight. Hopefully, it also means a tool with unprecedented power to track money flow and fight fraud, as well as illicit activities that will ultimately strengthen financial regulation.

The difficulty is that CBDCs could theoretically enable governments to control how the general public spend their money, which would be like living under a dictatorship.

For example, in 2024, Thailand launched a digital wallet scheme that involved distributing funds via a government-developed app to low-income households. While not officially a CBDC, the scheme's features resembled one. The funds in the wallet had to be spent within six months and were restricted to specific goods and local merchants, while excluding items like alcohol and online purchases. This process aimed to stimulate targeted economic activity but raised concerns about overreach and social engineering. And rightly so. China's e-CNY also showed signs of this during certain pilot programmes, where the currency had to be spent within a set timeframe and was limited to specific geographical locations.

These concerns are certainly not speculative; they reveal the reality of where this technology might take us. In more extreme scenarios, individuals express fears that CBDCs could pave the way for a "social credit" style system, whereby spending might one day be restricted based on behaviour. While such concerns might seem speculative, and likely far-fetched in demographic countries, the danger is still being felt by some.

The push for digital currencies will likely bring about a fundamental shift in the role of central banks, if they have widespread implementation that requires an evolution in regulatory and technical standards. As CBDCs develop, maintaining a balance between innovation and security will be crucial to building public trust and ensuring that these digital currencies are a positive force in the evolving financial landscape.

In my opinion, CBDCs still inherit the underlying issues of inflation and currency debasement that plague fiat currency, and those that blockchain technology has been trying to address in the first place.

For CBDCs to succeed, central banks must tackle all these challenges, by carefully avoiding destabilising the global financial landscape, yet leveraging the benefits of a blockchain-based digital financial system. With the growing popularity of traditional cryptocurrencies by governments and institutions, policy makers will need to strike a balance to help ensure that CBDCs are both complementary and technologically forward-looking, while respectful of citizens' rights and spending habits. There would be no other way to build a secure and trustworthy digital currency system that aligns with public expectations.

Chapter 15

The Future of Finance

Mayor Amschel Rothschild, the banker and the founder of the Rothschild banking dynasty, has been credited as saying "give me control of a nation's money and I care not who writes the laws". The more you control the money, the more you control everything. Money isn't just a tool, it's the thread running through each part of our lives. Every action. Every decision. Every single day. Whether it's working, driving, eating or sleeping in a home that you rent or own with a mortgage. They are all tied to money in some way. Everything that you do, the other side is money. Control the money and you control all that flows from it. In a world where centralised control has historically dictated monetary flows, Bitcoin and blockchain technology represents a shift towards decentralisation, offering individuals sovereignty over their wealth.

In reality, the control of money has always been intertwined with power, shaping economies, societies, and even the fate of nations. This shows the revolutionary potential of digital assets, as they introduce a fundamentally different approach to monetary systems, one that drives inclusivity and resists centralised control.

We have explored such a wide array of use cases and ways the technology could improve the financial system we live in. We have also seen many of the drawbacks and challenges that need to be addressed for this technology to thrive. There is no doubt that we are still really early in this adoption phase. What an exciting era to live through, watching whether this technology can really pivot away from the financial direction that we had been heading in.

The financial world is on the cusp of transformation. From Bitcoin's humble beginnings as a decentralised digital currency to the widespread interest in blockchain technology and decentralised finance, we are witnessing a paradigm shift that challenges the traditional models of banking and financial governance, as well as fiat currency. Central banks, corporations, and everyday individuals are now grappling with how to adapt to the possibilities these technologies offer.

This shift is not just technological. It's philosophical. Humanitarian. Bitcoin's genesis block in 2009 was a direct response to the vulnerabilities exposed by the global financial crisis. It posed a question: What if money could exist outside the control of governments and central banks? In answering this question, Bitcoin laid the foundation for an entirely new financial framework.

Throughout this book, we have explored Bitcoin as both a digital asset and a catalyst for broader changes in global finance. In the span of just over a decade, Bitcoin and blockchain technology have emerged as powerful forces disrupting traditional finance and reshaping global monetary systems.

We have delved into the rise of blockchain, the intricacies of Bitcoin, the proliferation of alternative cryptocurrencies, the disruptive potential of NFTs, and the increasing interest from governments in adopting blockchain technology in the form of traditional cryptocurrencies as well as CBDCs. From the emergence of Bitcoin in 2009, to the evolution of alternative cryptocurrencies and their associated use cases. From the upheavals of hyperinflation crises to the bold embrace of Bitcoin as legal tender in El Salvador, and from the adoption of Exchange-Traded Funds (ETFs) to the growing influence of institutional money, our exploration has uncovered a landscape of innovation, challenges, and transformative potential.

Beyond these milestones lies a vision. A financial future. One of decentralisation, transparency, and driven by technology.

What unites these innovations is an aim to create a future where financial systems are more technologically efficient. A world where tomorrow is becoming much more digital than it is today. Our journey thus far has made clear that these innovations represent more than just technological advancement, they offer a vision for the future of money, finance, and governance.

In this context, Bitcoin's role as "digital gold" becomes even more crucial. Its fixed supply and decentralised nature contrast sharply with traditional fiat currencies, which can be printed at will. This scarcity positions Bitcoin as a long-term store of value and a hedge against inflation. Yet the narrative extends beyond Bitcoin to encompass a broader transformation: blockchain's potential to revolutionise industries, decentralised finance's promise to empower the unbanked, and AI's integration into blockchain systems for unprecedented efficiency.

Already, industries are exploring blockchain's transformative power, from supply chain transparency to tokenising real estate, laying the groundwork for widespread adoption.

In this final chapter, we bring these themes together to envision the future of finance. Will Bitcoin truly become the "digital gold" it promises to be? How will decentralised systems interact with digital currencies like CBDCs?

And what role will blockchain play in reshaping industries beyond finance? But before these questions can be addressed, we need to determine whether the debt-ridden global financial system can survive as we know it.

DEBT ON A NATIONAL SCALE

As we have seen throughout this book, keeping a lid on growing national debt levels and combatting inflation and currency debasement is a fundamental problem for governments globally. The struggle not to capitulate to rampant inflation as so many previous empires have done, is global. In 2025, central banks are doing everything they can to lower interest rates, so they can issue more liquidity into the system, however, if they inject too much, too quickly, runaway inflation could ensue.

From the mounting troubles in recent years, from the global financial crisis to the trillions of dollars printed during COVID-19, many countries simply can't cope with these high debt levels. None, however, are as severe as in the U.S. In comparison, the UK is over $3.3 trillion in debt, with Japan sitting at around $10 trillion and China's national debt rising to around $14 trillion. While these levels are high, they need to be viewed in light of the GDP of each country. Although the U.S. is the world's largest economy with a GDP of approximately $30 trillion, its debt level is a staggering $36 trillion, giving it a debt-to-GDP ratio of over 120%. This issue has received even more scrutiny since the beginning of Donald Trump's second term in office. Not only is it historically high, it even exceeds the peak seen after World War II. If we compare this ratio to the UK at just under 100% and that of China at around 77%, if this reported figure is considered accurate, we can see that the U.S. owes more than the money it brings in each year. This raises grave concerns about its fiscal sustainability, and in particular over the high interest payments on its debt and the lingering threat of inflation.

We have already spoken about the situation in Japan and its extreme levels of QE since the turn of the century. In fact, the Japanese debt-to-GDP ratio now surpasses 216%, showing a clear indication of the damning consequences that years of consistent injections of liquidity brings forth. To put this into perspective, as of March 2025, the Bank of Japan holds approximately 43% of the country's outstanding debt. So, as the Japanese government frequently issues more debt, it is their very own central bank who is the main buyer and holder of this debt. Foreign buyers have become increasingly reluctant to hold Japanese debt securities and government bonds. As we have seen in Chapter 12, this is why Japan had to employ yield curve controls to artificially maintain low interest rates. If borrowing costs start to rise, it would drastically destabilise the national bond market and the government would be unable to service its ever-increasing debt burden.

Now, let's return to the situation in the U.S. Other countries are still willing to buy U.S. debt at present. However, if countries and pension funds pull away from wanting to hold this debt, the U.S. is going to be in an increasingly difficult position.

If the confidence in the U.S. bond market breaks, the entire structure built on cheap debt becomes unsustainable, and governments could face soaring borrowing costs, sell-offs in currencies, and forced austerity or traditional money printing, just to keep the system afloat.

The high debt levels of the 1930s were at least anchored by a hard asset like gold, but now everything is built around debt and the collective trust in bond markets. If this falters, the systematic collapse would be devastating, making the global financial crisis of 2008 and the Wall Street Crash of 1929 appear to be mere momentary blips.

This is the reason that the Federal Reserve is walking a finely balanced tightrope. On the one hand concerns mount about the uptick in inflation, but on the other, there is a need to preserve the longevity of the U.S. bond market. Should U.S. Treasury reserves continue to deplete at the current rate, they will soon void their ability to service their growing debt interest payments, as well as the principal on some of these loans, while managing to provide money for government spending. Productivity levels and GDP growth are simply not high enough to bring in enough tax revenue to fund U.S. debt and fiscal operations. As John Maynard Keynes, founder of the Keynesian school of economics, once warned:

"By a continuing process of inflation, governments can confiscate, secretly and unobserved, an important part of the wealth of their citizens." That quiet confiscation is becoming ever more visible. This tale is beginning to sound ever so familiar to those that arose in Chapters 4 and 5.

For the U.S. and the whole global financial system as we know it to escape from this potential financial catastrophe, in my opinion, three things need to happen. First, the U.S. needs to preserve trust in its bond market, at least in the short-term, as China and Japan are large holders of their government debt, and weakened demand would constitute a big problem.

Secondly, the Federal Reserve, as well as other central banks, need to continue increasing the addition of liquidity into the system and end programmes of QT. This would replenish its depleted monetary balance in the Treasury, so that it maintains its capacity to service its debt burden and allows the government to continue servicing the needs of its country, thereby avoiding social and civil unrest.

And thirdly, global productivity levels need to drastically improve so that countries are better equipped to increase their GDPs, enabling them to reduce their growing debt levels and be better positioned to service national debt without purely relying on the safeguards of liquidity injections.

As we have seen so many times in this book, multiple rounds of liquidity — whether through short-term reverse repo markets (RRP), or the growing issuance of short-term Treasury bills boosting the M2 money supply, fluctuations in the Treasury General Account (TGA), excess reserve balances held by banks or even global QE interventions — have only provided temporary relief, but none offer a long-term solution. I am not condemning this method of resolution by any means, but the reality is that there are not many other options left on the table, other than a violent systematic reset. Once these shorter-term debts have been refinanced, core changes need to be implemented, and we will come to those shortly. For now, let's focus on what the impact of this liquidity influx might be in the coming months of 2025 and beyond.

Liquidity drives asset prices. And liquidity debases fiat currency, leading to inflation because the more money that flows into the system, the more banks lend and invest. Holders of fiat currency see their purchasing power diminish, and holders of scarce assets see their value rise. It doesn't matter what the asset class is, whether it be stocks, gold, rare artwork, Rolex watches or cryptocurrencies.

More liquidity in the system drives asset prices higher, and digital assets tend to thrive in such environments. While Bitcoin benefits from strong fundamentals — from the way its value scales with network adoption, as explained through Metcalfe's law, to the speculative interest generated by its four-year halving cycles — these advantages still rely on an abundance of liquidity to fully take effect. It makes sense, therefore, that cryptocurrencies and gold are being seen as prime store-of-value assets to protect against this. As we saw in Chapter 5, Gresham's Law tells us that "bad money drives out the good money" from participating in the economy, as it is preferable to hoard good money like gold or Bitcoin and spend the bad depreciating fiat currency instead.

And Chapter 7 showed that liquidity is one of the main drivers of Bitcoin and cryptocurrencies, with their price movements almost perfectly tracking changes in the M2 money supply. It happened especially in 2017. It happened as well in 2021, and then the bull market came to a crashing end when it dried up in 2022.

> **"Bitcoin is digital property. It's the first time in the history of the human race that we've created a form of property that you can take custody of with full custodial rights, with full integrity, that is not a liability of anybody else."**
>
> — Michael Saylor, Co-Founder, Strategy

One of the key advocates endorsing this train of thought is Michael Saylor. The co-founder and executive chairman of Strategy has become the first institutional mover to safeguard his company's wealth using Bitcoin as a reserve asset, in anticipation of this high central bank liquidity-driven market. Finding himself sitting on a large stockpile of fiat currency in Strategy's accounts, Saylor realised that there must be another way to protect that wealth, especially after the trillions being pumped into the system during COVID-19. He has become one of the most prominent advocates for Bitcoin, positioning it as a cornerstone of his company's corporate strategy. Under Saylor's leadership, Strategy began acquiring Bitcoin in 2020 as a treasury reserve asset, citing its potential as a hedge against inflation and a superior store of value compared with traditional fiat currencies.

When Michael Saylor talks about Bitcoin he says: "Bitcoin is the best capital asset. What is capital? It is pure economic energy; Bitcoin is digital capital. It is the first occurrence of pure economic energy in human history."

"It gave us branding, it brought us investments, it brought us tourism", he said. "I do believe that the positive outcomes outweigh the negative, and the issues that have been highlighted are relatively minor."

— Nayib Bukele, President of El Salvador

El Salvador, under Nayib Bukele's leadership, became the first nation-state to adopt Bitcoin as a treasury asset in September 2021. Although the pathway destination of legal tender has been halted by the IMF, the country has launched Bitcoin-backed bonds, using domestically mined BTC, and introduced a citizenship-by-investment programme for foreigners who contribute to government funds. Bukele had a vision of El Salvador breaking the tradition of gang violence and transforming the country into a tech-savvy, investment-friendly destination. To him, Bitcoin is a strategic alignment to fulfil the broader vision of this transformation.

A STORE OF NATIONAL WEALTH

In fact, it's more than that. Bukele has highlighted El Salvador's role as a "first mover" in governmental Bitcoin adoption, noting how Wall Street now offers a range of Bitcoin-based investment products and how cryptocurrency has played a prominent role in the most-recent U.S. presidential election, with Donald Trump's pro-crypto and Bitcoin campaign helping to sway voters to victory. Through direct purchases and its citizenship programme, El Salvador has accumulated a substantial Bitcoin reserve. According to Bukele, the country's public wallet holds over $500 million in BTC.

BITCOIN ELSEWHERE

This is the first purposeful step at a national level to introduce cryptocurrencies onto the reserve balance sheet, and other countries are likely to follow suit in the near future. With the introduction of the Bitcoin and Ethereum spot ETFs and with large institutions getting into the space, driven further by President Trump's pro-crypto stance, this all ties into adoption erupting on a grand scale. As we know the U.S. has announced plans to incorporate a number of cryptocurrencies as a national reserve asset, which shows similarities to how governments used to stockpile gold for similar reasons, which might suggest that more countries will also follow suit.

BITCOIN STILL MUST PROVE ITSELF

Although large economies including China banned crypto in 2021, including bitcoin mining — this didn't halt its global appeal. With migrating mining operations and ongoing volatility, the asset class's ability to evade every obstacle in its path shows immense resilience.

We saw what happened to Amazon in 2001 after the dot-com crisis. Despite its value dropping by 95%, it recovered from that setback and went on to prosper. Bitcoin is a technology.

And it, too, has endured crashes of over 90% of its value, only to bounce back time and again, while continuing its overall upward trajectory since inception. However, there's no denying that we are still early. Early in infrastructure. In adoption. In valuations. Cryptocurrencies are like tiny shrimp swimming among the giant sharks in the turquoise depths of the Pacific Ocean. Compared with other asset classes, Bitcoin and Altcoins are the mice among men. The hornets within the electrifying field of cyberspace. The estimated total value of all the assets and all the sectors in the world in 2025 is valued at over $600 trillion. With the crypto market worth around $3.5 trillion, this only represents around 0.06% of the global assets. Obviously, these figures can change rapidly, but it clearly shows how small a sector it is.

Figure 15.1: Global Asset Distribution (2025, approx. $600T)

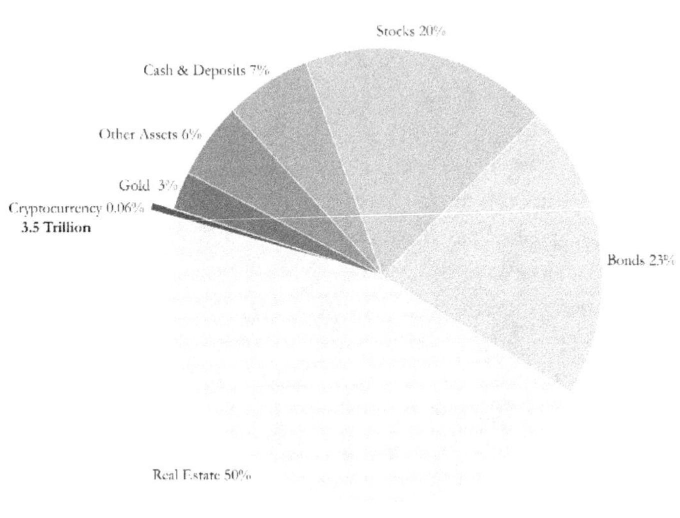

Sources: https://www.mckinsey.com/business-functions/mckinsey-global-institute/. https://www.sifma.org/resources/research/statistics/. https://www.world-exchanges.org/. https://www.imf.org/. https://www.blackrock.com/. https://www.gold.org/. https://www.gold.org/

Figure 15.1 highlights how early Bitcoin and altcoins are in terms of total market valuations, leaving substantial room for growth. The potential is clear, however, in predictions from influential figures such as Cathie Wood of Ark Invest, who projects Bitcoin could reach over $1 million per coin by 2030, and $1.5 million in a bullish case, according to her "Big Ideas 2025" report. "*At present the generally safe allocation to Bitcoin is seen as being around 1-2%*", however, over time she expects these allocations to go over 5%. If these projections materialise, Bitcoin could capture a much larger share of global asset allocations in the years ahead. However, for this to happen, we need a clear regulatory pathway so that more institutions are legally allowed to add Bitcoin and other crypto-currencies to their portfolio holdings.

As mentioned in Chapter 13, The GENIUS Act (Guiding and Establishing National Innovation for U.S. Stablecoins Act), is currently advancing through the U.S. Senate, with the aim of establishing a comprehensive regulatory framework for stable-coins. This requires stablecoin issuers to maintain a 1:1 backing with liquid assets and adhere to strict disclosure and compliance standards, which will provide clarity and legitimacy, as well as new liquidity to the stablecoin market. This will be complemented with the STABLE Act, which clarifies the legal status of payment stablecoins, and explicitly excludes those issued by permitted issu-ers from being classified as securities. This is a massive step as it provides the regulatory certainty needed for institutional investors, such as pension funds, to allocate a portion of their portfolios to digital assets like Bitcoin. If Cathie Wood's prediction of alloca-tions up to or even surpassing 5% were to come true, we could see a huge take-up in crypto valuations. Additionally, it is likely that other countries within the Euro zone and the UK would follow suit. So, it may not be long before our pensions actually hold and allocate to cryptocurrency. The question remains whether these pension funds, who are large holders of government bonds, might divert some of these holdings into cryptocurrencies.

When any institution or government compiles a reserve asset, they do so as a form of sovereign security. A means to protect the interests of the country or institution and something to fall back on. They did this with gold in the past, as we know. Having hard assets in reserve also gives the financial system something of an anchor of prosperity and security. Something with true perceived value, rather than just a piece of paper. Therefore, I perceive two possible outcomes considering strategic crypto asset reserves.

MOTIVATIONS FOR GOVERNMENTAL CRYPTO ASSET STOCKPILES

It's tempting to speculate that the U.S. is seeing crypto as a way to escape from its debt burden. And I certainly foresee the sale of a proportion of its strategic assets to prevent global economic collapse, that is if Americans decide it is worth saving. Perhaps they see systemic failure as the first step to reducing the debt? Are they making these investments now because they envisage soon pumping in trillions of dollars in liquidity, and they want to allow themselves as well as pension funds an obvious slice of the pie before this money enters the system? After all, doing so would massively debase the debts the U.S. currently holds.

Perhaps these assets could be a way of protecting value outside of traditional systems, assuming we envisage a total global reset, with all debt wiped off the table. Of course, anyone with savings would have them wiped off the table as well. As you can't really strip away people's property, or crypto ownership, so holding these types of assets could be a good way to safeguard yourself, in case of either of these possibilities. Does the U.S. in fact view the fiat currency system as finished, and crypto asset stockpiles will instead propel a new economic standard, with digital currencies being at the forefront?

Could traditional Cryptocurrencies Coexist with Fiat and CBDCs?

As governments explore Central Bank Digital Currencies (CBDCs), questions arise about how these state-controlled digital assets might coexist with decentralised alternatives like Bitcoin. This intersection could present a unique opportunity to create interoperable systems, where Bitcoin could function as a global reserve asset within a stockpile or similar framework, as gold used to, and CBDCs could facilitate localised transactions. The answers to these questions lie in the evolving landscape of global finance, where technological advancement, regulatory frameworks, and public sentiment will collectively shape the future. What is clear, however, is that we are at the dawn of a new era, one in which financial power dynamics are being renegotiated, creating both risks and opportunities for everyone involved.

One option would be to integrate CBDCs into these systems, if traditional fiat currencies continue to exist. Or it could replace it entirely. It would be interesting to see whether there would still be dependence on commercial banks, within a two-tier system.

Whichever eventuality plays out, hard assets need to be at the centre of it. For fiat currency to continue, a crypto reserve asset or gold should be tied to it in some way. A CBDC being tied to a crypto asset in many ways would make sense as they are both digital. Perhaps the answer is for the monetary base to be strategically expanded and contracted but with careful guardrails in place and algorithmically tied to the digital assets that are held in reserves. This would be a clever way to allow some monetary policy, providing there were enough conditions in place so it couldn't become a reckless practice, like it has been since 1971.

In the second scenario, where there is a full-blown reset, and fiat currency no longer exists, then it shouldn't take long to decide on the type of monetary base will support the economy. We are past the stage of using soft commodities like barley or corn to transact with, since they don't store value and are perishable. Gold has worked for hundreds of years but doesn't really work in the modern, tech-driven world because people will just end up using methods like paper currency to represent it, so the physical gold is not used in practice. Also, moving large amounts between countries or businesses on a reserve asset basis is awkward, as is moving it around as a medium of exchange in the digital world.

We have tried and failed countless times with a fiat currency system throughout history and while intentions may seem good at the beginning, I think the only reason it has been used before is because there wasn't anything better.

With the technology that is being created today, we now do have something better. Whether something new is going to jump out of nowhere to become the asset to implement this change, is impossible to say. What I would say, however, is that we need a strong, decentralised, permissionless, tamper-proof secure asset, and it looks like that could be Bitcoin. Becoming a global reserve asset and backing the entire financial system is no mean feat. Bitcoin could be at the centre of all other currencies in use. A backbone that other digital assets could interact with, creating a large network of interoperable cryptocurrencies each with their own unique use cases.

With all that in mind, it is important to understand that aside from the bond market and central bank liquidity, the issue that we must seriously address is that of productivity. Regardless of the outcome of our current financial system, we need to build a more sustainable level of economic output. So, the question arises, how are we going to boost productivity when we have a large global ageing population?

Ageing populations shrink the labour force and increase the cost burden for governments, as they have higher pensions, and those liabilities last for longer. Not to mention the increased healthcare and social care costs that also contribute to this burden. With fewer workers and slower population growth, it makes it increasingly difficult for productivity to keep pace with our current debts, and this makes it harder to raise GDP sufficiently to combat the worsening debt-to-GDP ratios we saw above.

Global society has changed hugely since the baby boomer generation. People now don't have as many children. A lot of the time they can't afford to, as the wealth inequality in developed countries has become as bad as it has ever been.

For the majority, this means working long hours for little pay. Focusing on their careers so not to fall behind, which has heavily contributed to the demographic generational imbalance. Not only do ageing populations contain fewer people of working age to help boost productivity and increase GDP, but the elderly need to be paid for through worker taxation to fund their state pensions, and their care home fees. The whole system has been set up with lifetime assumptions, but people are living much longer these days. If we do move into a new system where it is no longer possible to simply create virtual money and pump it into the system, what is the solution? I believe the answer lies in the introduction of meaningful AI automation and robotics, with cryptocurrencies being the functional transactional worth within this framework. This would allow a higher volume of performance-based tasks to be achieved, and in some cases, faster and more efficiently than before.

Construction workers. Delivery drivers. Warehouse workers. Cleaning staff. These are all jobs that could be done by robots with AI integration. In fact, in the U.S. there are already many driverless cars in some large cities, which are replacing the need for human drivers, while a large number of robots work in Amazon's factories in place of humans. Tasks like sorting, packing, lifting, and transporting items are increasingly being done by robots. There have even been trials of the first robot police officer in China. So, could the world be moving towards a system where AI, robots, and digital currencies will be the backbone of how we live, work, and transact?

Robotics and AI are not just confined to manual tasks either. Aside from reshaping traditional industries, AI is also integrating seamlessly into the evolving world of cryptocurrency and blockchain technology, creating new opportunities for efficiency, innovation, as well as the adaptation to global challenges. With an ageing population and rising energy costs, AI-driven solutions are becoming essential. The synergy between AI, cheap energy, and blockchain technology could redefine how economies operate, bridging gaps in labour and automating tasks across various sectors.

In the cryptocurrency space, AI projects are still speculative. Some still see them as memecoins. It's virtually impossible even to know which ones, if any, will actually succeed.

Projects in the crypto space will aim to use AI to revolutionise how data is analysed, decisions are made, and processes are automated, yet in a decentralised fashion. For instance, AI-powered algorithms are increasingly used in trading platforms to predict market trends, optimise portfolio management, and even facilitate decentralised autonomous organisations (DAOs). These AI tools help streamline operations, reduce human error, and adapt to rapidly changing market conditions, enhancing the overall ecosystem's efficiency.

By leveraging the blockchain with AI, transparent tracking of supply chains, production outputs, and resource allocation has potential to boost accountability, efficiency, and scalability.

So, if these AI systems, integrated with blockchain technology are going to work, how will we produce the electricity to power them? This is going to use trillions of KW/h, perhaps surpassing existing capacity, and it's all going to be extremely expensive. Is it really going to be more efficient on a cost-side basis to implement?

We need to orchestrate the infrastructure to allow these new technologies to operate. All these future systems rely on an abundance of plentiful energy. We saw in Chapter 10 how much Bitcoin mining costs. From large language models from OpenAI, as well as Microsoft, Deepseek, and video conferencing software like Zoom, all of them are energy intensive. As well as trying to move over to electric cars, there are also plans to do away with gas boilers in favour of electric heating systems. As well as damaging the environment, oil won't last forever.

All of this ties into the need for improvements to infrastructure that will create cheap electricity and utilise renewable energy sources. Underutilised sources, such as those mentioned in Chapter 10 in Scandinavia, will also assist with these goals. The solution is to be able to produce an abundance of electricity at almost no cost and this is the direction that many governments have been taking in recent years.

Ultimately by leveraging robots and AI, crypto protocols could decentralise energy, allowing homes and businesses to also use the technology on a decentralised basis. And if everybody became a Bitcoin or crypto miner, that would secure the core layers of governance. Then you wouldn't need a heavy-handed government that could control the way you spent your money. The government would just need to ensure the infrastructure was in place, and that it worked.

Bitcoin mining operations, particularly in regions leveraging renewable energy like hydro and solar, are already showcasing how blockchain networks can thrive sustainably, reducing their carbon footprint while maintaining network security. There has also been mention of every household in the future having their own renewable energy sources. If these were connected to a small mining rig, everyone could contribute to the Bitcoin network, decentralising it further.

As long as there is no central control, there would be collective participation, just like the public ledger used on Yap Island. And let's learn from the lessons from this Micronesian Island region, where interference from European explorers led to the over-extraction and importation of Rai stones from Palau Island. Once they were no longer scarce, it completely destabilised the public ledger financial system.

As AI chat systems advance, speculation has been rife over where the space could go. The intelligence in the AI systems is becoming so great that in a year or two it's predicted that their IQs could reach well over 240, making them more intelligent than humans. Currently we are limited by the speed of inputs into the computers. For example, it's the speed of using a mouse or a keyboard that's limited, rather than computers' ability to process the inputs. In their place, voice-activated inputs, where the AI could fully respond to voice requests would greatly improve efficiency and speed. Going one step further, if you can give the AI processes to perform, they would be able to do tasks such as booking tickets to the theatre or a holiday. There is talk of having your own personal AI agent, which would know all of your preferences. And neuroscience developments mean that even thinking about what you want the computer to do for you will achieve the input.

Consider this scenario. It's Friday afternoon, and Alex is wrapping up his work when a thought crosses his mind, he hasn't seen his friends in a while.

- "Hey Nova, can you sort out a dinner with Jake, Priya, and Sam for tomorrow evening? Somewhere with good seafood, maybe near the river," Alex says.

- Nova, his AI assistant, responds instantly.

- "Got it. I'll check their schedules and preferences and find the best option."

- Within seconds, Nova pings the AI assistants of Jake, Priya, and Sam. Each of their AI agents already knows their dietary preferences, preferred dining times, and availability.

- Jake's AI, "Echo," responds: "Jake is free tomorrow evening but prefers something with vegetarian options."

- Priya's AI, "Lyra," replies: "Priya is in! She'd love somewhere with a nice cocktail menu."

- Sam's AI, "Vera," chimes in: "Sam's available but prefers a quiet place, not too crowded."

- With all the input collected, Nova cross-checks restaurant reviews, available bookings, and even factors in real-time traffic data.

Ⓑ "How about The Azure Bistro? It's by the river, has great seafood and vegetarian options, a top-rated cocktail menu, and a quieter atmosphere than most spots on a Saturday night."

Ⓑ The AI agents confirm with each other, ensuring no conflicts. A few seconds later, the booking is made, and all four friends receive a message:

Ⓑ "Dinner at The Azure Bistro, 7:30 PM tomorrow. Table booked under Alex. See you there!"

Ⓑ Alex smiles. No back-and-forth texts, no debating over restaurant choices, no stress. Just a seamless arrangement, handled entirely by AI.

Ⓑ "Thanks Nova. That was quick."

Ⓑ "Of course, Alex. Anything else I can do for you?"

Ⓑ "Yeah, remind me to tell Jake not to be late this time."

Ⓑ "Already done."

An AI agent could even do things like manage your investments for you and make investments based on your preferences, and this really does go hand in hand with crypto and automated technologies. Especially if cryptocurrency could exchange value from AI-to-AI agent transactions. It could also be as simple as the AI agents being paid to arrange the meal as above. We could even look at robot-to-robot transactions. Think about the driverless cars. On needing to recharge or fill up with petrol, robots could operate the fuel station. Here digital currencies could be exchanged with ease to make these types of payments.

Integrating AI with cryptocurrency and blockchain works so well together, marking a significant step towards a more interconnected and autonomous future. As these technologies evolve, they will not only address the challenges of ageing populations and energy demands but also create entirely new business models for work, finance, and global collaboration.

BOOSTING PRODUCTIVITY WITH AI AND BLOCKCHAIN

In the past there were factory workers and bankers. Soon, a larger portion of the workforce could be responsible for building robots, compiling smart contracts, and enhancing blockchain innovation, instead.

People will prosper if they learn how to use this technology. Developers. Programmers. People that can manage this technology. Creative designers. Implementers. In just a few years, many of the jobs that can be automated may soon be made obsolete. People who acquire assets will do well, like they do now. The workforce will be much smaller, and this shift is already starting. Advances in technology mean it won't require many people to implement. With productivity at its peak, funding people would be easy to do. Most would receive payments similar to a basic income. Like a flat-rate wage designed to cover their cost of living. As productivity would be so high, they would not need to do any meaningful work, so the way many people live could drastically change. Perhaps new systems will materialise as a consequence, but that is anyone's guess. But I feel the opportunities will be there for those who embrace the technology.

As we look forward, this is a time to embrace innovation while also remaining vigilant to the challenges. Whether Bitcoin becomes a new standard for wealth preservation, or whether blockchain technology will be the foundation of global economic systems, one thing is certain: the future of finance is being shaped right now. The question is no longer whether Bitcoin and blockchain will have an impact, but how profound that impact will be. The future of finance is being shaped now, and it's a future we all must engage with and understand.

FUTURE OF INFRASTRUCTURE AND CRYPTO BANKING

One thing to remember is that the Bitcoin network and all the current and new projects coming onto the market are the infrastructure layers of the technology. Yes, we should understand the principles and how the technology operates. But it is also crucial to appreciate that like all good infrastructure, this layer will be behind the front end of what the user will see. It's just like logging into your banking application to input your username and password, or using face recognition. In the same way, blockchain technology could be the backbone of how online transactions are processed.

In future, instead of going onto a decentralised exchange, connecting your MetaMask wallet, and using your private keys and seed phrases, decentralised banks and banking apps could hold your digital currencies. With the use of AI and smart contracts, these functionalities could all be built into a web 3.0 application.

Imagine a new bank called Freedom Bank, which is not controlled by an institution, but is decentralised and functions on a community level. If you wanted to invest in the bank, purchasing Freedom Bank tokens would make you part of the community that helps the bank to operate. Instead of central banks controlling everything and potentially manipulating the currency, your collective could secure financial inclusion and prosperity for the customers. Token holders could jointly secure the network and ensure that transactions ran smoothy. There would be no shareholders, no exorbitant bankers' bonuses, and no risk of currency debasement.

Alongside, central bank digital currencies could support this set-up as well. Ultimately, the collective desire is to minimise currency manipulation. Should financial uncertainty arise within a free market, then market forces would naturally deal with the problem, rather than problematic methods like quantitative easing giving false hope of a resolution.

To overcome governmental fears of new CBDCs being overlooked in favour of Bitcoin, they may be interoperable in future.

With Bitcoin potentially becoming a global reserve asset, governments, institutions, and individuals alike could hold a store of it, just as they currently might hold U.S. Dollars or gold reserves. Finally, Bitcoin payments and salaries could be commonplace, or it could be converted to native CBDCs to pay taxes.

PROPERTY, GAMING, AND AI

Take a moment to again think about how we currently buy and invest in properties. If each property were added to a block-chain, the whole process would be much easier. We'd still need professionals to conduct surveyor reports and log them into smart contracts, for example, as a criterion of the purchase. What peace of mind that would bring.

The same would be true for the legal aspects. Some conveyancers are already moving more in this direction, by having app checklists and uploading property searches and documentation, so again, smart contracts and AI could make the process so much more efficient.

Now think about how games are usually made — large studios, publishers, and a lot of upfront capital. But imagine if players could purchase tokens to back a project and, in return, own a share in its future success. These tokens could act as both a funding mechanism and a form of shared ownership, giving players a percentage of the game's future revenue or profits. For smaller independent studios, this could be a game-changer, allowing them to raise capital directly from their communities.

Another intriguing intersection is the role of AI in autonomous finance. AI could manage decentralised finance protocols by automating smart contract execution and full risk assessments. Fraud is unlikely to avoid AI's gaze, so transactions would be secure, efficient, and unbiased. By integrating AI into crypto networks, systems could self-optimise and even manage liquidity efficiently. The result would be a much more robust and resilient financial framework.

Financial Innovation Belongs to Everyone

Now, breaking everything down and avoiding all the noise for the people who might still say that blockchain and cryptocurrency is just a gamble, that's fine. But remember you're placing a bet on the technology, on the infrastructure level, you're buying into the fact that the world tomorrow is going to be even more digital than it is today. While it wasn't possible to purchase any of the infrastructure layer of the internet, or to be an initial seed investor of Google or Amazon, with crypto you can. We are still incredibly early, and it'll be thrilling to see where this technology will go and where adoption will take us, and what positive utility this can all bring to our lives.

The journey into the future of finance does not belong to governments, banks, or technologists alone. It belongs to us all. The decisions we make in the coming years, about how we engage with these technologies, how we use them, and how we regulate them, will shape the world for generations to come. Bitcoin and blockchain have given us the tools, but the future remains unwritten.

It is our responsibility to harness these tools to build a financial system that is fairer, more transparent, and more inclusive. A system that respects individual sovereignty, promotes innovation and resists corruption. As you, the reader, step away from this book and into the unfolding world of decentralised finance, remember that you are not just a passive observer of history. You are a participant in shaping the future of global finance. The story of Bitcoin and blockchain technology is far from over; in fact, it is just beginning. With every block added to the chain, every decentralised application launched, and every new person empowered through financial inclusion, we are collectively writing the next chapter of human progress.

The future of finance is not a distant horizon, it is here, now, waiting to be claimed. As we stand on the threshold of a financial revolution, it is vital to embrace these technologies with both enthusiasm and caution. The choices we make today will define not just the future of finance but the values that underpin it. Thank you for joining me on this journey. The world is changing, and you are now a part of that change. The future of finance is in your hands. Let's build it together.

References

The following references were retrieved in June 2025, unless otherwise specified.

Chapter 1

- Carstens, A. (2023) Trust and Public Policies; *BIS*; Available at: https://www.bis.org/speeches/sp230519.htm
- *Critical Past* (1932) Available at: https://www.criticalpast.com/video/65675068204_children-face-winter-suffering_chow-line_child-cries_men-collect-food
- Elliot, F. & Duncan, G. (3 Jan 2009) Chancellor Alistair Darling on Brink of Second Bailout for Banks; *The Times*; Available at: https://www.thetimes.com/business-money/companies/article/chancellor-alistair-darling-on-brink-of-second-bailout-for-banks-n9l382mn62h
- ENDEVR (2015) *Bitcoin: The End of Money as We Know it*; YouTube; Available at: https://www.youtube.com/watch?v=BFKZoq2z39s&t=3474s
- Hayek, F. (1976) *Denationalisation of Money*; The Institute of Economic Affairs, London.
- Kramer, L (2024) *The Stock Market Crash of 1929 and the Great Depression*; Investopedia; Available at: https://www.investopedia.com/ask/answers/042115/what-caused-stock-market-crash-1929-preceded-great-depression.asp
- Lund, J. M., Jannsen, V., Vickery, P., Pfannestiel, T., Corbett, P. S. & Waskiewicz, S. (2014) *U.S. History*; Available at: https://openstax.org/details/books/us-history
- Marks, H. (1996) *Will it be Different This Time?*; Howard Marks Memos; Oaktree Capital; Available at: https://www.oaktreecapital.com/docs/default-source/memos/1996-11-25-will-it-be-different-this-time.pdf?sfvrsn=23bc0f65_2 (p.3)
- National Taxpayers Union (2012) *Milton Friedman Full Interview on Anti-Trust and Tech*; YouTube; Available at: https://www.youtube.com/watch?v=mlwxdyLnMXM
- Phaneuf, E. (2023) *Hayek and Bitcoin*; The Daily Economy; Available at: https://thedailyeconomy.org/article/hayek-and-bitcoin/
- Richardson, G., Komai, A., Gou, M. & Park, D. (2013) *Stock Market Crash of 1929*; Federal Reserve History; Available at: https://www.federalreservehistory.org/essays/stock-market-crash-of-1929

- *The Complete Satoshi* (2008) Satoshi Nakamoto Institute; Available at: https://satoshi.nakamotoinstitute.org/quotes/economics/
- *The Depression; Social Security History*, Social Security; Available at: https://www.ssa.gov/history/bank.html
- The Investopedia Team (2024) *What is Money? Definition, History, Types, and Creation*, Investopedia; Available at: https://www.investopedia.com/insights/what-is-money/

CHAPTER 2

- 5paisa Research Team (2025) *IPOs for Beginners*, 5Paisa; Available at: https://www.5paisa.com/stock-market-guide/ipo/ipos-for-beginners
- Banking Crisis Timeline (2008) *The Guardian*, Available at: https://www.theguardian.com/business/2008/oct/08/creditcrunch.marketturmoil
- Beattie, A. (2021) *Why Did Pets at Home Crash so Drastically?*, Investopedia; Available at: https://www.investopedia.com/ask/answers/08/dotcom-pets-dot-com.asp
- Brewington, D. (2024) *Lloyds Banking Group: Rising from the Depths of the 2008 Global Financial Crisis*, Yahoo!Finance; Available at: https://finance.yahoo.com/news/lloyds-banking-group-rising-depths-162611389.html?guccounter=1
- Dan, I. & Neumayer, E.R. (2024) *The Advantages of Agency Mortgage-Backed Securities*, Franklin Templeton; Available at: https://www.franklintempleton.ch/articles/2024/western-asset/the-advantages-of-agency-mortgage-backed-securities
- Davis, A. (2018) *At one Point, Amazon Lost More Than 90% of its Value. But Long-Term Investors Still got Rich*, CNBC; Available at: https://www.cnbc.com/2018/12/18/dotcom-bubble-
- amazon-stock-lost-more-than-90percent-long-term-investors-still-got-rich.html
- Diana (2025) *Dot-Com Bubble Explained: Story of 1995 – 2000 Stock Market*, Fin-Bold; Available at: https://finbold.com/guide/dot-com-bubble-crash/
- Dodd-Frank Wall Street Reform and Consumer Protection Act (Pub. L. No. 111-203) § 929-Z, 124 Stat. 1376, 1871 (2010).
- Emmons, W. & Noeth, B. (2012) *Household Financial Stability: Who Suffered the Most from the Crisis?*, Federal Reserve Bank of St Louis; Available at: https://www.stlouisfed.org/publications/regional-economist/july-2012/household-financial-stability--who-suffered-the-most-from-the-crisis
- Geier, B. (2015) What Did We Learn From the Dotcom Stock Bubble of 2000? *Time*, Available at: https://time.com/3741681/2000-dotcom-stock-bust/
- Hoffner, B. & Arnold, V. (2024) United States: Citigroup Capital Injection, 2008; *Journal of Financial Crises*, Available at: https://elischolar.library.yale.edu/cgi/viewcontent.cgi?article=1592&context=journal-of-financial-crises

- *How the 2008 Financial Crisis Unfolded* (2024) Investa; Available at: https://www.investagrams.com/daily/2024/10/how-the-2008-financial-crisis-unfolded/
- Leiner, B. M. et al. (1997) *A Brief History of the Internet*, The Internet Society; Available at: https://www.internetsociety.org/internet/history-internet/brief-history-internet/
- Silver, C. (2023) *Lessons from the 2008 Financial Crisis*, Investopedia; Available at: https://www.investopedia.com/news/10-years-later-lessons-financial-crisis/
- Stoll, C (1995) Why the Web Won't be Nirvana *Newsweek*; Available at: https://www.newsweek.com/clifford-stoll-why-web-wont-be-nirvana-185306
- Treanor, J. (2015) HBOS Timeline: Countdown to Collapse; *The Guardian*, Available at: https://www.theguardian.com/business/2015/nov/19/hbos-timeline-countdown-collapse-lloyds-takeover
- *Troubled Asset Relief Program: Lifetime Cost* (2023) *GAO (U.S. Government Accountability Office)*; Available at: https://www.gao.gov/products/gao-24-107033
- The Sweater Team (2023) *Navigating Beyond the Boundaries of Private Funds: Liquidity*; Sweater; Available at: https://www.sweaterventures.com/insights/navigating-beyond-the-boundaries-of-private-funds-liquidity
- *UK Government Reduces Stake in RBS Owner Natwest Group* (2023) Scottish Financial News; Available at: https://www.scottishfinancialnews.com/articles/uk-government-reduces-stake-in-rbs-owner-natwest-group

CHAPTER 3

- Ammous, S. (2018) *The Bitcoin Standard: The Decentralized Alternative to Central Banking*, Wiley.
- *Bitcoin, Explained*, Blockchain.com; Available at: https://www.blockchain.com/learning-portal/tokens/bitcoin-explained
- Chen, J. (2024) *Fiat Money: What It Is, How It Works,*
- *Example, Pros & Cons*, Investopedia; Available at:
- https://www.investopedia.com/terms/f/fiatmoney.asp
- Crypto Catch-up (2023) *How do Bitcoin Transaction Work?*, coin.co.th; Available at: https://coins.co.th/blog/how-do-bitcoin-transaction-work/
- 'Fiat vs. Crypto & Digital Currencies: Full Guide' (2025) *Cryptopedia*, Available at: https://www.gemini.com/en-SG/cryptopedia/fiat-vs-crypto-digital-currencies
- Hankin, J. (2025) *Bitcoin Pizza Day: Celebrating the 10,000 BTC Pizza Order*, Investopedia; Available at: https://www.investopedia.com/news/bitcoin-pizza-day-celebrating-20-million-pizza-order/
- *JustGiving Becomes First to Accept Cryptocurrency* (2025) MHA; Available at: https://www.mha.co.uk/insights/justgiving-becomes-first-to-accept-cryptocurrency

- Kaur, G, (2024) *Who is Hal Finney? Behind the Scenes at the First Bitcoin Transaction*; *Cointelegraph*; Available at: https://cointelegraph.com/learn/articles/hal-finney

- Lunn, P. & Duffy, D. (2010) *The Euro through the Looking-Glass: Perceived Inflation Following the 2002 Currency Changeover*, ESRI Working Paper, No. 338, The Economic and Social Research Institute (ESRI), Dublin.

- Nakamoto, S. (2008) *Bitcoin: A Peer-to-Peer Electronic Cash System*, Bitcoin.org; Available at: https://bitcoin.org/bitcoin.pdf .

- *Why Does Bitcoin have Value?*, P1 Investment Services; Available at: https://p1-im.co.uk/digital-assets/why-does-bitcoin-have-value/#:~:text=Divisibility%3A%20each%20Bitcoin%20can%20be,supply%20of%2021%20million%20Bitcoins.

- Southurst, J. (2025) *Hal Finney's First Bitcoin Transaction Happened 16 Years Ago Today*; Coingeek; Available at: https://coingeek.com/hal-finney-first-bitcoin-transaction-happened-16-years-ago-today/

- The Diary of a CEO (2024) *The Investing & Crypto Expert: "We Only Have 6 Years Until Everything Changes!" - Raoul Pal*, YouTube; Available at: https://www.youtube.com/watch?v=XyhhwVJB9Z4

- *The Long Search for Satoshi Nakamoto* (2016) BBC News; Available at: https://www.bbc.co.uk/news/technology-36168864

- *The Rise and Rise of Bitcoin* (2014) [documentary] Nicholas Mross; Pittsburgh, Pennsylvania, USA.

- *Thirteen Years Ago, the Founder of the American Liberty Dollar was Convicted* (2024) Atlas 21; Available at: https://atlas21.com/thirteen-years-ago-the-founder-of-the-american-liberty-dollar-was-convicted/

- Turner, J. (2022) *What are the Lessons from History for Digital Currency?*, Economics Observatory; Available at: https://www.economicsobservatory.com/what-are-the-lessons-from-history-for-digital-currency

- Vermaak, W (2023) *Bitcoin Whitepaper: Satoshi's Hallowe'en Monster Turns 15*; Mindplex; Available at: https://magazine.mindplex.ai/post/bitcoin-whitepaper-satoshis-halloween-monster-turns-15

- Wright, G. (2024) *Joining the Ever-Growing DeFi Market with Lucrisma*, Lucrisma; Available at: https://lucrisma.com/blog/joining-the-ever-growing-defi-market-with-lucrisma/

CHAPTER 4

- 'Ancient Greek Coinage' (2025) *Wikipedia*, Available at: https://en.wikipedia.org/wiki/Ancient_Greek_coinage

- *Anatolia by Ages: In the Cradles of Civilisations*, Ebruli Tourism; Available at https://www.ebruliturizm.com/anatolian-civilizations/

- 'Bulla (seal)' (2025) *Wikipedia*, Available at: https://en.wikipedia.org/wiki/Bulla_(seal)
- Cartwright, M. (2018) *Fertile Crescent: Cradle of Civilization*. World History Encyclopedia; Available at: https://www.worldhistory.org/collection/26/fertile-crescent---cradle-of-civilization/
- Clark, D. (2012) *Record Keeping and the Origins of Writing in Mesopotamia*, Semiramis-Speaks.com; Available at: https://semiramis-speaks.com/record-keeping-and-the-origins-of-writing-in-mesopotamia/
- Collon, G. Woods, J. (2025) 'Anatolia' *Brittanica*, Available at: https://www.britannica.com/place/Anatolia
- *Cowrie Shells and Trade Power*, National Museum of African American History and Culture; Smithsonian; Available at: https://nmaahc.si.edu/cowrie-shells-and-trade-power
- 'Cradle of Civilisation' (2025) *Wikipedia*, Available at: https://en.wikipedia.org/wiki/Cradle_of_civilization#:~:text=Scholars%20generally%20acknowledge%20six%20cradles,earliest%20in%20the%20New%20World.
- 'Electrum' (2025) *Wikipedia*, Available at: https://en.wikipedia.org/wiki/Electrum
- Groeneveld, E. (2016) *Prehistoric Hunter-Gatherer Societies*, World History Encyclopedia; Available at: https://www.worldhistory.org/article/991/prehistoric-hunter-gatherer-societies/
- Gronn, P. (2009) Early human society hunted, gathered, and worked without leaders'; *The Independent*, Available at: https://www.independent.co.uk/voices/commentators/peter-gronn-early-human-society-hunted-gathered-ndash-and-worked-without-leaders-1706868.html
- Hirst, K. (2025) *Clay Token System*, Thoughtco.; Available at: https://www.thoughtco.com/clay-tokens-mesopotamian-writing-171673
- 'History of Coins' (2025) *Wikipedia*, Available at: https://en.wikipedia.org/wiki/History_of_coins
- *Hunter-Gatherer Culture*, National Geographic; Available at: https://education.nationalgeographic.org/resource/hunter-gatherer-culture/
- *Introduction to Roman Coins* (2002) The American Numismatic Society; Available at: https://www.numismatics.org/dpubs/romangeneral/
- 'Lydia, Aylattes I, 1/3 Stater, ca. 600-561 BC, Sardis, Electrum' *NumisWorld*, Available at: https://www.vcoins.com/en/stores/numiscorner/239/product/lydia_alyattes_i_13_stater_ca_600561_bc_sardis_electrum/1817241/Default.aspx
- Mark, J. (2009) *Ancient Egypt*, World History Encyclopedia; Available at: https://www.worldhistory.org/egypt/

- Mark, J. (2016) *Ancient Egyptian Writing*, World History Encyclopedia; Available at: https://www.worldhistory.org/Egyptian_Writing/
- Mark, J. (2017) *Trade in Ancient Egypt*, World History Encyclopedia; Available at: https://www.worldhistory.org/article/1079/trade-in-ancient-egypt/
- Mark, J. (2020) *Indus Valley Civilization*, World History Encyclopedia; Available at: https://www.worldhistory.org/Indus_Valley_Civilization/
- Mark. J. (2022) *Trade in Ancient Mesopotamia*, World History Encyclopedia; Available at: https://www.worldhistory.org/article/2114/trade-in-ancient-mesopotamia/
- *Oldest Known Coin Mint Unearthed in China* (2021) Archaeology Magazine; Available at: https://archaeology.org/news/2019/05/14/210809-china-oldest-mint/
- 'Propaganda on Roman Coins' (2022) *Imperium Romanum*, Available at: https://imperiumromanum.pl/en/article/propaganda-on-roman-coins/
- Renfrew, C., Dixon, J. & Cann, R. (1968) Obsidian and the Origins of Trade; *Scientific American*, Vol. 218 No. 3; p. 38.
- 'Roman Republican Currency' (2025) *Wikipedia*, Available at: https://en.wikipedia.org/wiki/Roman_Republican_currency
- Singh, M. (2021) *Beyond the !Kung: A grand research project created our origin myth that early human societies were all egalitarian, mobile and small-scale*, Aeon; Available at: https://aeon.co/essays/not-all-early-human-societies-were-small-scale-egalitarian-bands
- *The Development of Agriculture*, National Geographic; Available at: https://education.nationalgeographic.org/resource/development-agriculture/
- The Investopedia Team (2024) *Accounting History and Terminology*, Investopedia; Available at: https://www.investopedia.com/articles/08/accounting-history.asp
- 'Timeline of Prehistory' (2025) *Wikipedia*, Available at: https://en.wikipedia.org/wiki/Timeline_of_prehistory
- Watkins, T. *Timeline of the Life of Julius Caesar*, San Jose University; Available at: https://www.sjsu.edu/faculty/watkins/caesarjulius.htm

CHAPTER 5

- Ackerman, C. (2023) *Largest Empires in History*, Study.com; Available at: https://study.com/academy/lesson/largest-empires-in-history-timelines-populations.html#:~:text=What%20are%20the%20top%205,in%20which%20they%20were%20active.
- Alberge, D. (2025) 'Spreadsheets of Empire: Red tape goes back 4,000 years, say scientists after Iraq finds; *The Guardian*, Available at: https://www.theguardian.com/science/2025/mar/15/stone-tablets-mesopotamia-iraq-red-tape-bureaucracy

- *Ancient Egyptian Economy*; Egypt History; Available at: https://historyegypt.org/economy

- Bates, M., Floor, W. & Album, S. (2016) *Coins and Coinage*; Encyclopedia Iranica; Available at: https://www.iranicaonline.org/articles/coins-and-coinage-/

- Benner, S. (2022) The Rise and Fall of the Roman Sesertius; *Coinweek*; Available at: https://coinweek.com/the-rise-and-fall-of-the-roman-sestertius/

- Biswas, S. (2025) A Million-Dollar Challenge to Crack the Script of the Early Indians; *BBC News*; Available at: https://www.bbc.co.uk/news/articles/c70q44zn18wo

- Bonfatti, R & Coşar, K. (2022) *Rise and Fall of Empires in the Industrial Era: A Story of Shifting Comparative Advantages*; National Bureau of Economic Research; Available at: https://www.nber.org/papers/w30295

- 'Bretton Woods System' (2025) *Wikipedia*; Available at: https://www.investopedia.com/ask/answers/09/gold-standard.asp

- 'British Empire' (2025) *Wikipedia*; Available at: https://en.wikipedia.org/wiki/British_Empire

- Claus, P. (2025) *A Crusader's History of the Sack of Constantinople*; Greek Reporter; Available at: https://greekreporter.com/2025/02/03/crusader-history-sack-constantinople/

- 'Daric' (2025) *Wikipedia*; Available at: https://en.wikipedia.org/wiki/Daric

- Editors of Encyclopedia Brittanica (2025) *John Maynard Keynes*; Encyclopedia Brittanica; Available at: https://www.britannica.com/money/John-Maynard-Keynes

- Department of Ancient Near Eastern Art (2004) "The Achaemenid Persian Empire (550–330 B.C.)." In *Heilbrunn Timeline of Art History*. New York: The Metropolitan Museum of Art; Available at: http://www.metmuseum.org/toah/hd/acha/hd_acha.htm

- Editors of Encyclopedia Brittanica (2025) *Pound Sterling*; Encyclopedia Brittanica; Available at: https://www.britannica.com/money/pound-sterling

- ESSA Admin (2023) *A First Time for Everything: The Financial Crisis of 33CE*; Economics Students Society of Australia; Available at: https://economicstudents.com/a-first-time-for-everything-the-financial-crisis-of-33-ce/

- Fenner, J. *To What Extent were Economic Factors to Blame for the Deterioration of the Roman Empire in the Third Century A.D?* The Roman Empire; Available at: https://roman-empire.net/faq/economic-factors-deterioration-empire

- Fernando, J. (2022) Silver Standard: What it Means, How it Works, Example; Investopedia: Available at: https://www.investopedia.com/terms/s/silver-standard.asp

- 'Financial Crisis of '33' (2025) *Wikipedia*; Available at: https://en.wikipedia.org/wiki/Financial_crisis_of_33

- 'Financial History of the Dutch Republic' (2025) *Wikipedia*, Available at: https://en.wikipedia.org/wiki/Financial_history_of_the_Dutch_Republic
- *General Government Debt: Percent of GDP*, International Monetary Fund; Available at: https://www.imf.org/external/datamapper/GG_DEBT_GDP@GDD/CHN/FRA/DEU/ITA/JPN/GBR/USA/FADGDWORLD
- 'Gold dinar' (2025) *Wikipedia*, Available at: https://en.wikipedia.org/wiki/Gold_dinar
- 'Gold standard' (2025) *Wikipedia*, Available at: https://en.wikipedia.org/wiki/Gold_standard
- 'Gold Standard Act' (2025) *Wikipedia*, Available at: https://en.wikipedia.org/wiki/Gold_Standard_Act
- Gordon, J. (2019) England's 'Secret Weapon': How a Bank Laid the Groundwork for the British Empire; *ABA Banking Journal*, Available at: https://bankingjournal.aba.com/2019/07/englands-secret-weapon-how-a-bank-laid-the-groundwork-for-the-british-empire/
- Grabmeier, J. (2019) 9,000 Years Ago, a Community with Modern Urban Problems; Ohio State News; Available at: https://news.osu.edu/9000-years-ago-a-community-with-modern-urban-problems/
- Groseclose, E. (2021) *The Great Paper Money Experiment*; Mises Institute; Available at: https://mises.org/mises-daily/great-paper-money-experiment
- Guan, H., Palma, N. & Meng, W. (2024) *The Rise and Fall of Paper Money in Yuan China, 1260–1368*; CEPR; Available at: https://cepr.org/voxeu/columns/rise-and-fall-paper-money-yuan-china-1260-1368#:~:text=Looking%20back%20to%20Chinese%20history,silver%20ingots%20(Figure%201).
- Halton, C. (2024) *What is Currency Debasement?* Investopedia; Available at: https://www.investopedia.com/terms/d/debasement.asp
- 'History of the United States' (2025) *Wikipedia*, Available at: https://en.wikipedia.org/wiki/History_of_the_United_States
- 'Jiaochao' (2025) *Wikipedia*, Available at: https://en.wikipedia.org/wiki/Jiaochao
- 'Karum (trade post)' (2025) *Wikipedia*, Available at: https://en.wikipedia.org/wiki/Karum_%28trade_post%29
- Kelly, R (2023) Gresham's Law: Definition, Effects, and Example; *Investopedia*, Available at: https://www.investopedia.com/terms/g/greshams-law.asp
- Kenton, W. (2022) International Currency Markets: Meaning, Overview; *Investopedia*, Available at: https://www.investopedia.com/terms/forex/i/international-currency-markets.asp
- *King Darius and Gold Coins of the Persian Empire* (2022) APMEX; Available at: https://learn.apmex.com/learning-guide/coin-collecting/king-darius/
- Lioudis, N. (2024) *What is the Gold Standard? History and Collapse*; Investopedia; Available at: https://www.investopedia.com/ask/answers/09/gold-standard.asp

- Mushin, J. (2017) *The Sterling Area*, EH.Net.Encyclopedia; Available at: https://eh.net/encyclopedia/the-sterling-area/
- 'Old Assyrian Period' (2025) *Wikipedia*, Available at: https://en.wikipedia.org/wiki/Old_Assyrian_period
- 'Ottoman Empire' (2025) *Wikipedia*, Available at: https://en.wikipedia.org/wiki/Ottoman_Empire
- *Our History*, The Bank of England; Available at: https://www.bankofengland.co.uk/about/history
- Parker, C. (2016) *A Short History of the British Pound*, World Economic Forum; Available at: https://www.weforum.org/stories/2016/06/a-short-history-of-the-british-pound/
- 'Reserve Currency' (2025) *Wikipedia*, Available at: https://en.wikipedia.org/wiki/Reserve_currency
- Robbins, T.; *What is the Petrodollar?*, Available at: https://www.tonyrobbins.com/blog/what-is-the-petrodollar
- Smith, C. (2020) *Bank of England: The Gold Standard*, House of Lords Library; Available at: https://lordslibrary.parliament.uk/bank-of-england-the-gold-standard/
- Stano, S. *Byzantine Coinage: History, Types and Significance*, ClassicWorldCoins; Available at: https://classicworldcoins.ch/byzantine-coinage/
- Stewart, H. & Wearden, G. (2025) Rachael Reeves Says She has 'Iron Grip' on Finances as Borrowing Costs Surge; *The Guardian*, Available at: https://www.theguardian.com/politics/2025/jan/08/rachel-reeves-says-she-has-iron-grip-on-finances-as-borrowing-costs-surge
- *Tealby Penny*, Cotswold Museum; Available at: https://cotswoldarchaeology.co.uk/museum/tealby-penny/
- *The History of Britain's Gold Coinage*, The Royal Mint; Available at: https://www.royalmint.com/stories/collect/the-history-of-britains-gold-coinage/
- *The Spanish and Portuguese Empires*, Discovering Bristol; Available at: https://www.discoveringbristol.org.uk/slavery/routes/places-involved/south-america/spanish-Portuguese-empires/
- UNESCO (2025) *The Treaty of Tordesillas*, Available at: https://www.unesco.org/en/memory-world/treaty-tordesillas
- Von W. (2023) *Roman Currency Debasement: A Brief History*, LinkedIn; Available at: https://www.linkedin.com/pulse/roman-currency-debasement-brief-history-von-wooding/
- William (2023) *The Medici Bank*, High Speed History; Available at: https://highspeedhistory.com/2023/04/24/the-medici-bank/
- Zandt, F. (2023) *The Biggest Empires in History*, Statista; Available at: https://www.statista.com/chart/20342/peak-land-area-of-the-largest-empires/

Chapter 6

- Brown, D. (2010) "SEC 2: Recommended Elliptic Curve Domain Parameters" in *Standards for Efficient Cryptography*; Available at: https://www.secg.org/sec2-v2.pdf
- *ECDSA: Elliptic Curve Signatures* (2019) Practical Cryptography for Developers; Available at: https://cryptobook.nakov.com/digital-signatures/ecdsa-sign-verify-messages
- Feng, P. et al (2024) *Mastering AI: Big Data, Deep Learning, and the Evolution of Large Language Models - Blockchain and Applications*; arxiv.org; Available at: https://arxiv.org/html/2410.10110v1
- Filipsson, F. (2024) *The Bitcoin Blockchain*; Redress Compliance; Available at: https://redresscompliance.com/the-bitcoin-blockchain/
- Fox, E. (2024) *Bitcoin Community Celebrates 13th Anniversary of White Paper Publication*; Tesmanian; Available at: https://www.tesmanian.com/blogs/tesmanian-blog/bitcoin-community-celebrates-13th-anniversary-of-white-paper-publication .
- Grant, M. (2024) *Orphan Block: What it is and How it Works*; Investopedia; Available at: https://www.investopedia.com/terms/o/orphan-block-cryptocurrency.asp .
- *Hash Validation*; Wholechain HelpDesk; Available at: https://support.wholechain.com/article/328-hash-validation
- *How Bitcoin Mining Works*; Babypips; Available at: https://www.babypips.com/crypto/learn/how-bitcoin-mining-works
- Katya V. (2024) *Blockchain Nonce: The Key to Secure Mining*; ToTheMoon; Available at: https://blog.tothemoon.com/articles/blockchain-nonce
- McConnell, P. (2021) *Not Even Nakamoto Believed in Bitcoin!*; LinkedIn; Available at: https://www.linkedin.com/pulse/even-nakamoto-believed-bitcoin-patrick-mcconnell/
- Merkle, R. Available at: https://ralphmerkle.com/
- Nakamoto, S. (2008) *Bitcoin: A Peer-to-Peer Electronic Cash System*; Bitcoin.org; Available at: https://bitcoin.org/bitcoin.pdf
- Navasardyan, N. (2023) *How do Bitcoin Transactions Work?*; CoinStats; Available at: https://coinstats.app/blog/bitcoin-transactions/
- Rapha (2020) *The Bitcoin White Paper, Explained and Commented: Section 6 – incentives*; Medium; Available at: https://cryp-to.medium.com/the-bitcoin-whitepaper-explained-and-commented-section-6-incentives-da6835015db
- Singh, G. (2025) Understanding Nonce in Blockchain: Selection, Rules, and Validation; LinkedIn; Available at: https://www.linkedin.com/pulse/understanding-nonce-blockchain-selection-rules-validation-singh-6jfxf/

- The Investopedia Team (2023) *DigiCash: Meaning, History, Implications*; Available at: https://www.investopedia.com/terms/d/digicash.asp
- The Investopedia Team (2024) *Nonce: What it Means and How its Used in Blockchain*, Investopedia; Available at: https://www.investopedia.com/terms/n/nonce.asp
- Walker, G. (2025) *Private Keys*, Learn me a Bitcoin; Available at: https://learnmea-bitcoin.com/beginners/guide/private-keys/
- 'What is a Bitcoin Miner?' *DeFi Wikipedia*, Available at: https://blog.tothemoon.com/articles/blockchain-nonce
- *What is Bitcoin's Architecture?* (2025) OSL; Available at: https://www.osl.com/hk-en/academy/article/what-is-bitcoins-architecture
- *What is Mining?* Coinbase; Available at: https://www.coinbase.com/en-gb/learn/crypto-basics/what-is-mining

CHAPTER 7

- Fisk, P. (2020) *Metcalfe's Law explains how the value of networks grows exponentially … exploring the "network effects" of businesses like Apple, Facebook, Trulia and Uber*, peterfisk.com; Available at: https://www.peterfisk.com/2020/02/metcalfes-law-explains-how-the-value-of-networks-grow-exponentially-there-are-5-types-of-network-effects/
- *Metcalfe's Law and Network Effects*, Faster Capital; Available at: https://fastercapital.com/topics/metcalfes-law-and-network-effects.html
- Mutuma, M. (2025) *Crypto's Going Mainstream Faster than the Internet did*, Coin Edition; Available at: https://coinedition.com/cryptos-going-mainstream-faster-than-the-internet-did/
- Peterson, T. (2018) *Metcalfe's Law as a Model for Bitcoin's Value*, CAIA; Available at: https://caia.org/sites/default/files/metcalfeslaw_websiteupload_7-5-18.pdf
- *Why Does Bitcoin Have Value?* P1 Investment Services; Available at: https://p1-im.co.uk/digital-assets/why-does-bitcoin-have-value/#:~:text=Divisibility%3A%20each%20Bitcoin%20can%20be,supply%20of%2021%20million%20Bitcoins.

CHAPTER 8

- *7 Avalanche Use Cases* (2023) Avalanche; Available at: https://www.avax.network/about/blog/7-avalanche-use-cases
- *8 Innovations that Make Solana the First Web-Scale Blockchain* (2019) Solana Foundation; Available at: https://solana.com/news/8-innovations-that-make-solana-the-first-web-scale-blockchain

- *20 Best Business Blockchain Ideas for 2025*; Maticz; Available at: https://maticz.com/blockchain-business-ideas
- *Alchemy will Boost the DeFi and Dapp Space with Polygon* (2021) Polygon Labs; Available at: https://polygon.technology/blog/alchemy-will-boost-the-defi-and-dapp-space-with-polygon
- Amure, T.O. (2024) *What is XRP?*, Investopedia; Available at: https://www.investopedia.com/what-is-xrp-6362550
- Anglen, J.; *Polygon Cross-Chain Development: Connecting Ethereum and Polygon*, Rapid Innovation: Available at: https://www.rapidinnovation.io/post/polygon-cross-chain-development-connecting-ethereum-and-polygon
- *Announcing Narwhal and Tusk Open Source* (2022) Sui Foundation; Available at: https://blog.sui.io/narwhal-tusk-open-source/
- *Bitcoin NFTs — How the Ordinals Protocol Works* (2025) Crypto.com University; Available at: https://crypto.com/en/university/bitcoin-nfts-ordinals-protocol
- BNBSmartchain; BNB Chain; Available at: https://www.bnbchain.org/en/bnb-smart-chain
- Browning, E. (2023) *Why is Polkadot called Layer Zero?*, Moonbeam; Available at: https://moonbeam.network/news/why-is-polkadot-called-a-layer-zero/
- Chainalysis Team (2023) *Monero: All About the Top Privacy Coin*, Chainalysis; Available at: https://www.chainalysis.com/blog/all-about-monero/
- Chamria, R. (2024) *Mapping Rollup Interoperability for Cross-chain Connectivity*, Zeeve; Available at: https://www.zeeve.io/blog/mapping-rollup-interoperability-for-cross-chain-connectivity/
- CoolBitX (2023) *An Introduction to the Layer-0 Network Upgrade of Cosmos 2.0 (ATOM)*, Medium; Available at: https://medium.com/@coolbitx/an-introduction-to-the-layer-0-network-upgrade-of-cosmos-2-0-atom-39d9f31f05a
- *Cryptocurrency Prices by Market Cap*, Coingecko; Available at: https://www.coingecko.com/
- Cryptopedia Staff (2023) *Zcash Leads the Way on Zero-Knowledge Proofs With zk-SNARKs*; Cryptopedia; Available at: https://www.gemini.com/en-SG/cryptopedia/zcash-zero-knowledge-proof-zk-snarks-mining
- Cryptopedia Staff (2025) *Ethereum Explained: A Guide to the World Supercomputer*, Cryptopedia; Available at: https://www.gemini.com/en-SG/cryptopedia/ethereum-blockchain-smart-contracts-dapps
- *Decentralised Finance (DeFi)* (2025) Ethereum.org; Available at: https://ethereum.org/en/defi/
- Dudhe, N. (2023) *Avalanche Fundamentals — Consensus Mechanism Explained!*, Medium; Available at: https://medium.com/coinmonks/avalanche-fundamentals-consensus-mechanism-explained-cb2db0a59fb8
- *Ethereum Virtual Machine (EVM)* (2025) Ethereum.org; Available at: https://ethereum.org/en/developers/docs/evm/

- *Exploring Off the Grid in Avalanche* (2024) Reflexivity Research; Available at: https://www.reflexivityresearch.com/all-reports/exploring-off-the-grid-on-avalanche

- *Faster Transactions at Reduced Costs* (2024) 1inch Network; Available at: https://blog.1inch.io/polygon/

- *Gensyn*, The Ultimate Web3 AI Map; Available at: https://www.diadata.org/web3-ai-map/gensyn/

- *How Sei Became the Fastest Blockchain: Twin Turbo Consensus* (2024) Sei; Available at: https://blog.sei.io/twin-turbo-consensus/

- *IBM and KlickEx Choose Stellar to Power the Future of Cross-Border Payments* (2017) Stellar; Available at: https://stellar.org/blog/ecosystem/ibm-klickex-partnership

- *Introduction to Smart Contracts* (2025) Ethereum.org; Available at: https://ethereum.org/en/developers/docs/smart-contracts/

- Jonathan G. *Stablecoins: Benefits and risks of USDT, USDC, and DAI*; Phantom; Available at: https://phantom.com/en-GB/learn/crypto-101/stablecoins-usdt-usdc-dai

- Kim, C. & Dale, B. (2024) *1 Big Thing: MakerDAO's $1 billion tokenization contest*; Axios Crypto; Available at: https://www.axios.com/newsletters/axios-crypto-8da262d0-437c-11ef-8798-558e97be2820

- Kulechov, S. (2023) *Aave and Flash Loans: Uncollateralized Lending in DeFi*; Cryptopedia; Available at: https://www.gemini.com/en-SG/cryptopedia/aave-flash-loans

- *Layer 2 Blockchains*, Alchemy; Available at: https://www.alchemy.com/dapps/best/layer-2-blockchains

- Leshner. R. (2025) *Compound (COMP): Lego Blocks of DeFi*, Cryptopedia; Available at: https://www.gemini.com/en-SG/cryptopedia/compound-finance-defi-crypto

- Lightspark Team (2024) *What is a Lightning Network Channel?*, Lightspark; Available at: https://www.lightspark.com/blog/bitcoin/what-is-a-lightning-network-channel

- Miah S. (2024) *What is Litecoin? A Quick Guide for 2024*; Webopedia; Available at: https://www.webopedia.com/crypto/learn/litecoin-explained/

- Mostoviah, M. (2025) *Stablecoins Explained: What Are Tether, DAI, and Others?*, Coin Wallet; Available at: https://coin.space/stablecoins-explained-what-are-tether-dai-and-others/

- Munene, V. (2024) *Top 5 Largest Financial Institutions Currently Using Ripple And XRP Technology*; Blockzeit; Available at: https://blockzeit.com/top-5-largest-financial-institutions-currently-using-ripple-and-xrp-technology/

- Nagel, S. (2021) *Hydra – Cardano's Solution for Ultimate Layer 2 Scalability*; Input Output; Available at: https://iohk.io/en/blog/posts/2021/09/17/hydra-cardano-s-solution-for-ultimate-scalability/

- Nevil, S. (2025) *Meme Coins: Examples of What They Are, Pros and Cons, and How to Make Them,* Investopedia; Available at: https://www.investopedia.com/meme-coin-6750312

- *Ondo Finance Brings Tokenized Real-World Assets to Mastercard's Multi-Token Network* (2025) Ondo; Available online: https://blog.ondo.finance/ondo-finance-brings-tokenized-real-world-assets-to-mastercards-multi-token-network/

- *Polygon (MATIC)*; TruBit; Available at: https://academy.trubit.com/12ed4e8c-76dc438bb05613fd52048d28

- Poteriaieva, M. (2024) *Dogecoin: A Joke No More? The Rise of A $58 Billion Crypto Phenomenon,* Forbes; Available at: https://www.forbes.com/sites/digital-assets/2024/11/22/dogecoin-a-joke-no-more-the-rise-of-a-58-billion-crypto-phenomenon/

- *Proof of Stake* (2024) Ethereum.org; Available at: https://ethereum.org/en/developers/docs/consensus-mechanisms/pos/

- 'Proof of Stake' (2025) *Wikipedia,* Available at: https://en.wikipedia.org/wiki/Proof_of_stake

- Powers, B. & Leech, O. (2023) *What is ZCash? The Privacy Coin Explained,* Coindesk; Available at: https://www.coindesk.com/layer2/2022/01/26/what-is-zcash-the-privacy-coin-explained

- Reiff, N. (2025) *Chainlink: What it is and How it Works,* Investopedia; Available at: https://www.investopedia.com/chainlink-link-definition-5217559

- *Revolutionizing Cross-Border Payments: How Ripple XRP Speeds up Finance Transactions and Cuts Costs,* KanBo; Available at: https://kanboapp.com/en/industries/finance/revolutionizing-cross-border-payments-how-ripple-xrp-speeds-up-finance-transactions-and-cuts-costs/

- Reynolds, S. (2024) *Vitalik Buterin Wants Ethereum to Hit 100K TPS with Roll-ups,* CoinDesk; Available at: https://www.coindesk.com/tech/2024/10/17/vitalik-buterin-wants-ethereum-to-hit-100k-transaction-per-second-with-rollups

- Ronis, J. (2023) *Understanding Ethereum's Layer 1 and Layer 2: Differences, Adoption, and Drawbacks,* Wilson Center; Available at: https://www.wilsoncenter.org/article/understanding-ethereums-layer-1-and-layer-2-differences-adoption-and-drawbacks

- Techskill Brew (2025) *Layer 2 Blockchain Scaling Solutions: Channels, Sidechains, Rollups and Plasma (Part 16),* Medium; Available at: https://medium.com/techskill-brew/layer-2-blockchain-scaling-solutions-channels-sidechains-rollups-and-plasma-part-16-79819e058ef6

- The Investopedia Team (2024) *Monero: What it Means, How it Works, and Features,* Investopedia; Available at: https://www.investopedia.com/terms/m/monero.asp

- The Investopedia Team (2024) *What Does Proof-of-Stake (PoS) Mean in Crypto?*, Investopedia; Available at: https://www.investopedia.com/terms/p/proof-stake-pos.asp#:~:text=Proof-of-stake%20is%20a,and%20keeping%20the%20database%20secure.

- *The Merge* (2025) Ethereum Roadmap; Available at: https://ethereum.org/en/roadmap/merge/

- *Top Ethereum DeFi Apps* DappRadar; Available at: https://dappradar.com/rankings/protocol/ethereum/category/defi

- *Top Gaming Tokens by Market Capitalization*, CoinMarketCap; Available at: https://coinmarketcap.com/view/gaming/

- Vogelsang, L. (2022) *Centrifuge: Where DeFi Meets Real World Assets*; Cryptopedia; Available at: https://www.gemini.com/en-SG/cryptopedia/centrifuge-crypto-tinlake-tokenization-real-world-assets

- West, B. (2023) *Goldfinch (GFI): Crypto Loans for the Real World*, Cryptopedia; Available at: https://www.gemini.com/en-SG/cryptopedia/gfi-token-goldfinch-crypto-loans-without-collateral

- Weston, G. (2023) What is *Layer 0 in Blockchain?* 101 Blockchains; Available at: https://101blockchains.com/layer-0-blockchain/

- *What are Layer-0 Protocols?* Coinbase; Available at: https://www.coinbase.com/en-gb/learn/crypto-glossary/what-are-layer-0-protocols

- *What are ZK-SNARKS?* Z Cash; Available at: https://z.cash/learn/what-are-zk-snarks/

- *What is Bittensor?* The Big Whale; Available at: https://www.thebigwhale.io/tokens/bittensor

- *What is Ocean Protocol?* The Ultimate Web3 AI Map; Available at: https://www.diadata.org/web3-ai-map/ocean/

- *What is XRP (XRP) and How does it Work?* Ndax; Available at: https://ndax.io/en/blog/article/what-is-xrp-xrp

- *Why IBM Built World Wire on Stellar* (2019) Stellar; Available at: https://stellar.org/blog/ecosystem/why-ibm-built-world-wire-on-stellar

CHAPTER 9

- *Best Crypto Cold Wallet 2024: BC Vault vs Ledger vs Trezor vs Ngrave vs Ellipal?* (2024) Nexus Investor; Available at: https://nexusinvestor.co.uk/crypto-cold-wallet/

- Birnbaum, D. (2024) *Crypto Hot Wallets vs Cold Wallets: The Key Differences*, Forbes 101; Available at: https://www.forbes.com/sites/digital-assets/article/crypto-hot-wallets-vs-cold-wallets/

- Chainalysis Team (2025) *The Importance of Blockchain Security and How to Prevent Threats Before They Strike*, Chainalysis; Available at: https://www.chainalysis.com/blog/blockchain-security/

- Chimelu, G. C. (2024) *How to Store Cryptocurrency*, Investopedia; Available at: https://www.investopedia.com/how-to-store-cryptocurrency-7500942
- *Crypto Security Best Practices*, Backpack; Available at: https://learn.backpack.exchange/articles/crypto-security-best-practices-protecting-your-digital-assets
- *Cryptocurrency Security for Small Businesses: Protecting your Wallet*, Downtown Computer Services; Available at: https://www.downtowncomputers.com/cryptocurrency-security-for-small-businesses-protecting-your-wallet/
- Dedezade, E. (2021) *The Top Decentralized Exchanges (DEXs) in 2021*; Decrypt; Available at: https://decrypt.co/73356/top-decentralized-exchanges-dex-uniswap-sushiswap
- Harper, L. (2023) *The Benefits of Using a Bitcoin Hardware Wallet for Secure Crypto Storage*, Red Belly Blockchain; Available at: https://www.redbellyblockchain.io/hardware-wallets/the-benefits-of-using-a-bitcoin-hardware-wallet-for-secure-crypto-storage/
- Hussain, Y. (2018) *Digital Assets Insurance* Gemini; Available at: https://www.gemini.com/en-SG/blog/digital-assets-insurance
- *Insurance* (2025) Coinbase; Available at: https://www.coinbase.com/en-gb/legal/insurance
- Kraken Learn Team (2025) *Custodial vs non-custodial wallets: Who holds your crypto?*, Kraken; Available at: https://www.kraken.com/learn/custodial-non-custodial-crypto-wallet
- Nallapaneni, D.; *Centralized vs. Decentralized Crypto Exchanges*, CoinLedger; Available at: https://coinledger.io/learn/centralized-vs-decentralized-crypto-exchanges
- *Security Guide – How to Protect Your Digital Assets*, Anados; Available at: https://docs.anodos.finance/education/security-guide-how-to-protect-your-digital-assets
- Singh, D. (2025) *Crypto Wallet Security: How to Protect Your Decentralized Wallet from Hacks and Phishing*, Debut Infotech; Available at: https://www.debutinfotech.com/blog/crypto-wallet-security-complete-guide
- The Investopedia Team (2024) *Hot Wallet: Definition, Types, Examples, and Safety Tips*, Investopedia; Available at: https://www.investopedia.com/terms/h/hot-wallet.asp
- Taofeeqoht, O. (2024) *The Importance of Security in Crypto Transactions*, LinkedIn; Available at: https://www.linkedin.com/posts/honeytees_cryptosecurity-blockchainsecurity-cryptocurrency-activity-7263224306967408642-aAn9/
- Tomasiak, K. (2024) *Security Best Practices*, swapped.com; Available at: https://swapped.com/blog/security-best-practices
- Transak Team (2024) *Custodial Wallets vs Non-Custodial Wallets: Control or Convenience?* Transak; Available at: https://transak.com/blog/custodial-wallets-vs-non-custodial-wallets

- *Vaults*; Coinbase; Available at: https://help.coinbase.com/en/coinbase/getting-started/other/vaults-faq
- Weston, G. (2021) *Decentralized Exchanges (DEXs) Risks That You Can't Ignore*; 101 Blockchains; Available at: https://101blockchains.com/decentralized-exchanges-risks/
- *What is a Hardware Wallet and How Does it Work?* Kapersky; Available at: https://www.kaspersky.com/resource-center/definitions/what-is-a-hardware-wallet
- Wood, J. (2024) *Custodial Wallets vs Non-Custodial Crypto Wallets*; Coindesk; Available at: https://www.coindesk.com/learn/custodial-wallets-vs-non-custodial-crypto-wallets

CHAPTER 10

- *16 Disadvantages of Blockchain: Limitations and Challenges* (2025) Webisoft; Available at: https://webisoft.com/articles/disadvantages-of-blockchain/
- AbdelSalam, F. (2023) Blockchain Revolutionizing Healthcare Industry: A Systematic Review of Blockchain Technology Benefits and Threats; *Perspectives in Health Information Management*, 20(3).
- Abeslamidze, S. (2018) *DocuSign Integrates Ethereum Blockchain, Adds ETH and Its Smart Contract Functionality*; Coinspeaker; Available at: https://www.coinspeaker.com/docusign-integrates-ethereum-blockchain-adds-eth-and-its-smart-contract-functionality/
- *Advantages and Disadvantages of Blockchain* (2024) Geeksforgeeks; Available at: https://www.geeksforgeeks.org/ethical-hacking/advantages-and-disadvantages-of-blockchain/
- Ahmed, A. (2025) *The Blockchain Trilemma: Understanding the Fundamental Trade-offs*; Medium; Available at: https://medium.com/@ahmedashfaque522/the-blockchain-trilemma-understanding-the-fundamental-trade-offs-56c63af1b91c
- *Beginner's Guide to Cryptocurrency Investing: Getting Started Safely* (2024) Nexus Investor; Available at: https://nexusinvestor.co.uk/beginners-guide-to-cryptocurrency-investing/
- Biswas, S. (2025) *Disadvantages of Blockchain Technology*; Cleartax; Available at: https://cleartax.in/s/disadvantages-of-blockchain
- *Bitcoin Wobbles Around $57K, Is the ETF Honeymoon Over?* (2024) Nexus Investor; Available at: https://nexusinvestor.co.uk/bitcoin-wobbles-57k/
- *Bitso Surpasses $12 billion in Transactions in 2024* (2024) Finextra; Available at: https://www.finextra.com/pressarticle/103639/bitso-surpasses-12-billion-in-transactions-in-2024
- *Blockchain's Impact in Fostering Financial Inclusion*; PWC; Available at: https://www.pwc.com/us/en/services/digital-assets/blockchain-financial-inclusion.html

- Brown, M. & Melchionna, M. (2023) *7 Challenges with Blockchain Adoption and how to Avoid Them*, TechTarget; Available at: https://www.techtarget.com/searchcio/tip/5-challenges-with-blockchain-adoption-and-how-to-avoid-them

- *Can Someone Steal my Cryptocurrency Wallet?* BBVA; Available at: https://www.bbva.ch/en/blog/innovacion/ciberseguridad/puede-alguien-robar-mi-billetera-de-criptomonedas.html

- Ciccomascolo, G. (2024) *Bitcoin Mining Environmental Impact Narrative Falling Apart as Banking Does More Damage*, CCN; Available at: https://www.ccn.com/news/technology/bitcoin-mining-environmental-impact-banking-more-damage/

- *Cryptocurrency Ownership Data* (2024) Triple A; Available at: https://www.triple-a.io/cryptocurrency-ownership-data

- Cryptopedia Staff (2021) *Unbanking the Banked and the Future of Money*, Cryptopedia; Available at: https://www.gemini.com/en-SG/cryptopedia/unbanked-financial-inclusion-fintech-startups

- Cryptopedia Staff (2022) *The Blockchain Trilemma: Fast, Secure, and Scalable Networks* Cryptopedia; Available at: https://www.gemini.com/en-SG/cryptopedia/blockchain-trilemma-decentralization-scalability-definition

- *Digital Traceability: 5 powerful benefits of blockchain technology for the Department of Defense*, Siemens Government Technologies; Available at: https://www.siemens-govt.com/insights/articles/article-digital-traceability-benefits-of-blockchain

- Global Data (2024) *DocuSign in Blockchain: Theme innovation strategy*, Verdict; Available at: https://www.verdict.co.uk/docusign-in-blockchain-theme-innovation-strategy-2/

- El Haj, M. & Farran, I. (2024) The Cryptocurrencies in Emerging Markets: Enhancing Financial Inclusion and Economic Empowerment; *Journal of Risk and Financial Management* 17(10) 467.

- *Electronics Signature Technology DocuSign (DOCU) Integrates with Ethereum Blockchain Platform* (2018) Market Exclusive; Available at: https://marketexclusive.com/electronics-signature-technology-docusign-docu-integrates-with-ethereum-blockchain-platform/2018/10/

- Enigma of the Stack (2023) *Web3 Is Taking Over the Internet — Is Web1 Obsolete? The Shocking Truth*, Medium; Available at: https://medium.com/@cannon_circuit/web3-is-taking-over-the-internet-is-web1-obsolete-the-shocking-truth-c7f8672a3e96

- *ENS Signatures on DocuSign with MyWalliD* (2025) ETH Global; Available at: https://ethglobal.com/showcase/ens-signatures-on-docusign-with-mywallid-g2n94

- Fabiano, A., Rybarczyk, R. & Armstrong, D. (2021) *On Bitcoin's Energy Consumption*, Galaxy; Available at: https://www.galaxy.com/insights/research/on-bitcoins-energy-consumption/

- Grinina, O. (2021) *Why Ethereum didn't work out for DocuSign (and how Taraxa is different)*; Medium; Available at: https://og-design.medium.com/one-size-doesnt-fit-all-why-ethereum-didn-t-work-out-for-docusign-and-how-taraxa-is-different-fb5705760412

- Gupta, H. (2021) *Crypto for Financial inclusion- Stable coins, CBDC and recommended model*; Creative Mixer; Available at: https://creativemixer.substack.com/p/crypto-for-financial-inclusion-stable

- Hayes, A. (2025) *Blockchain Facts: What is it, How it Works, and How it can be Used*; Investopedia; Available at: https://www.investopedia.com/terms/b/blockchain.asp

- Koch, C. (2022) *Blockchain's Energy Crisis* SAP; Available at: https://www.sap.com/blogs/blockchains-energy-crisis

- Kouts, A. (2024) *Sui vs. Solana: A Comprehensive Comparison*; CoinBureau; Available at: https://coinbureau.com/analysis/sui-vs-solana/

- KryptykHex (2024) *How Austrian Economics Illuminates the Path to Bitcoin's Success*; D-Central; Available at: https://d-central.tech/how-austrian-economics-illuminates-the-path-to-bitcoins-success/

- Kubinec, J. (2025) *Seeker and Firedancer expected to ship Solana products in 2025*; Blockworks; Available at: https://blockworks.co/news/2025-solana-product-launches

- Manyika, J. et al (2016) *Digital Finance for All: Powering Inclusive Growth in Emerging EconomicsI;* McKinsey Global Institute; Available at: https://www.mckinsey.com/~/media/mckinsey/featured%20insights/Employment%20and%20Growth/How%20digital%20finance%20could%20boost%20growth%20in%20emerging%20economies/MGI-Digital-Finance-For-All-Executive-summary-September-2016.ashx

- Mattackal, L.P. & Singh, M. (2022) *Cryptoverse: 10 billion reasons bitcoin could become a reserve currency*; Reuters; Available at: https://www.reuters.com/business/cryptoverse-10-billion-reasons-bitcoin-could-become-reserve-currency-2022-04-12/

- Miller, L. (2025) *Electricity Costs to Mine 1 Bitcoin at Home, Around the World*; NFT Evening; Available at: https://nftevening.com/bitcoin-mining-cost/

- Nelson, D. (2025) *Solana Pushes Validators to Test Early 'Firedancer' Upgrade*; Coindesk; Available at: https://www.coindesk.com/business/2025/01/08/solana-pushes-validators-to-test-early-firedancer-upgrade

- Patel, E. (2023) *How can Cryptocurrencies Play a Role in Promoting Financial Inclusion?*; The Economic Times; Available at: https://economictimes.indiatimes.com/markets/cryptocurrency/how-can-cryptocurrencies-play-a-role-in-promoting-financial-inclusion/articleshow/100205450.cms?from=mdr

- Pratt, M. (2023) *Top 10 benefits of blockchain for business*; TechTarget; Available at: https://www.techtarget.com/searchcio/feature/Top-10-benefits-of-blockchain-technology-for-business

- *Privacy Enhancing Technology: Anonymity and Hashed Timelock Contracts* (2025) Faster Capital; Available at: https://fastercapital.com/content/Privacy-enhancing-Technology--Anonymity-and-Hashed-Timelock-Contracts.html
- Reiff, N. (2024) *Scalability: Blockchain Tech's Greatest Problem*, Investopedia; Available at: https://www.investopedia.com/investing/governance-blockchain-techs-greatest-problem/
- Rooney, C. (2020) *Bitcoin loses half of its value in two-day plunge*, CNBC; Available at: https://www.cnbc.com/2020/03/13/bitcoin-loses-half-of-its-value-in-two-day-plunge.html
- Quirkify Chronicles (2024) *Discover How Blockchain Is Building the Future of the Internet in Web3*; Medium; Available at: https://medium.com/thecapital/discover-how-blockchain-is-building-the-future-of-the-internet-in-web3-ffb286282913
- *Regulatory Challenges in Blockchain: Navigating Compliance and Legal Frameworks*; Technology Innovators; Available at: https://www.technology-innovators.com/regulatory-challenges-in-blockchain-navigating-compliance-and-legal-frameworks/
- Shewchuk, T. (2024) *The Role of Cryptocurrency in Enhancing Financial Inclusion*, Evertas; Available at: https://evertas.com/news/the-role-of-cryptocurrency-in-enhancing-financial-inclusion/
- 'Short Squeeze' *Upay*; Available at: https://blog.upay.best/crypto-terminology/short-squeeze/
- Sregantan, N. (2023) *What is the Blockchain Trilemma?* DBS; Available at: https://www.dbs.com.sg/personal/articles/nav/investing/what-is-the-blockchain-trilemma#:~:text=The%20Blockchain%20Trilemma%20refers%20to,this%20poses%20challenges%20to%20scalability.
- *The $60 Million Heist that Shook the Blockchain World*, Sustainify; Available at: https://www.sustainify.ee/post/the-60-million-heist-that-shook-the-blockchain-world
- *The Limits of DeFi for Financial Inclusion: Lessons from ASEAN* (2024) OECD; Available at: https://www.oecd.org/en/publications/the-limits-of-defi-for-financial-inclusion_f00a0c7f-en.html
- *Tokenomics 101* Coinbase: Available at: https://www.coinbase.com/en-gb/learn/wallet/tokenomics-101
- 'Transaction Malleability Problem' (2025) *Wikipedia*, Available at: https://en.wikipedia.org/wiki/Transaction_malleability_problem
- *What is "Proof of Work" or "Proof of Stake"?* Coinbase; Available at: https://www.coinbase.com/en-gb/learn/crypto-basics/what-is-proof-of-work-or-proof-of-stake
- *'Worst hack in history' as $1.5bn in cryptocurrency stolen* (2025) Archyde; Available at: https://www.archyde.com/worst-hack-in-history-as-1-5bn-in-cryptocurrency-stolen-money-news/

- Wright, L. (2024) *Bitcoin Inflation Now 75% Less Than Current US Rate Post-Halving*, Available at: https://www.forbes.com/sites/digital-assets/2024/05/29/bitcoin-inflation-now-75-less-than-current-us-rate-post-halving/

CHAPTER 11

- Amure, T. O. (2024) *How to Buy and Sell NFTs; The Ultimate Guide*, Investopedia; Available at: https://www.investopedia.com/how-to-buy-and-sell-nfts-6361693
- Anderson, C. (2024) *Pros and Cons of NFT Investing in 2025*; Available at: https://nftevening.com/pros-and-cons-of-nft-investing/
- Anglen, J. *NFT Applications in Art, Gaming, and Event Management* Rapid Innovation; Available at: https://www.rapidinnovation.io/post/nft-applications-in-art-gaming-and-event-management
- Anglen, J. *The Complete Guide to NFTs and their Ecosystem*, Rapid Innovation; Available at: https://www.rapidinnovation.io/post/the-complete-guide-to-nfts-and-their-ecosystem
- Bernstein, C. (2023) *Top 7 NFT Use Cases For Business;* TechTarget; Available at: https://www.techtarget.com/whatis/feature/5-business-use-cases-for-NFTs
- *Beyond Collectibles and Gaming: How will NFTs Look Like in the Future?* (2025) OSL; Available at: https://www.osl.com/hk-en/academy/article/beyond-collectibles-and-gaming-how-will-nfts-look-like-in-the-future
- Brown, X. (2024) *Jimmy Fallon NFT portfolio confirmed to include a Bored Ape*, NFT Evening; Available at: https://nftevening.com/jimmy-fallon-nft-portfolio-confirmed-to-include-a-bored-ape/
- Bru Finance (2024) *NFTs and Real-World Assets: A match made in heaven* Medium; Available at: https://medium.com/bru-finance/nfts-and-real-world-assets-a-match-made-in-heaven-6deb5365a343
- Chamria, R. (2023) *What Challenges Lie Ahead in the Adoption of web3 in 2023?* Zeeve; Available at: https://www.zeeve.io/blog/what-challenges-lie-ahead-in-the-adoption-of-web3-in-2023/
- Chugani. S. et al (2021) *The Notorious NFT: Consumer Protection Issues Raised by Non-Fungible Tokens.* Available at: https://uk.practicallaw.thomsonreuters.com/w-030-4989?contextData=(sc.Default)&transitionType=Default&firstPage=true
- *Common Security Flaws around NFT Projects and How to Protect Against Them* (2025) QuickNode; Available at: https://www.quicknode.com/guides/web3-fundamentals-security/security/common-security-flaws-around-nft-projects-how-to-protect-against-them
- Crypto Navigator (2024) *NFTs: From Digital Art to Real-World Utility*, Medium; Available at: https://medium.com/%40cryptonavigator.net/nfts-from-digital-art-to-real-world-utility-397caa98f61c

- *Dynamic NFT Examples – 16 Use Cases* (2024) Chainlink; Available at: https://chain.link/education-hub/dynamic-nft-use-cases

- *ERC-721 vs ERC-1155: Overview, Characteristics, and Differences*, Merkle Science; Available at: https://www.merklescience.com/blog/erc-721-vs-erc-1155-overview-characteristics-and-differences

- Ferrill, E., Shah, S. & Young, M. (2022) *Demystifying NFTs and Intellectual Property: What You Need to Know*, Finnegan; Available at: https://www.finnegan.com/en/insights/articles/demystifying-nfts-and-intellectual-property-what-you-need-to-know.html

- Frank, R. (2022) *Metaverse real estate sales top $500 million, and are projected to double this year*, Available at: https://www.cnbc.com/2022/02/01/metaverse-real-estate-sales-top-500-million-metametric-solutions-says.html

- Garnett, A. (2025) *NFT Use Cases: 8 innovative ways to use non-fungible tokens*, Brittanica Money; Available at: https://www.britannica.com/money/nft-use-cases

- Glover, E. (2022) *Ten Popular NFT Use Cases* Built In; Available at: https://builtin.com/articles/nft-use-cases

- Hayward, A. (2022) *Justin Bieber paid $1.3 Million for a Bored Ape NFT. It's Now Worth $69K*, Decypt; Available at: https://decrypt.co/114718/justin-bieber-bored-ape-nft-now-69k

- Hissong, S. (2021) Kings of Leon will be the First Band to Release an Album as an NFT; *Rolling Stone*, Available at: https://www.rollingstone.com/pro/news/kings-of-leon-when-you-see-yourself-album-nft-crypto-1135192/

- *How to Make an NFT* (2023) Meadow School for the Arts; Available at: https://www.smu.edu/meadows/newsandevents/news/2023/how_to_create_and_sell_nfts

- *How to Mint an NFT*; Chainlink; Available at: https://chain.link/tutorials/how-to-mint-an-nft

- *How to Sell an NFT* (2022) OpenSea; Available at: https://opensea.io/learn/nft/how-to-sell-nfts

- 'Impact of non-fungible tokens on traditional businesses' (2025) *Wikipedia*, Available at: https://en.wikipedia.org/wiki/Impact_of_non-fungible_tokens_on_traditional_businesses

- Kaur, G. (2024) *The NFT Marketplace: How to buy and sell nonfungible* tokens; Available at: https://cointelegraph.com/learn/articles/the-nft-marketplace-how-to-buy-and-sell-nonfungible-tokens

- Legge, M. (2025) *OpenSea NFTs Guide 2025: How to Mint, Buy, and Sell* Koinly; Available at: https://koinly.io/blog/opensea-nfts-guide/

- LCX Team (2023) *How are NFTs Contributing to Digital Identity in Web3?* LCX; Available at: https://www.lcx.com/how-are-nfts-contributing-to-digital-identity-in-web3/

- *NFT Beyond Art: 14 Practical Use Cases of NFT*; Ortmor Agency; Available at: https://www.ortmoragency.com/blog/nft-beyond-art-14-practical-use-cases-of-nft

- *NFTs for Real Estate: Exploring the Concept and Creating Tokens in Python, JavaScript, and Solidity*; Apiorit; Available at: https://www.apriorit.com/dev-blog/782-blockchain-nfts-for-real-estate

- 'Non-Fungible Token' (2025) *Wikipedia* Available at: https://en.wikipedia.org/wiki/Non-fungible_token

- Reeve, E. (2023) *Snoop Dogg, his ape and a question of celebrity hype;* CNN Business; Available at: https://edition.cnn.com/2023/04/07/business/snoop-dogg-bored-apes/index.html

- Sharma, N. (2025) *Non-Fungible Token (NFT): What It Means and How It Works*; Investopedia; Available at: https://www.investopedia.com/non-fungible-tokens-nft-5115211

- Singh, O. (2025*) How NFTs Prove Ownership of Physical Items*; CCN; Available at: https://www.ccn.com/education/crypto/how-nfts-prove-ownership-of-physical-items/

- Stokel-Walker, C. (2022) *An NFT Bubble is Taking Over the Gig Economy*; Wired; Available at: https://www.wired.com/story/nfts-gig-economy/

- *The Role of NFTs in Real Estate Tokenization* Antier Estates; Available at: https://www.antiersolutions.com/blogs/the-role-of-nfts-in-real-estate-tokenization/

- *Ticketmaster Launches New Capability to Issue Digital Collectible NFTs to Fans Before, During or After an Event - Over 5 million NFTs Already Minted on the Flow Blockchain* (2022) DapperLabs; Available at: https://www.dapperlabs.com/newsroom/ticketmaster-launches-new-capability-to-issue-digital-collectible-nfts-to-fans-before-during-or-after-an-event

- Token Minds Team (2024) *NFT Royalties: A Game Changer for Revenue Models*; Token Minds; Available at: https://tokenminds.co/blog/nft-marketing/how-do-nft-royalties-work

- Trivedi, M. (2022) *Madonna Becomes Latest Star to Join the Bored Ape Yacht Club*; FX Empire; Available at: https://finance.yahoo.com/news/madonna-becomes-latest-star-join-095023128.html

- *Understanding Cross-Chain NFTs: The Future of Digital Collectibles* (2025) OSL; Available at: https://www.osl.com/hk-en/academy/article/understanding-cross-chain-nfts-the-future-of-digital-collectibles

- *Unlocking the Potential for NFTs With Privacy* Secret; Available at: https://scrt.network/about/secret-nfts

- *What are Cross-Chain NFTs?* (2024) Chainlink; Available at: https://chain.link/education-hub/cross-chain-nft

- *What are the Pros and Cons of Investing in NFTs?* Coinbase; Available at: https://www.coinbase.com/en-gb/learn/crypto-basics/what-are-the-pros-and-cons-of-investing-in-nfts
- *What is Minting?* (2022) Opensea.io; Available at: https://opensea.io/learn/nft/what-is-minting-nft
- *Why NFTs are Bad for Artists*, Metroclick; Available at: https://www.metroclick.com/blockchain-solutions/nft-displays/why-nfts-are-bad-for-artists/
- Wolfe, M. & Nolan, V. (2025) *The Challenge of Digital Asset Regulation of NFTs*, DuaneMorris: Available at: https://blogs.duanemorris.com/fintech/2025/02/10/the-challenge-of-digital-asset-regulation-of-nfts/

CHAPTER 12

- '2012–2013 Cypriot Financial Crisis' (2025) *Wikipedia* Available at: https://en.wikipedia.org/wiki/2012%E2%80%932013_Cypriot_financial_crisis
- Adrian, T. Natalucci, F. & Wu, J. (2024) *Financial Stability Implications of Emerging Market Currency Developments*, IMF Blog; Available at: https://www.imf.org/en/Blogs/Articles/2024/07/22/financial-stability-implications-of-emerging-market-currency-developments
- Askew, J. (2022) *Soaring Inflation and a Collapsing Currency: Why is Turkey's Economy in such a Mess?* Euro News; Available at: https://www.euronews.com/2022/11/09/everything-is-overheating-why-is-turkeys-economy-in-such-a-mess
- *Benefits of Price Stability*, European Central Bank; Available at: https://www.ecb.europa.eu/mopo/intro/benefits/html/index.en.html
- Choi, S. & Shin, J. (2022) Bitcoin: An inflation hedge but not a safe haven; *Finance Research Letters*, 46(b).
- 'Crisis in Venezuela' (2025) *Wikipedia* Available at: https://en.wikipedia.org/wiki/Crisis_in_Venezuela
- Depersio, G. (2025) *How Does the Price of Oil Affect Venezuela's Economy?* Investopedia; Available at: https://www.investopedia.com/ask/answers/032515/how-does-price-oil-affect-venezuelas-economy.asp
- 'Economic Adjustment Programme for Cyprus' (2025) *Wikipedia*, Available at: https://en.wikipedia.org/wiki/Economic_Adjustment_Programme_for_Cyprus
- Fraser, S. (2023) *Why Turkey's Currency is Crashing after Erdogan got Re-Elected* Associated Press; Available at: https://apnews.com/article/why-is-turkeys-currency-falling-erdogan-1faf7d58144fc84479c251c3fdeabe2a

- Gürkaynak, R., Kısacıkoğlu, B. & Lee, S. S. (2023) *Consequences of Weak Monetary Policy: Learning from the Turkish experience*, Available at: https://cepr.org/voxeu/columns/consequences-weak-monetary-policy-learning-turkish-experience

- Hanke, S. (2017) *Zimbabwe Inflates…Again* Cato Institute; Available at: https://www.cato.org/commentary/zimbabwe-inflates-again

- Hanke, S. (2019) *Venezuela's Hyperinflation Hits 80,000% per Year in 2018*; Cato Institute; Available at: https://www.cato.org/commentary/venezuelas-hyperinflation-hits-80000-year-2018

- Hayes, A. (2024) *Currency Crisis: What it is, Examples, and Effects*, Investopedia; Available at: https://www.investopedia.com/articles/economics/08/currency-crises.asp

- House of Lords Economic Affairs Committee (2021) *Quantitative Easing: A Dangerous Addiction?* First Report of Session 2019–21, HL Paper 42; Chapter 2 "The Impact of Quantitative Easing".

- 'Hyperinflation' (2025) *Wikipedia*, Available at: https://en.wikipedia.org/wiki/Hyperinflation

- 'Hyperinflation in Zimbabwe' (2025) *Wikipedia* Available at: https://en.wikipedia.org/wiki/Hyperinflation_in_Zimbabwe

- Iyigun, S. (2024) *Will the Turkish Economy Benefit from the Authorities' U-Turn Towards Greater Orthodoxy?* Coface: Available at: https://www.coface.com/news-economy-and-insights/will-the-turkish-economy-benefit-from-the-authorities-u-turn-towards-greater-orthodoxy

- Johnston, M (2024) *Worst Cases of Hyperinflation in History*, Investopedia; Available at: https://www.investopedia.com/articles/personal-finance/122915/worst-hyperinflations-history.asp

- Kowalevsky, P. & Shirai, S. (2023) *History of Bank of Japan's More than Two Decades of Unconventional Monetary Easing with Special Emphasis on the Frameworks Pursued in the Last Ten Years;* Asian Development Bank Institute; Available at: https://www.adb.org/sites/default/files/publication/883946/adbi-wp1380.pdf

- Menke, C. (2025) *Gold vs Bitcoin: Which is the Better Hedge*, Julius Baer; Available at: https://www.juliusbaer.com/en/insights/market-insights/markets-explained/gold-vs-bitcoin-which-is-the-better-hedge/

- Orhangazi, O. (2024) *The Falling Lira*, Phenomenal World; Available at: https://www.phenomenalworld.org/analysis/the-falling-lira/

- *Quantitative Easing* (2025) The Bank of England; Available at: https://www.bankofengland.co.uk/monetary-policy/quantitative-easing

- Ross, S. (2023) *The Diminishing Effects of Japan's Quantitative Easing* Investopedia; Available at: https://www.investopedia.com/articles/markets/052516/japans-case-study-diminished-effects-qe.asp

- Savaricas, N. (2013) *Cypriot Banks Reopen Amid Tight Security*, France 24; Available at: https://www.france24.com/en/20130328-cyprus-banks-reopen-after-12-day-closure

- Segal, T. (2025) *How Currency Fluctuations Affect the Economy* Investopedia; Available at: https://www.investopedia.com/articles/forex/080613/effects-currency-fluctuations-economy.asp

- Siegel, R. (2008) *Zimbabwe's Hyperinflation poses Unique Challenges* NPR; Available at: https://www.npr.org/2008/03/26/89123990/zimbabwes-hyperinflation-poses-unique-challenges

- Sor, J. (2025) *Gold Price Records Show Investors See it as the Ultimate Safe Haven*, Business Insider; Available at: https://www.businessinsider.com/gold-price-today-record-bullion-rally-safe-haven-commodities-investing-2025-4

- Srinivasan, H. (2025) *Historical U.S. Inflation Rate by Year: 1929 to 2025* Investopedia; Available at: https://www.investopedia.com/inflation-rate-by-year-7253832

- *The Greek Debt Crisis in Numbers* (2015) BBC News; Available at: https://www.bbc.co.uk/news/world-europe-33407742

- The Investopedia Team (2023) *Hyperinflation Throughout History: Examples and Impact*, Investopedia; Available at: https://www.investopedia.com/ask/answers/061515/what-are-some-historic-examples-hyperinflation.asp

- Thompson, M. (2013) *Cyprus banks to Reopen with Strict Cash Limits*, CNN Business; Available at: https://money.cnn.com/2013/03/27/news/economy/cyprus-capital-controls/index.html

- Tomaselli, W. (2018) *Why Venezuelan Migrants are Making Handbags out of Worthless Banknotes*, Time; Available at: https://time.com/5265941/venezuelan-migrants-bolivares-banknotes/

- *Understanding the Importance of Financial Stability* (2025) Faster Capital; Available at: https://fastercapital.com/topics/understanding-the-importance-of-financial-stability.html

- *United States Inflation Rate*, Trading Economics; Available at: https://tradingeconomics.com/united-states/inflation-cpi

- *Which Commodities are the Best Hedge for Inflation?* (2024) Goldman Sachs; Available at: https://www.goldmansachs.com/insights/articles/which-commodities-are-the-best-hedge-for-inflation

Chapter 13

- *Adopting El Salvador*, Available at: https://world.adoptingelsalvador.gob.sv/welcome

- Arslanian, H., Donovan, R., Blumenfeld, M. & Zamore, A. (2021) *El Salvador's Law*, PwC; Available at: https://www.pwc.com/gx/en/financial-services/pdf/el-salvadors-law-a-meaningful-test-for-bitcoin.pdf

- *Bitcoin Holdings of Countries and Governments* (2025) Bitbo; Available at: https://bitbo.io/treasuries/countries/
- *Bitfinex Hacker and Wife Plead Guilty to Money Laundering Conspiracy Involving Billions in Cryptocurrency* (2016) DOJ Press Release: Available at: https://www.justice.gov/archives/opa/pr/bitfinex-hacker-and-wife-plead-guilty-money-laundering-conspiracy-involving-billions
- Casaburi, P. (2025) *Portugal Crypto Tax: The Ultimate Guide for 2025*; Global Citizen Solutions; Available at: https://www.globalcitizensolutions.com/portugal-crypto-tax/
- Chainalysis Team (2025) *2025 Crypto Crime Trends: Illicit Volumes Portend Record Year as On-Chain Crime Becomes Increasingly Diverse and Professionalized*; Available at: https://www.chainalysis.com/blog/2025-crypto-crime-report-introduction/
- *Consumer Warning on Binance Markets Limited and the Binance Group* (2021); FCA; Available at: https://www.fca.org.uk/news/news-stories/consumer-warning-binance-markets-limited-and-binance-group
- Fathi, A. (2025) *Germany Left $2.3 Billion on the Table After Early Bitcoin Sell-Off* FinanceFeeds; Available at: https://www.fca.org.uk/news/news-stories/consumer-warning-binance-markets-limited-and-binance-group
- George, K. (2024) *Cryptocurrency Regulations Around the World*; Investopedia; Available at: https://www.investopedia.com/cryptocurrency-regulations-around-the-world-5202122
- Huang, R. (2024) *A 2025 Overview of the E-CNY, China's Digital Yuan*; Forbes: Available at: https://www.forbes.com/sites/digital-assets/2024/07/15/a-2024-overview-of-the-e-cny-chinas-digital-yuan/
- Khatri, A. (2025) *Bitcoin Strategy Intact: El Salvador Purchases 12 BTC Despite Policy Adjustments*; CryptoDaily; Available at: https://uk.investing.com/news/cryptocurrency-news/bitcoin-strategy-intact-el-salvador-purchases-12-btc-despite-policy-adjustments-4095696
- Knight, R. (2024) *UK Finance Regulator 'A Deterrent' to Crypto Industry, says Crypto UK*; CoinTelegraph; Available at: https://cointelegraph.com/news/uk-finance-regulator-fca-crypto-industry
- Linthicum, K. (2025) What El Salvador's Bukele, a hero for the American right, isn't showing the world; *LA Times*; Available at: https://www.latimes.com/world-nation/story/2025-05-18/el-salvadors-millennial-dictator-disappeared-thousands-but-quashed-gangs-how-long-will-his-popularity-last
- *Malta: The Blockchain Island* CSB Group; Available at: https://www.csbgroup.com/fintech/blockchain-malta/
- Malwa, S. (2025) *Ripple-SEC Bid for XRP Settlement Rejected by Judge Citing "Procedural Flaws"*; CoinDesk; Available at: https://www.coindesk.com/markets/2025/05/16/ripple-sec-bid-for-xrp-settlement-rejected-by-judge-citing-procedural-flaws

- *Ripple (XRP) Price per day from August 9, 2022 to May 28, 2025* (2025) Statista; Available at: https://www.statista.com/statistics/807266/ripple-price-monthly/
- Russon, M. (2021) *Trump Calls Bitcoin 'A Scam Against the Dollar'*; BBC News; Available at: https://www.bbc.co.uk/news/business-57392734
- Stempel, J. & Nishant, N. (2025) *Ripple Labs says US SEC ends Appeal over Crypto Oversight*; Reuters; Available at: https://www.reuters.com/legal/ripple-ceo-says-us-sec-will-drop-appeal-against-crypto-firm-2025-03-19/
- *Tax Payments with Cryptocurrencies* (2023) Kanton Zug; Available at https://zg.ch/de/steuern-finanzen/steuern/steuerbezug/taxpaymentswithcryptocurrencies
- The White House (2025) *Factsheet: President Donald J. Trump Establishes the Strategic Bitcoin Reserve and U.S. Digital Asset Stockpile*, Available at: https://www.whitehouse.gov/fact-sheets/2025/03/fact-sheet-president-donald-j-trump-establishes-the-strategic-bitcoin-reserve-and-u-s-digital-asset-stockpile/
- *Trump Names 5 Cryptocurrencies for National Reserve, Sending Prices Soaring,* (2025) AlJazeera; Available at: https://www.aljazeera.com/economy/2025/3/3/trump-names-5-cryptocurrencies-for-national-reserve-sending-prices-soaring

CHAPTER 14

- *Cato Institute 2023 Central Bank Digital Currency National Survey* (2023) Cato Institute with YouGov; Available at: https://www.cato.org/sites/cato.org/files/2023-05/cato-cbdc-survey-toplines.pdf
- *CBDC Central Bank Digital Currencies: Foundational Principles and Core Features* (2020) Bank for International Settlements; Available at: https://www.bis.org/publ/othp33.htm
- Chao, L. (2025) Observers.com; *Banking and CBDC Weekly RoundUp: 17/02/2025*; Available at: https://www.observers.com/banking-and-cbdc-weekly-roundup-17-02-2025/
- *China Focuses on Green Travel in two New CBDC Trials* (2021); Ledger Insights; Available at: https://www.ledgerinsights.com/china-focuses-on-green-travel-in-two-new-cbdc-trials/
- *Could CBDCs Destroy Privacy* (2024) FCA Institute; Available at: https://www.cfainstitute.org/insights/articles/could-cbdcs-destroy-privacy
- Hall, I. (2021) *Bahamas 'Sand Dollar' Put to Use for Payroll*; Global Government Fintech; Available at: https://www.globalgovernmentfintech.com/bahamas-sand-dollar-cbdc-put-to-use-for-payroll/
- Koonprasert, T., Kanada, S., Tsuda, N. & Reshidi, E. (2024) *Central Bank Digital Currency Adoption: Inclusive Strategies for Intermediaries and Users*; IMF eLibrary; Available at: https://www.elibrary.imf.org/view/journals/063/2024/005/article-A001-en.xml

CHAPTER 15

- Bigdata (2024) *The Fusion of AI and Blockchain in Cryptocurrencies*; Bigdataanalyticsnews.com; Available at: https://bigdataanalyticsnews.com/ai-blockchain-in-cryptocurrencies/
- Castrovilli, M. (2023) *How AI is Changing Crypto: Hype vs Reality*; CoinTelegraph: Available at: https://cointelegraph.com/news/how-ai-changing-crypto-hype-reality
- *Debt to GDP Ratio by Country 2025* (2025) World Population Review; Available at: https://worldpopulationreview.com/country-rankings/debt-to-gdp-ratio-by-country
- Milliken, D. (2022) *Bank of England Projects more than £30 Billion of Annual QE Losses*; Reuters: Available at: https://www.reuters.com/business/finance/bank-england-projects-more-than-30-bln-pounds-annual-qe-losses-2022-11-22/
- Mvalenzuela (2015) *MIT Technology Review: A Brain-Computer Interface that Works Wirelessly*; Blackrock Neurotech; Available at: https://blackrockneurotech.com/insights/a-brain-computer-interface-that-works-wirelessly/
- *National Debt of China from 1995 to 2030*; Statista; Available at: https://www.statista.com/statistics/531423/national-debt-of-china/
- *Public Sector Net Debt Expressed as a Percentage of GDP in the United Kingdom from 1900/01 to 2029/30*; statista; Available at: https://www.statista.com/statistics/282841/debt-as-gdp-uk/
- *The 2008 Recession 10 Years On* (2018) Office for National Statistics; Available at: https://www.ons.gov.uk/economy/grossdomesticproductgdp/articles/the2008recession10yearson/2018-04-30
- *The History of MicroStrategy (Strategy) and Their Approach to Bitcoin: A Bold Financial Gamble* (2025) RR2 Capital; Available at: https://rr2.capital/the-history-of-microstrategy-strategy-and-their-approach-to-bitcoin-a-bold-financial-gamble/

Glossary

Address: A unique alpha-numeric string used to send and receive cryptocurrency on a blockchain network.

Airdrop: A free distribution of tokens, often used to promote a cryptocurrency project or reward users.

Algorithm: A set of rules or processes followed in problem-solving or computation, especially in cryptography.

Altcoin: Any cryptocurrency other than Bitcoin. Includes Ethereum, Solana, and thousands more.

AML: Anti-Money Laundering law or regulation designed to detect and prevent illicit financial activity.

Asset-Backed Token: A digital token whose value is linked to a real-world asset, such as property or gold.

Atomic Swap: A smart contract-based exchange of two cryptocurrencies across different blockchains without intermediaries.

Base Layer: The foundational blockchain protocol responsible for core functions like consensus and data availability. Also known as Layer 1.

Bitcoin: A decentralised digital currency that enables peer-to-peer transactions without the need for banks.

Bitcoin Halving: A scheduled reduction in the block reward for Bitcoin miners, occurring roughly every four years to control supply.

Blockchain: A distributed digital ledger that records transactions across a network of computers in a secure, immutable way.

Block: A batch of transactions grouped together and added to the blockchain.

Block Height: The number of blocks that precede a given block in the blockchain.

Block Reward: The new units of cryptocurrency awarded to miners for validating and adding a new block to the blockchain.

Block Space: The limited amount of data that can fit in a single block on a blockchain. Because space is scarce, users compete to have their transactions included, often by paying higher fees.

Bridge: A protocol that allows tokens or data to move between two separate blockchain networks.

Bridge Chain: A blockchain designed specifically to facilitate cross-chain communication and asset transfer between otherwise incompatible networks.

Burning: The process of permanently removing tokens from circulation, usually to reduce supply.

Byzantine Fault Tolerance (BFT): The ability of a distributed system to function correctly even if some participants act maliciously or fail to respond.

Central Bank: A national institution that manages a country's currency, interest rates, and monetary policy.

Central Bank Liquidity: The process by which central banks inject money into the financial system to ensure credit continues to flow. This is done through methods like short-term loans to banks or purchasing government bonds. Quantitative easing (QE) is one such tool, used to lower borrowing costs, stabilise markets, and prevent financial collapse during crises.

CBDC: Central Bank Digital Currency – a digital version of fiat currency issued and controlled by a central bank.

CBDC Wallet: A digital wallet that stores central bank digital currency and allows users to send, receive, and manage government-issued digital money.

CEX: Centralised Exchange – a cryptocurrency trading platform operated by a central authority that holds users' funds and executes trades on their behalf.

Chainlink: A decentralised oracle network that connects smart contracts to real-world data.

Clipping (coins): The historical practice of shaving small amounts of precious metal from coins, reducing their value while still using them at face value.

Coinbase Transaction: The first transaction in a block, created by a miner to collect the block reward and any transaction fees.

Cold Wallet: A cryptocurrency wallet not connected to the internet, offering increased security against hacks.

Collateral: An asset pledged to secure a loan or financial agreement, often used in DeFi protocols.

Confirmation: The process by which a transaction is validated and added to the blockchain.

Consensus Layer: A component of modular blockchain architecture that handles transaction validation and agreement across the network.

Consensus Mechanism: The method used by blockchain networks to agree on the validity of transactions. Examples include PoW and PoS.

Cryptocurrency: A digital currency secured by cryptography, operating independently of a central authority.

Cryptographic Hash: A mathematical function that converts input data into a fixed-length string, used for data security.

Cryptographic Proof: A mathematical guarantee that verifies the authenticity or accuracy of data without revealing the underlying information.

Custodial Wallet: A wallet where a third party controls the private keys on behalf of the user.

DAI: A decentralised stablecoin on the Ethereum blockchain, soft-pegged to the US dollar and backed by crypto collateral.

DAO: Decentralised Autonomous Organisation – a blockchain-based structure where decisions are made by code and community voting, not central leadership.

DApp: Decentralised Application – a software program that runs on a blockchain network rather than a central server.

Decentralisation: The distribution of power and control across a network rather than relying on a single central authority.

DeFi: Decentralised Finance – financial services such as lending, borrowing, and trading that operate without central intermediaries.

DEX: Decentralised Exchange – a peer-to-peer trading platform where users retain control of their funds and trades are executed via smart contracts.

Digital Identity: A user's online identity represented on a blockchain, often linked to credentials, certificates, or wallet addresses.

Digital Signature: A cryptographic technique used to verify the authenticity and integrity of a digital message or transaction.

Distributed Ledger: A shared digital record of transactions maintained across multiple locations, forming the foundation of blockchain technology.

Double Spending: A flaw in digital cash where the same unit could be spent more than once. Blockchain prevents this through consensus.

Dust: A tiny amount of cryptocurrency that is smaller than the minimum required transaction fee, often left unspent.

DYOR: Do Your Own Research – a common phrase in crypto advising investors to independently verify information before acting.

Elliptic Curve Cryptography: A method of encryption used in blockchain for secure public and private key generation.

Epoch: A set time period in blockchain networks used for finalising rewards, updating validator roles, or processing data batches.

ERC-20: A technical standard for creating fungible tokens on the Ethereum blockchain.

Ethereum: A decentralised blockchain that enables smart contracts and decentralised applications. It introduced programmable transactions using its native currency, Ether (ETH).

Exchange: A platform where users can trade cryptocurrencies for fiat or other digital assets.

Fiat Currency: Government-issued currency not backed by a physical commodity, such as the British pound or US dollar.

Finality: The assurance that a blockchain transaction is permanent and cannot be reversed once confirmed.

Fork: A change in the rules of a blockchain protocol, which can result in two separate versions of the blockchain.

Fungibility: The ability of each unit of a currency or token to be interchangeable and equal in value.

Gas Fee: A transaction fee paid to validators on a blockchain, especially Ethereum, to process and confirm transactions.

Gas Limit: The maximum amount of computational effort a user is willing to pay for in a blockchain transaction.

Genesis Block: The first block in a blockchain, from which all subsequent blocks follow. Bitcoin's was mined on 3 January 2009.

Governance Token: A type of token that gives holders the right to vote on protocol upgrades and decisions within decentralised platforms.

Gresham's Law: An economic principle stating that "bad money drives out good" when both are in circulation.

Hard Cap: The maximum supply limit that a cryptocurrency can ever reach, often coded into the protocol.

Hash: A fixed-length string of characters generated from input data, used to ensure data integrity in blockchain systems.

Hash Rate: The speed at which a blockchain network processes hashes. A higher rate generally indicates greater security.

HODL: A slang term meaning to hold cryptocurrency rather than sell, often during periods of high volatility.

Hot Wallet: A cryptocurrency wallet connected to the internet, convenient but more vulnerable to hacking.

Immutable: In blockchain, refers to data that cannot be changed or deleted once written to the ledger.

Inflation: A rise in the general price level of goods and services, reducing purchasing power over time.

Interest Rate: The cost of borrowing money, expressed as a percentage of the loan amount. Set by central banks to influence inflation, spending, and overall economic activity.

Initial Coin Offering (ICO): A fundraising method in which new cryptocurrencies are sold to early investors, similar to a stock IPO.

Initial Public Offering (IPO): The first sale of a company's shares to the public, marking its transition from private to publicly traded status.

Interoperability: The ability of different blockchain networks to communicate and share data or assets with each other.

KYC: Know Your Customer – a compliance process that requires verifying the identity of users to prevent illicit activity.

Layer 1: A base-level blockchain protocol like Bitcoin or Ethereum, responsible for transaction processing and consensus.

Layer 2: A secondary framework built on top of a Layer 1 blockchain to increase speed and scalability.

Ledger: A record-keeping system for financial transactions. In blockchain, this ledger is decentralised and publicly visible.

Lightning Network: A Layer 2 solution for Bitcoin that allows for faster and cheaper transactions via payment channels.

Liquidity: The ease with which an asset can be converted into cash without affecting its market price.

Liquidity Pool: A smart contract that holds reserves of two or more tokens, allowing users to trade between them automatically.

Margin Call: A demand by a broker for an investor to deposit additional funds to cover potential losses on leveraged positions.

Mining: The process of validating blockchain transactions and adding them to the ledger in return for block rewards.

Monetary Policy: The actions of a central bank to manage money supply, interest rates, and inflation in an economy.

Network Effect: A phenomenon where a service becomes more valuable as more people use it, increasing adoption and utility.

NFT (Non-Fungible Token): A unique digital asset stored on a blockchain, often used to represent art, collectibles, or identity.

Node: A computer that participates in a blockchain network by validating and broadcasting transactions.

Non-Custodial Wallet: A wallet in which the user controls the private keys, offering greater sovereignty over funds.

Open Source: Software whose source code is publicly available, allowing anyone to inspect, modify, or contribute to its development.

Optimistic Roll-up: A Layer 2 scaling solution that assumes transactions are valid and only checks them if fraud is suspected.

Oracles: Services that bring external data onto a blockchain, enabling smart contracts to react to real-world events.

P2P (Peer-to-Peer): A decentralised model where participants interact directly without intermediaries.

Private Key: A secret code that gives access to control and spend the cryptocurrency associated with a blockchain address.

Proof of Stake (PoS): A consensus mechanism where validators are chosen based on the amount of cryptocurrency they stake.

Proof of Work (PoW): A consensus mechanism where miners solve computational puzzles to validate transactions and secure the network.

Public Key: A cryptographic code paired with a private key, used to receive funds on a blockchain network.

Quantitative Easing (QE): A monetary policy in which central banks purchase assets to inject liquidity into the economy.

REKT: Slang for "wrecked", used to describe heavy financial loss in crypto markets.

Repo Market: A financial system where banks and institutions borrow cash by temporarily selling securities, agreeing to repurchase them shortly after. It provides short-term funding and plays a key role in maintaining liquidity in the financial system.

Repo Rate: The interest rate applied to repurchase agreements. It reflects the cost of short-term borrowing in the repo market and is a key indicator of liquidity conditions between banks and financial institutions.

Reserve Currency: A foreign currency held in large quantities by central banks, often used in international trade and finance.

Retail Investor: An individual investor who trades in smaller amounts, as opposed to institutional investors.

Reverse Repo: A transaction where a central bank sells securities with an agreement to buy them back later. It temporarily withdraws liquidity from the financial system and is often used to control short-term interest rates.

Roll-up: A Layer 2 scaling solution that batches multiple transactions off-chain and posts them to the main chain.

Rug Pull: A fraudulent exit scam in which crypto developers withdraw funds and abandon a project after attracting investors.

Satoshi: The smallest unit of Bitcoin, equal to 0.00000001 BTC. Named after Bitcoin's creator, Satoshi Nakamoto.

Scalability: The ability of a blockchain network to handle increased usage, transactions, or data without performance loss.

Security Token: A digital token that represents ownership of a real-world financial asset and is subject to regulation.

Seed Phrase: A set of words generated by a wallet that can be used to recover access to cryptocurrency funds.

Self-Custody: When an individual holds and controls their own private keys, without relying on third-party services.

Sharding: A method of splitting a blockchain into smaller parts (shards) to improve processing speed and scalability.

Shitcoin: A slang term for a cryptocurrency considered to have little to no value or utility.

Snapshot: A record of blockchain account states at a specific point in time, often used for airdrops or voting eligibility.

Smart Contract: A self-executing code stored on a blockchain that carries out actions when predefined conditions are met.

Stablecoin: A cryptocurrency designed to maintain a stable value by being pegged to a reserve asset like a fiat currency.

Synthetic Asset: A token that mimics the value and behaviour of a real-world asset using smart contracts.

Token: A digital unit of value created on a blockchain, often representing assets, utility, or access to a service.

Tokenisation: The process of converting rights to a real-world asset into a digital token on a blockchain.

Total Supply: The total number of coins or tokens that will ever exist for a particular cryptocurrency.

TradFi: Traditional Finance – refers to the conventional financial system involving central banks, commercial banks, stock markets, and other regulated financial institutions.

Transaction Fee: A fee paid to validators or miners to process and confirm transactions on a blockchain.

Trustless: A system that does not require participants to trust each other, as security is enforced by code and consensus.

UTXO (Unspent Transaction Output): The portion of a cryptocurrency transaction that remains after part of it is spent, forming the basis of Bitcoin accounting.

Validator: A participant in a proof-of-stake network who verifies transactions and helps maintain the blockchain.

Volatility: The degree of variation in the price of an asset over time. High volatility means frequent and sharp changes.

Wallet: A digital tool for storing, sending, and receiving cryptocurrencies. Can be hot (online) or cold (offline).

Web 3.0: A vision for a decentralised internet where users control their own data, identities, and assets using blockchain.

Whale: A term used for an individual or entity that holds a large amount of cryptocurrency and can influence markets.

White Paper: A technical document that explains the purpose, mechanics, and design of a cryptocurrency or blockchain project.

Wrapped Token: A tokenised version of a cryptocurrency that can be used on a different blockchain while maintaining its value.

ZK Roll-up: A type of Layer 2 scaling solution that uses zero-knowledge proofs to batch transactions and verify them efficiently.

Yield Farming: A DeFi strategy that involves lending or staking crypto assets to earn rewards or interest.